What GOD *said to* DEW *in 2002*

D.E. WILLIAMS

Quantum Discovery
A LITERARY AGENCY

What God Said To Dew in 2002
Copyright © 2023 by D.E. Williams

ISBN
978-1-959314-95-0 (Paperback)
978-1-959314-96-7 (eBook)
978-1-959314-94-3 (Hardcover)

Table of Contents

Preface

Everyone has a unique gift or skill within them. When that unique gift or skill is exercised and shared, it will enrich the lives of those around you and produce prosperity for the sharing individual. I believe the words within these pages are derived from my unique gift. Here I am sharing it with you.

These words flowed out of me like the waters at a waterfall. Because of the times we are in, I thought it best not to edit it to make it political correct. The book was first copyrighted and published in 2002. This is a reprint of the original, unedited version. The books' content is prophetic, and the present-day circumstance of the American citizenry is eerily reflective of the words within these pages. The statistics and figures have not been updated. However, not much has changed since the time of this book's first printing. I am confident that, with few exceptions, the changes in these figures is proportional to the degree that the message remains the same.

What GOD said to DEW in 2002

This book is about the essence of our existence and the perpetuation of our species, the human animal. It is about taking a "time-out" from your day-to-day existence to reflect on yourself, the lives around you, and your planet. It is about accepting the challenge of perpetuating humanity, social structure, and civilization. It is about everyone's destiny, both individually and collectively. There is a connection between social and spiritual circumstances, though we perceive each as being separate aspect of reality. There is a very real connection between social order and the divine system of Nature. It is defined within the context of our spirituality. In other words, it is our connection to the system of Nature that links us together as a species, and therefore, the actions of our lives are connected to the system of Nature as well. Because each of us as living beings can attribute our origin to one source, we must embrace our connection to all that has the divine energy of that source flowing through it, seeking to balance our collective existence through tolerance and compromise. This is to include all living things.

Embrace these words within the context of "GOD" being everything, the one source of everything, the beginning, the all-powerful. For me personally, the birth and development of these writings has been a very spiritual experience. Within these pages are concepts and ideas that may appear to be in conflict with your current belief system and state of mind. In this case, "state of mind" is synonymous with perspective. Do not interpret these words in a completely subjective way, to the degree that you become offended. Do not allow yourself to become offended or threatened by these words or you will close your mind to any truth they may convey. Think of this book as you would any "self-help" book. The purpose of which is to give you information that, when added to your own knowledge of yourself, will allow you to change aspects of your being for the better through conscious, purposeful effort. It is important that you the reader evaluate the following words within the context of how they relate to the realities of your present circumstance of existence. However, it must be done objectively. All humans are the same at the depths of their being, as a member of a species group. Human difference occurs on a subjective level related to factors like intellectual development, opportunity, individual circumstance, desire, etc. Therefore, you must recognize that the truths I point out are to be viewed in a general sense. As you compare yourself to any likeness I may refer to within these pages, you may "feel" that you differ. Recognize and examine the reality that the "feeling" in question is the result of an interpretation you make based upon your current perspective. This perspective is heavily influenced by what you know and understand. The truth is, not one of us humans knows all there is to know about the reality within which we exist. So take this truth and use it to keep your mind open. Keep it open to the possibility that there is something to be gained from interpreting these words objectively.

I would like to take this opportunity to express my most sincere apologies to any and all religious groups, ethnic groups, and individuals that I may unintentionally offend by expressing what I believe to be the truth of existence. Build your forgiveness upon the foundation of the reality that others are committing atrocious crimes against society like robbery, rape, and murder. The words within this text are truly meant to help each of us embrace the reality of the one true "GOD." Do not judge me as harshly as you would a robber, rapist, or murderer. My purpose is directed at bringing you closer to "GOD," rather than taking anything from you. As these words came to me, I feared those who would classify this text, particularly because of my assertion that the words were given to me by "GOD." As I released my fears to the Will of "GOD," I realized that these times mandate that individuals must make definitive determinations of what is true and what is not. Individuals can no longer allow others to define truth for them by manipulating their interpretation of reality through word selection and influential imagery. It is not up to me or anyone else to classify these words or place them into context for you. What "GOD" said to do is share these words with you. It will then become the responsibility of the individual to decide the value of these words, based on the comparative truth contained within their souls (within their hearts).

Everything, objectively and subjectively, relates to one positive truth. The primary elements of this truth are energy, movement, and polarity. Once we all truly recognize the benefit and blessing of positive flowing energy, positive thought, and positive action, then we can strive together as a nation for a standard of living that truly allows us to exercise our liberty. This would be a near-utopian existence. On the other hand, we can continue to think in a divided manner, maintaining a divided perspective and living in a divided society. This way of thinking provides a foundation for selfishness and greed. Selfishness and greed separate each of us from the collective. This will continue to lead to distrust, envy, and hatred. In the end, through a combination of chaos within our social system, foreign and domestic terrorism, natural disaster, and ultimately civil war, the United States will no longer exist. Those fortunate enough to have survived will never again enjoy the plentiful, "free" America we now know.

So read these words for enjoyment and insight. However, understand that you must make a decision about yourself, reality, and the Divine Energy of Life. Not one of us knows all there is to know about "GOD" or truth. However, our bodies tell us spirituality is real in the subtlest of ways. Each of us must listen and believe in our "inner self," i.e. our soul. Trust in the reality that since the holy books of our species parallel what is within these pages, and the author (me) says in no uncertain terms that "GOD" has sent these words, perhaps, this is for real (a co-incidence is two incidences of truth). Recognize that seeking to deal with reality objectively and seeking to use positive flowing energy to achieve positive resolution is a good thing. Based upon this, simply because you know it will only help and not hurt, you will try to have hope. You will try to maintain a positive attitude. You will try to behave within the context of the definition of civilized, which is the group of words that explain the current standard of human behavior. Each individual is in pursuit of long-lasting personal satisfaction. To achieve it, one uses their energy to move in either a positive (direction) way or a negative way. For all to enjoy long-lasting personal satisfaction, each person needs to choose to move in a positive (direction) way while pursuing balance through the use of compromise and tolerance.

One of the most important truths to keep in mind is that as long as the Earth keeps spinning, time will continue to pass. Things will continue to happen whether we consciously recognize them or not. They may work out beneficially, or detrimentally, but they will happen. Americans as a whole are a successful people, so we have up until now prospered. We may continue to stumble ahead into prosperity as a nation. However, any American with their eyes truly open to the realities of our existence can see the turmoil that lies before us. Do not underestimate the devastation of the events that makeup damnation. We need to wake up to the reality of our circumstance both in terms of ourselves as united Americans, and as a human species on the global scale. As Americans, we can solidify and perpetuate the standard of living we have achieved. We can also maintain the liberty we as a nation have inherited from the blood and energy of the builders of this great society. To do this, we as a citizenry must embrace each other as countrymen, as brothers and sisters, as a family. This must be done regardless of ethnic background because the truth is that the actual builders of this nation were individuals that came from all corners of the planet. Only here is it possible to have true and boundless liberty to live and express oneself as desired. Only in America do we have the freedom to indulge our creativity by trying new and different things, which lends itself to our individual growth. This means that only here does humanity have the opportunity to fully manifest a positive, utopian existence.

The reason for the very formation of this nation was greatly due to the need for freedom of religious expression. To think that we can exist without "GOD" in our thoughts, when it is this very divine energy that gives us life itself (without which nothing, materially, monetarily, or otherwise matters), is a fool's notion. Without time or breath, you as an individual do not exist, and life goes on without you, the memory of you soon forgotten. Time and breath are true blessings. The point to recognizing the gift of each breath is that because of the magnitude of that gift, regardless of individual circumstance, as long as each of us breathes (i.e. is alive) we are fortunate. This allows individuals to appreciate all the little things about living that are often taken for granted. You can appreciate the reality that all in life beyond breath is gain. This appreciation for the opportunity to live must be the foundation upon which we build our understanding. Nothing individuals will do can ever be equal to the gift of life, so each of us is always humbly indebted to the Divine Energy of Life for flowing through us. Without that breath, nothing else for us is real.

We must come together as brethren of a truly united nation. For this to occur, we need a "rebirth" of our understanding with regard to what our reality truly is. In essence, our consciousness must evolve to the level where our interpretation of the truth is clear and common. It must be common because we are all one species, i.e. the human community. As is evident relative to our current way of life, the embracing of religion, or more aptly put, spirituality, is what creates and perpetuates a sense of community. We come together in church to worship and fellowship with shared beliefs. These are truths we must not ignore. Even though in one community there are many churches of different denominations, it does not matter because religion is the celebration of the goodness within the people of a sect. Separate denominations merely denote the different ways in which we express and practice our spirituality. We can maintain this separation while still accepting the truth that there is only one "GOD." The divine truth is the true word of "GOD" embraces the goodness of our entire species, i.e. all of humankind. Churches, no matter their affiliation, strengthen us as a human community. It is spiritual awareness that is the foundation of moral and ethical application. These teachings give us the formula for the creation of our character. The holy books of our species tell us that the humans' actions are to be directed towards what is good and righteous. This truth is given to us through the realities of the teachings and actions of those guided to the positive way. Our spirituality has a physical foundation that corresponds to what we know through the sciences. We must all be humbled by the fact that not one of us knows all there is to know about that which gives us life. Therefore, it is obvious that there is still knowledge and wisdom to be gained relative to our spiritual Nature.

To receive these words in earnest, each of us must let down the barriers that have been created in our minds by ego, misinterpretation, and the physical stimulation of our material existence. Each of us must feel these words in your heart. Weigh the truth of each and every one of them and recognize that there is still room in every person's life for enlightenment. We have reached the period of our existence where each one of us, each and every individual, must now recognize reality and face the responsibilities we as individuals have to it. There are definitive choices to be made about the direction of our actions. These revelations are designed to make the right choices clear to all that are prepared to recognize their existence from the perspective of pure truth. All life was created as a part of a divine system. We have numerous labels that are applied to the task of identifying that system, as we perceive it. Labels like religion, spirituality, and Nature. Each person must open their mind up so that they can perceive the truth beyond the barrier of these labels. Accept the possibility that there is truth that lies beyond human knowledge. Trust the love that we as humans repress for fear of being made vulnerable by the depth of our emotional connection to each other. Have hope for the perpetuation and prosperity of humanity and have faith in the word of "GOD." In Second Timothy 3:5, it says that in the last day's men "having a form of godliness but denying the power thereof: from such turn away."

This "form of godliness" is our conscious mind. Each of us who has given up hope is denying the power of our minds, "denying the power thereof." Being aware makes each of us responsible. By turning away from responsibility, we are turning away from (the discipline we can generate in) our minds, and the power thereof.

Many people have a difficult time accepting new ideas and philosophies, even though they truly want to be open-minded. Individuals develop intellectually to whatever degree circumstance and desire allow, then many circle their faculties around the understanding they have gained just to get through their everyday lives. Some people close their minds unintentionally. They close themselves off to possibilities because it makes them vulnerable and requires additional energy to deal with varied possibilities. for the remaining time you invest in sharing and interpreting for yourself the truth in these words that were given to me for you, I hope you will do so with an open and eager mind. "Open" to the degree that you understand there is a meaning to the energy of life on our planet that you yourself have missed. Because you do not understand the meaning of the very force that gives your life, you therefore cannot know all there is to know about yourself or the selves around you. For this reason alone you must be humbled, yes, <u>humbled</u>, by the reality and truth that you do not know it all, and there is still wisdom for you to seek. This is not admitting stupidity or an inability to learn. This is the expression of humility in the face of the awesome power of "GOD." This is reverence. Accepting this releases us from the pressure we feel relative to the endeavor of embracing new ideas and concepts. as well, "eager" to the degree that you know in your heart that by finding and embracing the understanding that will deliver you to a meaningful existence, you will also bring to your life all the satisfaction, direction, and salvation that all individuals are consciously or unconsciously seeking for ourselves.

In addition, I hope you will read this work from an objective point of view, because it is my hope that there is something within these pages to enhance every reader's life. At the very least, as a book of amusement kept in the bookrack next to the toilet, read to relieve the stress brought on by the strain ☺. At the other end of the spectrum of desires, perhaps these words will aid you in elevating your consciousness and intellect to a higher level of awareness. The part of the message that gives me the most energy is that this is not just a call to salvation. This is a call to riches that you have never imagined. There will be riches for the body, mind, and soul. The corporations along with the help of the politicians have already amassed the material riches. Now they must be shared amongst those who generated and contributed to this wealth (body). The sharing of resources will reduce the unnecessary stress in our lives, allowing us to grow towards truth (mind). As well, each of us will experience the spiritual richness promised to us by "GOD." This enrichment will manifest itself as the peace of mind and salvation (soul) we all seek. Imagine an existence without the stress of worrying about how you will survive, and without the stress of worrying about heaven or hell. Do not let the negative vibrations (trials and tribulations) of today remove the hope that radiates from the positive vibrations (seemingly endless possibilities) of tomorrow. Tomorrow is the first day of the rest of your life. If you decide to take control of your actions, or more rightly put, exert your influence over your reality, you can have an effect on it. Once a moment transpires, it becomes part of the past. We are to learn from these past moments. Each of us must take these lessons of life and move forward. Do not let the mistakes of the past paralyze the flow of your life. We all must have hope.

As you progress in these writings, you will find that I frequently refer to sections of the Bible that concur with the point I am making. It is important to read the Holy Scriptures so that each can see the truth, and the truth will be <u>felt</u> as well, as awakening occurs. I do believe that the text of the Bible has been manipulated, and I know that it is incomplete. However, these are holy writings, and ingesting them will produce revelation. From reading these words in earnest, what is divinely true will be revealed. There are many analogies within these pages. An analogy is a partial similarity between like features of two things, on which a comparison can be based.

In logic, an analogy is considered a form of reasoning in which one thing is inferred to be similar to another thing in a certain respect, based on the known similarity between the things in other respects. Analogies are descriptive examples of the divine truth that there is <u>one system of existence</u>. To be able to relate one circumstance of reality containing one set of elements to another circumstance containing an entirely different set of elements and finding common truth therein is indicative of the fact that there is only one system of existence. In an analogy, one comparatively applies completely different elements to a similar system of actions or conditions.

This project was almost done before I associated my use of "parables" or analogous stories, with the many prophets, including Jesus Christ, who used this tool to convey their messages in a way that was more clearly understandable by the masses. In an effort to create a common perspective that will lead to a common understanding of divine truth, I use analogies to bring to light the similarities and common aspects of the system of realities before us. A clearer understanding of the <u>physical</u> reality of our spirituality can be derived from the examination of its analogous relationship to the electromagnetic energy generated by the spinning of our Earth. A clearer understanding of the <u>conceptual</u> reality of the systems that make life work can be derived from the examination of its analogous relationship these systems have to the Atom. The Atom is the foundation of both the spiritual and physical reality, which together comprises existence.

I have learned how to rightly channel the energy of "GOD" (the Divine Energy of Life) and use it to my benefit here on Earth. This knowledge has been revealed to me through reading the Holy Scriptures, and contemplating GODs' existence within the context of human reality. As the energy and system of "GOD" truly exists, we must be able to understand that existence as well as that power, relative to our present understanding of reality in general. Since life continues to draw energy from a source, that source must continually exist. The Holy Scriptures are a profound work inspired by "GOD" to lead us to right action. However, since the time those words were recorded, the humans' knowledge and understanding of reality has grown, as has its ability to communicate it. Therefore, so too our knowledge and understanding of "GOD" should grow as well. This truth has been the fuel that sustained my contemplation. In truly understanding and utilizing the energy and power of "GOD," the element of faith is the key. It is the key that unlocks the energy and power of "GOD" that lies within each of us. Faith allows one to channel the limited energy each individual has so that person is able to optimize his or her potential. It is through the indulgence of personal faith and contemplation that the power within each of us is released. Through faith, I have come to understand that there is a purpose to the existence of each life. As well, each individual life has something specific to contribute to the "whole" that serves to enhance and perpetuate what we call "reality." This is true whether we are talking about a blade of grass or an elephant. In human terms, this means that each of us truly has a God-given gift that we are to share with those around us. This "gift" is released by the faith that we have. This faith we must have in ourselves as well as in the Will of "GOD."

We, as a species, do not always recognize that we must remain open to a continued evaluation of our collective reality, in hopes of gaining a greater understanding of what the unbiased truth is. The words "GOD" has given me are meant to bring about a clearer understanding of our spiritual Nature. It is an understanding that can be embraced by people of all religious followings and secular practices.

It places "GOD" within a context of understanding that can be easily understood and embraced. Our understanding of "GOD" within the context of the "Divine Energy of Life" will transcend religious and secular beliefs and practices. While recognizing the word "GOD" as the name for the generally acknowledged supreme being, understand deep within yourself that your interpretation of this entity is limited by your own knowledge. Whether we are referring to the energy that "He" is or that "life force" within living things, whatever we choose to label it, the power of "GOD" is real.

Many of us, young and old, are searching for an understanding of our existence relative to our spirituality. There are many different reasons for this. One such reason is that not one of us can escape recognizing this part of ourselves. In addition, those of us that embrace our internal perceptions can truly sense the need to find this part of ourselves. We recognize our need for direction at this particular time in human existence. There are far too many of us still having a problem with recognizing and/or embracing the existence of "GOD." one reason may be that it has become increasingly more difficult for those born into more current times to embrace most existing "religious" doctrines, because of the influence their knowledge of science and tangible reality has had upon their perspectives. Most organized religions base the adhesion to moral code upon the fear that individuals will suffer in the "afterlife." They will "burn in hell" if they do not obey the rules set forth by that religious body. However, individuals can feel a truth within themselves that leads them to have wants/desires that transcend the parameters of existing religious constraints. They also are finding it difficult to continue believing in the hellish punishment at the basis of most religions. This notion of "hell" causes many individuals to shy away from recognizing a structured form of religious belief. They seem satisfied with their adopted "I'll believe it when I see it" attitude. What is needed is a clearer understanding of our spirituality. One that is more truthfully related to our understanding of what we know to be true about our physical existence and ourselves. What individuals are searching for is "divine" truth. They are searching for "revelation." To understand and benefit from our spirituality, we must seek it out. In essence, we must listen for "GOD" from within ourselves. Within the Holy Scripture at First John 4:13 it says, "Hereby know we that we dwell in "Him," and "He" in us, because "He" hath given us of "his" spirit." That "spirit" is the Divine Energy of Life.

The true understanding of "GOD" eludes us because we separate the knowledge of reality we possess into categories. For example, many of us look to the Bible for the full explanation of our spirituality. Yet, we use general science, chemistry, mathematics, and physics to define the systems and properties of our existence. What we must do is put the truths within the Bible together with the truths of our reality, to determine the "whole" truth. These other truths are the truths of science, of physics, of mathematics, of chemistry, of philosophy, and more. Because there is only <u>one</u> existence, there must be <u>one</u> explanation of it. This means that all bits of knowledge make up one "whole" truth. What we must do is place reality in its proper context of understanding. We must accept the truth that there is one single source of all creation. Our limited understanding has caused us to interpret this source within a context that allows us to think of it as a human personification. Humans are "in the image" of "GOD." "GOD" is not in the image of the human. When the human walks erect, it looks like a primate. When a human walks on all four appendages, it looks like an ass (I mean donkey ☺) or a dog. If "GOD" had a form like ours, then many animals were "in the image of "GOD," not just the human. Therefore, personifying "GOD" is not a correct interpretation of this divine entity.

One of the faults of such an interpretation is that it allows us to attach an ethnicity or a group characteristic to this personification. This in turn allows each different group to have its own version of what is truly a single entity. Another fault that affects each of us on a subconscious level is that in thinking of the Supreme Being as a human personification, we create the opportunity for our individual disobedience to the Will of "GOD." To the degree that humans are in the image of "GOD," they are like individual Gods themselves. The power of such a revelation manifests itself within the ego box of the mind in such a way that at a given moment in time, every individual feels all-powerful. It is within that moment that an individual will embrace his or her will (desire) as though it is all that matters. They will do what they desire to do even if it conflicts with or violates the positive code of conduct to which each of us is to adhere. That person will disregard GODs' Will because at that moment, that individual feels like "GOD." They then pursue their own will, and perhaps even think of it as GODs' Will.

For the purpose of opening our minds, we must replace the label "GOD," with the label "Divine Energy of Life." By doing this, we remove the subjective interpretation of our spirituality and replace it with an objective interpretation to which we can all relate. We must move beyond religion with respect to understanding the divine entity. We must open our minds up to other more descriptive sets of words or labels when endeavoring to understand what "spiritual" means. Each of us must face the truth that it is blatant arrogance to assume the human species has defined "GOD" and there is no more about this divine entity to be learned. The human species does not even know how it came to be, but it has resigned itself to accepting an understanding of "GOD" that was developed at a time when human understanding was in its infancy.

While not seeking to define "GOD" in entirety, each of us must accept that "GOD" is energy of divine form. The composition of "his" being is significant and relevant to our understanding of "him." So that there is a clear understanding upon which to base the perspective from which these writings are interpreted, recognize that "GOD" is a label. It is a word that can be and will be used by me interchangeably with "the Divine Energy of Life." "GOD" is in each of us in the form of the spirit, the Divine Energy of Life. The human can identify and/or explain everything of texture inside the human body (or temple). The only element within the body the human cannot fully explain or recreate is the source of the energy that makes the heart beat in rhythm. That is other than to say it is electrical in nature. The source of our creation is "GOD" (the Divine Energy of Life). Just as this is a spiritual reality, there is a worldly (scientific) reality that our creation and existence in general is based upon and can be expressed in one simple term. That term is "energy."

This leads to the following inference: as our creation and existence is energy manifested into matter, the divine truth is that our origin is energy. Our creator, "GOD," has a form that by our definition cannot resemble the fleshy human in any realistic way. This is because, unless you are prepared to debate the possibility of other dimensions, GODs' place of origin is beyond the boundaries of Earth's atmosphere, what we term "outer" space. To the humans' understanding, nothing of living matter as we perceive it can exist under those environmental conditions. As we are energy, our creator must be, to the limits of human understanding, energy in some divine form. "GOD" uses energy to manifest and sustain "his" creations, as we perceive them. "His" form is unknown and cannot truly be determined by humans. I submit that the label given to me by "GOD" for that which we are derived from, the Divine Energy of Life, should be deemed acceptable and accurate as it relates to the full expression of the truth that has been revealed to me.

Civilized, metropolitan lifestyles have led many of us to a perception wherein the definition of "human" is such that it is not an animal. Because of this, many of us have an interpretation of reality that occurs out of context. Since many humans do not consider themselves animals in a real sense, they move about as though they are separate from Nature. Because of this, humans do not understand their individual lives relative to the system of Nature to which they owe that life. There is a connection between the system of social order, the system of human spirituality, and the system of Nature. If we do not make this connection, then the interpretation of the one reality is perceived as occurring in two different, separate contexts. In addition, because of a pursuit of self-gratification, the priority assigned to the required actions (responsibilities) related to each of these "realities" is misplaced. Again, we can label our two interpretations of the one reality as the worldly reality and the spiritual reality. The worldly reality we interpret to be our material world. It is the earthly existence within which we function on a daily basis. Our interpretation of what would be the spiritual reality is incomplete, fragmented, and misunderstood. It is incomplete because we do not see that it is the "whole" picture and encompasses every aspect of existence. It is the one reality. Our interpretation of it is fragmented because there are aspects of our existence that are naturally occurring that we consider as being separate manifestations of reality. The truth is that all naturally occurring phenomena are a part of spirituality.

Our spirituality is misunderstood because the truth has been given to us repeatedly through the words that "GOD" has sent to us, and we have yet to see the meaning held within them. The intent of this collection of words is to rectify this unfortunate circumstance of existence.

It is a physical (scientific) reality that our creation, as well as existence in general, is based on and can be expressed by one simple term. Again, that term is "energy." It is the energy that makes everything move. The foundation of this energy is the Atom. The Atom is the basis for the design of every element and system of existence that followed its creation. Relative to the systems of existence, every one of them is based upon the elements of that particular system revolving around a central source of radiant energy that in essence, has influence over; has power over; has <u>authority</u> over those elements that revolve around it. There are three major systems within our existence that generate authority to which each individual member of the human species is to yield. One major system is that of **social order.** Social order is the system of movement by which the interdependent group achieves continuity, as each member exercises their respective individuality. It is constituted by smaller systems like that of the individual, the family, business, the community, etc. Another major system is that of **human spirituality.** It is the understanding within which the system of human movement interrelates and connects with the movements of all other living things on our Earth. Human spirituality is the system of movement within which our species exercises its responsibility to the divine system. Lastly, there is the major system within our existence we have labeled, "**Nature.**" It is the system of movement whereby all living things work together to produce the energy and conditions necessary to perpetuate the earthly existence. Nature is the system that produces the earthly energy that drives every other system on our planet. Each one of these systems is the result of the actions set in motion by the Divine Energy of Life.

Human Reality and Truth

We are well into the new millennium. Some think of it as a new beginning. Others see it as the beginning of the end of humanity. Neither interpretation is truly wrong because the future is still to be determined (chosen). The question is, determined (chosen) by whom? Shall individuals, corporations, or governments determine the future of the human species? Most individuals believe they determine their own destiny. They believe this because their minds have been conditioned to function within restricted parameters. Within these, parameters, their interpretation and the resulting perspective is limited by the selfishness and greed that results from thinking of existence only in terms of how it relates to their daily life. Individual destiny is merely a part of human destiny. Whatever human destiny is, that is the destiny of the individual human as well. Corporations and governments are determining our future on this planet, and we individual humans are allowing them to do so. We actually empower them to lead us to our slaughter. This is because we choose not to expend the energy and effort it takes to be responsible for more than ourselves as individuals. The Holy Scriptures indicate that a "body" will lead humanity into damnation. As individuals, in general, we do not concern ourselves with the collective future of humanity or the rest of the life upon our Earth. People are so caught up in their own lives, that they feel they do not need to worry about the world around them. Do not be seduced into thinking that there is not someone worrying about it. Do not naively believe that there is not one individual, or group of individuals, planning the future of life on our planet relative to the available resources. One or perhaps more persons out there <u>are</u> concentrating on what to do with the future of this planet and its resources.

There will come a moment in this new millennium when the individuals of the human family will reach the fork in the road of our existence. The terrorist acts against the twin towers at the world trade center and the pentagon are signs indicating this fork in the road is fast approaching. From these horrible occurrences, it is clear to the consciousness of all humanity what actions are good and what actions are evil. The movements considered good and those considered evil within the human species were exposed by these occurrences. Each individual saw the effects of love, joy, compassion, sharing, nurturing, patience, discipline, perseverance, sacrifice, compromise, tolerance, and godliness exemplified before their opened eyes. As well, each individual saw the effects of selfishness, greed, indifference, rage, revenge, ethnic hatred, depravity, intolerance, and ungodliness' exemplified before their opened eyes. Now, humanity will have to choose its direction from only two possibilities. The two choices of direction can be termed "right" or "wrong," or they can be termed "positive" or "negative."

The decision-making process of which direction each of us as individuals will choose must begin now. When the time actually comes to make our final choice as individuals, not one of us will have time to ponder. Now is the time to learn of what and who you truly are, and on which path of the journey of life you wish to travel.

There are many signs that Bible prophecy says will identify the "terminal" generation. One such sign is recorded by Daniel: "but thou, o Daniel, shut up the words, and seal the book, even to the time of the end: many shall run to and fro, and knowledge shall be increased" (Daniel 12:4). The translation of this scripture indeed indicates that the terminal generation shall experience a notably significant increase in knowledge, what some have labeled a "knowledge explosion." From the time of Adam and Eve until into the 1900s, humans either walked or rode horses to get around. In the span of a few decades, our species has seen the creation of everything from automobiles, trains, and planes, to the space shuttle. The fields of medicine and science have given humankind miracle drugs and machines that have revolutionized our existence. The greatest evidence of this prophecy come true is the "information superhighway."

In a home or office, at the touch of a button, anyone can immerse themselves in a sea of information and knowledge via the internet. In Second Timothy 3:1-5 of the Holy Scriptures, the apostle Paul describes the state of society that will initiate the "end times":

"....in the last day's perilous times shall come. (humans) shall be lovers of their own selves, covetous (greedy), boasters, proud, blasphemers, disobedient to parents, unthankful (ungrateful), unholy, without natural affection (love), trucebreakers (malicious and vengeful), false accusers (abusive and slanderous), incontinent (unrestrained; uncontrolled, especially with regard to sexual desire), fierce (savagely violent), despisers of those that are good, traitors, heady (insincere and deceitful), high-minded (shallow and childish), lovers of pleasures more than lovers of "GOD." (Humans) having a form of godliness (consciousness), but denying the power thereof, (and) from such (responsibility) turn away." This is a mirror image of the current state of American society. The choice made by Americans, followed by the other societies of the world, will determine the direction the journey of our existence will take and will ultimately shape our fate as a species. All who are legal American citizens share the responsibility for our present circumstance, and whatever destiny we will face as a nation.

The scripture in Genesis 11:6 indicates the unlimited power the human wields when it possesses thorough use of words because it is attributed to "GOD." The verse is, "and the lord said, behold, the people is one, and they have all one language; and this they begin to do (building the tower of babel): and now nothing will be restrained from them, which they have imagined to do." From this, we can infer that our natural progression led us to have one language. As well, we can also conclude it was the humans' arrogance that brought about the need for various tongues. As well, we can also infer from this that we can accomplish anything we set our minds to because of the power of words. In February of 1995, it was reported that the world's 6,000 languages were dying off quickly, leaving only a select few. Spiritually speaking, the human species is returning to one of the circumstances "GOD" originally set for us all. It is us all communicating as a single unit. It is natural for us all to have the ability to understand one another, and this is to lead to greatness within the context of our subordinate position to our creator. We must embrace the opportunity before us. To do that, we must combine knowledge with wisdom and insight, as we expand our vocabulary in an effort to interpret the realities we face more fully. One of those realities is the authority of "GOD."

The death of these other languages is largely due to technological advancement. Satellite television, cellular and digital telephones, and the internet allow people to speak to each other all over the world instantly. This all drives the need for the use of language(s) many understand. The "universal" language is turning out to be English. If English is to be the language of the world, how does that reflect upon the significance of the American population? The place of the first universal language was babel. Babel experienced the ire (wrath) of "GOD" because of the arrogance derived from great progress and presumed self-sufficiency. Its inhabitants considered themselves better than their neighboring brethren in both the technical and social realms of existence. The same wrath befell the new Babylon and for the same reasons. Both defied the tenets of "GOD." Does not Americas' attitude and posture fit the same mold? The parallels are truly too similar to ignore.

Prophecy must be taken into consideration. This is because it is true that a determination, identification, or "prediction" can be made of the path that will lead to a specific result, by identifying the "actions" that will lead to that conclusion. A person can infer that they will earn a degree in the future, if they complete the "work" or "actions" that will lead to that end. Identifying what it is we want, or where we want to be in life, and performing the "actions" that will lead to that end determine the path of our lives. "History" is based upon the "actions" or events of the past. The future is defined by the actions that lead to it. Prophecy is a vision of the future that is based upon not only a revelation or divine truth, but also a conscious understanding of where actions lead. Place this understanding with a revelation and a map of future events can be defined. All prophecy has indicated the end is near. Each one of us can feel the intensity and fear of its approach in our hearts.

We do not realize the true nature of these feelings because we attribute them to the level of uncertainty, violent behavior, and chaos that exist in our lives and in our society. Nevertheless, this truth is evident because individuals are all starting to seek out some understanding of "religion" or spirituality in their own respective ways. As a part of these events, there are spiritual reactions that we are to manifest to avoid damnation. For the word "reaction," we can substitute "required action." These things are what are required of us as a part of Nature's system.

The human species has to evolve. I believe the next stage of human evolution begins within the conscious mind. Because of this, we are going to be aware as it takes place. A key element of awareness is recognition. It is a conscious application of the mind. As is Nature's way, evolution does not occur because of choice. Though our species will be aware during the process, our evolution is not up for debate. There is no choice of whether it should begin or not, whether it should take place or not. Evolution is a stage of life and a part of human destiny. What each of us must come to understand is that this evolution is Nature's way of perpetuating our collective existence. Those that evolve will live, and those that do not will likely die. Those that live will create for themselves a utopian living condition.

Truth be told, the process has already begun. It is happening right under our noses and right before our eyes. As I said would be the case, we are aware of it. However, as a collective, we have not examined this occurrence relative to the evolution of our species within the context of Nature, even though we often use the term "evolution" when discussing elements of what has begun. We are in the first stages of this evolutionary process, and it is taking place within the conscious mind. It begins with the evolution of communication, and this highlights the renewed importance of words. The information superhighway is the primary factor of the next stage of developed communication. I may be wrong, but I believe that very few really understand the impact that this new technology will have on our lives. imagine, by exerting no more energy than is required to push a button, individuals will have access to full libraries (printed words!) of knowledge on any subject matter of interest to them. The realization of the information superhighway means that mental application will become more specific and profound. People interested in attaining knowledge within a given discipline will become smarter in that area, because of the wider availability of information to utilize in the learning process. Life will become more intensely competitive because of this circumstance of reality. This is all the result of collections of words that already exist. The ease with which we can access them will bring about this change. With our current educational support system, an individual has to make a greater effort and expend what some consider substantial energy in pursuit of knowledge. With most humans, the more work it takes to attain something, the less it is reached for. With the advent of this "information superhighway," all knowledge will be at our fingertips. It will provide us with the most information a person has ever had about life. This will make our interpretation of our existence much more clear. It will also make the need for objectivity in both the foundation of the mind (perspective), and the action of the mind (interpretation) more significant and relevant.

In truth, the computer and the information superhighway are forcing the evolution of the human consciousness upon us. The computer is changing the way we communicate and the way we think. It changes the way we communicate for obvious reasons. It changes the way we think because of how it affects our personal and professional lives. Because of this, our minds, our concepts, our consciousness must evolve also. How will the computer have such a great impact on our lives? Say, for example, a computer is installed in someone's work area and it is meant to relieve that person of some part of his or her work routine. That part of their routine was something they <u>had</u> to think about because most human action is the result of thought. Therefore, since that person will no longer have to think about that task, their mind is free to think about something else. The more involved computers become in our day-to-day tasks, the less thought we will have to devote to daily accomplishments. This in turn will allow us more of an opportunity to pursue personal interests and growth.

Each of us must consciously participate in the process of our own evolution because much of it takes place within the minds of our species. To begin the process of human evolution as a collective, each of us must have a mindset that is objective.

Because evolution is a part of Nature that most times takes decades to transpire, most humans have not interpreted the changes that have occurred in the structure of our existence as human evolution. Look at the length of time it has taken to make the computer become a stable part of our everyday lives. The integration of the computer into our lives has occurred over a period of decades, and it was divinely destined to set the stage for the beginning of the process of the evolution of our individual and collective consciousness. Each of us must recognize the spiritual aspect of this "evolution of the mind," because we need to gain an understanding of our individual and collective direction so that we can avoid the damnation of the "end times." This happening is not merely the result of random occurrence. This is truly divine destiny. If these events are interpreted and placed within the proper context, it is evident that we are in the period biblically referred to as the "end times." We can embrace this revelation and allow it to lead us to our salvation. Or we can live the lie and follow it to our collective destruction (i.e. damnation). How do we prevent the age of computers from overwhelming and destroying humanity? We save ourselves by accepting all of the realities and responsibilities of our existence. One of those realities is that we are supposed to run machines, not the other way around. Therefore, if computers and technology in general advance to a degree that they are considered more precise than the human mind, then the human must accept the responsibility of developing its mind. We humans must evolve in conscious understanding to maintain the ability to get the most out of our creations. We start by doing what is right (action directed in a positive direction) and accepting the responsibilities that are inherent to our existence. These are individual, family, social, and spiritual responsibilities.

With education, we are to gain a better understanding of our reality. We can only arrive at a truthful understanding if our examination of the realities before us is done from the proper perspective. As we learn, we must build upon our current perspective to facilitate our arriving at a more truthful understanding. If we were to examine the nature of human existence, the will and intellect associated with the conscious mind could not be excluded. The conscious, cognitive part of our brain gives our species dominion over the rest of the animal kingdom. Other animals have brains, the enlarged and greatly modified part of the central nervous system contained in the cranium of vertebrates, but none as advanced and complex as that of the human. The humans' brain contains the power of expressive consciousness. With this, the human is aware of its own existence, feelings, and thoughts. The state of consciousness also gives the human the ability to identify external objects and conditions, as well as imagine new ones. It gives them the capacity to reason, the power to draw logical conclusions and make inferences. "Inference" is one of the most important qualities of human mental ability. In any case, our state of consciousness not only allows us to recognize, but also to examine existence. This examination is to lead to an interpretation we have labeled "truth." During examination, each of us must <u>always</u> remain conscious of the fact that not one of us knows all there is to know about existence. Therefore, the conclusions a person comes to are not based upon the "whole" truth. This is not to imply that one's interpretation of reality has been untruthful. However, it has been incomplete. Each of us must remain open-minded when it comes to interpreting what is learned and experienced. Allowing the mind to close around only what one chooses to believe has led to perspectives that are heavily affected by personal bias. The effect of personal bias upon individual interpretation and the resulting perspective is keeping many from recognizing what it truly means to exist.

Most other animal species have one level of awareness. The human animal's interpretation of existence occurs within the context of two stages of awareness. There is a perceptual difference in how the human experiences existence. This difference is the result of the existence of the conscious mind. All animals recognize, but the human does a more in-depth examination in an effort to ascertain truth. This results in the human making two interpretations of the reality it perceives. One interpretation is of the physical or earthly existence within the context of the human as an animal. We have labeled this interpretation "reality." The other interpretation is derived from the humans' consciousness (that part of the mind that is in the image of "GOD"). We have labeled this interpretation "truth." An example of how existence occurs on two perceptive levels for "word-using" and "non-word-using" animals can be illustrated by the review of this circumstance of existence: take a human and a squirrel and place them both in a living room full of furniture. When the squirrel goes about the room, it may jump on the coffee table, it may avoid the coffee table, but it will recognize the reality that there is a structure in that room of which it needs to be aware. However, the human perceives that same reality differently. It recognizes the structures in the room. The humans' examination brings us to ascertain a truth. That truth is our determination that one such structure is a coffee table, which to our understanding brings aesthetic and practical benefit to our existence. This is an example of how one circumstance of existence is perceived and interpreted on two separate levels of understanding.

In recognizing this, it is evident that our analysis of human existence needs to be less superficial and more specific. Reality occurs within a context that is specific and relevant to all life. Truth occurs within a context that is specific and relevant to only human life. We can actually label the context within which these interpretations can be categorized and more readily understood. They are the interpretations of the "worldly reality" and of the "spiritual reality." Yet, it must be understood that these two interpretations of what exists must make up one understanding. There is the recognition of reality, where existence is what it is. Generally speaking, this is the worldly reality. It is the objective perception of existence that can be recognized by both "word-using" and "non-word-using" species. This objective perception is the circumstances of existence being interpreted literally. How most other "non-human" animal species experience existence would be categorized and labeled by us as reality. This is the objective recognition of existence. Then there is the examination of reality, which leads to the truth. In a general sense, this is the spiritual reality. This is the second "level" of interpretation. It is where that same element of existence is subjected to the "conscious" deciphering of its relevance and significance, which is to conclude with a developed understanding. This understanding is the foundation of our perspective. Truth comes from the interpretation of existence within the context of what humans consider significant and relevant. Truth describes the area of understanding where existence is subject to review by the conscious mind. Truth is the interpretation of reality that is relevant and significant to the human. It refers to the meaning that the human consciousness attaches to reality. It is existence given meaning by the interpretation derived from human consciousness.

Truth, and our recognition of it, is the basis for the actions or movements that each human has. Based on the truths that we accept as we experience existence, we choose the actions our bodies will have. What we "do" is based upon what we choose to believe is true. Within the confines of what we interpret to be the "wild" aspects of Nature, the actions of the beings that inhabit these areas are balanced as a natural occurrence within the context of the system of Nature. Within the confines of what we interpret to be the "civilized" aspects of Nature, the actions of the beings that inhabit these areas are balanced as the result of choice, because human action (or behavior) is controlled by our conscious minds as beings with free will. These choices and the resulting actions are very much a part of the system of Nature. The system that makes Nature work is equally relevant to our functioning in harmony with all that exists. What is characteristic of "GOD" is characteristic of Nature. What is characteristic of Nature is characteristic of the human. Balance, harmony, creation, regeneration, cycles, energy, and responsibility are characteristics that are inherent to all that has the Divine Energy of Life flowing through it.

We fail to make this association because we have grown to recognize Nature as something "exterior" to ourselves. This is a grave misinterpretation of ourselves, as well as a misunderstanding of our true place in reality. We perceive ourselves as being "more" than animals. This is because we are not recognizing the complete definition of the word "animal" and its relative significance. Our interpretations of reality have become less complete, as our lives have become more self-centered. Because of this, the understanding that develops from that interpretation is incomplete as well. Consider the fact that the word "being" is defined as existence, as opposed to nonexistence. It is to have reality in time, space, or idea. It is anything that exists actually or potentially. However, as we look closer at this word, we find that the suffix "ing" is defined as "the act of doing the action expressed in the root verb." That root verb is "be." It means, "To exist." From this, one can conclude that there is more to living than just occupying time and space. To have life is to have action, i.e. the act of doing what is necessary to exist. The term "human being" implies the nature of the humans' existence. It is the human going about the task of existing and doing. This label refers to "man, woman, or child" and nowhere within this definition is there an inference that the human is not an animal. Therefore, because this is true, the human cannot think of himself or herself as not being a part of the system of Nature.

"Existence" is an objective term that is the label for <u>all</u> that has occurred. Fully interpreting this statement, existence is not the result of mental conception, but is a physical manifestation. It is the result of action. It is the label for what occurs in time whether or not there is a human presence. "Reality" is the label for one of the humans' interpretations of its perception of existence. Personal feeling or belief cannot be allowed to become an influential factor in this interpretation. Our interpretation of reality must be an objective one. Once the influence of personal feelings and beliefs has become a factor, we have a subjective interpretation and reality ceases to be reality. Our interpretation of existence cannot be derived from what we would like to "think." It must be derived from what is actual and factual, because it must be able to be perceived and interpreted the same way by others. Truth is the most fallible interpretation of existence because it is the result of human understanding. It is therefore subject to an individual's state of mind. Truth is the collection of words the human uses to define, understand, and communicate reality. We do not write or speak reality; we write or speak the truth. Reality is not words or other symbols. Reality is what is manifested through action. We must open our minds so that we interpret existence beyond our own relevance to it. Reality is individually perceived and interpreted into truth, and this is from where individual perspective is derived. Yet, we must recognize that we cannot alter our perceptions of reality. Therefore, we should not alter our interpretation of it. Humans have a tendency to manipulate the interpretations we have of our perceptions. What is being manipulated is the truth. We cannot manipulate our interpretations of reality so that they fit into our subjectively created "fantasy worlds," and still have the facts of those moments conform to what is true. Because reality is objective, our interpretation of it must not be skewed by our personal feelings or desires. Our interpretations of our perceptions must be objective and without bias, so that they can be translated into the truth.

There is a real obligation created by every truth or bit of knowledge. It is true that there is an obligation created by being alive. For the human, both reality and truth create responsibilities we must accept. Reality and truth are only relevant and significant to the human species, other animals do not "think" within the context of these terms. Therefore, only the human is obligated by its awareness of both reality and truth. We must be responsible. The truth that occurs in the context of the worldly reality is supposed to be evident and universally perceived by all humans. These truths cannot be changed just as reality cannot be changed. Examples of these truths are science, a piece of fruit, or the result of an event in time. By our actions, we cannot defy the existing laws of science. We cannot change an existing apple into a pear, and we cannot change the results of the past. We are bound by the truth in these realities.

The truth that occurs in the context of spiritual reality is a bit more involved. To one degree or another, it is supposed to be subjectively perceived by each individual. It occurs within the context of how that individual relates to the truths of the worldly reality, and how that individual fits into the grand scheme of things. Examples of these truths are what we think, how we act, what we do. However, one thing is clear, we are bound by the reality that the spiritual aspect of existence is true. We think, we act, and we do. Therefore, it is we, each of us as individuals, who are responsible for the physical results of those occurrences. To deny this is to close off the mind and heart to what is the truth.

As the evolution of the conscious mind occurs, our reasoning process must follow this path: as we perceive existence, we must recognize that those moments of reality should be completely interpreted, which is to place them in both a worldly (objective) and spiritual (subjective) context. There is an interpretation that is relevant to the human within the context of its physical "self." In addition, there is an interpretation that is relevant to the human within the context of its conscious "self." It is that part of ourselves we currently label the "soul." The humans' understanding of existence must be derived from two interpretations, leading to one perspective. In understanding this, we can use comparisons that describe two separate things coming together to produce one in a way that occurs throughout our existence. For example, it is hydrogen and oxygen that come together to produce one element, water. It is a sperm and an egg that come together to produce one life. It is the two sides of the brain that make up one mind. This last reality is evident in that the human brain is split into two hemispheres, the left and right sides.

In a broad sense, these "sides" process information in a way that is indicative of how we should interpret reality. The left hemisphere is the side of objectivity. It is more logical, verbal, and able to deal with things in sequence, one truth at a time (step-by-step). This is the side that is "plugged into" reality. We have created a label for our conscious awareness of our significance and relevance to the interpretation derived from this side of the brain, it is the term "self." The right hemisphere is the subjective side. It is more emotionally intuitive, skilled at spatial relations (pertaining to, involving, or having the nature of space), and able to deal with things all at once (the big picture). This is the side that is "plugged into" spirituality. The label we have created for our conscious awareness of our significance and relevance to the interpretations derived from this side of the brain is the term "soul." The left side goes about the task of understanding words and finding their meaning, it deals with things in a structured fashion. The right side appreciates humor, imagery, and emotional content. It is also the side that the brain relies upon to perform perceptual tasks and is able to deal with the entirety of circumstance, the whole truth. When a person performs a perceptual task, brainwaves, blood flow, and glucose consumption reveal increased activity in the right hemisphere. When a person speaks or calculates, activity increases in the left hemisphere. These hemispheres reveal the physical and spiritual aspects of the mind, and they are physical realities. The human brain is physically split into an objective, physical hemisphere, and a subjective, spiritual hemisphere. Yet, it is to be used as one brain. Likewise, we must take into account both interpretations of existence to form one perspective.

Because our perceptions of worldly reality are based upon more tangible and pronounced elements of existence, we place a higher emphasis on the interpretation of the "self" as we seek understanding. This is much more of a priority than we place on what we would consider our spiritual reality and the interpretation of the "soul." However, the revelation is that spiritual reality has domain over any subordinate reality that is conceived of by the human consciousness. It is within the context of spiritual reality that the system of existence occurs. It is this "spiritual reality" that provides the energy that keeps our Earth spinning in a circle. This same energy keeps hearts pumping and brains functioning. This "spiritual reality" produced all of the systems that make Nature work. so, humans must come to the understanding that while the responsibilities of our worldly reality may seem more pressing and immediate, the responsibilities of our spiritual reality, and the interpretation derived from the soul, are vital to our existence on a much more relevant and significant scale. The daily responsibilities of our existence are included within the context of spiritual reality, but they are subordinate in priority. For this reason, we must embrace the revelation that maintaining two separate perspectives must end.

Within the Holy Scriptures in James 1:8 it says, "A double-minded man is unstable in all his ways." To restore stability to our collective existence, we must accept the single truth of our divine roots. We must recognize and understand the context in which all reality is spiritual, and the "whole" truth of existence is a never-ending pursuit. We must continue to "do" the things necessary to maintain our physical existence, while recognizing there is more to the meaning of what we do than personal satisfaction. The relevance and significance of that meaning, i.e. that spiritual reality, will be there whether we choose to see it or not. What we must do is reach the point in human existence where recognizing the complete truth is no longer optional. The human species must develop a pattern of collective decision-making that is reflective of an objective understanding of the truth. Moreover, we must seek to bring about positive results as we act upon those decisions.

We comprehend the concept of an unyielding truth when it is applied to physical reality. We must broaden our objectivity to recognize this concept as it relates to our spiritual Nature. Some of us still have difficulty with even accepting spirituality as a true part of our existence, and we must all get past this obstacle before we can place our spiritual Nature into context. We can overcome this handicap if we recognize that the circumstances that we perceive need to be interpreted relative to the two "levels" of one understanding, which we have interpreted as two separate realities. Because we are physical beings in a tangible existence, the stimulation of our senses is an overwhelming experience. This is why one-half of our consciousness so dominates our being, that of the self. Spiritual reality is the foundation of existence, by virtue of the divine energy that sustains it. We interpret spiritual reality as a more subtle manifestation because it has no mass for us to perceive with our physical senses. However, if we open our minds to the oneness of all that exists, we will see that spiritual reality does have mass because everything that exists is the result of it. Everything that exists is the result of what we can interchangeably label "GOD," the Divine Energy of Life, or the Divine System of Nature. The choice of which label to use can differ. However, because each term refers to the same entity, our resulting understanding and perspective will be a common one.

The element of balance allows the Divine System of Nature to work correctly or rightly. It is also the element that allows every part of the system to work correctly or rightly. We can see this if we truly look at reality, but it is true whether we recognize it or not. Our physical body is balanced, for the most part, symmetrical. Our brain is balanced, having two sides equaling a whole. Likewise, our understanding must be balanced. Though we have the ability to choose, we are bound by the laws of the Divine System of Nature to seek or pursue balance. In recognizing this, it is the responsibility of each individual to learn what is necessary to produce this balanced understanding. One very important thing we must learn is the balance between objectivity and subjectivity. Without an understanding of the balance between the "self" and the "soul," a person is reacting to only half of the story.

The major fear that each of us must overcome is the fear of ourselves, i.e. our recognition of our entire being. There are so many of us that are afraid to listen to ourselves. This is because we are afraid we will find out how much energy and how much potential lies within our respective beings. We are afraid to find out that only the individual is responsible for controlling that energy and potential, making only the individual ultimately responsible for what happens to him or her in life. The notion that we must control and understand all our actions overwhelms most of us. We fear having to be responsible for such an awesomely powerful being as ourselves. This fear keeps most of us from desiring to get that deeply into ourselves. The first example of this that comes to mind is the fear of solitude, manifesting itself in the need to have the television or radio on whenever an individual is alone in some space.

By having something going on or a sound in the background whenever individuals are alone, they are distracting themselves away from where their mind would go if it were not focused on or distracted by something. Each of us must embrace our opportunities to experience solitude, and where it takes us. We must get over the fear of having to control the awesome power and potential that is within each of us. This power is the only true power each of us has, and it is truly a blessing from "GOD." To take full advantage of this power, we must come to a clearer understanding of ourselves, and use this knowledge to its fullest, positive potential. We cannot reach a clearer understanding without words, and we cannot use knowledge without producing action. What does this mean? We must become more literate, and our behavior must be right(eous).

We recognize the reality of "self" and do not have much difficulty defining it to our understanding. The problem is that the "self" is recognized as being the sum of all that individuals are. It is merely the first stage of awareness and interpretation of a very complex being. The interpretation of the "self" is related to the reality that exists around each of us. It is the knowledge that is derived from physical matter, which makes up the tangible world. Humans are supposed to have a second stage of awareness and interpretation. Deep inside each of us, this is known to be true. This second stage of awareness and interpretation occurs at the level of the "soul." The knowledge derived from the "soul" is what reality means to us as individuals. It is what reality means, i.e. truth, this is what is "felt" and "sensed" by us. It is the revelation of our individual significance to existence.

There are two important elements of our spiritual Nature that each of us must embrace more fully. One is the interpretive ability inside of us that allows us to determine accurately what is good and what is bad, what is right and what is wrong, what is positive and what is negative. This is the divinely (positively) energized set of feelings, emotions, intuitions, and other sensory perceptions that are to guide all our conscious actions. The other is the truth that as an individual, each of us is a unique member of the group that is our species. Within this "uniqueness" lies the special gift we are to share with those around us that will perpetuate positive change or growth. These things are there within each of us whether we recognize and embrace them or not. We recognize the reality of the "soul" to the degree that we know it exists. However, because to this point it has not been satisfactorily defined or understood, we do not embrace its complete relevance to our existence. Each human has but one brain. It consists of two halves, which are distinctly separated. Humans have but one consciousness. The "self" and the "soul" are the two halves of this consciousness.

The soul is divinely connected to the Divine Energy of Life, and it is within the context of the soul's manifestation that we experience "GOD." The soul is the area of our being that encompasses our "personal" relationship with "GOD." The soul is the pathway or conscious "link" between the human and the Divine Energy of Life. All of these revelations are brought forth by the ingestion of words. As an individual learns more words, his or her understanding grows proportionally to that person's vocabulary. There is no greater truth than the one that dwells within each of us. Sigmund Freud recognized the levels of perception and labeled them "the ego" and "the super-ego." The words he used to express this truth were the result of his interpretation of his perceptions. John F. Kennedy urged us all to stop being selfish and greedy, and to help each other when he said, "it is not what your country can do for you, but what you can do for your country." "GOD" has sent us many prophets and teachers to help us to the truth. Their messages are all the same, just expressed at different levels of depth, and with different interpretations of perceptions. Some of these notable people were Gautama Buddha, Mohandas Gandhi, and dr. martin Luther king. There are many other men and women too numerous to mention.

There are reasons why we have not completely embraced the truths these individuals have brought to us. For one, they were merely humans like each of us. Their words are interpreted within the context of only the first stage of interpretation. Hence, they are given the same weight as the words spoken by the individuals doing the interpreting. We have not connected their words to spiritual reality. Therefore, the true meaning in them is lost.

It is not until the truth of those words is "felt" that the relevance and significance of them are truly embraced. As well, some of us have made derogatory judgments of these individuals based on their human frailties. These judgments undermine the trust that is necessary to believe. These judgments are also derived from our lack of depth when we are interpreting reality. Every human being has weaknesses, and therefore, each of us will transgress. Because of this, are we <u>not</u> to believe in the knowledge they bear? We have also disregarded the truths they have given us because of selfishness and greed. This is also the result of there not being a second stage of awareness and interpretation taking place within our minds. Our subjectivity is supposed to be limited to our understanding of ourselves. It is not something we are supposed to impose upon the elements surrounding us (reality).

What must we do? Each of us must be objective. Five of our basic senses are of sight, hearing, smell, taste, and touch. These senses are stimulated by the elements of reality that we are exposed to during the course of our lives. We then interpret these experiences. In the quest to experience, the human allows the most pronounced, overwhelming aspect of its existence, the tangible world, to dominate its life. We desire most the experience of sensation that produces the more satisfying response in us. The essence of pleasure is sensation, and we are always seeking stimulation to create it. Because of this, we manipulate our perception of some circumstances so that they are more "satisfying" to interpret. In effect, for subjective reasons, we are pleasurably stimulating our minds by manipulating the truth. We must examine this reality and recognize that there needs to be a more balanced meaning to the lives of beings with gifts such as we have. The lives of humans are meant for much more than simply self-stimulation. Wild animals would respond to sensation just as we do in a given circumstance. As conscious "animals" having civilized behavior, we must transcend the stimulation of our basic physical senses to a level of existence where our personal satisfaction occurs on higher planes. This is mind over matter. For example, there is a great deal of satisfying stimulation to be derived from the energy that is produced when making people happy. It can be better and more invigorating than any food, sex, or drug-induced feeling of euphoria if the sensation is interpreted from the proper perspective. That perspective is positive and objective.

We must allow the objectively interpreted (true) circumstances of existence to shape our perspective, not the interpretation of circumstances that we subjectively manipulate. This manipulation occurs as either a conscious act or an unconscious one. It is sometimes done as a result of some bias or pre-judgment. It is sometimes done because of a lack of knowledge. It is sometimes done because individuals are concentrating their thoughts and actions within the confines of the first level of human interpretation, that of the physical self and the five senses. We must no longer view reality from our individually biased, selfish, self-indulgent perspectives, but must accept all that is reality with sincere objectivity. We must interpret every realization with regard to its objective implication, and <u>then</u> its subjective implication relevant to us spiritually. The latter will unfold the truth it holds for us as individuals. One way of interpreting what is meant when one is "shallow" is that a person does not allow his or her examination of reality to occur on a level any deeper than that of the physical "self." Each of us "mentally" lives in our own individualized world. What we must do is be deeper. We must open our minds up so that we all look at reality for what it is. This means expending more energy than we do now because we must think more than we presently do. When individuals open their minds up, that is what it is to come out of their subjectively created world. Whether it is a snobbish world, a racist world, or simply a biased world, we must live in reality as it is, each of us taking responsibility for making our life positive and/or right.

Objectivity is the "common" state of mind that humanity must embrace to come to a better understanding of the truth. In other words, to understand reality truthfully one must be objective. True understanding is a process that develops over a period of time, so one's objectivity must be constant.

This need for constant objectivity is reinforced by our recognition of the significance and relevance of the circumstance we label as a "precedent." "Precedent" is defined as an act or instance capable of being used as a guide or standard in evaluating future actions. A precedent is a preceding instance or case that may serve as an example for or a justification in subsequent cases. It is an act or instance that may be used as an example in dealing with subsequent similar instances. It is the recognition of something as a reality, and the taking of the ramifications of this revelation into consideration as the establishment of understanding takes place. A precedent truly is a moment of reality, a true occurrence. Once something is recognized as being real, it must become a factor in the process of understanding, if what is sought is the truth. Once something occurs or exists, the truth in that instance cannot be ignored. To close the mind to the truth held in a moment of experience is a subjective act that cuts individuals off from understanding the truth of a moment. Ignoring or not taking into account the truth within each moment of precedent is to perpetuate hypocrisy or falsehood. To start to put an end to hypocrisy, each of us must recognize the relevance and significance of each moment of reality before us, each precedent. With this in mind, let us proceed to recognize and examine some crucial aspects of human perspective to derive a greater understanding of our existence, as well as what "GOD's" way actually is.

Our Earth is responsible for reality, but not existence. We do not and possibly cannot know all there is to know about existence. "Reality" is the label for the humans' perception and interpretation of the time and space it recognizes. Reality is not the definition of existence. "Reality" occurs within the context of this circle we are on, i.e. our Earth, and the Divine System of Nature. In addition, it is whatever we experience (perceive and interpret) as we travel beyond our Earth's atmosphere. "Existence" is everything that has come to be within the Universe. Relative to our Earth and the average human being, reality must be dealt with objectively. This is because reality relates to the Earth, its systems, and everything within it. What we think about what happens around us does not affect what happens. Therefore, when we interpret what happens, what we think should not alter that interpretation. Our actions do affect what happens around us. To effect a positive change in the world around us, we must react positively to the events of our existence. Each of us must seek to have positive action. We are a part of the Earth's system, and we must perform our part so that the system functions properly, regardless of whether or not we personally benefit or profit. We must only seek to do the "right" thing.

Existence in its totality is subjective because it relates to the individual and his/her place in the Universe. For example, as a moment in time is interpreted, each of us must recognize that because it occurs within the realm of reality (i.e. what we know to be real), we must interpret the facts of the moment. This is objectivity. Yet, because that moment is also a part of the Universe which we do not have full knowledge of, we must also "consider" how that moment and we as individuals fit into the "big picture." This "big picture" is divine or spiritual in nature. To fulfill our part in the "big picture," we must start thinking of ourselves as "spiritual" beings and recognize that we must do the best we can in every waking moment of our lives. We must be positive beings relative to polarity, by thinking positive and doing positive things. Each of us must seek to understand the significance and relevance of the realities we face to determine the path our journey through life is to take. We must then take our two interpretations of that moment and develop not two, but one perspective. This is because we are not just a part of the Earth and reality, but also a part of the Universe and all of existence. We must conclude that there is only one true reality, and we must all subscribe to it.

This may be a bit confusing. Perhaps things will become clearer if we examine human existence within the context of an analogous relationship with mirror images. We have established that for the human, existence has two interpretations that are true and are to lead to one perspective. One is the context of understanding in which the human considers itself as a physical being, i.e. an animal, and it experiences existence on that physical plane relative to day-to-day life. The other is the context within which the human has conscious awareness of itself, causing it to examine what it has experienced. This is another plane of existence. As an individual looks in the mirror, they recognize that they are standing on the Earth in a very real sense. This is the physical context of existence. That person understands that they must do what is required of them in this earthly existence. Yet, they also recognize that their image, a very real yet subtle and intangible aspect of them also exists, within a dimension that they know exists, but they do not truly understand.

One way to interpret this analogous experience would be from a largely subjective perspective. From this point of view, one could arrive at a personal conclusion based on what is perceived. That conclusion would be that this side of the mirror, this earthly existence, is the only dimension in need of concern, because the other side of the mirror, that reflective dimension, does not "physically" affect this one, as far as is known. From that perspective, a person deals with the worldly aspects of life as they happen, relative to how they choose to understand it. If something occurs that is not understood, that individual is not open to the possibility that the occurrence could be relevant and significant to that area of his or her existence that is not understood. In effect, that person is dismissing the other aspect of existence, keeping it separate from his or her process of understanding. If there were an action required of them relative to the area of existence they have dismissed, it goes unfulfilled.

Each of us must be more objective and open-minded. That person in front of that mirror must accept the reality that he or she exists both in a physical sense and on the intangible plane where the image occurs. Individuals can use the labels "worldly reality" and "spiritual reality" for each respective interpretation. While recognizing both aspects of existence, that person still needs to continue to act within the context of their daily life. He or she must also maintain recognition of the fact that they know about that image in the mirror, i.e. that other dimension of existence. As well, that person must embrace the fact that he or she cannot <u>truly</u> dismiss its relevance or significance to their life. There must be recognition of two dimensions of existence, one that requires things of that person of which they are aware, and one about which he or she is not completely sure. So that person fulfills the requirements he or she is aware of, and he or she keeps in mind the fact that there is more to life to be understood.

Within this worldly, physical dimension, it is easy to accept that having positive action is better than having negative action because the results of this movement can be experienced with the physical senses. Suppose that all that was known about the intangible dimension where the image was located was that positive was the required direction for all movement related to the individual casting the image. Then, it would only make sense that having positive action or movement be sought whether that individual understands why or not. This is because if the circumstance is relevant to the worldly and tangible dimension, positive is known to be the required direction for that person's action or movement.

If that person does not understand the circumstance, it may be because it is relevant to the spiritual and intangible dimension, in which case full comprehension probably will not occur. However, positive is still the required direction for that person's actions regardless of what they want to believe because it corresponds to what that person is supposed to do in a worldly sense. Moreover, because a truly reliable source (a Bible perhaps) indicates this is required as well.

When things happen that are not understood, that person can consider the fact that these things could possibly be relevant and significant within the context of that aspect of existence that is somewhat obscure. By being open to the consideration of this possibility, an individual actually maintains only one perspective based on what is known and unknown.

To be open-minded, is to be objective. if it were known that the right response for anything related to that "somewhat obscure" aspect of existence was to do the positive thing, a complete understanding of the workings of that area of existence would be unnecessary with regard to fulfilling one's responsibility to it. This is what each of us must embrace.

Reality must be interpreted as objectively, as its definition implies. Truth cannot be ascertained from a subjective interpretation of existence, because there is no room for the consideration of all possible relevant factors of evaluation in this narrow mindset. There is consideration given to only those factors that result from the conceptions of the individual, which are confined to the limits of that individual's interpretation, understanding, and experience. The truths derived from a wholly subjective interpretation of existence are bits, fragments that serve to validate the perspective that that individual wishes to have. Having an overly subjective perspective is the result of a person's need to create his or her own personal reality. That individual wants to create his or her own world to live in, so that he or she can be the center of it. The nature of our species and social structure dictate otherwise. There is only one reality. It includes all that exists. What has created this state of mind in the human that can be likened to it having its head stuck in the sand like an ostrich? It is the human's lack of humility. It is the perception that the Universe revolves around an individual because he or she is at the center of it. It is the ego that says that this interpretation and perspective is the only interpretation and perspective that exists.

Say a giant the size of the world's tallest building was to suddenly appear and go roaming around the Earth. Humans would appear to the giant much the same way ants appear to us. They have a social structure, places to live, roads, etc. They also work very hard. We work seemingly as hard, but probably accomplish a lot less and with much more disorganization. In any case, in this instance we could no longer think of ourselves as being the center of the Universe, even if we wanted to. The point is that one being is superior to another only within the scope of its knowledge of itself. To have an ego (which is a natural component of our consciousness) and always be humble would appear to be a contradiction at first glance. To place the ego in its proper context, think of it as a little box or a small room in the recesses of the conscious mind. It is a place given to each individual by "GOD," for the purpose of re-energizing and re-focusing ourselves. The ego is the only place an individual is supposed to go and indulge himself or herself in self-glorification. However, as the location of the room would indicate, this is a private matter. No other individual should have to deal with this "ego," and an individual should not go into that room <u>excessively</u> themselves. The individual should enter it only in those times when they need to reflect on their accomplishments and redefine their direction.

Because of a number of reasons, one of which is a true lack of understanding, a lot of us humans have chosen to live in these "ego boxes." This means they are living in a world with very confining boundaries and one that places each individual at the center of focus. Objective truth cannot penetrate the walls of this box. These truths can only be perceived when one emerges from this shut-off place. This ego box is no more relevant to who an individual really is than what they think of themselves. It is what each of us does, i.e. our actions, which truly define us as individuals. A person can think they are president, but if they steal cars, that person is a car thief. A person can think they are a priest, but if they molest children, that person is a pedophile. A person can think they are mature, but if they act childish, that person is immature. When a person chooses to recognize only partial truth, whether it is subjective or otherwise, they are only deceiving themselves. Within the Holy Scriptures at James 1:23 it says, "…be ye doers of the word, and not hearers only, deceiving your own selves." The objective truth does not disappear because a person closed their eyes to it. Others can still see it and act upon it. Each of us must wake up by coming out of the darkness and into the light. Denying reality is lying to oneself. Each of us must stop lying to ourselves.

I may seem to say the following more often than is necessary; it is because this point is a very important stepping-stone to the evolution of the humans' conception of existence. Perspective is an individual circumstance relative to the state of one's ideas and mindset. It is the factor that determines how information will be processed and understood. There are two frames of mind that profoundly affect the nature of one's perspective. They are the state of objectivity and state of subjectivity. It can be very confusing to discern when an individual is to be either objective or subjective during their moments of existence. The conscious mind is complex, so individuals must recognize that any description of one of the mind's "states" must also be complex. Let us examine some of these descriptive labels to determine what is significant and relevant about them. Objectivity could be viewed as a state of "open-mindedness," where one's reasoning process is free from personal feelings or prejudice, and conclusions are based on fact. One could almost say that subjectivity is a state of "narrow-mindedness," but that would not be a complete truth. To be subjective is to base one's conclusions on what is perceived to be true, while placing an excessive amount of emphasis on such factors as personal moods, attitudes, prejudices, and opinions. However, subjectivity is a necessary part of our psyche. Many of us understand subjectivity to be a negative element of our being, because of the bias that is created within this mindset. Yet, there is a positive aspect of subjectivity, this is related to our subjective wants/desires. Like objectivity and many other words, there are different interpretations and applications of the meanings these words have. The significance and relevance of each is determined by the context of the circumstance to which it is to be applied.

Three pairs of terms identify fields of thought that have a profound effect on how our perspective is formed. These terms are the "self" and the "soul," "objective" and "subjective," along with "objectivism" and "subjectivism." The terms "objectivism" and "subjectivism" are relevant to our understanding of human interpretation. However, within the context of this book, they cannot be strictly compared to the terms "objective" and "subjective" even though all four terms are obviously related because they share their respective roots. This is because objective and subjective are words with singularly defined uses, while objectivism and subjectivism are the labels for technical philosophic doctrines. Objectivism is the doctrine that implies that reality is external to the mind, the view that human knowledge is universally valid. It is not human knowledge that is universally valid. It is the circumstances of existence that are universally valid. The circumstances of existence would occur whether or not the human was around to perceive it. Since all human knowledge is derived from the circumstances of existence, that knowledge is universally valid.

Subjectivism is the doctrine that implies that the good and the right can be distinguished and judged only by individual feeling. Individual feeling is a physical manifestation of that person's spiritual Nature. The vibrations of our bodies that our mind interprets (i.e. hunches, gut feelings, first impressions, impulses, intuitions, emotions, and extra sensory perceptions) are natural to us, meaning they are a part of us. Each of these is an element of our divine guidance system that is within our bodies, and each is exhibited in individual ways within each person. It is not simply that judgment can only be made by individual feeling, rather, what is good and right can be determined based upon what is individually "felt." The human individual can feel what is good and right for them by utilizing its collective sensory abilities. The doctrines of objectivism and subjectivism are not separate. Together they are the collection of words that explain the "levels" of human awareness and interpretation. Again, we humans interpret these levels as the "self" and the "soul." They are indeed levels, or stages of interpretation. Of the six terms, three are related to the first level, and three to the second. The three related to the first level of interpretation are self, objectivism, objective. The three related to the second level of interpretation are the soul, subjectivism, and subjective. Let us examine these terms relative to their relationship to the stages of interpretation.

The first level of awareness and interpretation is an objective one. It is the most pronounced "stage" of awareness and interpretation because it occurs within the context of the "self." It is specifically related to the worldly reality. At the level of the "self," we become aware of our terrestrial existence and interpret it into reality. The self is affected by the external forces of existence, i.e. "matter." The first line of perception of these external forces is the body. We experience these perceptions through the (five) senses of the body. Therefore, the "self" is the "physical" way the human encounters experiences. It is the level where the manifestation of objective truth occurs.

Objectivism is the doctrine that indicates reality, i.e. the circumstance of existence itself, is external to the mind. Objectivism is the label for the truth of what each of us is to do as we experience. Each of us is to interpret what we encounter objectively, or outside of ourselves and our subjectivity. Being objective is to have a reasoning process that is free from personal feelings or prejudice, allowing our understanding to be based on fact. At the first level of interpretation, what we are processing is a series of objective circumstances. Being objective means that we must interpret them as such. What causes the problem here is that within the individual, the "self" has become overwhelmed by sensation and/or the desire for it. This leads to a manifestation of selfishness and/or greed that result from the pursuit of satisfaction on the level of our existence that is supposed to be objective, rather than subjective. At this point, individuals do not come into a "second" stage of interpretation, because both objectivity and subjectivity are occurring at once. This places the mind in a position of having to decipher truth and feeling simultaneously.

The second level of awareness and interpretation is a subjective one. It is the most misunderstood stage of awareness and interpretation because it occurs within the context of the "soul." It is specifically related to spiritual reality. This is because the ability to subjectively understand, infer, reason, and create is what brings each of us into a likeness with "GOD." The area of our being that is considered the "soul" is where the consciousness attaches personal meaning to the impressions perceived by the senses. This is obviously a more profound interpretation because it is derived from an examination that goes beyond the stimulation of the senses themselves. It is the level where the manifestation of subjective truth occurs. Subjectivism describes how our feelings can tell us right from wrong (positive from negative). The aspect of our being that manifests this ability is the soul. Being subjective is defined as interpreting reality with an excessive amount of emphasis on such factors as personal moods, attitudes, prejudices, opinions and the like. Subjectivity should only be considered excessive when in transcends the second level of interpretation and occurs on the first level as well.

At the second stage of interpretation, you are <u>supposed</u> to be seeking out your "inner" most thoughts, hunches, gut feelings, impressions, impulses, intuitions, emotions, and extra sensory perceptions. These elements tell us what is right or wrong from within. Therefore, to place emphasis on these things is not wrong. What is wrong or negative, is to be subjective at the first level of awareness. What is also wrong or negative, is to allow your subjective impressions to be overly influenced by our worldly reality. Each individual must realize that as physical beings, externally produced sensations that stimulate our senses are very overwhelming when compared to the subtleties of mental stimulation. Subjectivity is a manifestation of the soul. Each individual must recognize that he or she must keep subjectivity separate from the first stage of interpretation, so that one of the "influential" factors indicating right or wrong is not overwhelmed by the sensation produced by one of the five senses. Because once this happens, a person is not truly responding from within (where "GOD" is), that person is responding from "without," without "GOD."

Truths are objective and feelings are subjective. While all of existence is spiritual in nature, our first stage of recognition must deal with the objective truth relative to the immediate circumstances we face. We must respond to those truths with positive action. We must then examine those circumstances more deeply to discern the spiritual relevance within them. By "spiritual relevance," I mean how those circumstances relate to a given individual and their journey through the natural world of this planet. Our positive wants/desires are spiritual in nature because they are a part of our natural being.

Our wants/desires is the motivational tool of our life force, used to guide us to fulfill our individual destinies. To reach this level of understanding, we must perceive our reality beyond a superficial interpretation. Our interpretation of our experiences must be deeper than the first stage of awareness. For example, if we only understand our personal wants/desires at the superficial, first stage of awareness, our interpretation becomes overwhelmingly influenced by the sensations produced by the exterior world. We then interpret our wants/desires to be simply the thoughts and urges that push us toward what will satisfy us for a given series of moments. What drives us to move toward things is deeper than that. If we do not gain a better understanding of ourselves relative to the natural world around us and grow more toward reacting to the truth objectively, our reactions will get more and more subjective to satisfy those wants/desires within the context of worldly reality. This generates selfishness and greed.

During our lives, we are not to pursue our wants/desires first, we are to first act and react positively to what is the truth, and then seek personal satisfaction. When we pursue personal satisfaction before truth, the second stage of interpretation never truly occurs. Rather, our recognition of reality becomes a singular process that includes both objectivity and subjectivity. When they both occur at the same stage of interpretation, our subjectivity is influenced more by the self than the soul, more by worldly reality than by spiritual reality. There is no recognition of the spiritual interpretation of reality. From this, we ultimately develop two perspectives of reality, because we never actually deal with the spiritual relevance of our experiences. Therefore, because we recognize that a spiritual relevance is "possibly" there, it remains in our conscious and subconscious mind as a separate perspective from how we "ordinarily" interpret things. It surfaces whenever spirituality or religion becomes an issue for us. Whether it occurs out of need, because of some general conversation we have with someone, or because we are attending Sunday morning mass.

If we allow both stages of interpretation to occur within their proper contexts, we are truly left with one perspective that has recognized both the spiritual reality and the worldly reality. Subjectivity should not occur until the second level of interpretation, and within the context of the soul rather than the self. We must be objective when interpreting the external world, and subjective when interpreting our relevance to it. For example, in terms of defining oneself at the first stage of interpretation, the question to answer would be "<u>what</u> am I?" Besides being an individual animal within the human species, the answer is determined by the result of that person's actions. It <u>is</u> how that person objectively fits into reality. As we progress on to the next stage of interpretation, to define oneself at this level, the question to answer would be, "<u>who</u> am I?" The answer is the result of an understanding of the truth about oneself and is subject to constant interpretation. This is accomplished through the "subjective" analysis of one's own consciousness. It is how that person <u>wants/desires</u> to fit into reality.

What each of us must do is never lose sight of the common aspect of existence. An individual's interpretation of existence should be the same as everyone's, which is what it means to be objective. One must limit their subjectivity to a secondary examination of reality. A person's primary examination must occur within a context that applies to a "norm," an average, or standard understanding of the circumstances, rather than imposing their personal subjectivity upon the common reality. The depth of one's understanding of truth depends on that person's level of objectivity. This refers to the priority of the individual's objectivity versus subjectivity, and the degree to which there is a balance between the two within his or her consciousness. To be "self" centered is to be overly (excessively) subject to the perceptions of the five physical senses. To be overly (excessively) "righteous," is to deny the inherent fallibility of the human. The system of Nature requires balance in all aspects of creation. The human consciousness is no exception.

The truth of one's understanding of their interpretations is based on the degree of objectivity on the part of the perceiver. Honor is based on the objectivity of one's interpretations, because it is measured by the standards of the human community within which one interacts. Truth is based on the objectivity of one's interpretations, because truth is objective in nature. Individual reality (i.e. the world a person lives in as perceived by that person) is based on the objectivity of that person's interpretations, because if it is based solely upon subjectivity, it becomes fantasy. <u>For it to be truthful, our understanding of reality must be built upon the foundation of objectivity</u>. Each individual human must recognize this in dealing with his or her respective life. This understanding must be applied during their thought process. Words are an expression of reality. To examine and understand existence objectively, each person must be prepared to recognize the truth conveyed by the words that result from the translation of individual perceptions.

Our personal interpretation of the existence we perceive is a system of three mental steps. The first step is the process of perceiving existence. The human's perceptions are based on the information it receives from the use of its primary senses, those being touch, sight, hearing, smell, and taste. This is how we receive impressions from the external circumstances that we encounter during our lives. The second step is the process of interpreting these perceptions. The final step is the process of allowing or disallowing an objective interpretation of existence to shape our state of mind. A difficulty arises after we have perceived existence. It is when our "subjective selves" or "egos," use the knowledge we acquire to perpetuate our feelings of self-importance. During this circumstance, we lose our objectivity and our perspectives become skewed by our manipulation of reality through our altered interpretation of it. We forget that "reality" is our interpretation of what is truly an objective existence. The perspective from which humans interpret the realities before them are shaped by and limited to the openness of a person's mind and his or her level of understanding. Therefore, for humans to interpret knowledge (which can also be expressed by the terms experience, reality, and truth) accurately, individuals would need to broaden their objectivity and the scope of their understanding of existence.

As individuals and as a society (the collective), our "system of thinking" does not include all its steps, and we are acting upon the thoughts that result from this incomplete process. Many of us are not thinking objectively first and are quickly losing our ability to be objective at all. Our subjectivity is supposed to occur within the confines of our objectivity, not the other way around. Spiritual reality has domain over any other reality perceived and interpreted by us. Worldly reality occurs within the confines of spiritual reality. However, as physical beings, we must act upon worldly reality first for us to survive. Therefore, we are to interpret our existence objectively first, determining the correct or right(eous) way to respond to it. Only then are we to look to the subjective interpretation to see how things relate to us as individuals. Unfortunately, our thoughts are monopolized with subjectivity. When an action occurs that we must interpret and react to, more often than not, our first thoughts focus upon what we think is positive for ourselves, rather than what is positive for that circumstance. In this way, we are acting upon our subjective interpretations of reality, seeking to satisfy ourselves within the context of the circumstances of the worldly reality. We satisfy our obligation to spiritual reality, to the Divine System of Nature, to "GOD," by doing what is correct, right(eous) or positive on all levels of occurrence in an objective sense. This must be done regardless of the personal ramifications.

Divinity or our spiritual Nature is real, and it has supreme domain over any subjective reality that is manifested in our minds as we perceive and interpret existence. We must recognize that the "actions" of "GOD," i.e. the Divine System of Nature, create the circumstances of our lives. Because the results of our lives are derived from a system, there can be pre-determination, and it can be said that the Divine

Energy of Life scripts our existence. Yet, each of us must also understand that within this system, some of its parts move freely or independently, though remaining within the goal of the system as a whole. It is the human that freely chooses how it will "react" to the "planned" circumstances it faces. Responsibility is the human's "reaction" to the action that is the gift of life.

We, the human population, as offspring from the Divine Energy of Life, must start seeing the nature of what time places before us as it truly is, and perceiving the meaning attached to it. That meaning we call "truth." Right now, our individual interests are shaping our perspectives. This is leading us to distort the truth by fragmenting it into bits of truth, to create the circumstance whereby the individual human can put itself before "GOD" by manipulating the reality "GOD himself" has created.

What follows are the principal elements of spirituality that my "GOD" has revealed to me, that I might share with my family across the globe. I know that my "GOD" is the same as everyone else's "GOD." Each of you must come to realize this and embrace these words. Yes, it is true. "GOD" has given me words to give to you. The message these words convey is "what "GOD" said to do," and this is the time to do it. Each of us must focus on the time ahead and the truths therein. Every individual must now make definitive choices. These are the choices of whether to believe or not to believe, to have faith or not to have faith.

The System of Nature

The Divine Energy of Life created the centerpiece of our earthly existence. It is the Atom. The smallest particle of matter is the Atom, and it is the essence of energy itself. Matter is the substance of which any physical object is composed, including ourselves. The Atom has at its core the *sphere-shaped* nucleus. The nucleus is positively charged by protons, and it contains electrically neutral neutrons. There are *rounded* negatively charged electrons whirling *around*, or orbiting (*circling*) the nucleus. The laws of science have defined a balance between the protons and electrons that is naturally occurring and produces energy. To one degree or another, every other system of existence is built upon the structure and action of this divine creation. Each system has elements or aspects of a reality, revolving around a central source of power. Our Earth is one of these elements of reality. The design for its creation is based upon the structure of the Atom, as is the human body. If you open your mind, the words to come will bare this truth out.

The Divine Energy of Life provides the power that sustains the *circular* rotation of our Earth. This *circular* movement not only produces energy, but also a magnetic field that causes polarization. One pole is the north or positive pole, and the other is the south or negative pole. A basic understanding of energy and magnetic properties such as polarization and fields of force is relevant to the understanding of our spiritual Nature. This is because energy and magnetism are inseparable aspects of the Divine System of Nature. The properties of "divine" energy include all that we know about energy, magnetism, electricity, and more. Yet, it is the principles of electromagnetic energy that are at the core of this life-giving source of power that we recognize as being spiritual in nature. The actions and interactions of matter, the movements of matter, occur by way of four basic kinds of force. These are the forces of gravitation, and electromagnetism, along with the strong and weak nuclear forces. All of these forces are dependent upon *circular* motion to one degree or another.

Nuclear forces are a 20th-century discovery, and they can only be studied within the context of nuclear physics. The recognition of nuclear force as a fundamental force of the system of Nature exemplifies the significance and relevance of the Atom to defining our existence on a spiritual level. The basis of the system of existence, or the foundation upon which it is built, is the "Atom." The makeup of the Atom provides the design for the Divine System of existence, and every other system created after it. The structure of the Atom could be compared to our solar system. The radiant source of positive energy represented by the nucleus of the Atom corresponds to the sun within our solar system. Whirling *around* the nucleus are the electrons and whirling *around* the sun are the planets of our system. Yet, if we recognize the Atom as the blueprint of the system of existence, then the comparison of the structure of the Atom must apply to all parts of the system, not just one area. Every system of natural or human construction is based upon the design of the Atom. Plant life, animal life, the human body, the family, business, government, social structure, everything that requires a system to function properly utilizes the general structure of the Atom for its formation.

Note that in the comparison using our solar system, there is a slight difference inherent in the two structures. The electrons whirl *around* the Atom from different angles, while the path of the planets is more linear. While the paths may be different, the general structure is the same. The relationship between the two can still be made and perceived if the mind is open to objective reality. Allow your objectivity to manifest itself as you continue through this text. One can make the same comparison between the Atom and our planet. This is a more complex relationship because the Earth "births" Atoms, in the form of life. With regard to the Earth, the source of radiant positive energy is the liquid core of the planet. The soil or the "ground" would represent the neutrons, which is electrically neutral. Whirling *around* the core are the negatively charged animals (electrons).

The whirling action is created because as the Earth is *round*, every inch of movement in any direction creates an "*arc*," or segment of *circular* movement. Therefore, as we continuously move about, in context, all animals are "whirling" *around* our Earth. The structure of animals can also be compared to the Atom.

Take for example the human. The radiant source of energy here is the brain, verified by the fact that the brain gives off measurable electric waves. The body is composed of 60% to 70% water. Hence, the action of the cells and fluids of our bodies can be said to "whirl" *around* the brain. In addition, the heart pumps fluid in a *circular* motion within the body. For the Atom to be true to its system of existence, the objects moving *around* the *orb* must move in harmony and without conflict. When this harmonious movement is interrupted by conflict, in the form of collision, destruction occurs. This is a natural aspect of the system of Atom s. We are composed of Atom s, so this holds true for us as well. If you extracted human action from the earthly picture, all movement would be considered in harmony with the Divine System of Nature because it would occur instinctively within the context of the balance of Nature, i.e. the food chain, etc. As the human is also an animal, its action must also be harmonious and in balance with the life around it. The difficulty here is that the human mind controls human action or behavior. Therefore, the human is responsible for consciously choosing the "right" or "positive" actions that correspond to the system of existence. Choosing the "wrong" or "negative" action will lead to conflict and destruction.

What we know of polarity, fields of force, and gravity are manifestations of electromagnetic elements that are prevalent throughout the Universe. The space between and around charged bodies in which their influence is felt is called an "electric field of force." The Earth is surrounded by such a field, as are we. Magnetic forces appear, in addition to electric forces, when electric charges are moving, as charged living things do. Here on our Earth, electric currents in the liquid core of our planet produce the magnetic field. The magnetic field of our planet is a dipole or two-poled field, just like that of a bar magnet. Basic electrical law tells us that a magnetically charged body of two poles at either extremity of a line of direction passing through its mass results in a positive and negative polarity. The Earth is one of these "charged bodies" and so is the human. Each has two poles. The "line of direction" passing through the Earth's mass is the axis and passing through the human's mass is the spine. The laws of electromagnetism indicate that which binds us to the planet, gravity, can be defined in terms of basic magnetism. The core of the Earth is positive, and the ground is neutral.

Relative to the laws of magnetism, only opposite poles attract. Therefore, the pole that binds us to the positive Earth is our negative pole. It is at the base of our spine, or the bottom of the line of direction. since we are two poled, the other pole located at the other end of the line of direction passing through our mass, the spine, to be magnetically and/or spiritually right in our polarization, would need to be positive. That location is our head. It is our brain, or more specifically, our mind. Within this context, to be spiritually correct or right(eous) requires that we have positive thoughts. Positive energy (in the form of positive thought) is supposed to radiate from this location of our bodies. A positive frame of mind motivates or moves us in a positive direction. The positive mental energy produced by a positive state of mind directs the motions of our bodies toward the positive resolution of the circumstances before us. Energy flowing in a positive direction is the physical foundation for the spiritual realities of our existence, as defined within the context of the physical sciences. The right understanding of this physical foundation of spiritual reality lies within our knowledge of magnetism and polarity. As "charged" and "bi-poled" beings, our physical existence is constructed around the principles of electromagnetism. Because our magnetic relationship to our Earth designates our negative pole as being located at the base of our spine, we are naturally and spiritually responsibility for maintaining a positive pole within our minds.

As the Earth is a direct reflection of the Atom, we know that the human has a negative charge as defined by the Earth's relationship to the Atom. Within this context, the living objects that move *around* the Earth have a negative charge because the electrons that move *around* the Atom have a negative charge. Spiritually speaking, this is why the human will never be without sin. The human can never get away from the negative aspect of its being. However, the nature of the action of the electrons (i.e. the direction in which they move) is positive because it is that movement makes the system of the Atom work correctly or rightly. When we reflect upon how positive and negative affect our lives, we recognize that when our energy flows in a positive direction, we feel alive, happy, energetic, and right. If this is what a positive flow of energy brings to our lives, reality indicates to us that the opposite would be true for a negative flow of energy. It depresses us and brings us down in much the same way that energy flowing in a positive direction brings us up. What we must recognize is that positive and negative are electromagnetic manifestations of the spiritual equivalent of good and evil, right and wrong. This is true for all animals, wild or civilized. One may ask, "How do wild animals emanate positive thought?" Their actions are also controlled by their minds, yet their movements are naturally occurring, instinctive and intuitive. What they do is a natural part of Nature's system. If their actions correspond with the system of Nature, then the "thoughts" that produce that action would be deemed "spiritually" right, or positive in polarity. Humans must direct their actions through their consciousness. Hence, it is up to them to choose to produce positive thought, which will lead to positive action. By producing negative thought and the resulting negative action, we are in effect, upsetting the balance of Nature.

The Path of Energy is the Circle

"What goes *around*, comes *around*." "*Around*," within this context, denotes the direction of the object in motion. Action or movement occurs in a direction. It travels a path. We label these paths with such terms as up or down, right or left, forward or back, east or west, and positive or negative, to name a few. For motion or action to occur, there must be energy present. No motion or action occurs by itself. There is always a source that is responsible for the occurrence of any movement or action. All movement must have a source of energy. The source of the energy that creates the actions of existence and time are interpreted by most humans to be divine or spiritual in nature. This energy must also travel a path of direction.

Divine motion produces divine energy. The motion that results from divine energy generates existence. Existence is the result of a system, or process. A process is "a systematic series of actions directed to some end." For example, within the human, the "systematic series of actions" are the functions of our cells and organs within the body. The "end" is our continuing to live. All that lives does so because of some "motion." That motion is a part of some physical "process" that sustains life. The label "divine" identifies the central source of creation. Though some of us call this source "GOD," my understanding takes "his" existence a bit further in that I recognize "his" actual form as being energy. Therefore, I can just as easily say it is the "Divine Energy of Life" that created everything in the Universe, and not be confused by my wording. In creating the condition of existence known as Earth, our creator utilized a system based upon energy and *circles*. The divine energy is the fuel for the necessary motion that produces the circumstance of existence. *Circles* are the foundation of the structures, cycles, and systems that produce the circumstance of existence.

The degree to which "circles" are relevant to the actions of existence is readily evident. To make that relationship clearer, we must look at the whole picture. This picture is of the Universe, the whole of creation, embracing all celestial bodies and all of space, i.e. the cosmos. Seemly all celestial bodies of mass, i.e. planets, stars, comets, meteoroids, asteroids, have a quasi-*spherical* shape. The circle is the common geometric symbol that is pervasive throughout the Universe. The circle is the primary format within which the actions of existence occur. If we make an effort to understand our reality within this context, things will truly become clearer than ever before. The circle's significance and relevance becomes more pronounced as we progress in these writings together. As you will see, the circle has a direct relationship to life and the creation of it.

The human has subdivided the Universe into what it terms "Galaxies." Of the Galaxies it has been able to discover, we humans have labeled ours the "Milky Way." Within this "Milky Way" is our own solar system. A group of *orbs* we call "planets" *revolving around* or *circling* a main source of radiant energy referred to as a *spherical* "star" and known to us as the "sun." Our home planet is the Earth. It is the third planet in a system of eight or nine. All of which maintain a *circular* rotation themselves (there is speculation that Pluto is not a planet, and its revolution is still in question), and a continuous *circular* path or *orbit around* our sun. An important point of fact is that these cosmic *revolutions* are the difference between life and death, because of the energy these revolutions produce. If a heavenly body does not spin in a *circle*, it is said to be dead. If it does spin in a *circle*, it sets in motion a chain of events (or connected moments) that can result in gravity, atmosphere, and life itself. Fortunately, our Earth is one of those spinning or revolving heavenly bodies. Moreover, make no mistake, if our Earth stopped turning in a *circle*, we would all die immediately. Taking all of this into account and realizing that we do not understand the relevance of all that exists around us, one can still conclude that there must truly be a relationship between what I will call the "energy of the circle" and creation.

Most of the aforementioned heavenly bodies either travel in circular paths around other *spinning orbs*, or they travel *around orbs* that emit energy. Others spin in a *circle* themselves. These are all relative manifestations of circles. Other examples of the significance of circles to existence are such things as a pulsar, which is believed to be a neutron star. It is an extremely dense, *spinning* object that sends out pulses of energy. A "black hole" is a region or object in space in which the gravitational pull is so great that even light cannot escape. It can cannibalize a neighboring star by pulling its matter into its gravitational field. That matter forms a *disc* around the black hole that *rotates* and builds up energy. Another example of the natural relationship between circles and the Universe are the results of an experiment performed during a space shuttle mission. In November of 1995, in an experiment designed to improve safety in space and to reduce pollution here on Earth, the Columbia's astronauts ignited drops of fuel in space. Most of the flames were round, instead of teardrop-shaped, because of the absence of gravity. Scholars and other learned men concur; the human would be but another wild animal that roams our Earth's wilderness, were it not for the blessings and benefits of the circle. The circle is the source of all power. Examples of this would be the wheel, the turbine, the electric circuit, the round sun, our orbit of the sun, the Earth, and the Earth's rotation. Our natural seasons come in circles, or cycles. Our day/night time periods are the result of our Earth making a circle. The most basic element of life and the foundation upon which all of existence is built is energy. The source of all energy can be traced back to some form of a circle. Regardless of what you may believe, the energy that sustains us all flows through a pathway between the Earth and us. This is true of both animals and plants. This energy is a direct result of the direction of the Earth's circular motion. Balanced circular motion produces energy. The balanced circular motion of our Earth on its axis produces energy. By having the balanced, internal circulatory motion that brings us to life, the human body also produces energy.

The divine truth about the Divine Energy of Life is that it has only a positive polarity. When the Divine Energy of Life "charges" or brings something to life, negative energy is a byproduct of this creative effort. This "byproduct" is an element of the production of existence, rather than a component of "the entity" itself. There is nothing with a negative connotation related to divinity. A good "real-world" example of this truth is the fact that individuals that have had "near-death experiences" report only sensing positive, serene vibrations. They use words like peace, love, and happiness to describe the experience. It is the divine motion of the planet that created negative because of the spinning action that generates the magnetic system and the resulting polarity. Relative to humanity, negative exists because the Earth or the material world exists. The positive energy for our existence is generated by movement on the physical plane through circular rotation, as evidenced by the Atom, the Earth, turbines, and the like. The one source that is responsible for creating all these things is "GOD." The Divine Energy of Life is the purest manifestation of positive energy. Because of this singular positive property, the movements that result from divine energy are to go in one single direction to be spiritually right. That direction is positive. This is as true as the Earth naturally spinning in only <u>one</u> direction. It is as true as time naturally only moving <u>forward</u>. It is as true as right is naturally only <u>one</u> direction. Good naturally only goes in one direction and the human must consciously choose that as its direction. These are positive actions. Charged bodies produce positive actions and results.

An electric charge in motion is called an electric circuit. Electricity is not the human's creation; we have discovered a way to reproduce and utilize an aspect of the divine energy source. I say this because it is very evident that energy, in the form of electricity, travels throughout our bodies. The measurement of energy produced by the heart is done through the use of electrical waves. The same goes for the measurement of activity from the brain. Electric signals travel through the nerves causing the muscles to react, resulting in human motion.

The human discovered what it understands is electricity, but we did not create it. If the human is an electrically charged body, then when it is in motion, it becomes an electric circuit. As our Earth is an electrically charged body, it too is an electric circuit. Therefore, in a broad sense, life on this planet are individual circuits that makeup one larger, more complex circuit.

Close examination of the nature of the divine motion of our planet, some of its characteristics are very apparent. Its motion is in one direction, and it is continuous. For our Earth to change direction, it would have to momentarily come to a complete stop. To come to a complete stop would mean the end of our existence, and to change direction would mean the same. For our current existence to be perpetuated, our Earth must continuously spin in one direction. The term "circuit" indicates that the flow or path of energy upon our planet is circular. To perpetuate our existence, we must perpetuate this circular motion of energy that is positive in nature. The continued existence of life is "perpetual motion." By thinking and acting positively, this is what we do. Think of the Earth as one living body in a Universe of other separate bodies. All living things that exist within the Earth's atmosphere are composed of Atom s. They contribute energy to the system of our Earth. This makes all living things a part of the natural system that makes the body of our Earth function. If the parts of the body do not function in harmony with each other, the system is interrupted. The body will then react by trying to eliminate that which is fouling the system by producing naturally occurring phenomenon aimed at eliminating the troublesome parts. With regard to our planet, these naturally occurring "antibodies" are the elements of our planet, i.e. earth, wind, water, and fire. These elements, with the exception of earth, are manifestations of the spinning action of the planet.

The Circuit

We can develop a better understanding of our spirituality once we embrace the fact that the word "spirituality" is simply a label. Its existence grew out of a need to identify something that was commonly recognized by all humans. In truth, spirituality is the label for our physical relationship to our Earth and the system of Nature. Spirituality can be more easily understood if it is interpreted within the context of the principles and laws that govern our physical movements. These principles and laws are explained within the context of electromagnetic energy. The information that follows is meant to bring about a better understanding through the general comparison between the life upon our Earth, and energy flow within an electrical circuit board. However, remember that life is a complex circumstance. Therefore, with regard to its comparison to an electrical circuit board, that circuit is a complex one. Also, keep in mind a unique aspect of human existence. Each individual has the capacity to direct the flow of his or her energy. Within the context of the comparison I am about to delve into, it would be as though the energy within the circuit had a "mind of its own," much like the way of fire moves. Within an electrical circuit, the path of energy is determined by the layout of the circuitry. This may be a factor that will lead you to an even greater understanding of this analogous relationship. However, it is not one that I have endeavored to explore.

A strong analogous relationship exists between the Earth, all of the life on it, and an electrical circuit. As the Earth and the human are charged bodies, as are all living things, they can be labeled as circuits individually and collectively. This is because an electric charge in motion is an electric circuit. It can be said that the Earth and all the life on it comprise a complete electrical circuit, wired not in series, but in parallel. In a spiritual sense, the circumstance of all life, and of human life in particular, is a complex state of existence. In an electrical sense, there are simple and complex circuits. However, there are laws that govern both types of circuits. Our Earth is a complex circuit. Within this complex circuit are perhaps trillions of individual circuits. The human animal is also a complex circuit. Within the grand circuitry of our Earth, the human circuit has many roles. Two of these roles are as a simple current path or conductor, through which energy flows, and as an electromotor, a producer or generator of energy.

A parallel circuit is defined as one having more than one current path connected to a common voltage source. Think of each individual life as a current path. The common voltage source is "GOD" (the Divine Energy of Life). "Circuit" is defined as the act or an instance of going or moving around, as in a circle. Electrically speaking, the circuit is the complete path of an electric current, including the generation apparatus, any intervening resistors and capacitors, as well as whatever else is left. The most important factor to understand relative to the path of the energy within this circuit is the direction in which it flows. The Divine Energy of Life flows in a circle. In other words, it flows in one direction. This direction is "positive." The path the Divine Energy of Life travels when it leaves the "source," travels through the circuitry of life, and returns to the "source," is a positive one. This energy (our energy) must maintain that path to complete this circuit. We alter this divine scheme by acting negatively because those actions divert the energy from its natural path. Acting negatively causes our natural system of existence to not work correctly or right(eous)ly.

Each individual life on our Earth is an energy conductor and generator. Within the complex circuitry of our planet, the human animal has many roles. Being dipole or two-poled charged bodies does not by definition conflict with the role of energy conductor or generator. While a conductor as a whole may be neutral, its various parts are not.

It is the movement of each and every living creature on our Earth that produces the energy that flows within the earthly circuit. As conductors of electric current, all forms of life can be compared to what are called "branches" within a parallel circuit. Each branch will carry a current that is a portion of the total current, in this case produced by our Earth. Two or more branches form a network, an interconnected system (in other words, a family or a community). The total current leaves the source and flows to a connecting point or junction, where it is distributed to the branches. Spiritually speaking, these "junctions" are the trees and plants around us. They give off the oxygen that we breathe into our bodies. Even fish need to breathe in oxygen to survive. The oxygen carries the current from the source. We breathe in the "electric field of force." This current flows through each of us. It then rejoins at another junction and flows back to the positive terminal of the source. We exhale carbon dioxide, which is absorbed by plant life and transferred to the Earth. Within this context, the positive terminal is a representation of the Earth's core. This is as true as an Atom is composed of electrons orbiting it, with a positively charged nucleus at its center, or as our solar system is composed of planets orbiting a positively charged sun at its center.

As animals are "moving objects," they can be spiritually defined within the context of Earth's circuitry. Within this definition, animals are not mere conductors of energy, they are also "electromotors," i.e. generators or producers of energy. The forces on current-carrying conductors are used to make "motors" that convert electrical, or in this case, mental energy to mechanical work, or action. Every electric motor is also an electric generator. Therefore, as we go about the "required action" of our lives, we generate energy to be utilized by living entities other than ourselves. As these other living entities are a part of Nature's system, they require energy flowing in a positive direction to function rightly within the system. However, if the direction of the energy we generate through our actions is negative, this adversely affects the natural functions of the divine ecosystem. All of the energy within the atmosphere of our planet travels a circuit, the path of a circle. This path has one direction, which is labeled "positive." Think of it in the same terms as in the way our Earth spins, in only one direction. By our actions, we determine whether the direction of the energy we produce is positive or negative. This is because we consciously choose our actions. If we think negative and act negative, then as conductors, we attract energy from a negative direction and give off energy in a negative direction. Whatever the direction of the energy we give it off, that is the direction from which we attract energy. The polarity of the energy we radiate is something we choose. It is based upon the choices we make that lead us to act.

As this energy flows, it creates "momentum." Apply the understanding of momentum in a spiritual context, and the importance of <u>repentance</u> and <u>penance</u> becomes clear. Positive actions and the resulting energy, perpetuate the Divine System of Nature, i.e. the spinning of our Earth. The opposite is also true. Negative actions and the resulting energy retard the workings of this system and the spinning action. There is a great deal of momentum created by the energy from the Divine Energy of Life, the Divine System of Nature, and the positive actions of the life on our planet. There is much more energy flowing in a positive direction being generated and conducted than there is energy flowing in a negative direction. It would take a huge amount of negative flowing energy to destroy the entire Divine System of Nature. However, it would take a far lesser amount to destroy any individual element of the system. The human species is one of these elements. Therefore, in the interest of self-preservation, we must minimize our negative thoughts and actions whenever possible. Should a negative circumstance occur, we must not lose sight of the truth that we must regain our positive direction as a way of minimizing the impact of any negative circumstance. By consciously repenting, we again radiate positive energy by allowing ourselves to mentally and physically get our energy flow back on the positive path from which we had strayed. By actively paying penance, we offset or balance out the adverse effect that our negatively flowing energies (and the resulting actions) have, by contributing positive flowing energy (through positive action) that would otherwise not have occurred. It would not have occurred if we simply accepted our negative action as a part of life, without recognizing the impact our actions have upon the world around us.

Sometimes human circumstance occurs in ways that seem to have no parameters of control, where an individual's actions are irrational, impulsive, and sometimes destructive. Is this because he or she does not have an understanding of the mind to the degree that they can constructively channel the energy generated by their thoughts? Electrically speaking, is that person's behavior the result of an energy (or thought) overload? Within an electric circuit, this sort of "overload" would create a short or break in the circuit. The effect of an open break in a parallel circuit would not necessarily disable the entire circuit. With regard to the human circuit, this means that an individual could continue to function, all the while dealing with this negative circumstance in his or her head. As well, society can continue to function while negative individuals have actions within our social system. Within the context of the earthly circuit, this means the uncontrolled actions of individuals alone will not bring about the destruction of <u>all</u> life. In the circumstance of a short or open break in the circuit, the current flow would not be reduced to zero (death), unless the open condition existed at some point electrically common to all other parts of the circuit. For the human, this could be the complete disregard of truth, or of "GOD," by all of humanity. For our Earth, it could be the uncontrolled destruction of all trees and plants, much like what is happening to the rain forests. In general, a short circuit will cause an increase in current and the possibility of component damage regardless of the type of circuit involved. In humans, is this an explanation for the increase in aggressive, sick behavior by those with "damaged" thoughts? Regarding our Earth, is this an explanation for the increase in seismic activity and overly destructive weather patterns?

Opens and shorts alike, if occurring in a branch circuit of a parallel network will result in an overall change in the equivalent resistance. This can cause undesirable effects in other parts of the circuit due to the corresponding change in the total current flow. Can this be defined in terms of the apathy, disregard, disrespect, discrimination, manipulation, and abuses occurring at an alarming rate in our society? If so, this implies that society does suffer because of the negative actions or behaviors of a few. On the other hand, perhaps it explains the erratic weather patterns being experienced around the globe. To prevent damage due to a short circuit, a fuse or overload relay is normally placed in the circuit in series with the more sensitive components or in series with the source. The fuse will open the circuit when the current (mental energy level) rises beyond functional capacity, causing the current to stop flowing. For us, this "fuse" is our faith in the word of "GOD." Scripture instructs us to release the burdens and pressures of our lives and allow our savior Jesus Christ to bear them. For our Earth, it is the eruption of volcanoes, among other things. A short usually causes components to fail in a circuit that is not properly fused or otherwise protected. Breaks and shorts in the human circuit can be likened to individuals breaking from normal, positive behavior and resorting to violent, destructive, negative activities. Worship, fellowship, humility, and belief in the oneness of "GOD" and of humanity serve to reinforce the strength and control of our minds over the temptations and powers of our bodies.

Within a motor, there are resistors. The spiritual equivalent of an electrical resistor is something that limits a human's full acceptance of its spiritual Nature. Unfortunately, parallel circuits must contain two or more resistors that are not connected in series, meaning they function independently of each other. Commencing at the voltage source (earth) and tracing counterclockwise (the direction of our Earth's rotation as perceived when standing on the surface) around the circuit, two complete and separate paths can be identified in which current can flow. One path is traced from the source through a resistance (R1) and back to the source. The other is traced from the source through another resistance (R2) and back to the source. Spiritually speaking, we could label these "resistors" selfishness (R1), and greed (R2), the two roots to which all our species' faults can be traced. Placed into context, it is as though there are two "physical" receptors within the brain that, when stimulated by the energy of reality, produce stimulation that causes the reactions we label as "selfish" and "greedy."

Resistance is a key factor in electric circuitry. This is also true with regard to our spiritual reality. Our earthly circuitry was created to work right(eous)ly, with the energy flowing in a positive direction. The resistance is greater along this path because the energy was expected to travel this path naturally. There is less resistance along the negative path because the divine design did not intend energy to take that path. However, the flow of energy will always follow the path of least resistance, and surely, that is not the right(eous) path. As humans, we take the easy way because of this ease of motion, this path of least resistance. Within an electric circuit, the flow of positive energy is <u>directed through</u> the resistors to complete the circuit. <u>Through</u> these resistors is the natural, more difficult path of our energy (be they thoughts or actions). The easier path would be wherever these resistors (selfishness and greed) diverted our energy to go. Each of us must direct our energy fully through the areas of our minds that manifest our thoughts of selfishness and greed. In this way, we will not produce the actions that thoughts of selfishness and greed generate. In the interest of "completing our circuit" or living up to our spiritual responsibilities, we must also consciously "get through" or direct our thoughts and actions through the resistance of our lives. We must not allow selfishness and greed to divert our actions from the correct, right(eous) path.

In dealing with this, we must also embrace the reality that time is the most valuable human commodity, and we do not have an infinite amount of it. Therefore, when we do something, i.e. when we direct our energy, it must be done the right, positive way. This is so that we conform to the Divine System of Nature and do not waste time by having to repeat a process in an effort to get to where we were headed in the first place. We must do things the right(eous) way, regardless of how difficult it may seem. In this way, we not only use our limited energy and time in the most efficient way, but we make our results a more stable part of reality. When not all of the steps of a process are taken, individuals may get where they want to go more easily. However, if it is not the right way, it must be done again, or the result will not withstand the pressure of time (the centrifugal force generated by the passing of days). These are some of the important factors that must be taken into consideration when choosing a direction for our actions.

When a "branch" increases its resistance, it does not affect the current flow of another branch, but it does reduce its own branch current proportionally. The manner in which branch resistors are connected in a circuit, as well as their actual level of resistance, affects the total current flow. Conversely, the manner in which a community is connected, as well as their actual level of resistance, affects the strength of their spiritual power, i.e. the intensity of their energy to live. Separatism among people that severs positive, beneficial interaction, along with an absence of the acceptance of spiritual responsibility, determines their divine strength and the strength of their group. When a resistor is alone, its resistance is greater than when it is interconnected with others. In a spiritual context, can we perceive this as perhaps a reference to the need for shared beliefs and fellowship? This would mean houses of worship and prayer are very vital elements of human existence.

Every <u>known</u> energy source possesses internal resistance. The presence of internal resistance results in a diminished voltage supplied to the components that comprise the load. On the divine plane, is this a decrease in positive attitudes? This internal resistance results in a decrease in total current. Divine energy strengthens charged bodies. On the divine plane, is our "resistance" making us weak as a species and are we weakening the Earth itself in the process? Another result is an increase in total resistance. Is this an increase in disbelief in the reality of "GOD?" All these circumstances are present within our society today. The power emitted by the circuit is also affected. Our resistance to spiritual truth physically affects the Earth, as well as ourselves.

If there is a resistor within the circuit that can be identified, then we should also be able to identify the capacitor. The capacitor is the untapped resource of the mind. Within this resource is energy and knowledge that are waiting to be utilized for our benefit, and the existence of this power is scientifically documented. To utilize this resource, we must bring this advantage into play. We do that as we seek to better ourselves. As we learn, our minds store that energy in the form of knowledge, ability, and experience. As these "storage banks" become filled, the brain opens up more resources for us to use. By studying and learning words and numbers, together with having different experiences, the activity and blood flow increase the positive radiance of that mind. This is accomplished even by doing crossword puzzles, or anything else stimulates the mind in a positive way. This increased radiance has many benefits. It draws positive energy to that mind. It increases the positive nature of that individual. It increases the value of that individual to the lives around it. It causes that individual to grow. The list goes on and on...

From all this, we can place a basic part of human difficulty into perspective. What is wrong with us as a species is that we are not channeling our energy to freely flow through the pathways of our being as it is designed to do. We are blocking a component of the "circuit" by not embracing the true purpose and nature of our soul more fully. Because of this, we are not properly "grounded." In an electrical system with large current flows, when there is no proper ground, the circuit is open to a variety of problems and malfunctions. These "problems" and "malfunctions" are very evident within every area of earthly existence within which the human has a physical influence. These areas include all social systems and natural systems as well. In a single phrase, all these systems can be identified by the words "our Earth." To right the practical ills of our collective living condition, our spiritual connection to the Divine Energy of Life (our souls) must be elevated to the proper level of importance in our individual lives. We must embrace the Divine Energy of Life (or "GOD") as a collective. By doing this, the energy within our entire species will become joined and focused in the way that the Divine Energy of Life intended. From this correct, positive, right(eous) flow of energy, we can collectively create the perfect condition of existence. The label for this perfect condition of existence is "Utopia."

The Connection

All things upon this planet are linked in ways that are physically and chemically evident and can be understood within the context of natural science. For example, protoplasm, the physiochemical basis of living matter, is a substance of complex composition that forms the essential part of <u>both</u> plant and animal cells. A large proportion of the minerals of the planet are either a part of the chemical makeup of the living beings of our planet, or they are used to sustain them. No matter how you look at it, all things on this circle we call "earth" are interconnected. Our Earth is the source of all life of which we are aware. If the Earth did not exist, no life as we know it would exist in this space occupied by our planet, because it is the beginning and perpetual (localized) source of the life-giving energy. The system of motion that brings our Earth to life we have called "Nature." What does Nature have to do with our spirituality? The system of Nature is the foundation of our spirituality, with oxygen and plant life being key elements of our spirituality. Within the growth of all plants lies our connection to our Earth. Each of us knows the obvious connection between humans and plants, i.e. that plant life provides us with nourishment as well as the oxygen we breathe. Yet to gain a clearer understanding of the connective relationship humans have to plants, an objective examination yields much more wisdom. There is a worldly reality and a spiritual reality, and the oxygen around us connects it all together. The electric field of force of our electromagnetically charged planet is the oxygen, and it is derived from plant life. Plants draw their energy directly from the planet because they are rooted in the soil, making them (for the most part) stationary. Animals, and more specifically humans, are moving objects, but the source of their life-giving energy is still the Earth. Just as the roots of plants provide a pathway through which the energies of the Earth flow, animals too must have a pathway through which the energies of the Earth can flow.

The stability of a plant on our Earth is dependent upon the strength of its root, the pathway of energy flow between it and our Earth. The human's pathway to the energies of life is the brain. Some living organisms can utilize not only the life-giving energy that travels through their respective pathways, but also the knowledge or abilities that travel with it. This advantage exists within the context of the mind. Plants and animals move within the same parameters, i.e. the laws of Nature. Therefore, it is evident that to stabilize the humans' existence upon the Earth, the human must strengthen its pathway of energy flow between it and our Earth. This pathway is the mind. As we talk of strengthening the humans' individual existence, we must include the human species in its entirety because each of us is a member of this species, and we are socialized and interdependent. In the process of strengthening our individual minds, we must recognize that this must be a collective pursuit. The future of the human species depends upon the collective effort of each individual to bring about the circumstance of salvation. The human species is not unlike any other socialized species of the planet in that we are interdependent upon each other for our survival. This is the nature of human existence. Individuals must embrace the revelation that they are species of animal. The term "human" is simply the label by which we refer to ourselves. This is true regardless of how we classify our behavior. It is not that we are no longer animals. It is that we <u>have consciously developed into civilized animals</u>. We "grew" into a better state of existence. This is, however, still a "natural" occurrence. As an animal, we are a part of the Divine System of Nature. Irrespective of the structures we build, we are still a part of Nature. Therefore, we are forever bound by the rules and laws that govern our natural existence. The human must stop thinking of itself as being "outside" of Nature. As Nature is of divinity, the human, as well as all other living things, are of divinity. Human existence occurs within a spiritual context, and there are actions that are required of us. Those actions are positive movements. By recognizing our spiritual responsibilities, we will open our minds to a more inclusive truth. This "more inclusive truth" brings us closer to the "whole," or "holy" story.

Due to the state of human consciousness, for people to accept the nature and reality of our spirituality, most want to see some physical example to prove that it truly exists. It is unfortunate, but most humans need to have physical proof of something before they can completely believe in it. The human existence occurs on a physical plane. Because of this, the human relates best with that which has a physical reality, as do all other animals. This is one of the problems keeping each of us from embracing "GOD" as we all should. It is because the seemingly random physical manifestations noted in our past are not proof enough for most. The proof lies within the physical relationship of spirituality to our existence, as inferred by the physical realities of spirituality based on the electromagnetic relationship between life and the Earth. Our spirituality requires that we be a positive part of Nature's system in a very physical sense, irrespective of what we consciously perceive. Our consciousness is there to allow us to experience and interpret the stimulation of physical existence. During the course of our lives, we are to guide ourselves such that our actions are positive. Our consciousness is not some tool for us to use to manipulate the interpretations of the circumstances before us in order to satisfy our personal selfishness and greed. Our consciousness is a gift that allows us to reap satisfaction from our movements and interaction by way of understanding. Because the consciousness does not exist on this plane without the body, our physical requirements must come first. However, just as we must satisfy our immediate need for food, water, and shelter, we must satisfy the physical requirements of our being a part of the system of Nature. Our existence must be understood within the context of how energy flowing in a positive direction affects our mind (knowledge), body (action), and soul (guidance).

The spinning action of our planet and the resulting electromagnetic field is responsible for what we consider to be Nature's system, and the "divine" system that keeps us alive. Because of this, the rotation of our Earth can be referred to by the label "the Divine System of Nature." I use the label "Divine System of Nature" for a reason. It is true that our existence can be defined within the context of science relative to Nature. It is also true that our existence can be defined within a divine context relative to "GOD." As this is true, there are obvious connections between the patterns of Nature, and the patterns of divinity. From the right perspective, one can see the connection between what science tells of about our lives, and what the Holy Scriptures tell us. Each of us can feel what right is in a physical sense. We can feel "right" or "positive" as a sensation within our bodies. This is because right or positive is a physical manifestation of the earthly system of existence. The ability to feel what is correct, right, or positive, is an aspect of our makeup that our creator, commonly labeled "GOD," intended us to use to guide ourselves toward the resolution of the moments of our lives in the way that "He" desired.

All life on our Earth is also linked in ways that can be "felt," but some are too subtle to explain or even comprehension. Because of this subtlety, when this link is apparent, pronounced, or in full manifestation, it is either misinterpreted or ignored. This link occurs within the context of what we consider to be "Nature," but on a more profound level. This link is a part of our spirituality. All life on this planet is spiritually connected. Our spirituality is a physical part of our reality, defined within the context of electromagnetic energy. All life is connected by virtue of the fact that we are all a part of the Divine System of Nature. The term "Nature," among other things, describes "the principle or power that appears to guide existence." It is "the entire material Universe and its phenomena." the word "Nature" is derived from the humans' recognition of the fact that circumstances related to existence do not seem to occur at random, so the human has labeled this "system" of occurrences. In truth, "Nature" is used as a label for some part of reality that the human species recognizes but does not fully understand. Though probably without specific intent, this label allows the human to keep this "guiding power" within the context of the physical or worldly reality. It also allows the human to avoid having to face a truth. It is the truth that the "guiding power" of existence is divine by Nature, and there is a spiritual reality to which our species will be held accountable.

If Nature has a pattern or system, then there are required actions that are inherent to the system. These actions are divine by nature and definition. One could rightly label them "divine responsibilities." Do humans have a divine responsibility to meet their obligation to perpetuate the pattern or system that sustains them? The answer to this question is yes, because all that exists on the planet is a direct or indirect result of Nature, and therefore a part of its pattern or system. Is one of these required actions the truth that we must move in harmony with one another to conform to the system? The profound interconnection between the Atom and matter leads to the conclusion that harmony and balance are inherent to the perpetuation of the objective system of existence. Things that are inherent to Nature are inherent to all parts of Nature, including humans. Electrons, protons, Atom s, planets, and the like that are influenced by electromagnetic energy have "characteristics" that afford them the ability to avoid collision during their divine movements no matter their speed of travel. This ability is also inherent in humans, because they are composed of Atom s, and their movements are influenced by this energy as well. For the human to manifest this ability, it must result from conscious effort because the human's consciousness controls its interactive movements. This conscious effort by the human to manifest this inherent characteristic would be its avoidance of conflict through the positive thought associated with compromise and tolerance. This will allow us all to interact peacefully, within the context of our pursuit of our needs and wants/desires. To make things real, there are things we must do. We must perform our "required action," our responsibility. We must manifest. To achieve peace, we must manifest a state of equation and/or balance. I am not suggesting that collision or conflict will never occur or should never occur. What I am saying is that this sort of interaction among bits of matter is not the norm, so we should do everything in our power to avoid it.

Who each of us is as an individual is derived in part from our interpretations of the experiences that stimulate our senses. Our most obvious senses are those of sight, hearing, touch, taste, and smell. Another very important sense is that of balance. We must recognize that the sense of balance is as critical to our existence as any other sensation we are capable of. Equilibrium is a condition in which all acting influences are canceled by others. Equilibrium is also mental or emotional balance, or poise. Relative to human interaction, this condition of living is achieved through compromise and tolerance. Equilibrium results in a stable, balanced system of movement. It is a part of human Nature to seek out balance to achieve equilibrium. Put another way, it is natural for us to seek out a stable, balanced system of movement. A sense of equilibrium or sense of balance is inherent to all animals. Equilibrium is a natural part of the lives of all living beings. All animals need a sense of balance to have <u>directed</u> movement. It is the sense of which direction is up or down, forward or back, right or left, positive or negative, right or wrong. Existence is fundamentally based upon the balanced interaction of movements within various sets of laws, rules, and codes.

The necessity of recognizing spirituality is mandated by its relationship to physical reality. Spirituality is beyond being a mental concept. It is a part of our physical existence. It may be easier to understand and digest these revelations if they are interpreted from the perspective that the label "spirituality" is synonymous with "the Divine System of Nature." We recognize the physical realities of science within the context of the definitions explained through physics. However, we most often close our minds to the notion that these principles of science can be applied to the process of understanding the spiritual part of our nature. Partly because even through selfishness and greed, most humans recognize this application would force us to exist in a world of equality and balance. We could no longer be selfishly subjective because in recognizing and dealing with any part of reality, the primary response or reaction to "dealing with reality," is to respond objectively and truthful. As our actions are a part of the Divine System of Nature, our actions must correspond to what is correct or right with regard to each respective system of actions.

By recognizing our true spiritual connection to positive energy, we will be taping into a resource that we benefit from without fully understanding it. For example, doctors are agreeing with the benefit of and relationship between prayer and medical healing. This is actually physical proof of the connection between spiritual reality and worldly reality. They have found that people who go to church and pray have stronger immune systems that people who do not. Doctors are also saying that "worry" (i.e. stress) has a direct effect on the health and wellbeing of individuals. In Scripture, it states that we are to "release" our burdens. These are not coincidences. Truly, this is further proof that spirituality is a physical part of existence. What it is that they are discovering is that there is a connection between positive thought, positive action, and the humans' positive existence. We must live our lives such that "GOD" (the Divine Energy of Life) is paramount in our thoughts as we choose the direction for the motions of our bodies.

Each of us must understand and embrace the physical foundation upon which our spirituality is based. This foundation is positive energy. Through the pathway of connection between the divine source of energy and living things, this energy circulates, moving in one direction. That direction is positive. In understanding the concept of "in one direction," think of it in terms of the spinning of our planet. It spins in only one direction, and to change that direction would be disastrous. When this divine energy enters a living thing, it also is to move positively. As conscious beings, we humans must choose this as a direction for our actions. By doing this, each of us can correct the polarity of our thoughts and the impact those thoughts have on the direction of our actions. With this internal change, the "non-believer's" movements will become harmonious with those who embrace the principles of human spirituality in all its depth. In this instance, the individual does not have to recognize "GOD" directly, only his right(eous)ness. That individual will thereby be limiting his or her acceptance of the existence of spirituality to the context of the "Divine Energy of Life," that which is conveniently labeled "Nature." The spinning of the Earth manifests this energy. The energy that flows through each living thing, which gives it life, comes from the spinning of the Earth. However, recognize that the energy that spins our Earth has a source also. It is the energy of "GOD" (the Divine Energy of Life), and it exists on a plane outside of our physical perception.

How do we yield to the authority of Nature? The answer is by helping other living things besides ourselves. We help other living things by making it easier for them to move. We accomplish this by having actions (movements, behaviors) that go in the correct or right(eous) direction. That direction is positive. While each of us must continue to live up to our worldly responsibilities relevant to our daily lives, each of us must also recognize our natural responsibilities as well. Individuals must embrace the fact that, objectively speaking, each of us is but one of many energy generators and conductors within the system of electrical circuitry of our Earth. As such, it is necessary for each of us to generate energy of the correct or right polarity for the system of our Earth to operate correctly. We must have positive attitudes as we move in positive directions in the pursuit of positive goals.

Each of us must come to understand that "Nature" is simply a label for our interpretation of our living Earth's system. The system itself must be recognized objectively relative to humans as an animal species, rather than subjectively relative to some belief that humans are some other category of natural object existing outside of the system of Nature. Each of us must accept that we have a role to play in making the system of Nature work properly. That role is defined as our moving or acting in a positive, helpful, creative (productive) manner as we pursue individual, as well as collective growth and prosperity. We must all work together to make our immediate and planetary environments clean. We must set aside and preserve vast areas of natural environments in recognition of the revelation that these areas contribute greatly to the proper function of the Divine System of Nature. If we destroy everything natural around us, we will bring about damnation in a very real and spiritual sense. There are consequences for what we do to all the plants and trees, flowers, and other animal life. We must allow great areas of natural growth to flourish because this is how we are linked to the planet.

This is how we perpetuate our survival. "GOD" intended <u>everything</u> to be fruitful and to multiply. The vegetation of the planet helps to generate the system of Nature. If we make this planet barren, this planet will die. "GOD" created all the vegetation first to create the system of existence that supports life. We are supposed to live <u>within</u> that system of existence.

Throughout human existence, there are countless examples of how some humans have gone out and tried to change the spiritual beliefs of native populations and tribes that live in natural environments. However, those spiritual beliefs support those natives, and the vegetation flourishes around them. "GOD" said, "be fruitful and multiply." This directive was aimed at the plants first, then at the other animals, and then at ourselves. We are supposed to support the ecosystem around us to the degree that it is able to flourish, and we are not doing this to the best of our ability. In a newspaper article printed January 16, 2000, it quoted the state of the world 2000 report issued by Worldwatch institute as saying, "global economic trends during the 1990s were remarkably bullish, but environmental trends were disastrous." The report goes on to say that the global economy is outgrowing our Earth's ecosystem. We are digging out land and destroying rain forests full of trees and other plant growth as we blindly pursue profit and power. We must begin to restrict the expansion of populations to specific areas and learn to live within the greenery. As we become more prosperous, the opportunity to reach into the system of existence and save it is within our grasp. With our collective human knowledge and our resourcefulness, we can save our Earth and ourselves along with it. We have to do this now. It is the only chance we are going to get.

The System of Human Spirituality

The structure of the Atom provides the design for every element and system of existence that followed its creation. It is composed of a central source of radiant energy with its elements revolving around it. The central source of radiant energy has influence over; has power over; has <u>authority</u> over those elements that revolve around it. Relative to the Universe, the central source of radiant energy is "GOD." All of existence is an element of the system created by the Divine Energy of Life. Therefore, "GOD" has influence, power, and/or <u>authority</u> over everything within the Universe. Hence, all elements of the Universe yield to this authority as actions naturally occurrence. On a smaller scale, the core of our planet is the central source of radiant energy. Living things are elements of the system created by our Earth. Therefore, our Earth, or the system of Nature, has influence, power, and/ or <u>authority</u> over everything within its realm. Here too, all elements of our Earth, or the system of Nature, yield to this authority as actions naturally occurrence. However, human action is derived from choice. Therefore, each individual must choose to yield to the authorities that govern the respective actions one has.

Within the solitude of the human mind, not one of us is able to escape the realization that we are all connected in some way to a spiritual system. Our species cannot avoid the recognition of the spiritual aspects of our existence. It is real, whether or not we can place it within the proper context of understanding. So much so, the human has found it unavoidably necessary to acknowledge its spiritual Nature by manifesting it into a structured system of beliefs and practices, which we humans have called "religion." Whatever the human has labeled it, our spirituality is an aspect of ourselves that cannot be escaped. However, because of an overwhelming sense of self-importance, which is the ego out of proportion, we do not realize the true nature of that which we are aware. This is because we have limited our ability to interpret the knowledge within our grasp by closing our minds, which is how our egos got out of proportion in the first place. Many humans have relegated spiritual recognition to a periodic observance and have limited its profound power of blessing to a resource that is called upon when there are no other choices. What we must embrace as a collective is the revelation that if all of existence was created by one source that is divine in nature, we cannot disregard the implications this has upon our everyday lives. Simply because we do not have a complete understanding of something does not negate its relevance to our existence. There are properties, principles, and laws that apply to Nature that cannot be ignored or changed by humans. The same applies to the reality within which we live. As this is true, we must accept and embrace the fact that this applies to the spiritual aspects of our existence as well.

It is hard for some to grasp how physical, scientific reality occurs within the confines of a seemingly mystic, spiritual reality. in coming to terms with this, recognize the truth that if Moses went to the mountaintop to receive the Ten Commandments, as long as that event occurred upon our Earth, every element of that reality was still subject to the laws of physics. If Noah built the ark, every element of that reality was still subject to the laws of physics. Science occurs within the confines of spiritual reality. All science truly explains is the physical circumstances of existence. The truest meaning of the circumstances of existence can only be understood within the context of spiritual reality. To reach an understanding of spiritual reality, we must first come to accept that there is a divine plane of existence. Each of us must accept the truth that there is a "divine entity," i.e. a source of ultimate power on this plane. This divine entity is responsible for the existence of life. Humans have labeled this entity. We have called it "GOD."

To come to a common understanding of "GOD," each of us must change our perspective. The resulting perspective must be shared by our entire species. This is the way it is supposed to be, because reality is an objective occurrence. To achieve this common perspective, we must have a common interpretation of all the circumstances we perceive. The knowledge and understanding that will serve as the foundation upon which we build our new, common perspective is already before us. We must now open our minds so that we can put it all together. We start by recognizing that we humans are truly animals, and therefore, we are a part of the system of Nature. There are only three great divisions of natural objects on our Earth. They are the animal kingdom, the vegetable kingdom, and the mineral kingdom. The human is a member of a group of animals called "mammals," one of the classes of warm-blooded vertebrates whose females nourish their young from milk-secreting organs. The physical bodies of mammals are constructed about a skeletal bone structure. They have similar, and in some cases, identical internal organs as other members of this group, and they perform primarily the same functions. There is the presence of skin, hair (or fur), muscle, external limbs, and more importantly the blood, heart, and a brain. In fact, if one was to exclude the will and intellect associated with a conscious mind, one could certainly conclude the human is but one of many ordinary animal species that inhabit our Earth. There are those that would argue that the human is not an animal. However, one must agree that few could successfully convince the learned person that the human should be categorized as a member of either of the other kingdoms. The human being is truly an animal within the scope of the system of Nature.

As a whole, humans must recognize that we are unlike any other species on the planet, because of the level of our consciousness and the awareness it generates. If "GOD" created all life, but only the human in "his" image, it stands to reason that the aspect of our being that is unique to only the human is that part of us that is in the likeness of our creator. That aspect is the human consciousness, the mind. The need to broaden the horizons of the conscious mind (through both formal education and personal experience) is a spiritual as well as a physical responsibility we have to the system that gives us life, rather than simply the way to get ahead in life. We must come to a clearer understanding of the relevance and significance of words and behavior (human action) to our existence specifically, and to the system of Nature in general. With knowledge and understanding as the foundation, words and behavior are the building blocks for the evolution of the human consciousness. The key elements of all creation are energy (action), and information (knowledge, words).

There is only one "GOD," and I believe in this divine entity. "GOD" (the Divine Energy of Life) created everything that exists. I believe that "GOD" created the Universe, and our Earth in the process. "GOD" then singled out the Earth on which to create what humans know of as life. As I matured through childhood, it did not take long to recognize that the structured civilization of which I was a part had many different systems of belief all aimed at expressing recognition of what was surely the same entity. Knowing for myself that GODs' energy is real, I did not want to choose a belief system that did not conform to reality. For this reason, I began to look at the truths related to spirituality and religion. The Jewish faith is close to 4000 years old and was founded by Abraham. The Hindu religion came out of India somewhere around 1500 BC. The Buddhist religion is the result of a splinter sect from Hinduism founded by Prince Siddhartha Gautama (Buddha) in about 500 BC. Catholicism appeared in the year 33 AD. Mohammed started the Islamic religion in the area of Saudi Arabia at about 600 AD. The Eastern Orthodox Church separated from the Roman Catholic Church in about the year 1000 AD. Martin Luther created the Lutheran church in 1517, the result of a split from the Roman Catholic Church. The first Lutheran congregation in North America was founded in Wilmington, Delaware in 1638. Their faith is based on the Bible, and the Augsburg confession. King Henry The VIII started the Church of England in 1534 because a pope would not grant him a divorce. The tenets of this church are the supremacy of the Bible as the test of doctrine. Emphasis is place on the most essential Christian doctrines and creeds, and the Book of Common Prayer is used.

The Amish or Mennonite faith was founded in Switzerland in the 1500s. They seceded from the Zurich state church, and most immigrated to Pennsylvania in the eighteenth century. The Presbyterian religion was based on the teachings of john Calvin, brought to Scotland by john Knox in 1557, and to North America by Irish missionary Francis Makemie in 1706. They place their faith in the Bible. A religious group called the Unitarians was first developed in Europe in the 1500s. The Unitarian Universalist Association was the result of a merger between a denomination organized in 1779 called the Unitarian Universalist Association of America, and the American Unitarian Association that was founded in 1825. Members of this congregation profess no creed. Their strong social, ethical, and humanitarian concerns are manifested from the search for religious truth through the freedom of belief. Their efforts are aimed at the creation of a worldwide interfaith religious community.

The Congregationalists are a religious group that split from puritanism in England in the 1600s. The Baptist religion was founded by John Smith in Amsterdam in 1607. In the seventeenth century in England, George Fox preached against organized churches. The result of this was the formation of the religious Society of Friends, or the Quakers. Their faith is based on the "inner light." For them it is the voice of GODs' Holy Spirit experienced within each individual. The Reverend John Wesley began evangelistic preaching within the Church of England in 1738. John and Charles Wesley founded the Methodist religion in England in 1744. A separate Wesleyan Methodist Church was established in 1791. The Methodist Episcopal Church was founded in the United States of America in 1784, when Samuel Seabury was installed as its first bishop. The Mormon Church was founded by joseph smith in 1830.

Their faith is based on the Bible, the Book of Mormon, the doctrine and covenants, and the pearl of great price, all of which are considered scripture. The Seventh-Day Adventist Church is the result of the teachings of William Miller; it was founded in North America in 1863. The Salvation Army, which is actually a religious group, was founded by William Booth in England in 1865. Mary Baker Eddy founded the Christian Scientist religion in 1879. In Pennsylvania, the Jehovah's Witness religion was founded by Charles Taze Russell in the 1870s. The Pentecostal religion was begun in the United States in 1901. There are many other religious groups founded on beliefs that are considered "mainstream" and some that are not. I regret they are too numerous to mention. From this information, the conclusion that I came to was that the number of religious denominations resulted from the differences in culture, beliefs, opinions, and practices. However, one truth remains, there is only **one** "GOD," and almost every mainstream religious group recognizes that fact. Even tribal cultures that we "civilized" people label "primitive" tend to believe in a power that has supreme domain over any other deity they conceive. It seems that regardless of the method of worship, all religious doctrine leads back to the one "GOD" (the Divine Energy of Life).

During my developmental period, I was exposed to a few different religious belief systems. These were mainly Baptist, Catholic, Methodist, and the like. Each of these belief systems relies upon the King James Version of the Holy Bible for scripture. Seeing that there were other religious denominations indicated to me that the varying spiritual groups represented the humans' varying interpretation of reality. My "inner knowledge" confirmed GODs' existence for me. However, I realized that as I grew older I would have to make choices about the foundation of my faith in "GOD," based on my perceptions and interpretations of the realities before me. I would have to choose the method by which I would recognize and worship the supreme entity. I do not know what "religious" category the belief system that developed from this search of divine truth would be listed. One could perhaps label me a "Neo-Christian." I believe in the Holy Scriptures of the Bible as the living words of "GOD." The reason I know the scriptures are the living words of "GOD" is because I received all my blessings the way the Bible indicates, by doing what it instructs and influences us to do. I believe this while recognizing that one book cannot hold all the truth the human species is to have. Particularly in light of the understanding of what happens when words are translated into different "versions" of a truth. Our spirituality is a natural part of our being and our existence. It is a part of every individual on the planet. This is true regardless of their ethnic lineage, and regardless of what they believe.

There is a point of enlightenment that can be reached where the individual comes to understand the magnitude of all of existence. On this plane of understanding, one sees that their connection to what exists around them goes beyond the context of religion. However, it must not be forgotten that religion is the outgrowth of the human attempt to place into context the minute elements of its spirituality that it has come close to deciphering. For example, each of us has been made aware that the human will "never be without sin." relative to truly coming to an understanding of what this means, as well as what all older texts of spiritual doctrine mean, we must embrace the truth that there were fewer descriptive words when these translations were undertaken. A sin is surely an error in judgment. Using terms that are more descriptive in an effort to gain a broader understanding, we will find it true that "never being without sin" includes the truth that error is unavoidable. It is a part of being alive. From this, we can surmise that existence is not to be feared, therefore, no part of being alive should we fear. We should not fear making an error or faltering in anyway, for these produce the lessons we are to learn from and use to make ourselves better. When one begins to listen to themselves, and trust what they hear from that and feel from that, the path they choose is one without fear because it is "right" for them as an individual.

This all may sound like simply a matter of opinion. However, our spirituality is real. It is not subject to opinion, and it is not fully explained within the context of any single, structured religion.

Truly, with regard to an individual's spirituality, one cannot follow another to his or her awakening.

That person must go there alone and have their set of eyes opened. We do need to experience fellowship and share our positive energy. Each subgroup within our species should come together and has the right to share like beliefs in the reverence of the Divine Energy of Life. Churches are an integral part of human civilization. However, each of us is an individual. Hence, the "frequency" (this is relative to our movements and vibrations, and I will explain its relevance later) upon which our existence is based is one only the individual can truly perceive and relate to. Many do not recognize or otherwise practice their spirituality within a system of religious beliefs. However, our awareness of this part of our being is engrained within all members of our species. Believers and non-believers alike perform the actions required by the spiritual system whether they know it or not, and whether they admit it or not. Over time, there has developed many different religions, spiritual belief systems, dogmas, and theories that seek to define that aspect of our existence that we consider spiritual. It is the fact that we all do not share the same understanding of our spirituality that keeps our species from totally embracing our responsibility to each other and to Nature. The revelation we must face as a species is that our divine roots, our inherent connection to each other, along with our connection to our Earth and its systems, transcends any religious or secular belief system.

As a species group, we must begin our evolution by embracing our natural relationship with the world on which we live. This is defined within the context of "spirituality." Spirituality is defined in the dictionary as the state, quality, manner, or fact of being spiritual. Spiritual is defined as being of, relating to, consisting of, or having the nature of spirit; not tangible or material; of, concerned with, or affecting the soul; of, from, or relating to "GOD." What is missing from these definitions is the fact that the "spirit" that is referred to is actually the energy of "GOD." It is the "Divine Energy of Life." Spirituality is the label for the <u>system of actions</u> by which the Divine Energy of Life generates existence. All of existence, as well as the reality we perceive around us, is spiritual in nature. This is because our Earth was brought to life by this energy. This energy sustains life, as we know it. In addition, the Universe was created through the manifestation of this divine energy. From this, we can easily conclude that spirituality is natural to us as a species.

Existence is a term that not only covers everything the human can perceive, but also that which is real, yet beyond human perception or interpretation. The label "reality" encompasses all of existence that the human is aware of, i.e. all human knowledge. However, there is a huge body of knowledge beyond human awareness and comprehension. The label the human has conceived of to describe this knowledge is the "unknown." There is "truth" that lies beyond human knowledge, within this unknown realm. It is true that one needs to have knowledge of <u>all</u> the elements of a circumstance before an absolute understanding can be achieved. Therefore, complete understanding cannot exist if critical elements of a circumstance are "unknown." As individuals, there are things we know to be true, because of firsthand knowledge or proof in some factual way. There are also things we accept as true, that we have not experienced for ourselves and/or are not able to prove. Are we not to utilize the knowledge within the last circumstance until it can be proven to us? To the contrary, we accept the reality of the existence of this truth and utilize what we accept and believe to our benefit. There is a word for that acceptance in the English language. It is called **FAITH**. As we have faith in the word of man, we must have faith in the word of "GOD." As not all knowledge is comprehensible by the human consciousness, it is evident that faith is a vital element of human understanding. As we embrace it, we express the human's acceptance of his or her subordinate stature in the presence of the power, i.e. energy and knowledge of "GOD." To embrace faith is an exercise in humility, and a testament to the glory and authority of the Divine Energy of Life.

To create is to cause something to come into being, or to cause something to happen by intention or design. To have the human create is to have something evolve from one's own thought, imagination, or action. Our system of beliefs is such a thing. It is a creation. Our belief system is the result of the conclusions that come to mind, which are based upon what we perceive to be true. There is an interesting theory in philosophy. It is called the "Relativity of Knowledge." It is the theory that knowledge of what things really are, is not possible, since knowledge itself is dependent upon the subjective nature of the mind. As this relates to our perspective or state of mind, by allowing our individual process of reasoning to be influenced by our personal interests, prejudices, or emotions, we keep ourselves from recognizing what things really are. The actuality of knowledge or truth is relative to a person's ability to be objective. In the interest of broadening individual objectivity, persons must open their mind up to a less subjective interpretation of our earthly existence.

The truth is, our belief system is based upon bits and pieces of a "whole" truth. Therefore, each of us must face the fact that our belief system cannot be considered complete or fully correct. There is proof of this fact. The system that our whole way of life is built around cannot be considered complete and could possibly be incorrect because the whole truth of existence includes the story of the origin of the human being, and not a single human being knows what that story is in its entirety. The notion that we have a true, complete understanding of reality is truly a "leap of faith." Why would our federal government keep secret its knowledge of the existence of extraterrestrial beings? It is because the human belief system is built around the conclusion that the human is the "only" intelligent being in the Universe. To find out otherwise would shake and possibly destroy the foundation our belief system is based upon. This could easily destroy our way of living. When a mind is closed to new information, change, and possibility, the rationale of that mind <u>can</u> be destroyed by a truth not held within that closed mind. When a mind is exposed to truth that it is not prepared to accept or understand, it can lead to chaos. One truth we <u>must</u> recognize at this point is that our current system of beliefs, spanning all of the human species, is based upon "faith." Because we do not truly know from where we came, our minds are obviously void of <u>all</u> the truths of existence. Hence, the basis of our understanding of everything is built upon conclusions we have created within our minds. Within this context, the things we believe but have no proof for are accepted because of the inherent faith each of us has in our species. It is based upon faith in the human ability to "figure out" things with its mind, as well as to perceive and interpret with its senses. By opening the mind beyond the boundaries of current understanding and exercising this ability to have faith while digesting the truth in these words, each person can all be awakened to the reality of "GOD" (the Divine Energy of Life). During this experience, each of us will come to realize the simplicity of creating a harmonious existence. The label the human has created for this state of existence is "Utopia."

To understand the nature and ramification of these words, you must open your mind to recognize reality and interpret it truthfully without bias. What does it mean to "open your mind?" It is to humbly recognize that no matter what you believe to be true, because you do not know all there is to know about existence, you cannot limit your process of examination to take into consideration only what you know, you must be ready to embrace other possibilities. Moreover, whether or not you can conceive what those possibilities are, you must be <u>objective</u> to the degree that you consider the possibility that there is more meaning to be determined. It takes a strong, mature mind and a strong character to believe in something, but to understand that belief may fall short of the whole truth. It takes this same strength and maturity to come to a realization that those beliefs may be misplaced all together, and not allow that recognition to manifest itself into a paralyzing "doubt." This is an open mind. For example, consider this: the human is the only animal with a need to fashion articles of dress to protect his or her body from the Earth's elements. All other animal species have a more natural way of adapting. The human has a need to create an artificial environment for itself, via air conditioning and heating systems. These ways of adapting to our Earth's natural environment are "foreign" to the animal kingdom as a whole. The human also fashions other sophisticated tools and toys that are not needed and probably not desired by any other species on our planet.

Of all the animals that survive within our natural earthly environment, the human is the only one that has a pre-occupation with looking up at the stars. The human is the only animal species that looks to the stars with wonder in its eyes. When the human looks up, it recognizes the dimension of existence beyond the blue sky and clouds. It recognizes existence beyond a point perceive of by other animals. The human is the only animal interested in leaving our Earth's atmosphere. Humans are the only animal species that has exercised a willingness to leave the planet's atmosphere altogether. It is as though our species has some inherent knowledge of our ability to travel among the stars. Then there is still the matter of the missing link in the evolutionary chain between the most highly evolved primate and the modern human. One answer for these curious observations might be that the human is the only intelligent, sentient member of the Earth's animal kingdom. However, why is that? The religious community has an explanation for all of the above, but the scientific community does not. So, having laid the foundation for my plausible scientific explanation, let us see if I can fill in the gaps.

There is hard evidence that dates back centuries that strongly suggest beings from another world with humanoid form have visited our Earth. Picture this, beings from another planet traveling the galaxies on a research expedition, and they come across a world of lush vegetation and a wide variety of animal species that live in harmony with each other. The only killing that goes on is that which takes place within the structure of the food chain and the ecological balance. These "space explorers" begin making regular research visits that require stays of several months. Perhaps during the evening of one of these visits, after the day's work was completed, something out of the ordinary happened. The spacemen (spacewomen were not allowed on these trips because of the possible dangers) were sitting around the campfire outside the spaceship drinking spaceman hooch and telling cosmic fairy tales. While this was going on, one member of the party spots a group of primates curiously watching them from afar. As the night grows old and the level of intoxication rises, this spaceman's hormones start to remind him how long it has been since he has seen his mate. He tells his comrades that he is tired of taking matters in his own hands and has decided to capture one of these inquisitive primates to help him get that monkey off his back.

As his buddies look on, he accomplishes his task and succeeds in releasing his frustration. The others, not wanting to be left out in the cold, capture a "pal" for themselves. They then build a holding-pen to keep them captive and available. After a period, one of the researchers decides to check into the possible results of their "close encounters," and finds they are about to become "fathers" of yet another, very unique species to be added to the Earth's animal kingdom. Since they cannot detect any possible problems with allowing the delivery of this new species to occur naturally, they decided to pack up and leave (just like a man), intending to drop by from time-to-time check on the progress of their kin. This could explain our difference from the other members of the animal kingdom, and the whereabouts of the "missing link."

If this were true, could the Bible have been left as a guide for our behavior by these extraterrestrial beings? Perhaps it was because they knew that being created in "their" image ("...and "GOD" said, let us make man in <u>our</u> image, after <u>our</u> likeness..."), the conscious mind was great and had ego. There was a fear that at some point in the humans' existence, he or she might begin to believe that they were "GOD." To avoid this, they said "GOD" was something far greater than we were, and the entity dwelled in a place beyond our Earth's boundaries. If aliens were responsible for the composition of the Bible, the prophecies could be forewarning of how "they" planned to weed out the good from the bad at a point where they thought our spiritual consciousness could grow no more. The scriptures infer the destruction of most of humanity if it does not awake to true righteousness. The aliens could want us to develop into a positive part of the system within which we exist. To accomplish this, we must reach "their" level of understanding, where the needs of the collective supersede the wants/desires that result from individual selfishness and greed. If they are dissatisfied with our progress, perhaps the preconceived plan is to wipe this "experiment" out and start over with what is left. Whatever the story of creation is, the task before us is the same. Whether it is to fulfill our responsibility to "GOD" and the Divine System of Nature, or it is to show some group of alien superiors that we are worthy of continued existence, our creator wants us to develop rightly. We must grow into the best we can become as individuals and as a species, and we must do it using positive action.

The foundation of my personal belief system is not based upon an alien "intrusion" in our Earth's existing system of Nature. I know in my heart and soul that there is a GOD/Divine Energy of Life. It has been proven to me through spiritual manifestation. I see the powers of positive flowing energy working around me every day. Yet, I am capable of telling this story without destabilizing my faith in "GOD." It is the result of my understanding that not one of us knows the truth of creation. Therefore, the whole truth is yet to be known. I do know that the Holy Scriptures exist, and that positive is the direction of human action as indicated by this text and by what I "feel" inside myself. Regardless of what you believe, each of us must evolve to the next level of human consciousness if we are to survive. Each of us must believe in something. For the human to continue to exist, it must develop a strong, <u>common</u> belief system and an open mind. This belief system must be based on positive flowing energy and on what it creates, as well as how it relates to human action.

For our species, understanding is a process, a cycle, or a system of growth in terms of conscious awareness. Reality or the knowledge there of, is a matter of perception and interpretation. The interpretation is a direct reflection of the perspective of the person who is doing the interpreting. The human perspective is based upon an individual's personal understanding of the conclusions that person comes to as a result of perceiving and interpreting. Each of us must seek to have an objective understanding of a circumstance before we draw conclusions. Once a "conclusion" is reached, it must be used to adjust that person's perspective. This is a loop that must be traveled each time something is learned or experienced.

For all of us to perceive and interpret a circumstance from a common perspective, we must have a common, or shared understanding of reality. We must recognize and deal with the truth that this "shared understanding" will establish a link that will bind us all together with a rope created from words. Much like how the pledge of allegiance was intended to bind all Americans together as a unit. We must then recognize what it means to have things in common and to be bound together by that.

Having a "common bond" is a natural part of the human species relative to our being socialized and interdependent. This is true irrespective of our individual state of mind. As an animal species, we are as much a part of the system of Nature as is any other living thing. We may have left the caves and jungles behind, but we are still on this Earth. That makes us a part of the system of existence created by the spinning action of the planet. There is nothing wrong with thinking the same as another, or feeling the same as another, or being and doing the same as another. Similarity and commonality do not detract from individuality. They are in fact, aspects of being a member of our type of species. Understand that it is not necessary for all humans to think the same way. However, it is essential to our survival as a species for us to have a common understanding of reality.

We can begin to establish the foundation for this "common understanding" by recognizing that "creation" is the result of one system, and our existence is the result of this one system. Every action that occurs throughout the Universe is a part of this system. This also means that everything that occurs can be defined and understood within the context of either the "one" system, or a "subsystem" thereof. Everything occurs as a result of a step-by-step (systematic) process. The Will of "GOD," the system of "GOD," occurs within the context of positive flowing energy as defined within the natural laws of electromagnetism. Because of this, our actions must adhere to the positive or right(eous) directives of any and all systems. I am talking about the system of Nature, of the human body, of the family, of the government, etc. We must always seek to do what is right(eous) and positive, whether there is subjective understanding or not. This is the common understanding that our perspectives must be built on. It is the reality that while we may err in our interpretation of the truth, there can be no error in the perception of positive action versus negative action. Polarity is a "physical" property that does not change relative to perception. Therefore, there can be no mistake regarding what is truthfully right or wrong, if our judgments are based on the right(eous) interpretation of the truth. This "truth" includes not only the respective actions and their result within the context of positive or negative, but also what we know and feel to be positive as indicated by our senses. We must not rely solely on the words we see or hear, for they are always subject to manipulation and skewed interpretation. We must embrace the depths of our individual spirituality so that we can trust and rely more on our senses when interpreting. The one thing that does not change regardless of who is doing the perceiving, is polarity. So we must all embrace the divine energy and its polarized definitions of positive and negative action, so that we can all go in the same direction.

Because spirituality has a physical foundation, it must be accepted as a true aspect of reality, rather than a philosophical interpretation of a field of thought. To deny our spiritual responsibilities is to deny reality. The nature of the system of realities within which we exist requires certain actions of us. Required action can also be termed "responsibility." All life must perform its required action, or it ceases to thrive. It will also meet with an earlier than normal demise. We must perform our required actions and tend to our responsibilities, for the benefit of the individual, the family, the country, and the species. This is what "GOD" intended. One of these responsibilities is we must personally pursue knowledge to provide ourselves with a firm foundation upon which to base our beliefs. We cannot merely accept what others tell us as truth because we are then not utilizing the interpretive abilities that lie within each of us. As a group (i.e. a species), most of us limit the openness of our minds. Put more accurately, we limit the objectivity of our perspective to the degree that we do not always endeavor to perceive beyond the definitions of the labels or words that we use. We must recognize the truth that individuals wrote all of these definitions, so their meanings are limited to the interpretations and understanding of those human beings. While the definitions may be true, are they complete?

It is the ability to feel what is truly right(eous) and positive from within ourselves that makes definition complete. Each individual must use their senses to come to a more conscious understanding of the significance and relevance of the words that explain existence. We fool ourselves into thinking we deal with reality as a matter of course. Not many of us function in an objective reality. We dwell in our own subjective realities, and we allow these "fantasy worlds" to shape our perspectives. We allow these "fantasy worlds" to separate us as completely united members of this nation. As a species, all of humanity is one. As Americans, we are of one community. This is reality. We cannot and must not continue to allow differences in race, culture, or behavior to divide this nation and pit countrymen against countrymen. We must not continue to allow selfishness and greed to determine the direction of our actions.

My brothers and sisters, be you White, Black, Hispanic, Indian, Asian, Arabic or what have you, the time is upon us when we must accept difference as a naturally occurring reality. Within this context, we must put difference aside so that we may come together to deal with more important matters. The most important of which is the perpetuation of human existence. The word "extinction" does not only apply to other species of the planet. We too can fall prey to this circumstance of Nature. Each living organism naturally moves in a way that seeks to perpetuate and improve its state of existence. Paraphrasing, one can say that movement goes in one direction, and that direction is positive. Like the spinning of our Earth, this is a part of the system of Nature. Contrary to this, in a very real sense, the overall actions of the human species are leading us to the brink of self-destruction. For a living organism, this is not natural. It is not a part of the system of Nature. Again paraphrasing, you can say that type of movement is counter to Nature, i.e. opposite of it, or negative. The Earth never spins in the opposite direction, does it? Moreover, what would happen if it did? For all the "artificial" things that surround us, we are not able to shield ourselves from the reality that we are still a part of Nature, and therefore, subject to her laws and her wrath.

Just as from catastrophes and wars of the past, the terrorist attacks upon the world trade center and the pentagon united America. As a nation, we became a unit of citizenry, as should always be the case. The same holds true for our species. Once we can accept the notion that we humans are not the focal point of the Universe, we will be able to embrace each other with love as "GOD" intended. Does our entire planet have to fall under attack from beings of another planet before our species will come together? There are UFO sightings. The possibility exists that we may not be alone in the Universe. This together with the possibility that our Earth could be destroyed by the impact of an asteroid brings to light the realization that we are one community of human earthlings. We must look to our future with this added insight. We must all unite and work together, with the goodness of "GOD" in our hearts.

As individuals travel down the road that is the journey of their life, each must seek to walk in the proverbial footsteps of Jesus Christ. This is because we were fathered by the Divine Energy of Life. The divine truth is, the Divine Energy of Life is there whether one chooses to recognize it or not. This divine manifestation did not seek to create humans. It sought to create life. The human is the physical manifestation of "GOD," the messenger of knowledge and earthly creator of blessing. The individuals of our species conceptualize themselves as the destiny of existence. However, it is life itself that is actually the destiny of existence. Humans can do as they choose with the species. Just as other species upon the Earth have become extinct, our species can become extinct also. Life itself will continue to thrive on the planet, whether humans choose to be a part of it or not. We must consciously choose to be a part of it. Choices mandate responsibility. Masses of people will readily believe someone who claims to have seen the Virgin Mary, or UFOs, or whatever. Those people will expend energy and time setting up vigils to glimpse these things for themselves. Those individuals do this out of faith, whether it is recognized or not.

If faith makes those endeavors easy to justify, then deeply evaluate the words of this text as they relate to our present earthly conditions. Feel the truth of this message in your mind, body, and soul. Believe me when I tell you, the time for decisive commitment is now. Each of us must make the right choices for the future of life in our country, on the planet, and in the Universe.

We must open our minds so that we interpret existence in its true state. Each of us must embrace what is really the truth. By not recognizing the reality that as animals on this planet, we are all an inherent part of this divine system, we are missing the truth. Everything around us is created by or from Nature and is therefore a functioning part of the system of Nature. Many humans have chosen to think of themselves as not being an animal, in effect separating their existence from Nature. Doing this creates another reality within the mind, a material or physical reality. We have reached the moment in time where we as humans must recognize our place within the Divine System of Nature. Examining the relevance and significance of our individual and collective behavior to the system of Nature will lead us to this. What we "do," i.e. our actions, are a part of the equation of existence. There must be an inherent balance to each of our movements. This must relate to anything at all that we do. All of existence is a part of an equation that we are continually defining but never completely solving. To continually move forward through the equation of existence while not solving it requires that we always seek to balance the factors and elements involved, because balance is the foundation of equation. This means each of us must choose how our hands move, what steps our feet take, we must be aware of the impact of our every motion. This makes each of us, alone, responsible for the impact our actions have. From this perspective, one can see why instincts, intuitions, and good judgments based on the goodness of the heart or the truth therein, are so important in guiding our actions. This is true simply because there are so many moments of time and so many movements to consider.

We all must come to the place in our collective understanding where the Divine Energy of Life is recognized as the singular source of our existence. Each of us must concede to not knowing all there is to know about this entity. Within this concession, we must embrace the fact that the system of religious belief or spiritual practice each of us subscribes to is but an interpretation of what the human species collectively knows to be real. "GOD" (the Divine Energy of Life) gives us the divine energy that gives us life by producing the spinning action of our planet. From this spinning action is created a myriad of sub-systems that generate our lives and the conditions surrounding them. Each individual living thing is one of these sub-systems, and so are the actions of that living thing. Each is a part of the one large system, the system of Nature. Therefore, each of us must do what is right (eous) to fulfill our function within the Divine System of Nature.

We must open our eyes to the revelation that our collective interpretation of reality is subjective, in that our species feels existence was created for the satisfaction of humans. To look at reality objectively, from the vantage point of a cloud, looking down upon our Earth, it is easy to see that humans are but one of many species of animal that inhabit our Earth. One system of life, what we have labeled "Nature," supports every living entity of our planet. The continuous spinning of our Earth in one direction creates this system of Nature. We must look for the manifestations or works of "GOD" (or the label Allah, or the "Divine Energy of Life," or the "creator," or simply the energy thereof) to be exhibited and made real through the system of Nature. As well, we must interpret these works relative to their relationship to the system of Nature. This system contains every aspect of our existence, not just the forests and the other wilds. The elements of the system of Nature can truly be seen, heard, felt, smelled, tasted, and understood. Therefore, the system is real. Each of us must embrace the relevance of the system of Nature to our daily lives. We are dependent upon this spinning action to survive. Therefore, we are "subordinate" to the energy that sustains this motion. It is the same energy that brings life to the living organisms of our Earth. It is true that we have supreme dominion over our Earth, but this occurs within a humbly specific context of understanding. These words are meant to enlighten our entire species to this context of understanding.

The label "GOD" is a noun. It is the result of a need to identify something we as humans are aware and conscious of, and that we must express. We must accept the fact that this does not mean that the interpretation of that which we identify is right or complete. This is because the interpretation is limited by the boundaries of human understanding. Scientists are conceding to the truth that the creation of existence was and is the result of intelligent conception. Scientists are starting to favor a theory called "intelligent design." They say that existence is too complex, so a creator must have made the Universe. The more they learn, the more they question, and those questions invariably lead to discussions about "GOD." One scientist has been quoted as saying, "the more you learn about the physical Universe, the harder it is to avoid the conclusion that there is an intelligent designer." The inference is that the forces of the Universe are not a random occurrence. Despite the efforts of the research community, science itself has not been able to destroy the notion that intelligent design is an explanation for the existence of life. As more is learned through science, it all remains consistent with the concept of intelligent design.

Some philosophers have sought to use reason to demonstrate that there must be a "GOD." In the thirteenth century, St. Thomas Aquinas formulated the famous five ways by which GODs' existence can be demonstrated. The first way is the "unmoved mover" argument. We know that there is motion in the world; whatever is in motion is moved by another thing; this other thing also must be moved by something; to avoid an infinite regression, we must posit (which is to assume as fact) a "first mover," which is "GOD." The second way is the "nothing is caused by itself" argument. For example, a carpenter, who is caused by his parents, brings a table into being. Again, we cannot go on to infinity, so there must be a first cause, which is "GOD." The third way is the cosmological argument. All physical things, even mountains, boulders, and rivers come into being and go out of existence, no matter how long they last. Therefore, since time is infinite, there must be some time at which none of these things existed. It is a fact that "nothing" cannot cause anything. So, if there were nothing at that point in time, how could there be anything at all now? Thus, there must always have been at least one necessary thing that is eternal, which is "GOD." The fourth thing is that objects in the world have differing degrees of qualities such as goodness. However, speaking of more or less goodness makes sense only by comparison with what is the maximum goodness, i.e. perfection, which is "GOD." The fifth way is the teleological argument (argument from design). Things in the world move toward goals, just as the arrow does not move toward its goal except by the archer's directing it. Thus, there must be an intelligent designer who directs all things to their goals, and this is "GOD."

Some people believe in "GOD," and some people do not. The Divine Energy of Life, "GOD," whatever the label, the power thereof truly exists. If someone does not believe this is true, that means that person is wrong. They are wrong to the degree that they refuse to relinquish their personally subjective state of mind. A person's interpretation of existence may not acknowledge the Divine Energy of Life. However, they cannot close their minds to the existence of "GOD" because the truth is, they do not know all there is to know about existence. Because of this, we can truthfully say it is that person's level of understanding that limits their knowledge. Whether an atheist or one with a religious belief, one thing everyone must concede to in recognizing the existence of life on our planet is that there is a "life force." There is an energy that "powers" living organisms. The spiritual person sees it as a divine energy emanating from a single entity. The atheist sees it perhaps as simply chemical reactions that cause the heart to beat. However, the truth remains that in both cases electrical energy is present. Regardless of the interpretation, each of us should be humbled by this divine energy. This humility exists within the context of the appreciation one should have for the gift of their existence. Having awe and reverence for this power creates the circumstance for the humility that is the basis of faith. The humility that you face because you do not know it all, and therefore, cannot understand the "whole" truth, is the foundation of faith. There are aspects of reality that we must accept on faith.

Many people have difficulty with recognizing that a supreme entity truly exists. Such problems involve both perception and interpretation. No matter how this entity is perceived or interpreted, one thing will not change. "GOD" (the Divine Energy of Life) is a reality. One problem with interpretation has to do with impatience. In haste to have the answer quickly, the fact that understanding is a time-consuming process is ignored. There is a definite span of time that exists between the manifestation of the interpretation of an experience, and the moments of comprehension. The way to negotiate the system of understanding is to first recognize and accept the fact that the system of existence requires that we produce certain actions irrespective of individual thought. Those "responsibilities" must be met, regardless of what we think or feel. Those actions as well all must have a direction of movement. To be right, this direction is positive. Having good "intent" ensures that those actions will be of a positive Nature, or at the very least, a neutral Nature. This allows the mental energy required to direct your movements to be diverted to more pressing matters. Like developing a more complete understanding and deciphering that instance of GODs' blessing. Humans think that they need to understand everything as soon as possible, so that they can determine their course of actions or necessary responses. These reactions are usually motivated by what people think is in their best interests, not what is in the best interests of the circumstance itself. The best interest of the circumstance is served by doing the correct, right(eous), or positive thing, and by balancing the interests of all whom will be affected by the reaction to those occurrences with "the actor's" personal interests.

There are realities that exist right before our eyes. Yet, we choose to close our eyes and our minds to them. This has been done to preserve the subjective beliefs we as individuals wish to harbor. The time has come when we must open our eyes so that we see the truth in the realities that exist. We must recognize the truth, examine it, and understand it to the degree that it truly becomes a factor of our decision-making process. It is no longer possible for our species to move forward, while we ignore what is real and believe in many different versions of the truth. The collection of words intended to explain the "divine system" is contained within the holy books of our species. Closely examine the relationship between human action defined within the context of the physically real science of electromagnetic principles relative to positive and negative flowing energy, along with its relevance to the Earth. Then compare those tenets to the direction of human behavior relative to right and wrong within the context of our holy books. You will find that the divine truth is they are mirror images of each other. Our holy words are still with us because we still have the opportunity to embrace the salvation these words bring. This salvation lies within the truth.

The **truth** is everything. It is our whole existence. The full understanding of ourselves, both spiritually and physically, lies within our recognizing the truth. For example, the truth is that "magic" is the label for the art of producing a desired effect or result using various techniques that seemingly assure human control of supernatural agencies or the forces of Nature. As an objective person, do you subscribe to the notion that an individual could <u>control</u> some aspect of the supernatural, or the forces of Nature? The truth is, there is no "magic." What we have labeled "supernatural" and the "forces of Nature" are elements of spirituality. The truth of spirituality is that there is nothing magical about it. Among other things, the term "spirituality" represents the doctrine that explains the physical relationship (flow of energy) between living things and the Divine System of Nature. It is to be interpreted within the context of our truthful understanding of reality. The power of the Divine Energy of Life created all that exists, and it is not magic. It is real. It is the power of the Divine Energy of Life, "GOD," which created the human. When we seek to understand the reality of "GOD," we must do so within the context of what we know to be real, so that we may come to a truthful understanding.

"GOD" does not seek to hide from the human species. "GOD" wants to be known. Therefore, spirituality truly occurs on a plane that can be experienced by each of us. As well, it occurs within a context that all individuals can understand. By interpreting the works of "GOD" as magic, individuals are creating a subconscious barrier that keeps them from the full acceptance of "GOD."

This barrier also stifles that individual's ability to have faith in GODs' power. This is because most members of our species do not accept or believe in magic. What this also means is that if individuals are to embrace "GOD," establish faith in "his" words, and come together to develop a world that can truly be called "the kingdom of "GOD," it is the responsibility of us as a group to make this happen; ours alone. It will not be magically produced. It does not happen because we think it. It will not happen because we wish it. It will not happen simply because we pray it will. The power of "GOD" is made real through our species. We must do what is necessary. We must take action. We must manifest it. The truth about the world around us is that there is nothing magical about it either. Things do not magically appear or happen. If an individual wants something to occur, that person must perform the steps necessary to make it a reality. To think; to conceive; to want, these are the actions of the mind. The human response or reaction to these thoughts results in movement towards the means to resolve those thoughts. If we are to make changes to our lives and our social condition, we must choose the actions necessary to make this happen. If we are to become the best human beings our abilities will allow us to become, we must do what is necessary to bring about these changes. We must manifest it. Fantasy is merely a series of images of the mind, figments of the imagination. What is conceived or perceived by the mind is not real or true simply because it "occurs" to the mind. It has to have been manifested by action into moments, past, present, or future. To want or desire something does not make it a part of reality. It does not become true or real until it is manifested through effort requiring energy.

The human was created in the image of "GOD." However, the context within which this is understood is a direct result of the perspective a person has. The meaning of the term "image" needs to be interpreted as something more than would be derived from a superficial understanding of this descriptive term. Is it our physical appearance or composition that is "in the image of GOD"? Reality does not support this possibility. Therefore, it must be some other part of us that bears a resemblance to this divine entity. If one studied the physical characteristics of the human in relation to the other members of the animal kingdom, the right conclusion to be drawn is that the human is not unlike other animal species. If "GOD" created only us in "his" image, there should be some distinct difference between us humans and the other animals. This difference is the conscious mind, and the words that flow from it. Not the brain, other animals have brains. It is the consciousness itself, as well as the words it generates. The human is a unique being in that, not only is it an animal with characteristics that identify it as such, it is a being with characteristics that are associated with a dimension other than this physical plane. These characteristics are all manifested within the context of the mind. Our consciousness, perception, and intellect are what make us unique.

Wild animals are more directly connected to their spirituality because they exist in the "flow" of their environment, going through the motions of their existence instinctively and intuitively. The human consciousness gives us the power to reason. Because of this gift, our extreme Nature has caused us to apply reason to our entire circumstance of existence. Therefore, we tend to minimize or disregard the importance and relevant significance of the use of faith, together with our instincts and impressions (or feelings) during our decision-making process. By doing this, we are actually suppressing an aspect of our nature or of our spirituality. It is the ability to sense (esp. /intuition), to feel (emotion), and to know (cognition), that makes us godly. Our thoughts and feelings are the elements of our being that are "created in the image of "GOD." Our emotions, humor, intuitions, and all other manifestations of feelings and thoughts that originate from within us are expressions of our spiritual Nature. This truth infers that the conclusions we draw from our perceptions have some spiritual relevance. As this is true, we must recognize that this spiritual relevance is significant to reality. We must recognize that spirituality is the paramount factor of reality, over any other factor conceived of by a human.

Let us try to place the "likeness" that exists between "GOD" and the human being within the context of human understanding. "Will" is defined as the faculty of conscious and especially of deliberate action. It is the power of control the mind has over its own actions.

"Telekinesis" is the label we give to the movement of an inanimate body without apparent external cause. It is accomplished using the mind. If we applied the understanding derived from these definitions to the biblical story of creation, a clearer picture emerges. "GOD" being the ultimate energy, the power to create anything is "his." We know that the creation of life was not the result of a physical "hands-on" building process, i.e. it was not the result of manual labor. We consider it a manifestation of the system of Nature. Truly, it was GODs' Will, done. "GOD" (the Divine Energy of Life) is supreme energy with supreme consciousness. The action of divine creation can just as easily be labeled "supreme telekinesis." We can infer that within our context of understanding, GODs' effort of creation was accomplished through an act of divine "mind over matter." Relative to the "likeness" each of us has with "GOD" (the Divine Energy of Life), it is manifested through the existence and use of the human mind. The human mind holds the key to creation upon our Earth. Each of us must develop this tool so that we learn what it is we are to create as individuals.

"GOD" Gave Us the Word

Gregory the great is credited with having left us this truthful bit of wisdom: "we are to learn the mind of GOD from the words of GOD." It is through the words attributed to "GOD" by true prophets, our holy books, and Jesus Christ, that we are to learn of the divine aspects of reality. It is not "GOD" that the scriptures seek to have us understand. It is the "mind of GOD." By our understanding of the "mind of GOD," we come to understand what "minds" we as a species are supposed to have. Moreover, as our minds control our actions, it is our behavior that is relevant to and significantly affected by the word of "GOD." To recognize and understand the mind of "GOD," one must be literate enough to interpret and comprehend the meaning of the word. The word of "GOD" is actually <u>all true</u> and <u>positive </u>words. These words are to lead us to a standard of conduct that is true and positive. Our behavior is to meet this standard continuously, not whenever it suits us to do so. We must open our minds to what is true and positive about reality, and learn from it, to respond positively to it. For an individual to open their mind does not mean they have to discard their current beliefs. However, it does mean that person has to recognize that learning is a never-ending process. Once the mind is closed, the learning process ends.

In the interest of gaining a broader, common perspective, consider what lies beyond the limits of basic human understanding. An objective examination of some obvious perceptions can establish the divine truth that the words and numbers known to humankind have a spiritual relevance and significance. To understand this, each of us must use the fundamental tool of the human mind. That tool is inference. If "GOD" is responsible for the creation of all that exists, then it can be inferred that words could easily be considered to have spiritual relevance and significance. This is because everything that exists has a purpose. If the human is created in the image of "GOD," then we can infer that the words the human uses to communicate could be said to be characteristic of "GOD," thereby making them spiritually relevant and significant. If mental activity is the result of energy received through the connective pathway to the Divine Energy of Life, then we can infer that thoughts and ideas manifested from that divine energy are spiritual in nature. It would follow that the "vehicles" used to relay those concepts would be relevant and significant. Those vehicles are words and numbers. This also means the actions that result from contemplation have a divine relevance and significance. in the pursuit of truth or the facing of reality, to derive a conclusion from all this inference regarding both words and numbers would be to, at the very least, acknowledge that they have a spiritual relevance and significance to reality. Together, they comprise a part of the "one" divine knowledge or a part of the "whole" truth. This whole truth is the living word of "GOD."

Physics and mathematics are the words and numbers that help us more clearly define our physical reality. We need the symbols of both words and numbers to define and express reality and its systems in both the physical and spiritual context. As there are certain words that have particular significance in explaining the direction of the motions of our lives, certain numbers have such a profound relationship to defining our reality in a spiritual sense. For a good understanding of the relationship of numbers to the Divine System of Nature, or spirituality, I would suggest a book entitled "Numbers in Scripture," by E. W. Bullinger. Within the pages of that book, you will find very good explanations and examples of the relevance of numbers to our spiritual reality. Adding, subtracting, multiplying, and dividing are inherent elements of the Divine System of Nature. They occur naturally as a part of existence. Because of this, there must be equation and balance. Numbers are needed by the human to come to an understanding of this reality.

Numbers become necessary once there is more than one of anything. You need numbers to calculate, to compute, to equate and to balance. You need numbers to explain the circle, existence, and time. Numbers are the key to unlocking the mystery of perpetual motion and utopia. Perpetual motion and utopia are the continued existence of life, human and otherwise, within the most nearly perfect conditions of earthly existence.

Numbers are necessary to our understanding of all that is around us in a natural way, i.e. reality, Nature, science, etc. Numbers are so inherent to the Divine System of Nature, that all living things recognize their relevance to one degree or another. Numbers are a wonderful and exciting divine creation. There is so much beauty and perfection in their composition and use. However, many other animal species have a perception of numbers. They recognize the strength of numbers. They also understand the relevance of numbers relative to the group, and to loss. It is the use of words that is unique to the human species. Words are derived from that aspect of our being that is created in the image of "GOD." They are a manifestation of human consciousness.

Animals in the wild signal each other in times of danger to warn. They also use signals to indicate other states or circumstances. This imparting of signals is termed "communication," the transmission or exchange of information or knowledge. Humans also share this ability to communicate, most commonly accomplished through speech or writing. Speech is communication derived from vocalization, and writing is communication that results from graphic inscription. However, whether the format of human communication is spoken or written, it can be expressed in a simplified, singular form, the word.

Language is the creation that resulted from our need to communicate our feelings and thoughts. Our feelings and thoughts are a part of what comprises our being. Each of us must open our minds to the revelation that "GOD" is both divine energy and intelligence, proven by deed and by virtue of the willful creation of life in all its complexity. Our being in "his" image, that part of "Him" that each of us has must also be energy and intelligence. As a collective, we must recognize the real label that describes the manifestation of creation. That label is "consciousness." The relevant significance of this divine truth is that words are the expressions of our consciousness, that part of us that is most like "GOD." The nature of the divine significance of words, oral and written, is that the word was introduced to our existence by "GOD" (the Divine Energy of Life) as a means by which we could communicate the perceptions and impressions of our reality to each other. Words transcend the dimensions of worldly and spiritual realities. If a word is written on a piece of paper, the truth is that item has a value that is more profound than the paper and ink that comprise that item. This is true simply because it is a mode of communication given to us as a tool by our creator. Each of us needs to experience life with the depth that allows for the appreciation of such a small blessing. Each of us needs to be able to see the minute miracles that exist around us like words. It is then that an individual is able to embrace the realities and responsibilities that comprise existence. Words are a miracle, each and every one. From the word "the," "in," "me," "you," "are," "can," "must," and "please," to the word "supercalafragalisticexpialidocious." Every word is a divine gift and a blessing. Think the word supercalafragalisticexpialidocious is not a blessing? Think of all the joy and happiness that was brought about by the context of understanding associated with the use of this word.

Language is the product of the human's need to communicate with others of its species. Words are the basic components of human language. Whether written or in oral form, this is what meaningful human communication boils down to within this context. A series of properly used words form a sentence, which are words that together express a message. It is here where the complexity of communication surfaces. It is where flawed and incomplete interpretations of the truth occur. This is because each word in a structured sentence can be referred to as a "label" for another series of words that explain the meaning of the "label," what we call (or label) the definition of the word.

Some words have more than one definition, the choice of which is determined by the context, or perspective from which they are used. To compound the already complex circumstance of human communication, each of the descriptive phrases in the definition is composed of words, which again have individual meanings. And so it goes, around and around.

Another aspect of communication to recognize is that every single noun in existence is the result of a need to identify something of which we as humans are "conscious." Complicating matters even more, our misinterpretation of some realities we are conscious of has led us to label them with more than one name because at different times we interpret these realities from varying perspectives. An example would be the labels existence, time and reality, or truth and fact. To one degree or another, when these words are used in certain contexts, they are synonyms. There is also the use of slang, which is confusing because it sometimes encompasses using one word in place of another. There are many grammatically horrible examples of slang. However, let us look at a mild example like the word "hill." A hill is defined as, "a conspicuous, usually rounded, elevation of the Earth's surface, not as high as a mountain." However, most people, when riding in a car will refer to an elevation in the road in front of them as a "hill." A more accurately descriptive term would be an "incline." An incline refers to a surface (or plane) that slopes. Nevertheless, explain this to an average American citizen, and suggest they incorporate this understanding into their consciousness as they chose words, and they will say, "It doesn't matter because people know what I mean. It's a free country, I can talk any way I want." There is some truth in that reply. It is a free country, and you can talk any way you like, for now. However, the important thing is whether everyone knows what you mean or not. in this example, the possible repercussions of any miscommunication that could occur as a result of this constant juggling and re-inventing of terms that we practice is pretty much non-existent. However, in a circumstance of human interaction that is more complex, thereby containing more "communication bits," a misinterpretation can be very costly. This is one reason we must re-examine the definitions of the words we use, to re-establish our objectivity, as well as to focus and clarify our understanding. Our collective understanding of our individual relevance and significance to existence suffers because of how we subjectively manipulate our interpretation of words into a context to please ourselves. To be civilized is to be characterized by a high level of intellectual development. Intellect is measured relative to words. Therefore, we cannot move away from proper English and the full definitions of words, or the actions that result from either of them.

Also, remember that we do not have to be conscious of something for it to be real. It is necessary to accept the fact that each word is the "label" for some bit of information that the human must define to its understanding to express. It is also necessary to accept the truth that this does not mean that the humans' interpretation of information is always right or complete, because it is limited to the boundaries of human understanding. In general, we cannot simply accept the one-dimensional perception of existence we receive from the labels that describe it. We must take the knowledge, or definitions of reality, and apply them to the process of understanding. This is called "inference," and the human is obligated to use this ability because it is a part of its reality. <u>Everything</u> that exists can and must be used to achieve some positive end. We cannot simply accept knowledge with selective indifference. We must do things with all of it. At the very least, we must constantly consider the implications these definitions have on our actions. We must recognize that we must act, or react to these words responsibly with positive, decisive action. We must also recognize the reality that it is words, whether spoken or thought of, that get things done within the context of human existence on both an individual and collective basis. Words carry the meaning of the actions of the Universe into our consciousness, and between the members of our species. Words produce action. Humanity has proven in the past that it does not always correctly interpret the true meaning, wisdom, and perpetual value of the words in its possession.

If a deeper examination were made of not only the words of this text, but also of all the words in our collective and individual existence, limitless power and renewed value would be found. It is because the worth of those words is defined by each individual's understanding of them.

There is an adage that says, "Watch your thoughts they become words. Watch your words they become actions. Watch your actions they become habits. Watch your habits they become character. Watch your character it becomes your destiny." A thought is an occurrence that has no effect upon the world surrounding it until it is translated into our reality by acting upon that thought. a single movement or action affects not only the reality immediately surrounding it, but in can set in motion a change of movements, actions, or events that can have a more far-reaching impact on all of reality. If the human species is to fulfill its role within the Divine System of Nature, then it must do what socialized species do. That is to work (move or act; have motion) together for the betterment of the community. This is how sustenance is maintained for the individuals of that community. To accomplish this, the human must open its mind and fill it with words. Each individual of the human community must become literate, i.e. educated. As well, each of us must become objective in our understanding of our spiritual Nature so that a common perspective is formed. This is because the thoughts that result from that understanding lead to words. Those words lead to actions that affect every living thing on this orb. It is repetitive action that forms the basis of individual habit. Repeating those habits are how individual character is formed. Individual character is the truth of oneself. The actions derived from one's character lead to one's destiny. "Truth" is our ultimate destiny.

There are so many of us, myself included, who have in our possession what could easily be deemed "collections" of books that we have accumulated over a period of time. They have been saved with the understanding that if they are read again sometime in the future, the information inside those pages will enhance and/or enrich our lives even though we may have read them once already. Recognize this truth, then multiply that opportunity for enrichment by the volume(s) of data collected and stored by all government, business, private or academic agencies, institutions, and individuals of the human communities of our world. The result is an unimaginable wealth of knowledge from which insight and wisdom can be derived. What we as a collective species must do is take the time to re-examine the words that exist in those databases and elsewhere around us, and embrace the messages that are contained within them with a better sense of perception and depth, in a serious search for greater understanding. The "information superhighway" will provide all individuals with that opportunity by pooling all knowledge from varying disciplines into one easy to access database. Literacy is the key to the gateway of prosperity and salvation.

Each of us must begin to understand our individual and collective connection to everything that happens around us. By sounding and acting negatively, we truly are not fulfilling our natural function within the system of Nature, and we are negatively affecting the elements of Nature. This includes even the weather, because we are disrupting the electrical connection we have to this earthly reality. That connection is made real through the energy our movements generate. Our movements must all be correct, right (eous), or good, to produce energy of the proper polarity (flowing in the right(eous) direction) to fulfill our required part of this connected system. We must elevate our minds to recognize that our conscious awareness dictates the behavior of our bodies, and our bodies are supposed to do certain things on the surface of this planet.

Our thoughts control our actions. Therefore, a better understanding of words will lead us to produce the actions that will bring about the betterment of every element of our being. We must aspire to understand the meaning of everything. To do this, we must increase our vocabulary so that we can better understand the sentences that relate those meanings. In essence, we must be literate.

We must recognize the relevance of how we use words, and what effect those words have on the actions that follow. In America, the system or process of learning and understanding the written and spoken word requires that we first learn proper English diction. After we have acquired the ability to communicate correctly within the context of our country's language, then we can "sometimes" revert to the use of slang. If we constantly use slang and fragmented words, we are not allowing those words to be "naturally" completed. By not understanding the pronunciation or definition of words, we are not coming to a resolute understanding. If the pronunciation and understanding of the word is not complete, how can you expect the action that results from that word to be complete?

Here are three examples of how a more clear understanding of the meaning and usage of words will lead to the betterment of the elements of human composition. Relative to the human mind, by creating slang from proper words without first learning to use and be responsible to the proper word, we are in effect saying that a person does not have to do the right thing or be responsible. In effect, we are saying that individuals can do whatever they choose to do with anything they choose. An example of this is the street term (slang) "dis"; the full word it refers to is "disrespect." Those who use it are recognizing only a part of the word and only a part of its meaning. The user does not want another to "dis" him or her. However, the truth of the English language is that before there can be "disrespect," there must first be "respect." This reality implies a certain amount of responsibility on the part of all parties to first respect others. as is exemplified by the general behavior of those who most frequently use the slang term "dis," just as they are only using a part of the full word, their actions are only partly complete. Most of these individuals have no respect for other people, i.e. authority, society, other gangs, etc. Yet, they want to be given respect. Using only part of the word allows individuals to use its meaning without being responsible to it.

Relative to the body, let us examine the meaning and usage of the word "diet." The first definition that comes to mind when the word diet is uttered is related to weight loss. This definition is food and drink selected or limited by the amount a person eats for reducing weight. Because of our focus on weight loss, rarely do we consider the full definition of "diet" with regard to our health plan. We try this diet, and that diet, hoping to find the diet that allows for the quickest result. It is the successful "dieter" who has embraced the full definition of this word. It is the usual, habitual, or regular food and drink a person consumes. It is the consideration of food and drink in terms of its quantities, qualities, composition, and its effects on health. In truth, we must understand that a diet is not a short-term change in our eating habits. It is a long-term change aimed at producing a healthy body.

Relative to the soul, the meaning and use of the word "guidance" needs examining. Many pray or ask for guidance toward the resolution of circumstance. "Guidance" is the act or process of showing the way. In most instances, this request for guidance is actually an expression of the desire to give up control over one's actions, or the responsibility for those actions. Guidance is information. It is each individual's responsibility to control the motions of their bodies throughout the moments of their lives. This is done by using the information one is exposed to as a guide for those actions. To desire guidance is to want the information one deems pertinent to their direction through existence. With such knowledge, the individual is still responsible for the actions of their body.

As words are an essential part of the human existence, they are therefore a part of the Divine System of Nature. Using them is how we make our part of the system work. We must all become literate, we must all become knowledgeable, and we must all become good "under standers" and communicators. As we complete the words we use and come to a more full understanding, we bring understanding to a natural conclusion. This will facilitate the actions that result from those words being full and complete, making them a rightly functioning part of the system. This brings the circumstance of our existence to full circle. The system of Nature gave us positive flowing energy in the form of existence. To maintain the perpetuation of this flow, each of us must move (or follow the flow) in the positive direction. For our species, this positive direction is established by choice.

We must see every circumstance through to its end. We must resolve or seek resolution. The words must have a beginning and an end, for the actions to have a beginning and an end. The direction of these actions must be positive, so the thoughts that lead to them must be positive. We must all think positive, and we all know what that is. We know the words that are positive, and positive words produce positive actions. Some of those positive words are moral, ethical, honest, fair, civil, etc. So we have to think positive, talk positive, act positive, be positive. We must educate ourselves so that we are knowledgeable enough to produce and utilize the right words. The state of our mind that will lead to this positive perspective is objective. The direction of the actions that result from this mindset is positive. We must strive to be both objective and positive.

What this all means is that words are not simply something that we use to communicate, they are binders. Words bind humans to each other, which is what leads to social structure. Words bind humans to actions. These actions fulfill our requirements to the Divine System of Nature. The human label for this action of "binding" is responsibility, and responsibility is required action. Humans are responsible to each other, so there are certain actions that are required of each of us during our interactions. Humans are responsible to social structure and order, so there are certain actions that are required of each of us during our actions within society. Humans are responsible to the Divine System of Nature, so there are certain actions that are required of each of us during our existence upon our planet. The direction of the actions that satisfy these responsibilities, to be spiritually right and fit into the flow of the Divine System of Nature as defined by both our holy books and the electromagnetic foundation of existence, is positive. We must work toward growth (i.e. have positive movement) to make it easy for the proper changes to occur within ourselves as individuals and as a collective species of animal.

If words have a spiritual relevance and significance, then reality has a spiritual relevance and significance also, because words are the result of a need to communicate the perception of reality. This also means that each of us must recognize that every situation, every circumstance, every event, and every moment that life is in existence, every part of reality has some divine or spiritual relevance and significance. This may be hard to conceive of within the context of our current understanding of divinity and/or spirituality. However, if it is recognized that our species is a part of the Divine System of Nature because we are in scientific terms (words) "animals," the picture becomes a bit clearer. The Divine Energy of Life created the system of Nature to sustain life. As a living being on this circle, what we perceive as reality occurs relative to the spinning of our Earth. This spinning action is responsible for our existence. Therefore, all life on our planet exists within the confines of the Divine System of Nature. For all these reasons and more, we must embrace the relevance and significance of spirituality to our existence. What is this relevance and significance? If the Divine Energy of Life has domain over all of Nature because it all came from the Divine Energy of Life, one must conclude that "GOD" (or the principles of the Divine Energy of Life) is a part of every moment of human life and of all that exists.

If the "source" of divine energy has within it the intelligence to create all of this, along with a consciousness that the human consciousness is patterned after, then we can infer that there must be a reason for all of the effort other than boredom. As some humans interpret things, the creation of all that exists seems to have occurred over a very extended period of time. Therefore, existence could not possibly be an orchestrated circumstance with a purpose. Yet, we must not forget that time is a label that is relative to the humans' interpretation of its perception. Therefore, without the human, time as we know it does not exist. Other animals function within a <u>cycle</u> during the time that they are alive. however, it is not a conscious one to the degree that they recognize that it is literally as a span of moments, nor as it being "time" to do this, that, or the other thing. Theirs is a natural, instinctive, intuitive existence. If it were true that "GOD" created the scenario of our existence with a purpose, for "him" it could very well take place within what we would term "the blink of an eye."

Simply because this possibility exists, we must recognize the revelation of the circumstance, and the perspective that this realization creates. If this "blink of an eye" were possibly true, it would create a need for a broader spectrum of interpretation. We would also need a greater understanding of the possible relevance of the circumstance of "destiny" and incorporate that into our mindset. For all any one of us knows, there may very well be a purpose to human existence. Regardless of what that purpose is, every waking moment of our respective individual and collective lives, every action, religious or otherwise, has some spiritual relevance and significance.

Why did "GOD" create life in general, and the human in "his" image? What our species has labeled "GOD" is truly pure, positive energy unlike anything we imagine. A comparison manifested here on our Earth that can be made is with the energy at the tip of a welding rod. It is controlled. It is so white and bright, the naked eye cannot look at it. The heat of this energy is so intense it can burn through metal. This is but a fraction of the energy of which the Divine Energy of Life is composed. Imagine "GOD" (the Divine Energy of Life) as fire magnified a gazillion-trillion times, with an awareness or conscious control of that energy and power. In this form, our creator has knowledge of everything. However, if my interpretations are right, "he" does not have access to the knowledge derived from "experience." This is derived from seeing, hearing, touching, smelling, and tasting. If our "GOD" were truly composed of intense positive energy, these senses would not be present. Think of being burned by a match or some other source of fire. The intense heat supersedes all other sensation to the point of deadening the ability to sense. Within this context of understanding, it is my contention that "GOD" created living things to manifest "Himself" into this physical dimension. This was done for the sole purpose of experiencing this reality, to actually grow into more than "he" is already. This is accomplished by utilizing the knowledge gained throughout all the moments of time experienced by living organisms as well as human consciousness. The experiences of every blade of grass, every tree, every sea and land animal, is transferred back to "GOD" along the circuit (circular path) the Divine Energy of Life that keeps us alive travels. Just as in the comparison to a phone line, "GOD" sends us energy and knowledge, and we send back the same. Humans were created "in the image" of "GOD" as a means of "his" gaining knowledge by physically, through us, projecting "Himself" into this dimension.

As GODs' instrument in this endeavor, this is what we humans must do. Each of us must experience this reality as fully as possible, and grow by means of expanding our knowledge. This pursuit of experience or process of growth, is what we have labeled "living." It is supposed to occur within the context of how "GOD" intended it to work. Think of it as an experiment. Within the context of those thoughts, consider what would be the normal course of action if an experiment does not work. One would discard it and start anew. The process of discarding the experiment of our existence is "the end times." The outline for the system of actions (or behavior) that the experiment is to follow is contained within the pages of the holy books of our species, and the structure of each is patterned after the Atom. **This is our reality. T**he words within these holy books may seem to be the story of the history of the human species, but these words are actually meant to lead us to the actions that conform to the physical responsibilities we have to the system of Nature. The message within these holy books is sometimes difficult to interpret for various reasons. For example, what parts are to be taken literally, and what parts figuratively? Recognize that as any given prophet interpreted the revelations he or she was exposed to, the question remains, "did he or she choose the proper wording to define their experiences?" Whatever the answer is relative to an individual seer of divine truth, the essence of the message within these holy books is very clear and simple. It is that humans are to act in a positive manner. This divine truth is verifiable when it is understood on the basis of what science says is physically true about the system of Nature, and what we know about spirituality and divinity, if the examination is done from the proper perspective. That proper perspective is objective.

Opening one's mind up to the degree that the contemplation of reality includes all of the variables that can be conceived of is difficult. This is where we are humbled before "GOD," and must utilize the awesome power of faith to deal with what our minds can conceive. We must apply faith in the process of reconciling and rationalizing that "unknown" factor of circumstance that could possibly be relevant. That "unknown" factor does exist because none of us knows all there is to know, and this is verified because none of us knows the definition of the source that gives us life. This in itself is the only example of the truth of our humility that we need. Recognizing, processing, and applying this in perspective during the time of an individual's life can seem like an exhausting task, when it is projected across the spectrum of all mental application. However, the energy, mental capability, and awareness that we need to achieve this goal is hidden in the untapped resources of our minds. It is that capacity of the mind that science says we do not utilize. It is accessible through our combined movements, our activities. These are our spiritual activities, mental activities, and physical activities, all of which result in knowledge. For the human species, knowledge (words) is everything. Unless you "know," nothing really matters. Knowledge (words) is what aids the human in guiding its actions. The knowledge derived from our consciousness is the human contribution to its natural guidance system. Our feelings, impressions, and intuitions, along with the knowledge (words) we gain, are truly the spiritual elements that guide us through the motions of our lives. The contemplation each of us indulges in during the course of our daily lives as we experience and explore causes an increase in mental activity and capacity. Once we open up our mental resources, we must apply them or lose them.

We must understand that all of the knowledge and energy realized by the human species was given to it by "GOD" for the sole purpose of producing growth. Processing (which is a system) that knowledge produces individual growth. Sharing what we know and learn with the human collective, i.e. humanity, produces social (collective) growth or civilization. It is a natural occurrence to prosper when knowledge is attained and shared. From this individuals must infer that because it is a natural occurrence, it is GODs' purpose that knowledge (words) be shared in an effort to achieve a higher plane of understanding and prosperity. In our reverence of "GOD," as we do not know all there is to know, we must have faith in the divine order of things. To share knowledge naturally increases its value and capacity for benefit because as it is passed along, each individual who encounters it adds it too. Sharing knowledge will naturally give us the tools to solve the puzzle that is our destiny. Consider the truth within the following realities. One, our lives are revolving around the exchange of words. The majority of the jobs that fuel our economy are now based on the exchange of information, rather than labor. Two, the exchange of information and communication in general is now a primary aspect of our lives. It is what we do for work and play. Entertainment is fast becoming more visual and intellectual, as well as being computer oriented. Three, an example of this being our destiny is the fact that the information superhighway will tie all intellectual disciplines together, creating a database of all knowledge, in essence linking it together. The foundation this technology was built upon is an element of Nature, a single grain of sand. Sand is found on almost every shore of the sphere. Is knowledge that is derived from the resources of every corner of the planet <u>not</u> to be shared by <u>all</u> the planet's inhabitants? The answer is no, all knowledge is to be shared. These revelations must make us recognize the relevant importance of words and the significant part they play in our lives.

Scientific Empiricism is the label for a philosophy that emphasizes the logical unity of all sciences, as well as a systematic analysis of language. It has also been called the Unity of Science movement. We must all embrace the connection between disciplines of knowledge. Either through a lack of understanding or from purposeful manipulation, many of us limit the application of this understanding to the arena of thought one wishes to affect.

An example of this is our avoidance of the truth that the discipline of thought we label theology, spirituality or the reality of the Divine Energy of Life, is as relevant to human existence as physics, mathematics, psychology, or any other system of theories, rules, or principles by which the human has been enlightened. This is because all knowledge is connected. Each is a part of a whole truth, derived from one divine source. There is a pattern within which words flow. The pattern lies within the depth of understanding the connection of one word to another. It is evidenced where single words mean different things, depending upon the context in which they are used. This pattern, which includes the nature of "root" words and the utilization of words across intellectual disciplines, is at the core of our spirituality. It is the basis for the realization that all information and knowledge is linked together.

For example, most of us have heard the phrase, "…the fruits of labor." We also know that the following statement is attributed to the almighty, "…be fruitful and multiply." Most take the latter as referring to reproduction. However, with regard to the pattern I speak of, the connection to which I have referred is exemplified by the use of the word "fruit" in both instances. I submit that the (energy and) knowledge derived from the Divine Energy of Life is universal in that it applies to our entire existence. from this viewpoint, I think it is a safe inference to interpret the latter directive to mean that not only are we to procreate, but we are to work and prosper as a divine decree. This would be a part of the "whole" truth of this directive. The word "whole" came from the same root word that "holy" does. Just as we make our knowledge of mathematics, psychology, and other tenets a part of our reality, so too our knowledge of "GOD" (the Divine Energy of Life) must also be a part of our existence. This is because spiritual reality has domain over any other perception of reality interpreted by humans. We look to the holy books of our species for the full explanation of our spirituality. What we must do is put the truths of the Holy Scriptures together with all the other truths of our reality, to determine a more complete interpretation of the "whole" truth.

We must embrace our common goals as defined by the definition of species (science). We must allow the energy within us derived from the Divine System of Nature to spew forth in a positive direction by having the goodness of "GOD" in our hearts (spirituality). We must accept our responsibility to contribute with our actions (newton's laws of motion; physics) to the community (sociology). We must seek to understand and improve ourselves (psychology, philosophy, and astrology) so that we can get the most out of our existence and realize our wants/desires (humanity). Based on a truthful interpretation of this bit of wisdom, one can see the need to apply knowledge from all known disciplines to the task of evaluating the nature of human existence. The challenge we face is whether we can elevate our consciousness to the next plane or not. On this plane, good triumphs over evil. It is where our energy, flowing in a positive direction, overcomes the influences of negative attraction. This is accomplished by the human species embracing the reality of GODs' word. We are all GODs' children, regardless of our ethnic lineage, and we must have faith in "his" word while living out the ideals derived from the teachings of Jesus Christ.

Along with so many different religious belief systems, there are so many different interpretations of our holy books. Each group takes their interpretations as objective fact, rather than subjective belief. Then they allow these subjectively created facts to determine the direction of their actions. Books of history, of which the Bible is one, are to aid and guide us through the journey of our lives. They are not to strictly define the steps we are to take. We must react to the actions of reality in a positive manner, using the words of our past to show us the way to positive resolution. We must look at our existence objectively. As well, we must do what is positive to bring our wants/desires in balance with those with whom we interact. We must equate. The prophecy throughout the Bible, and/or prophecy in general, is all up for interpretation. Yet, an objective glance at the realities of our society and humanity as a whole easily indicate that our species is heading in a destructive direction.

It is one that could easily lead to what is described as "damnation." Irrespective of our interpretations of the written word, each of us can see the realities before us all. We must react to what we face in a positive manner if our moments are to have a positive resolution.

As each of us seeks to perfect or better our efforts relative to "GOD," we must embrace the fact that our spirituality is a natural part of our being. As well, our entire being is a part of Nature. We must open our minds beyond the subjective interpretations each of us has made. We must re-examine the words of our spiritual past and see the objective truth in them. We must do this with the understanding that there are a greater number of more specific descriptive words now than there was when these original writings were compiled. Therefore, utilizing our power to infer along with allowing our interpretation to take into consideration the "implied" meaning of certain words relative to the context of their use, the circumstance they are relevant to, and our greater vocabulary, we can and must come to a better understanding of what is true.

Each of us must then allow these truths to guide us in a positive direction as we collectively move into our future. Truth is the collection of words that explain and define reality. Because this is true, each of us must recognize the significance and relevance of words like socialized (species), civilized (existence), as well as positive and negative (direction), etc. In the process of recognizing the truth in these revelations, the necessity and practicality of faith must be acknowledged. Faith is a reality within the context of the humble position humans find themselves in as they seek to define and understand the Divine Energy of Life. Because no individual or group knows all there is to know about our reality or existence itself, we must accept and believe in things that we do not fully understand. Faith is not about understanding GODs' entire plan. It is about choosing "him," acting in truth with regard to what is known, and leaving the rest to "him." We may not understand the whole thing, but we must seek to understand the part that is relevant to us, and believe that "GOD" will take care of the rest. just as we are the guardians and supervisors of our children and they must obey us whether it makes sense to them at that moment or not; we are the children of "GOD," and we must obey "his" directives, whether we can rationalize and understand them or not. Just as with the child, who begins to understand the purpose of what he was directed to do as he matures and comes into greater understanding and wisdom, we too will be enlightened, as we progress into the truth of our spirituality. As the human deems the energy that produced and sustains life as being spiritual or divine, we must then recognize the supreme value of the books that define the nature of divine doctrine. These are the books that form the foundations for the world's religious belief systems, of which the Bible is one. In these books specifically, together with other books of knowledge, we have all the answers we need. They are just not arranged and presented in a fashion that can be interpreted in a manner to be everything for everybody.

We manifest the reality of positive energy every day. Humanity knows what right is. We know that a person just cannot do something any way they choose, that one must do it the "right" way. Right is an indication of direction. We are always to do the right thing the right way. In other words, we are always to do the positive thing the positive way. There is a system for everything. There are certain (all) words that are particularly relevant and significant with regard to human action. These words are a part of our vocabulary because they are labels for something we recognize. That truth means that what we recognize is real or a part of reality, so we must deal with or react to them. We identify "positive" and "negative," so they are real. We must recognize and effectively deal with them as a part of our reality. "Right" and "wrong," "positive" and "negative," "correct" and "incorrect," are a part of existence. We must understand their relevance and significance within their proper context. This is why perspective is so important. Many of us do understand the meaning of these and other words.

However, unless they are understood within the proper context, the true relevance and significance of their existence and use will be missed. This is not to say that from the current perspective people have, that their understanding is not true. It is to say that we are missing the "whole" story. The foundation of our understanding of reality is based upon fragments of one, whole truth.

These words can take each reader to another level of human understanding if their mind is open to change. There have been many righteous men in our collective past who were killed because of the words they spoke and the actions that followed those words. Their words produced fear. Do not fear any words from another human. Seek to understand and apply the truth within them. The words can only be manifested into reality by action. Do not condemn me for any of the words contained within these pages because each of us must accept the reality that no individual knows all there is to know. These words reflect the truth, whether or not each person believes them. Because this is true, contemplate the righteous possibilities within them. Take what is positive out of them and apply it. Our lives must always follow a positive path, always going in a positive direction. Every person will always have a choice of direction. We can all see the positive direction just by "sensing" reality. It is natural to us. Each person can face reality if possessing an open mind. Faith in the one "GOD" will keep us all from being afraid of reality. We need faith to allow us to open our minds without fear. There is truly nothing to fear, but fear itself. The whole point to recognizing our true spirituality is that without it, we will be afraid to confront and deal with the issues before us. Embracing the truth will cause us to do certain things. We resist the impulse to do what is right, because we want to do what we desire. Each of us can truly do both.

No individual should disregard the truth of some of these words because they make him or her recognize their own subjectivity and prejudice. These words are intended to stifle everyone's ability to be self-centered, selfish, and greedy. That is what they are supposed to do. Do not avoid the hard things that must be worked at to achieve. Someone once said, "What is easy is best, but what is best isn't easy." We must look at our "whole" reality with this in mind. We must all collectively change our direction, completely if necessary. We must all go in the same direction for salvation to be ours. All of us, in America and on the entire planet, must do positive things to go in a positive direction. If we all, i.e. our entire species, do this while sharing all our Earth's resources in a more balanced way, what we will create is utopia and near perfection. Individuals need only open their minds up beyond the boundaries of subjectivity, pessimism, arrogance, and ignorance. Just imagine what would happen if all the individuals of the whole world did positive things. Each of us is <u>supposed</u> to move in the positive direction. That is the path of our journey. It is the truth. We must all embrace the truth about the meaning of human life.

Our "thinking" is merely the mechanism that gets us to fulfill our required actions. Our required actions or responsibilities are the "works" we are to contribute to the Divine System of Nature. To make a choice, one must decide. One must use their powers of reason and inference to answer questions that are significant and relevant to the decision at hand. As the human uses reasoning and inference to determine the direction of its actions, each of us comes to a point where we begin to question. We begin to ask "why," "what," and "how." the core of human consciousness is query. Each individual develops a pattern of behavior based upon the answers that person accepts as true. If we are to truly understand why we are to be positive and pursue betterment or perfection, we must answer basic questions about our existence.

Let us begin with the question, "**what is the meaning of my (a human's) life?**" The answer to this very philosophical question will vary, because it is "subject" to interpretation based on the perspective of the individual who is seeking the answer. That perspective is built upon the foundation of what that individual <u>accepts</u> as true, not what is <u>completely</u> true. In an effort to establish a more universal perspective and interpretation, let us come to a common understanding of this particular question. We can do this by clearly defining the words of the sentence that forms the question. We will substitute the words of the definition in place of the actual word, so the question will be reduced to its purest form. W**hat**, is interrogatively used as a request for specific information. **Is,** defines the "third person singular of be." The definition of <u>be</u> is "to have existence, truth, or actuality." So then the use of **is** establishes a state of reality, truth, and/or existence. T**he**, is a definite article used to render a word more particular, specific, or individual. The word **meaning**, within this context, is synonymous with interpretation or significance/relevance. **Of,** translates into "pertaining to." **Life**, for the purposes of this analysis, is defined as, "the period of existence between birth and death." So then, the question now becomes, **"please reveal the interpretation of reality that is significant and relevant to the**

human, pertaining to the period of its existence between birth and death." The answer to this question is clearly, **TRUTH.**

Though the answer to that question is one word, the complexity of interpreting that one word can be immense. "Truth" is the <u>collection of words</u> the human uses to define, understand, and communicate reality. We do not write or speak reality; we write or speak the truth. Reality is not words or other symbols. Reality is what is manifested through action. The period between birth and death is composed of a series of moments. Within each moment, any single person can derive an infinite number of individual truths, depending upon what element(s) of that moment is examined. The shortcoming in our understanding of the truth is that the perspective that results from our interpretation of these individual truths does not incorporate the most profound truth. That "profound truth" is the fact that each individual truth is directly related to and derived from a complete, whole truth that not a single human being fully knows. If we never come to understand the true nature of what we know relative to the whole truth, the big picture as it were, we are doomed to continue our divisive, selfish and greedy ways.

What we must embrace as true and real is that there is only <u>one</u> whole truth, as there is only one genuine, all-inclusive existence. This "one" truth begins with the spinning of our planet. This is the first truth. Every other bit of human knowledge and every bit of human existence stems from this first truth. Without this first truth, there would be no other "truths" to follow. Think of it in terms of truth starting out as one complete circle. Imagine that this circle was then divided into many pieces, or bits of knowledge, having many different shapes and sizes. Those different pieces, or individual truths, are held within the minds of each individual human being. Each piece of truth must be added together to reproduce the original, whole truth. As we share our knowledge with each other, it grows. As we come together as a species, this growth and unity will restore the original shape. That original shape is the circle.

In coming to terms with our true, objective reality, we must all embrace the fact that the spinning of this planet produced the conditions from which life was able to emerge. It is the system of actions and reactions generated by energy produced from this rotation that is the perpetual source of life. The "sub-systems" derived from the primary system, like the primary system itself, are composed of variations of circles in the form of cycles and circular actions. Circles are the foundation upon which our spirituality, as well as all other systems of existence are built. This is true of the Atom, the internal workings of living beings such as ourselves, and time as we know it. Occurrence, circumstance, recognition, examination, inference, all these and more are all elements that take place because this planet spins in a circle. This spinning action is the phenomenon that links all living things with <u>one</u> system. The spinning of our planet generates what humans refer to as "time." The spinning of our planet generates this "one" system. Everything that lives on this planet does so because of this divine system we call "Nature." Living upon our Earth makes us a part of that system. The human consciousness, time, our perception of existence, are all contained within the system of Nature. Therefore, they are all elements and factors of the Divine System of Nature. Every moment on our Earth is a part of the process, a part of the system.

As stated earlier, there are two different dimensions and/or interpretations of existence to which humans are accountable. There is the tangible worldly reality, and there is the intangible spiritual reality.

Separately, they are "halves" of the whole truth. Each individual truth spans both interpretations of human existence, and humans are responsible to the whole truth. At any given time, the human chooses to be responsible to only one half of the whole truth. Most of us are always swinging back and forth between the objective, worldly truth, and the subjective, spiritual truth. The root of our social system's problems is that we have been choosing one or the other, when the reality is, there is only one whole truth. Even though we interpret our perceptions in two different ways, this does not negate the fact that there is still only one truth. By choosing to react to only part of the whole reality, we are not completing the circumstance. We are choosing between the truths, when reality dictates that we are responsible to both. The mind perceives the objective truth and the subjective truth regardless of our perspective. It takes discipline and control, along with the acceptance of responsibility, to come to the right conclusion based on the perspective that considers objective truth primary to, though including subjective truth.

The manipulation of truth must end. This can only occur if individuals start thinking <u>for</u> themselves, and rightly react to the positive and negative of reality. Manipulation is possible only when it is allowed to occur. It happens when one is exposed to "a" truth, or truth in fragments, instead of the whole truth, and that person accepts these bits without question. It occurs when we examine particular moments in time and leave other relevant moments out. It also occurs when the facts or words that relate to given moments are changed by someone manipulating our perceptions of those moments (i.e. words and images communicated to us in a variety of ways). Very good examples of sources of manipulation are the media via print and news telecasts, the television in general through its programming, movies, and commercials. These are all words and images. Once we are exposed to information, we cannot simply accept it as true without personal examination. It is our worldly and spiritual responsibility to evaluate what is perceived. Only then can we make the correct or right choice for the direction of our individual actions. Each of us must embrace the facts, or the truth, or what amounts to all the realities of the relevant moments before us. From a truly positive perspective, each of us must produce righteous action based upon what is real. We all know that we are purposely being exposed to incomplete truths, and that the purpose of this is to influence what we do. To blindly accept this information and follow the course of action that we are led to have, is to react like an animal that is not human. Perhaps that animal is more like a sheep, or a duck. We must be true to ourselves. By seeking to manifest into reality the goodness that is within our hearts, we can come to trust and listen to ourselves. Our actions must be guided by choices we make that are based upon guidance we receive from within ourselves, not guided by choices others make for us.

Let us examine for ourselves some other very basic questions whose answers we must utilize to more clearly define the positive, orderly course for our lives. These questions serve to clarify our understanding of the human system of existence. **"What is the nature of living things?"** In an effort to minimize misinterpretations, we can reduce the question to a simpler form. In doing this, the question becomes, "please reveal the fundamental characteristic that defines the actuality of animate existence?" The answer is **"to move, to have action, and to do."** The body is manifested by the Atom s that make up the cells, tissues, and organs. Each of these units has a corresponding system of motion associated with it, a system that "does" something through "motion." Just as the Atom has electrons that whirl around the source of radiant energy, i.e. the nucleus, so too is the living body and other living things structured. Within the human body the brain is the nucleus, it is the source of radiant energy. Though the mass of the body seems solid in form, it is made primarily of fluid, about 60% water. These fluids, which are composed of smaller particles, flow throughout the body. In a general or basic sense, it can be said that the particles that make up the fluids are actually "whirling" around the nucleus, or brain. The fundamental characteristic that is prevalent in every living thing is movement, or action.

The next pertinent question is, **"What is the goal of a human's movements during its existence?"** More clearly put, we ask, "please reveal the truth that pertains to the intent to which the human's efforts are to be directed during its period of existence?" "GOD" intended all living organisms to live. **The goal is to live. W**ithin the Divine System of Nature, to live is to grow. Growth is a process, a systematic series of actions directed to some end. For humans, the process of growth is directed at the three elements that compose the human being. These elements are the body, mind, and soul. Within the context of human existence, "live" does not simply mean exist. It means to grow, experience, and get better. We must embrace the truth that within the context of simply existing, one can sit in a chair for their entire life and be within the parameters of this phrase. However, to grow, one must <u>pursue</u> the nourishment for that growth, whether it is the growth of the body, mind, or soul.

To experience, one must <u>pursue</u> movement, by endeavoring to get out of the chair and do things. To get better, one must <u>pursue</u> positive enrichment for oneself. While an individual's personal definition of desired experience and enrichment may differ, what is common is the fact that "pursuit" is a primary element of "living." To grow is to move. To pursue is to move. Relative to the movement required for both growth and pursuit, that movement occurs in a direction, whether it is up, down, or sideways. If the desired effect of our pursuit is to produce a positive change in our lives, which is what growth is, then the direction of each of these pursuits must be positive. This means that the actions of the pursuit must be positive. Within this context, positive is synonymous with good. Therefore, it can be said that we should pursue "goodness." However, in the simplest terms, the goal of human action is growth or positive change.

Lastly, **"with its movements, what state of existence is the human to pursue to support its life?"** In other words, "please reveal the condition of reality which the human is to apply its energies and motions to, in an effort to sustain itself during the period between birth and death?" That condition is one that supports the individual human as he or she pursues their goal. Since the goal of human action should be growth or positive change, the state of existence the human pursues must also grow or positively change. The label for this state of existence is **"Civilization."** The human is constantly changing over the course of its life and that change is supposed to be positive. The human must seek to create for itself a condition of existence that supports this continuous effort. For humans, the system that supports growth and positive change is civilized society. The betterment of a society of individuals occurs within the context of civilization. Realistically speaking, pursuing a more perfect system of existence is what we do anyway. We just do not understand it within this context because it occurs on an individual, superficial level. Each of us pursues a condition of existence that allows us to move through our lives while having experienced the least amount of pain and the most possible pleasure. The entire period between birth and death is actually one of growth. What we must recognize is that we must direct this growth. As our bodies grow, we must consciously choose the proper types of food, or direction of eating, that will facilitate the most positive condition for its growth. As our minds grow, we must consciously choose the proper direction of understanding that will facilitate the most positive condition for its growth. This is also true of the soul. Each person is to work towards improving (perfecting) himself or herself as an individual, so that each of us can contribute to the whole what "GOD" intended to have shared with humanity. The "whole" is society, and our society is characterized as "civilized." Therefore, we must pursue the characteristics of civilization to optimize our individual ability to grow.

From the answers to these questions, we can work out a basic understanding of the nature and direction of human action that will lead to the creation of a more perfect union. As living beings, we must move. This movement is to be aimed at surviving, growing, and experiencing. Each individual member of the human species is to move and have direction. To do this without conflict, there must be a system in place to give structure to human movement and to support it. That system is civilization. The very creation of civilization is the result of our natural inclination to function within a system. Utopia is the state within which "GOD" intended living things to function. These two conditions of existence (civilization and utopia) together form the most ideal (perfect) environment for human growth. Growth is the goal of all living things.

As we recognize, obey, and aspire to the authority of "GOD," we find that it is our betterment that our actions are to be aimed at. Though there are three elements of human composition, the mind is the authority of the human individual. It is charged with the task of guiding the efforts derived from the body and soul. Our getting closer to "GOD" means getting closer to the truth. It is taking that truth and having action that corresponds to it. It is our mind that must interpret the perceptions of our senses.

Therefore, our perspective is very important to our ability to determine what a given truth really means. To understand what our bodies are to do takes clarity and growth of the mind. To understand what direction our souls are to lead us takes clarity and growth of the mind. The evolution of the human species or the betterment of ourselves as a collective according to the rules, codes, and laws of "GOD," begins within the human mind. Our ability to interpret and understand the circumstances that come before us must evolve. We must open our minds up to the degree that we truly recognize that <u>anything</u> is possible. Each of us must become more inclusive with regard to what is possible in our day-to-day lives. We must become less selective regarding what we believe about the truths that exist in the world around us. The difference between a closed mind and an open mind is the amount of "questioning" that takes place. We must continue to seek answers to the circumstances we face because each new moment of <u>our</u> individual lives is one <u>no other</u> person has experienced. For this reason alone, no individual can know all there is to know.

"GOD" and Symbols

The first two of the Ten Commandments relate to there being only one "GOD" that cannot be represented by a symbol. We cannot have a symbol or image that represents "GOD" (the Divine Energy of Life). Regardless of whether we use the label "it," "he," "GOD," or "the Divine Energy of Life," the source of our origin must be forever contemplated in the mind. This contemplation is composed of words, and words lead to actions. The process of contemplation keeps "GOD" and "his" doctrine alive in our hearts. Each of us must contemplate "GOD." Each of us must think about "his" righteousness along with the positive words and deeds of "his" most perfect creation in the body of Jesus Christ. Each of us must think about "his" perfection and aspire to it, being the best individuals we can be. Each of us must think. Think about the good things, the positive things. That is the positive energy. When each of us thinks about "GOD," Jesus Christ, and positive things, our body's reaction is to manifest positive action in response to our positive thoughts. Our body seeks to harmonize our actions with our thoughts.

Once we allow a symbol to represent "GOD," we can then separate our reality from "his" reality, which is what we have done. This leads to the feeling that the action of worshipping within the doctrine of the symbol is what satisfies our responsibility to "GOD." This is what has happened. A person or group of people can worship and celebrate the realities of "GOD" in the manner of their choosing. Yet, each of us must recognize the same "GOD," and we must relate directly to "GOD," not through some likeness of "him" or anything else. Therefore, it does not matter what we choose to believe with regard to the details of our religious doctrine. Even Mother Teresa uttered these sentiments. Naveen Chawla, her close friend and biographer, attributed this statement to Mother Teresa, "once you've found "GOD," it's up to you to decide how (in what manner or denominational context) to worship "Him." The truth that is evident throughout every interpretation of the Divine Energy of Life is the significance and relevance of righteousness and goodness. This truth indicates the path of direction for the actions of our lives. Moreover, because we are all GODs' children, this righteousness and goodness cannot be selectively applied as we choose. It must be universally applied.

Symbols are something we choose to stand for or represent something else. Symbols are the physical manifestations of the consciousness that give substance to our perceptions. Symbols solidify consciousness within the physical realm. They are the junction between that state of existence we consider divine, and what we consider our reality. Humans need symbols to relate to reality. However, we cannot allow symbols to define us, we must define ourselves through our actions. Therefore, we have to act true to ourselves as individuals and as a species group. We cannot be limited by the symbols that we have, and the doctrine or definition represented by a symbol must always remain greater than the symbol itself. We must think beyond the symbols that are manifested by our minds, and act on those thoughts in a positive manner.

It is the point at which Jesus Christ succumbed to death, that symbols became profoundly relevant to our acceptance and understanding of the divine aspect of existence. It was after his death that "religion" was created and that symbols arouse to represent religious doctrines "attributed" to the teachings of Jesus Christ. The spiritual doctrines developed by the human have been labeled "religion." Religion is regarded as a specific fundamental set of beliefs and practices generally agreed upon by a number of persons or sects. Therefore, religion is unique to human existence. It is not "natural" to the degree that it applies to GODs' other creatures. The symbol that represents the "Christian" religion is the cross, or crucifix. This symbol is the result of human creation.

It was not a symbol brought to us by our savior, Jesus Christ, nor did he bring us the Christian religion. Hence, there is no true divine connection between this symbol and "GOD," other than the fact that it was the device upon which our savior, Jesus Christ was put to death. Even viewed in today's practical terms, the cross is not a geometric symbol, so it has no physical relationship to the Universe.

GODs' second commandment to humanity specifically instructed us to "not make unto ("GOD") any graven image, or any likeness of anything…" "…thou shalt not bow down thyself to them, nor serve them…" we have such a representation in the cross, or crucifix. A perfect example of how symbols are the junction between the divine domain and the worldly domain would be the significance of the cross. It is a physical manifestation that the human consciously associates with divinity and/or spirituality. Yet here we have a perfect example of how we have allowed a symbol to become greater than the doctrine it represents. There are those of us who blindly follow the crucifix wherever it leads, regardless of who is "carrying" it. We do this rather than following the depth of the doctrine and the positive action this symbol is supposed to represent. It is this harmonious, positive action that corresponds to Bible doctrine and satisfies our responsibility to the Divine System of Nature. Few consciously recognize that the crucifix was truly an ancient instrument of death. It was used for execution. Condemned persons were fastened to this structure in a very harsh manner until they died. The Holy Scriptures tell us that the son of man, the divine manifestation known as Jesus Christ, was put to his death, i.e. killed, i.e. murdered upon such a structure. It is recognized that Jesus Christ was Hebrew. The crucifix is not, and nor is Christianity. The word symbol "Christian," like the crucifix, represents doctrines that were conceived of by humans after the death of Jesus Christ.

The cross is the direct result of the humans' need to have a symbol that represented the doctrine that was created by it. As this is true, obviously the human has misunderstood GODs' intent within the context of the second commandment. For to have a symbol that we look to for our salvation, means that we are not looking to "GOD" for it. With so many different religious doctrines, it is obvious that the human is truly lost when it comes to knowing the whole story of what we identify as divine or spiritual. However, throughout time and the related interpretations of it, there have been certain steadfast themes that seem to transcend the humans' lack of understanding. These are things like positive action, righteousness, harmony, love, trust, forgiveness, tolerance, acceptance, balance, and

the Holy Land. Richard and Philip were more concerned with their own deadly rivalry going on in England, than with the Holy Land. Because of these things, Jerusalem continued to stand.

The fourth, from 1202 to 1204, never reached the Holy Land. The fifth, from 1217 to 1221, was directed at Moslem strength in Egypt. The sixth, from 1228 to 1229, was characterized by the notable gains of Emperor Frederick II through negotiation rather than fighting. Through treaty, a ten-year truce was established, while Jerusalem, Nazareth, and Bethlehem were restored to the Christians. Louis IX of France led the seventh, from 1248 to 1254. Louis IX of France led the eighth and last notable Crusade, in 1270. It was cut short by his death. For a clearer understanding of this period of human history, you can find books on this subject in your local library. The point is that there is a period in human history that corresponds to the spreading of the cross.

Not one of us knows all there is to know about human history or existence in general. Whether the tale on the Hopi stone is true or not, the definition of symbols infers that the symbol of spirituality would represent that which it symbolizes. Our Earth is round like a circle. The energy that gives us life, i.e. the electromagnetic aspect of our reality, is derived from the system of our Earth. This system is based upon the principals of parallel circuitry. A circuit is the act or an instance of going or moving around, as in a circle. We would perish without the energy generated by the circular rotation of our Earth. The system of our spirituality is based on the circle. Circles are the centerpiece of our entire reality. If the Native American knew the story of the circle, it would follow that their approach to spirituality would be significant, since it would be representative of their understanding. The Native American lived in harmony with Nature. They kill for food, becoming a part of the natural ecosystem of the region they inhabited. They worshipped the Great Spirit, and lived in reverence of all that "he" created. The doctrine of spirituality that would be represented by the circle encompasses the harmonious interaction of reality in its entirety. It includes everything that exists upon the planet. The planet is the circle. What we label "spirituality" is the doctrine that defines the application of the Divine Energy of Life within the context of physical reality. Spirituality truly explains how all living things are connected to the system of our Earth. All living things are directly connected to Nature, and Nature manifests the naturally occurring earthly activities. Because none of us truly knows all of the answers, we must open our minds to the reality that it is possible and not so far a reach to infer a connection between our behavior, our actions, and this circular object gravity binds us to.

Those of us who are not atheists accept the fact, on faith, that all living things are GODs' creatures. We accept the fact, on faith, that "GOD" created the heavens and our Earth. We accept the fact, on faith, that "GOD" created the Universe, and that "he" is the source of the energy that keeps everything alive. However, beyond these things, we start to close our minds to the inferences and truths that lie deeper within the words we accept. We must accept the revelation that all living things upon this circular object we inhabit have a common connection that is profoundly interconnected with the environment within which we all exist.

We must accept the realities and inferences related to the understanding applied to the circle, i.e. its physical shape (geometric), and the concepts of the whole. Whether our perspective of spirituality is based on the belief in the Divine Energy of Life (as it relates to the physical reality of divinity), or "GOD" in the biblical sense, we must think in terms of the whole. We must think in terms of the whole individual, the whole family, the whole community, the whole nation, the whole species, and the whole planet. The circle represents the whole. We must start thinking about the system that makes all that interaction work in the correct, right(eous), or positive manner. We must utilize to our advantage the practical understanding of cycles, balance, and harmony.

The circle embodies the path traveled by divine energy in our reality. That path leads in one direction at a time, and that direction is either positive or negative. The aspect of our being that is connected to the Earth contains a receptor that tells each of us whether that action is positive or negative, once we are taught how to interpret it and understand it. This teaching is that of the difference between right and wrong. This is all part of the laws of Nature, the system of our Earth (this same sequence of events occurs throughout the animal kingdom.). We must consider and embrace everything that exists when we determine the course of our actions. We must seek to have a harmonious, positive interaction with everything around us. Instead of embracing "GOD" through the limited tenets of the cross, we must now expand our understanding to include an acceptance of the tenets of the circle. The circle is not to be the symbol of our "GOD," but the framework for understanding the doctrine of our spirituality. We must look beyond Jesus Christ to the father, the spirit, the divine energy, the source, and forge our own personal connection therewith. We must recognize that we are not unlike Jesus Christ, and must therefore make an effort to be as he was.

When the truths and tenets of spirituality within the context of "GOD" are compared with those within the context of Nature or the Divine Energy of Life, an objective analysis of both groups of words confirm that they are simply different sets of words that relay the same meaning. The foundation of that meaning is based upon positive and negative movement. The doctrine's purpose is to keep us learning the things that can be applied towards the building of a path to enlightenment and growth, in hopes of our becoming better than we were in that moment just gone, i.e. the past. Just as we are one species of animal made up of different groups, we can have different religions recognizing the same "GOD." However, each of us must embrace the fact that it is the "GOD." As well, each of us must accept the inherent kinship between all living things created from the truth. As the symbols for a man and woman suggest, we must connect the philosophies of the circle to those of the cross.

Once I was out enjoying myself during some of my leisure time, and I encountered a homeless man I had helped before with handouts a few times. I decided to test a few of my perceptions on him to see what he thought. After all, this was truly the "common man." As we got into the philosophies of GODs' true spirituality, he looked at me and said, "Yeah, it's just like a circle." This was an example of the fact that we all have the truth within us, and each of us can recognize it when we are shown the way to it. We just do not have the "stress-free" time to explore ourselves for this knowledge and apply its ramifications to our lives.

Negative Flowing Energy and
Action Within Context

Positive flowing energy is manifested within the human in many ways. We refer to it by such labels as pep, vim, vigor, vitality, happy, glad, invigorated, energetic, and the like. I do not think I need to explain what positive flowing energy is. It produces a good feeling within us. Positive flowing energy comes from humor, kindness, caring, thoughtfulness, and good deeds among other sources. Positive flowing energy is love. We must embrace positive flowing energy in every form it takes. We must use the positive flowing energy around us, not abuse it. We must use positive flowing energy around us to produce good works, instead of manipulating our divine energy into traveling in the opposite direction and producing bad works. We must use the positive flowing energy around us to generate positive flowing energy so that we ourselves, as well as every living thing around us moves forward and grows into the future.

Just as we recognize the existence of positive flowing energy and its effect upon our species, we must acknowledge and to some degree seek an understanding of negative flowing energy on this same level. We have a better understanding of positive flowing energy and the effect it has upon our lives, than we do of negative flowing energy and its effects. Most people tend not to objectively analyze negative states of mind or negative actions relative to energy, because we associate energy with its positive manifestations. While we readily associate labels like happy and pep with positive energy, rarely are the labels like "sad," "down," "angry," "depressed," and the like, associated with negative flowing energy.

Whether or not it is necessary to understand negative flowing energy to the same degree that one understands positive flowing energy is debatable. The rationale behind this is based upon many things. Human energy is limited by its physical properties and by time itself. Therefore, in the interest of one's own growth and prosperity, why should a person waste energy on negative pursuits of any kind, mental or physical? There is also the issue of having faith. Faith is what allows the individual to continue to "do," while still recognizing the unknown. Since there will always be an "unknown," one should not waste their limited time, energy, or thought, on trying to understand every little detail of existence. One of these "little details" is negative flowing energy. It can easily place it within the parameters of the "unknown." Not knowing does not absolve living things of the responsibility to continue to have positive movement. A strong faith in the Divine Energy of Life allows one to know what direction their actions are taking, whether a complete understanding of why exists or not. For everyone, there will <u>always</u> be an "unknown." In dealing with this fact, faith will allow each of us to move ahead with living without the worry or concern for things we do not understand or cannot control.

Every individual will have negative thoughts at some point during his or her life. However, every individual is responsible for seeing to it those thoughts do not lead to actions that adversely affect reality. This is because each person is a conscious, self-controlling human being. In recognizing our supreme dominion over this planet, we must also recognize our responsibility to the Divine System of Nature. We must embrace the reality that our earthly obligation is to generate positive energy. For humans, our thoughts control our actions. Our species has a label for the single source of negative flowing action. It is "Satan." We must maintain a vigil over our state of mind to the degree that the positive aspects of our reality, not the negative aspects, not some "Satan," are what influence our thoughts. We perceive this "Satan" as influencing thought, and therefore, action. However, each individual is charged with ultimate control over his or her body through the conscious mind, awareness, and will. We all must employ the realities of strength and discipline to controlling the actions of our body to avoid committing negative acts. The series of thoughts that maintain this directive will ultimately produce a positive state of mind.

Negative energy flows in a direction opposite to that of positive energy. It is contrary to the natural flow of energy within our earthly existence. One should not seek to utilize it. However, the manifestation of it within each individual cannot be avoided. This occurs within the context of the analogous relationship between the human and the foundation of creation, i.e. the Atom. The energy that every human uses to generate their actions comes from the same source. Whether those actions are positive or negative is determined by the choice each individual makes. There is a distinct difference between those generated actions that can be labeled "good works" and "bad works." By examining fire, perhaps a clearer understanding of the nature of good and bad works can be had. Human progress through the ages has been based upon our ability to manipulate or have authority over the energy source that resulted from the discovery of fire. Fire is the foundation upon which the civilized world was built. For example, fire in an evolved sense, is electric energy. Fire is indicative of how the action of energy can be positive or negative. Fire can be used constructively, which is positive. On the other hand, it can destroy, which is negative. The energy or fire within us has the same capacity for good or evil use. Fire produces both positive and negative action, and we must balance that out because we must always have fire. The same goes for the fire within us.

If we do not control and/or contain fire, then it can and will destroy us. Therefore, we <u>must</u> control and/or contain it, as well as the power produced from it. That is what we must do within ourselves. In other words, each of us must control and contain the energy that is within us. This is true of the positive flowing energy, as well as the negative flowing energy. We cannot get rid of the negative aspect of ourselves, because it is a part of us. Within this context, we cannot expect to be able to completely eliminate all of what we consider negative, because some of those things are a part of us. Just as fire sometimes needs to act indiscriminately to "live," we also have that capacity to indulge our fire. When this occurs in nature, it is followed by a rebirth. This rebirth occurs within us, in the form of a chosen course of action aimed at repentance and penance. Sometimes fire must get out and do something we place in the category of "wrong," but we must always regain control of the fire and do well with it. The same applies to us. That same fire burns within us. Sometimes we will transgress. We must limit these transgressions to our own personal indulgences, so that we limit the harm our energy can produce. To be successful at this, we must develop an understanding of this part of our nature.

Humans are animals first, making each of us a distinct part of a divine system. Human action or behavior is made possible by the energy produced by the spinning of the planet, and its action is a part of the divine system generated by this spinning action. Again, human action or human behavior is a part of the Divine System of Nature. When we try to understand our reality using just our intellect, we define correct in terms of "right" and "wrong." Within this context, the determination of right and wrong is fallible, because it is subject to the misuse of words. When we seek to understand our reality from a more physical or "spiritual" perspective, i.e. within the context of the Divine System of Nature, correct is better defined in terms of "positive" and "negative." This is because the Divine System of Nature is the result of the spinning of the Earth, the resulting magnetic field of force, and the polarized energy it produces. The determination of positive or negative is infallible, because it is a physical part of reality. To determine the right direction of human action, we must look to our "Nature" to provide us with the truth. Placed within the proper context of understanding, Nature is another word for truth.

There will always be trials and tribulations in our lives. Trials are the things we determine are negative about ourselves that must be overcome. Trials are the things we determine to be our personal weaknesses. These things we must seek to understand and curtail, by working to become better than we currently are through growth. This task is a part of every human's personal growth process. Because there is a negative charge related to every living being, there will always be negative action.

These actions are tribulations. Tribulations are the difficulties we encounter as we interact with the world around us. These things we must also overcome. They are obstacles that test our strength, discipline, and resolve. Every living creature faces only trials and tribulations that are, within the context of its species, equal to its ability to overcome. Death is not a tribulation. It is an element of the Divine System of Nature.

Each of us thinks of our hardships or our trials and tribulations as being tougher than those of other living things are. This is a subjective way of interpreting life. There is always someone, outside of our personal knowledge, who has a worse condition of living than we Americans do. Objectively speaking, how do you think it would feel to exist in a world where you could literally be stomped on by a giant? Imagine being crushed as an ant would be, under a gazillion ton shoe. We as humans step on ants without an afterthought. Imagine how it would feel to be a bee in a hive doing what is spiritually or naturally right, and suddenly have the most horrifically poisonous liquid toxin sprayed on your body and your shelter with the force of a fire hose. We humans do this to bees all the time. These things qualify as tribulations. Yet, these troubles do not destroy that creature's motivation to pursue their natural actions as a species group. We too, as members of the animal kingdom, cannot allow the troubles of our lives to keep us from performing the actions of our nature. We must recognize this because our consciousness directs our actions while being influenced by our spiritual Nature by way of instinct, intuition, and divine knowledge.

Existence is the result of one, all-inclusive system. Every living thing that exists is a part of that system. This means that all living things are interconnected to each other and linked to this one system. The system functions on the action or movement of the parts. Because it is a system built upon interdependent motion, there is no isolated movement. Every movement that occurs has an effect on the rest of the system. Every motion of an Atom has an effect upon the matter composed of it. Every motion of a cell has an effect on the organ composed of it. Every motion of an organ has an effect on the body within which it exists. Likewise, every motion that occurs within our Earth's atmosphere has an effect upon the Earth itself.

Our actions have an effect on other humans as well as everything around us. This includes the weather and our Earth. This is because we along with our actions are a part of the system of life, or Nature, or existence, or reality, or the divine plan. One can choose whatever label is suitable. The truth remains the same. Before denying the revelation that our actions or movements about the Earth have a physical relationship to the rotations of the Earth, consider things from this perspective. One could successfully argue the analogous physical similarities between a mouse running on a wheel, and the motion of our existence on the planet. In this example, there is one seemingly stationary object that moves (the mouse), and one moving circular object (the wheel). It is relatively the same as with a human walking about the Earth, one circular, seemingly stationary object that moves (the earth), and one moving object (the human). The divine truth is that in both cases, both objects must move for either to move (remember, if the Earth stopped spinning, all life would be destroyed). The mouse's movement atop the wheel produces source energy if it moves in the right or positive direction, and maintains the necessary balance. It is the natural movement of animals that produces the energy that sustains them. In both cases, energy is produced because of the movement or action by an object, in conjunction with a circular spinning object in balanced harmony with each other. Also in both cases, the action of the object atop the circular spinning object affects it greatly.

Nature can be described as the system of existence flowing in a positive direction. This is verified by the fact that the energy that sustains Nature's system comes from the Earth spinning in only one direction. This must be considered positive because it produces life. Hence, to be negative is against what is deemed natural. It takes more energy to go against a natural flow than it does to go with that flow. Imagine if the wheel that the mouse was on top of had another source of energy that sent it spinning in the same direction.

Within this context, the energy that was produced by the mouse's motion would only serve to augment the original source of energy, thereby perpetuating the motion of the wheel. In this instance, try to conceive the amount of energy that the mouse would have to expend if it decided to move in the direction opposite the one that was naturally occurring. The term for the direction of action opposite the "right" one would be "wrong." For the human, actions that fall into the category of wrongs may not be sins as defined by the Ten Commandments. Rather, they are transgressions, because once they become part of reality, the ramifications of those acts harm others besides ourselves. Transgression and sin disrupt the harmony of our movement and interaction, which literally hampers the rotation of our Earth. The buildup of this counter-productive energy will lead to our destruction by the forces of Nature. The things that can be used to carry out this destruction are the elements of Nature. They are water, fire, Earth, wind, other humans, or other living things and/or organisms. Each of these is but one of the forces of Nature.

If a stone is tossed into a freestanding quantity of water, it produces an effect in the water that starts at the point of contact and radiates outward from that point in a circular pattern. This is the case with all moving objects within our collective reality. Every physical occurrence produces what can be termed a "ripple effect." These occurrences have also been known as "spin-offs." Even with the Atom, there are little particles that come off it. What we can learn from this is that for every action that takes place, there will be a reaction. Within this reaction, there will be ramifications that reach beyond the physical entities that produce the action. Those entities may not be aware of these ramifications. That is another reason why we must act with goodness in our hearts, so that the ramifications, "spin-offs," or reactions to our actions do not harm others. When actions are produced that go in the negative direction, then the spin-offs from those deeds also go in that direction and they are detrimental to others. In this way, we are compounding an already negative circumstance.

Sin

Negative movement or action is contrary to the Divine System of Nature. Yet, each human must embrace the fact that each member of our species will transgress, because the human cannot eliminate the negative aspect of its being. This negative aspect is exemplified in our comparative relationship with the Atom. Within this context, just as the electrons are negatively charged, humans in the analogous position of electrons are negatively charged as well. However, the action of the electrons is positive, and our action must be correspondent to this reality as well. Therefore, we must reconcile ourselves to the never-ending presence of transgression and sin, seeking to minimize their occurrence. When either of them does occur, we must place that occurrence within its proper context and learn from it. Rather than simply accepting the direction in which negative action takes us, we must seek to understand the root of that negative occurrence. From this knowledge, we must learn how to avoid this deflection from the right(eous) path in the future. We must learn from our mistakes, and consciously fight against making them again. We must recognize that this is a part of our growth process and progress from there.

In First John 3:4 it says, "...sin is the transgression of the law." The basic use of the label "Sin" is as a noun, identifying the result of the negative action of the human species that is the most detrimental to the natural order of things, i.e. the Divine System of Nature. Transgression is the label for the actual negative action, which is the result of the weakness inherent in the human species. When not held in check, this weakness leads to the manifestation of sin. Sin is the failure to comply with what is righteous within the context of "GOD." It is a violation of code or law committed against either "GOD," or against another being. Transgression is the failure to comply with what is right within the context of human existence. It is a negative act within the realm of our worldly existence. There is a reason for making this distinction. The human must seek to <u>eliminate sinful acts</u> from its behavior. We must recognize "GOD" (the Divine Energy of Life) respectfully and humbly. We must have faith in "his" whole truth and "his" divine plan. We must obey the divine law. However, there will always be transgression. We must act righteously during our personal interactions, so as not to commit a wrong against another.

Energized by the Divine Energy of Life, the action of the balanced rotation of our Earth added to the balanced combination of other planetary elements causes the reaction that produces the balanced conditions that generate and sustain life. The air is a mixture of gases that forms the atmosphere, consisting chiefly of the gases oxygen and nitrogen. If the balanced combination of these gaseous elements is upset in some way, there is an end to life through suffocation. The water is a transparent, odorless, tasteless liquid that constitutes rain, oceans, lakes, springs, etc. It is a compound of hydrogen and oxygen. If the balanced combination of these elements is upset, there is an end to life through thirst. If the balanced condition of the combination of elements within the Earth's soil is upset, there is an end to life through starvation.

If a chemical analysis was done on any living or natural object of this planet, it would be founded to be composed of the elements of our Earth. This includes the life on the surface of the planet, and life submerged under the waters of the planet. It is the action and reaction of the various chemical elements of the planet subjected to given balanced conditions that are responsible for it all. One could safely conclude from these realities that as a rule, all of existence that occurs on this planet is a circumstance of time, based upon action and balance. Therefore, because what naturally happens on our Earth can be referred to as the "system" of Nature, all parts of that system are subject to this rule.

Whatever happens must occur within the context of what we have labeled "time," because of action and balance. To upset a balanced condition would be to introduce excess as an element of that condition. <u>Excess</u> is the element of reality that is most detrimental to the system of existence, i.e. the Divine System of Nature. In recognizing that balance is the key element of the system of existence for living things, it is also clear that the element of excess is detrimental to this system. The holy books of our species indicate that we must balance our lives with the lives of others. Excess is the essence of selfishness and greed. Excess is the primary building block for what is wrong or negative. An example of this in a physical sense is apparent in the principles of electricity. "Negative" electricity is the electricity present in a body or substance that has an <u>excess</u> of electrons.

Our lives as human beings are unlike any in the known Universe. With the five senses "GOD" has given each of us, we have the opportunity to perceive the moments of our lives in the stimulating context of "self." Over the course of time, the wonder of this state of awareness has caused our consciousness to exist on a plane of self-satisfaction. Because of this, it seems as though humanity is more inclined to embrace the philosophy of the "pleasure principle" as a way of life. This is the concentration of the ego (or mind) on securing a maximum of pleasure with a minimum of pain and effort. In essence, what this means is that by thinking about securing pleasure without pain, our efforts or works are <u>directed</u> toward that end or result. This is a very subjective, selfish, greedy way to exist. We must direct our efforts toward more realistic, balanced goals. A more objective, truthful approach to life would be to embrace the "reality principle." This is the adjustment of the ego (or mind) to meet the requirements of the external world, while still recognizing that there is pleasure to be had. Thinking this way would have our efforts or works directed at satisfying the requirements of our lives first, and then pursuing the pleasure life has to offer. The pursuit of self-gratifying pleasure first is shortsighted. It has led us to act with selfishness and greed to compete for the pleasures of our existence.

Most of the difficulties that exist within our species are the result of three things. Those three things are the lack of knowledge, and the manifestation of both selfishness and greed. Because the human species collectively thinks of itself as being the center of the Universe, it will not embrace the one divine truth that should be at the foundation of all that individuals seek to understand. This revelation is the fact that not a single human being knows all there is to know about existence. Without this foundation, many of the things we do know are misinterpreted. To be more specific, our lack of knowledge of the "whole" truth has not only caused the misinterpretation of a lot of general information, but also of the context within which we are to satisfy our needs, wants, and desires. We have allowed our personal pursuit of satisfaction to manifest itself into selfishness and greed.

Selfishness and greed are the two most destructive elements of human reality, and they are the basis of most all that is negative within the human mind, or wrong with human action. Selfishness is the excessive indulgence of oneself in "subjectivity." Subjectivity is a conscious choice to disregard the natural balance of the mental senses. It causes us to interpret reality such that we as individuals are at the center of it. To this degree, it is as though we are individual GODs', and the Universe is subject to our personal whims and desires. Greed is the excessive indulgence of oneself in "materialism." Greed is a conscious choice to disregard the natural balance of the physical senses. It causes us to behave such that our actions are focused upon satisfying our personal wants/desires at the expense of everything around us. Materialism, or more aptly put, egoism, is selfishness and greed manifested into reality. Selfishness and greed are contrary to the characteristic Nature inherent to members of a socialized species. The characteristic Nature inherent to members of a socialized species is to commit personal effort toward the goal of collective benefit or mutual, balanced satisfaction.

Relative to the Holy Scriptures, there are categories of action that lead to the violation of the Ten Commandments. Recognizing and understanding the nature of each category of action is vital to staying on the path of righteousness. The seven cardinal sins, or deadly sins as they are more commonly known, are the categories of the actions that serve as the catalyst for violating the Ten Commandments. The basis of all of these occurrences is imbalance, or more directly put, **excess**.

The first of these cardinal offenses is pride, an undue sense of one's own superiority; it is a sin of excess. The manifestation of pride will lead one to place himself or herself above "GOD." The second is covetousness, to be excessively desirous and greedy; it is a sin of excess. This will lead to stealing. The third is lust, an excessive sexual appetite, especially seeking immediate or ruthless satisfaction; it is a sin of excess. This will lead to adultery. The fourth is gluttony, the act or habit of indulging in anything excessively; it is a sin of excess. This will lead one to break any or all of the Commandments. The fifth is envy, a feeling of resentment or discontent over another person's superior attainments, endowments, or possessions; it is a sin of excess. This will lead to bearing false witness against a neighbor, among other things. The sixth is anger, a strong feeling of displeasure and belligerence aroused by a real or supposed wrong; it is a sin of excess. This will lead one to break any or all of the Commandments. The seventh is sloth, this simply means laziness; it is a sin of excess. This will lead one to steal from and covet the neighbor's possessions.

Every human will commit sin during its lifetime. By our daily actions, we invariably break one or more of the Ten Commandments. Whether it is leaving work early without permission (stealing), or consciously stepping on an ant (murder), humans exist in a constant state of sin. During the course of our lives, each of us will be confronted with the temptation to react to some of the circumstances we are confronted with subjectively. Temptation is the result of the humans' weakness in the face of the perceived joy of sensation and satisfaction. There are three categories of temptation that lead the human astray. They are the lust of the flesh, the lust of the eyes, and the pride of life. "Lust" is the label for a passionate or overmastering (excessive) desire. The lust of the flesh is the overpowering (excessive) desire to stimulate the senses of the body through touch, chiefly by sexual means. The lust of the eyes is the overwhelming (excessive) desire to stimulate the senses of the body by the acquisition of that which titillates the sense of sight. The pride of life leads the human to believe itself to be greater (excessive) than another, placing itself first above other humans, then above "GOD," by the manifestation of thoughts that are self-glorifying. These thoughts are the interpretations of the perceptions of the senses. Our will is undermined by the weaknesses of our flesh. Without mental strength and discipline, along with a commitment to doing what is right (which is the essence of honor), we are easily dominated by sensation. Temptation should be looked upon as a test of the strength of human will and resolve. The temptations of life are a test of our character. We must strive to resolve all of our trials and tribulations with positive actions. However, because of the length of our lives together with our negatively charged bodies and the humans' subjective Nature, we will sometimes fail. Those failures we must recognize as weakness, and we must use these instances as lessons. We must learn that we are to grow from those experiences so that we do not repeat them. The first time something happens, it is an experience and a lesson. The second time the same thing happens, it is an error in judgment.

In the pursuit of perfection and righteousness, individuals must limit the occurrence of transgression, and make little allowance for excesses. There will be times when each of us will think about indulging ourselves in a selfish manner, and perhaps think about sinful acts. Yet, if people will truly embrace the goodness of "GOD" that lies within them, this will help in those moments. In a physical sense, this "help" will be manifested through positive flowing energy and positive thought. Following the path of positive flowing energy can be deemed as following a "spiritual flow." Each of us must work to remain within our positive, spiritual flow. This means to listen to our heart, heed our impressions and intuition, and make judgments based on what is right.

There may be times when individuals knowingly commit a transgression that person is able to reconcile within themselves and their spirituality. That person may be able to justify a personal indulgence as a selfish desire. That person may be able to reconcile it within his or her spirituality because that action will not harm another or directly disrespect "GOD." In these moments, an individual may consciously choose to indulge himself or herself in an endeavor that may contain elements of risk for them. Any indulgence of this sort must be considered an excessive behavior, and is therefore a transgression. One must still truthfully repent for that transgression in earnest. To understand these things, each of us must open our mind up to a broader awareness and commit our abilities to applying the knowledge of truth each of us possesses. Each of us must think in larger dimensions than the one in which we currently function. To aspire to perfection means that each of us must think about everything we do. Each of us must seek to make the right choices "continuously". Each of us must act in truth. To make the right choice is to act in truth. To act in truth is to produce responsible action (i.e. required action, divine action).

"GOD" (the Divine Energy of Life) made the direction of negative action very simple for the human to recognize by giving it knowledge of "boundaries." The awareness of these boundaries is apparent in two forms. One is physical. Each of us can actually "feel" when something is right or wrong for us. We can "sense" whether it is good or bad for us, positive or negative. This is the manifestation of the part of our being that is trying to guide us in the right direction, using energy that produces these sensations. It is an aspect of our spirituality. The other form is words, words that form the doctrines of morality and ethics. More profound words are found within the holy books of our species. For the human to act in righteousness, it had but to obey the Ten Commandments, and have the goodness of "GOD" within its heart.

Absolution

The releasing of the contemplation of committed sins and transgressions allows each of us to keep moving forward in a positive direction without the retarding burden of worry and concern that result from having gone in the wrong direction. Each of us must constantly strive towards that goal of perfection (being the best one can be), no matter what mistakes we make or how we falter. The message of repentance is that if we hold GODs' truths in the highest regard and we live our lives aspiring to achieve goodness, perfection, and balance, we are forgiven for the mistakes and transgressions we manifest during the journey of our lives. We are susceptible to the temptations before us that stimulate our five senses. A human cannot go through its entire lifespan without succumbing to one temptation or another. We must learn from the error of our ways, make penance, and continue our pursuit of perfection in the proverbial eyes of "GOD."

Each of us must understand the implication of our transgression on the lives around us and realize that we were being selfish (not humble) to knowingly indulge in transgression and sin. As a society, to reconcile ourselves to these realities, a limited allowance must be made for our indulgence. For this, each of us must embrace the reality of spirituality and faith. The human will not ever exist without sin. To expect everyone to live without committing a transgression is unrealistic. The human must seek to calibrate its transgression to the goodness of "GOD" within the heart and soul, and the human will then manifest the existence that is expected of it. Individuals must calibrate their existence, seeking a balance that will equal a positive life for themselves. This will lead to prosperity, as defined by an individual's perspective and desires. Any persons that focus on and recognize "GOD" can achieve their greatest wants/desires, the urgings of their hearts. GODs' system will bless each of us if we live in truth. In more physically real terms, positive flowing energy producing positive action will bring about positive (prosperous) results. Each of us is "GOD," to the limits of our existence and our abilities. We can call this being the "human manifestation of GOD." As we seek perfection, that is as close as we, as individuals, can get to the Divine Energy of Life.

Repentance is a key element of the pursuit of human perfection. As the human will never be without transgression, it should therefore be in a constant state of repentance. This revelation must be consciously applied during the human process of making choices and judgments. It is a factor of human humility. To repent is to feel remorse or regret for something one has done or failed to do. Repentance is the act turning with sorrow from a past course of action. The human has accepted the revelation of repentance. But its interpretation, like other aspects of existence, occurs within the context of both spiritual and worldly realities. Contrition is a feeling of repentance for sin, with an intention to make amends, arising from a love of "GOD" and the consideration of "his" goodness. This is an objective recognition of the truth. Attrition is a similar feeling of repentance, resulting from inferior motives, as fear of punishment, divine or otherwise. This is a subjective recognition of the truth. As individuals, we must always seek the objective interpretation first.

Penance is a feeling of sorrow for sin or fault, which is indicated clearly by some outward act. The "outward act" of penance is an action that restores the directed of energy that is disrupted by the occurrence of negative action. Think of it in terms of a spinning ball, or more relatively speaking, the spinning Earth. The orb can only spin in one direction at a time. Within the context of our Earth, we know that this direction is positive because it produces life and growth. Because of our understanding of Nature and science, we know the energy that causes this spinning action is also positive. As the orb continues to spin, it establishes a degree of momentum. Electrically speaking, if positive energy flows in one direction, negative energy flows in the opposite direction.

As we breathe in the "field of force," the energy generated by our actions becomes absorbed into the Divine System of Nature. If our actions are positive, as they should be, this aids the Divine System of Nature, and in essence the spinning of our Earth. Our existence is truly an electrical system or circuit. Our positive actions produce and perpetuate the flow of energy in the right direction that the energy is to flow within this earthly circuit. In this way, we are perpetuating and aiding the system (the Earth's spinning) in its existence.

If our actions are negative, the flow of this energy is contrary or opposite of that which is required to sustain the current direction of the spin. The production of this negative flowing energy does not abruptly change the direction of the spin, because the orb has built up a high degree of momentum. However, it does start to hamper or slow the spinning as the negative energy accumulates. This is exemplified by what can be termed as the "malfunctions of Nature," i.e. some of the natural destruction that occurs outside of the pattern of Nature. The positive energy created by all of humanity having the goodness of "GOD" in our hearts will decrease the strain placed on our rotating Earth (or the system of Nature), serving as "oil on the tracks." When we indulge in excesses that result in our not maintaining our relative position in the divine flow (continual movement of positive flowing energy), those excesses or those excessive behaviors are what disrupt our spirituality. The divine flow, in essence, refers to the very rotation of the Earth and the systems it generates. As we adversely affect the living Earth, there are always negative repercussions from our excessive actions that adversely affect us. These "repercussions" are usually manifested by way of the elements of our planet, i.e. Earth, wind, water, fire, other living things. These elements serve as the living Earth's "antibodies," used in much the same manner as the antibodies of the human body.

Within this context, we must open our minds to an important truth. We are a part of the system or pattern of Nature, which is in essence life. The profound characteristic of life is action. Therefore, what we do, i.e. our actions, are our functional part of the system. As all of Nature is interconnected, our actions or behaviors have a direct affect, albeit subtle and cumulative, on the natural world around us. This includes the wildlife, environment, atmosphere, geology, and the climate. Just as a baby in its mother's womb has a subtle effect on the wellbeing of its mother, we have an effect on the wellbeing of our Earth. Our very creation is the result of the interactive movements of the elements of our Earth. The Earth "birthed" our species. The energy produced by our actions, which result from what our thoughts have us do, affects the environment around us. To understand how the exchange of energy takes place, examine the connection between humans and plants. We depend upon plants and trees to provide us with the oxygen that we need to survive. This transference of gases takes place unseen by the eye. This holds true for the Earth's life-giving energy. It is an unseen transference of energy. It is true that many of the natural catastrophes we face are the result of a long buildup of "ill effects."

We can all feel the coming of the "end," and we can see that it is the human's pattern of movement that is about to bring about that "end." It is not a coincidence that from a spiritual and secular perspective, the humans' actions are bringing about what could be labeled the "end times," and at the point in time depicted in revelations. our actions have an effect on weather patterns and geologic activity because within the context of our reality, our actions include atmospheric and ocean pollution, destruction of rain forests, mining and other excavation, etc., all upsetting the balance of Nature. However, there is more to this story. Do not discount the physical reality that the production of negative flowing energy through negative thought and action, like our erratic, violent behavior, has translated into erratic, violent weather patterns and geologic activity. All of existence is connected. This includes the human and the Earth. Related to identifying the period known as the "end times," the lore indicates that worldwide weather patterns will change to a degree where the weather conditions will not correspond to the seasons in which they occur. As well, it is the actions of the human to which these changes are attributed. If we look around the world, it is obvious to both nonprofessional and scientist that the weather patterns of a given region do not rightly match what would be considered the normal weather pattern of that region.

Take note of the word "patterns." Over time, when activity is repeated again and again, gradually, this pattern becomes accepted as normal. Because of this acceptance, we do not recognize the true relevance of the occurrence of such activity. This is because we stop evaluating the relevance and significance of the pertinent circumstances. We see these patterns and associate them with what is normal. However, we are not recognizing the reality that these erratic patterns are not truly normal, just frequent. There is a union between our Earth and the living things upon it, and it is supposed to be a good, positive, right(eous) one.

Because of the realities before us all, our species must change its attitude toward itself and the planet. As we recognize the reality that we are the superior animal species on the planet, we must recognize the revelation that what makes us superior is our conscious awareness. This awareness also makes us responsible for our actions and the effects that they have on what exists around us. The human individual will not live infinitely. Each of our lives is limited in the physical sense. If the human individual continues to live without fully considering the ramifications of its actions, the human species truly becomes vulnerable to annihilation and extinction. This could result from natural disaster, human ignorance, or some combination of the two. As members of one divine species, we must seek to produce a harmonious coexistence throughout Nature. Each nation, each cultural group, must balance their needs with the needs of the global community and the planet. We must recognize that the Earth is indeed a living organism, and therefore requires a balanced system of actions to sustain it. We are a part of that system. Thus, we must face our responsibility to the system of life and meet our obligations to it. Every socialized species has a communal activity that benefits the collective. The nature of that activity differs from species to species, like bees collecting nectar, or ants building communities. Because we are an intellectual species, our communal activity is mental (philosophical), as well as physical. We must embrace this reality. We will have to mature psychologically in order to handle things more realistically. A factor in maturing or "growing up" is that each of us accepts our responsibilities. We may see ourselves as adults when measured by physical standards. However, when we look at current social standards, we all must grow even more if we are to meet the needs of this new millennium. This is a part of progress and of evolution. Everyone knows that to excel at any discipline to a level of greatness, a commitment must be made to that discipline. Therefore, to be great at living, we must make a commitment to our lives.

How do we yield to the authority of human spirituality? Each of us must come to understand that "human spirituality" is simply a label for our interpretation of how we fit into the system of existence. The system itself must be recognized objectively rather than subjectively relative to a particular religious or secular belief. Each of us must accept that we have a role to play in making the spiritual system work properly. That role is defined as our moving or acting in a positive, correct, right(eous) manner as we pursue individual, as well as collective growth and prosperity. It is important to understand that human spirituality is not that much different from the spirituality that applies to any other socialized species of animal upon our Earth. We work, we play, we commune, we protect, we fight, we procreate, we nurture, we live, and we die. What is different is that the human is conscious to the degree that it recognizes the system of actions that comprise the rhythmic existence that we have labeled "spirituality." What separates human spirituality from that of other animals is conscious awareness. As such, humans are responsible to this awareness because it allows us to "know." Conscious awareness allows up to infer or foresee the outcome of having movement in the wrong direction and it allows us to choose and/or create an alternative. This is from where our position of dominion, authority, or responsibility is derived. Our conscious awareness makes us responsible for the protective safety of our scope of influence. That realm encompasses our entire planet. Each of us must act accordingly.

Each of us must recognize the relevance of polarity to our movements. Each of us must embrace the revelation that we are to move in a correct, right (eous), or positive manner. This is the essence of the message contained within the holy books of our species, transcending the many varied interpretations of those words. Energy flowing in a positive direction is the physical foundation for the spiritual realities of our existence, as defined within the context of the physical sciences. The right understanding of this physical foundation of spiritual reality lies within our knowledge of electromagnetism and the resulting polarity. As "charged" and "di-pole" beings, our physical existence is constructed around the principles of electromagnetism. Because our magnetic relationship to our Earth designates our negative pole as being located at the base of our spine relative to our physical composition, we are naturally and spiritually responsible for maintaining a positive pole within our minds because of our ability to choose.

Many messengers have, in the past and are continuing to, relay to us all the words that indicate that positive thought and positive attitude are the keys to prosperity. Numerous people are always saying that we should be doing positive things, we should read, we should get an education, etc. The consensus is that this is the way to get ahead in life. It is, but there is more truth in this reality that is significant and relevant. This pursuit of betterment is what we are supposed to do to satisfy our spiritual responsibility as a living organism. From the proper perspective, one can interpret the entire future of humanity as depending upon the human attitude because it directly affects the direction of human action and the outcome of human behavior (our habits). Individual human action or behavior is the result of individual human thought. Words lead to actions both positive and negative. Positive action is correct, righteous action. The nature of life is directed motion. Life has motion because energy (divine energy) is the basis of all that is living. Life is directed because spiritual energy is based upon electromagnetism, and therefore moves relative to polarity, i.e. travels a specific direction. That direction is positive.

By making choices based upon what we know to be correct or right, we can all move in the same direction during our lives. On the surface, it may seem impractical to think that all of humanity can move in the same direction. However, this can be easily understood if it is interpreted from the proper perspective. The truth is, there are only three possible choices for the direction of human action, and only two that actually involve movement. Those two choices are positive or negative. One other choice is to remain neutral, which is to do nothing, or not have action. Believe it or not, all human beings are supposed to react to a given circumstance the same way. They are to do positive or right(eous) things. This can be referred to as "positive (perfect) resolution." The following are very simple examples of this: (1) first, the circumstance is that there is a cup on the floor that needs to be moved. A positive response would be to pick up the cup and place it in the sink. A neutral response would be to do nothing. A negative response would be to kick the cup across the floor. However, with regard to the positive response, one person might pick the cup up with their right hand, because they are right-handed. Another person might use their left hand, because they are left-handed. A person with no arms might use their feet instead. The response is the same, positive, but the approach is individual. (2) The circumstance is that a person is seen trying to flag down vehicles because his or her car is disabled by the side of the road. A positive response would be to give aid to that person. A neutral response would be to do nothing. A negative response would be to increase his or her hardship. With regard to the positive response, one person might stop and physically render assistance. Another might give the person a lift to the next service station. Still another might use a cellular phone to notify the police of a stranded citizen. These are all positive responses, but acted out in different ways. (3) The circumstance is a hate group comes to a town to recruit members. A positive response is to show opposition in a positive manner. The neutral response is to do nothing. A negative response would be to either join them or harm them. Again, regarding the positive response, one could protest their presence. Another could choose to debate them. Still another might start a counter-recruitment drive aimed at establishing an organization that brings us all together.

What is "right" for one person may not be "right" for another. However, there is no mistaking positive action and the result that follows, from negative action and the effect it produces. In the general scheme of things, it does not matter what a person may think, or what biases that person may have. It does not matter if the cup is white, black, red, yellow, or fuchsia. It does not matter whether or not persons like the color of the cup, or the cup itself. Moving the cup from the floor satisfies the requirements of that respective circumstance in a positive manner. The truth is, what is right or positive is not affected by, or subject to biases. If we all seek to perform the actions that are positive, a positive state of mind will be developed. This is because our thoughts produce our actions. Therefore, if one continually seeks to produce positive action, eventually, that person's state of mind will be such that his or her mind will view things in a positive manner, to facilitate the production of positive action.

Within the Holy Scriptures at proverbs 16:3, you will find this: "commit thy works unto the lord, and thy thoughts shall be established." According to the system of Nature, the human must move or act because of the thoughts it produces. Having thought is an action. The movement that results from thought is the human "reaction." Hence, because the human will have action that it is consciously aware of, it must be responsible for choosing the "right," or positive action, regardless of its subjectivity. Dr. Martin Luther king stated the need for America to change certain laws. He said that changing the laws might not change the "hearts" of men, but it will change the "habits" of men. If the habits of men were changed, soon after the men would have a change of heart. From this, we must gain the understanding that it is not our minds that we must immediately change. It is our actions that we must first change. What we must do is change the direction of our actions, our behavior, i.e. our habits.

In the process of constantly producing positive actions, our state of mind would become consistently positive. If right actions are what we seek to produce, to have those actions occur requires the right thought. So, the right frame of mind will be manifested through the pursuit of a responsible, positive course of action. The priority of living is to act or move, as exhibited by all living things including the humans. It is not to think, even though in the human as in many other animals, it is thought that produces most behavioral actions. For humans, faith and trust allow us to act righteously without first deciphering our subjective concerns. We must react to the objective truth of any given circumstance we face with positive action. It is very difficult to live in a moment, and analyze it at the same time. We must act and react positively, so that we "do the right thing." Then we must seek out the wisdom of the moment that we will derive from the process of understanding. If we act and react positively, this will end the decay of our social systems, and go a long way in the right direction toward making repairs to our state of being. While this "good" is going on, the stable living condition positive action provides will create the time necessary for a new "process of understanding." If we all start doing positive things, positive thoughts will follow.

It would be too difficult for all of America to suddenly subscribe to the same set of beliefs. However, each of us can clearly see the difference between positive and negative action, and we can understand the truth and benefit of positive action. Therefore, it would be an easier task on a mass scale to change the direction of our actions. The humans' actions are the result of its thoughts. Therefore, if our actions are positive, and our thoughts lead to those actions, our directive thoughts will be positive. If all of our actions are positive, and most all of our thoughts are positive, then eventually, our hearts or our "Nature" will all be positive also.

An individual may have thoughts that are prejudice or bias. However, that person cannot allow those thoughts to determine his or her course of action. Individual action must be based upon what is good, right(eous), and positive for that moment. What this will eventually lead to is a change in the way that an individual thinks. If a person's mind is open to growth, and that person acts and reacts in a positive manner, that person's negative way of thinking will dissipate.

When each of us interacts with those that we have "negative" opinions or thoughts about, and the interaction is full of positive actions, we will begin to see the truth. The truth is that we have many more similarities than differences. The similarities are deep, while the differences are superficial. Positive action will allow us all to come together as a species.

We must embrace spirituality to the degree that it is truly a part of our daily lives, because the spinning of our planet is truly a part of our daily lives. This means that spiritual understanding has more than moral implications upon our lives. The need to understand and embrace our spirituality has physical and biological roots as well. This is due to the truth that what we term "spirituality" is actually the label for the entire system of our Earth. Each individual must recognize that our spirituality is based upon magnetoelectric energy. Our bodies are magnoelectrically charged by energy from a source we have labeled as "divine." As we recognize the fact of our being alive, we must do so within the context of the conscious recognition of our spirituality. We must get in touch with our spirituality because this planet has created a Magnoelectric system of existence, and we are a critical part of it. Religion has narrowed our interpretation of the events and circumstances of human existence. It has overshadowed the all-inclusive recognition of our responsibility to the system of our Earth. This system is the Divine System of Nature. The human species has reached the point in its existence where its understanding of spirituality must exceed the limits of religious barriers.

Our spirituality is based upon positive and negative energy, and the motion thereof. Sometimes a person's attitude is positive, and sometimes it is negative, depending on what they have been going through. Look at that last sentence and see if you can recognize the implication of choice in it. It exists in the thought process that produces the conclusion that a state of mind occurs "sometimes." In that sentence, the word "depends" is indicative of that individual's perception of their lack of control and choice. It truly does "depend" upon the individual's perspective. By not exercising or "working" for control of the mind, an individual gives up the ability to choose positive over negative, and their attitude is determined by what their body is going through. Enlightenment is a process. It occurs on a step-by-step (systematic) basis. To achieve it, each of us must begin somewhere. That beginning is now.

The Soul

One cannot come to understand the true nature of human spirituality without having reconciled oneself to the relevance and significance of that which we have labeled the "soul." To a degree, it is unfortunate for the human species that we were blessed with both the free will to make choices and the strength of mind to create. This is because these very gifts manifest the selfishness and greed that lead the human to close itself off from the truth that dwells within each of us. having both been created in the image of "GOD" and having the Divine Energy of Life flowing through our bodies, each of us has the two components of the divine entity within us as well. These components are positive energy and innate knowledge. In separating ourselves from Nature, we humans have come up with different terms that refer to the same elements of our being. We use some terms if we are speaking within a spiritual context, and others within a worldly context. Within a worldly context, with regard to the positive energy, the label we use to identify that is the "spirit." With regard to the innate knowledge, it is thought of as the "heart." The awareness of the heart manifests the spiritual "ability" to direct oneself rightly through the course of one's life. Each of us has the ability to "feel" what right or wrong is on an individual basis, i.e. what is positive or negative. It is the ability an individual has to guide himself or herself with the feelings or impressions derived from instinct, intuition, and extrasensory perception. Along with this knowledge comes an inherent spiritual awareness of a higher power that is present in all of us. It is evidenced by our need to have created a system to worship this power called "religion." Within a spiritual context, a single term truthfully identifies the two GOD-like components within each human being. That term is the "soul." The soul is an individual's divine guidance system.

The soul has many components that affect us as we live. The label "soul" identifies the pathway through which the positive energy that keeps us alive passes. It is the pathway through which we are guided in a positive direction. All living things possess this pathway. The reason the human thinks it may be the only animal with a soul is because it has the ability to translate the knowledge received through this pathway into words. In essence, this knowledge becomes a "voice" from within, which is uniquely possessed by our species because words are unique to our species. The soul encompasses the link between ourselves and what it is that created us. Once this divine energy enters the human body, it makes us "alive." The natural condition of being "alive" manifests the human senses. Our senses are a part of the group of components contained within that which we label the soul. We must come to understand the true relevance and significance of all our senses. As well, each of us must recognize and embrace the importance of the other components of the soul. These are our feelings, emotions, and sensory perceptions, as well as our impressions and vibrations. Each of us must learn to interpret what we feel and otherwise sense more deeply, as well as the impact this has on the direction of our actions. Our emotions like happiness and sadness are truly indicators we are to utilize to steer ourselves through the course of our lives.

By coming to a true, deep understanding of oneself in terms of motivations, personal characteristics, wants and desires, and by trusting what is felt, each person will manifest the being "GOD" intended them to become. To truly gain benefit from the blessing of life, one must allow the goodness within his or her own self to come forth. As well, he or she must have faith and trust in what they derive from the Divine Energy of Life. Individuals must believe in their own instinctive impressions and intuitive inclinations. All of our feelings, emotions, intuitions, and psychic abilities, all of our mental and physical sensors are labels for references to our spiritual pathway and the knowledge or awareness transmitted by it. A person's divine cognition and having goodness of heart, along with good and positive judgments, are the best system of guidance one can rely upon when making decisions in the course of everyday life.

When a person analyzes a given circumstance, most think there is a need to use their mental capabilities to try to "figure out" and cover all of the "angles." This uses time and energy. Most interactive moments are instances of spontaneity. To respond correctly or right instantaneously, one should react honestly or true. This occurs when a person reacts naturally and positively. Reacting this way also allows a person to maximize all the inherent benefits and potential of those moments. That is a blessing inherent to our spirituality. As one strives toward perfection using faith, trust, goodness, and positive (or perfect) resolution, that person manifests the ability to maximize the advantages available to them.

The human is a very "complex" being. So to try to gain insight into how individuals should guide themselves through the journey that is their life, let us compare the human to a complex vehicle (body) that travels. To gain a better understanding of how the divine guidance system, i.e. the soul is to work, think of the body relative to an analogous comparison of it to a large transportation vessel. In this comparison, the larger vessel can be either a passenger plane or an ocean liner. In either case, the fully operational system of guidance within these vessels has a separate component (someone) that is responsible for steering the craft. This is a pilot or helmsman. also, for complex vessels, there is a separate component (someone) that is responsible for guiding the ship's path by interpreting the signs on the map that lead to the desired destination. This is the navigator. By embracing the truth within this analogous relationship, we might find it easier to understand our role in GODs' divine order. When individuals ask or pray to the "divine entity" for guidance, there is a reality here that must be recognized. It is that there are roles here that are clearly defined. Guidance is the responsibility of the navigator, which in this case is the soul. In turn, individuals must themselves consciously use their mind to "pilot" or direct their vessels, i.e. their bodies. Each of us is responsible for "steering" our own "craft," which is our physical self. In other words, we are responsible for directing the actions of our bodies. "GOD" will direct our respective courses by providing the signs of understanding that will lead each of us to the destination of our truly positive desire.

Within this context, one can see the importance of being able to interpret what I label as the "signs of divinity." To understand this, one need only recognize the reality of this circumstance. The "craft" that is being steered is the body of the individual, so the signs of direction are relevant and significant to that individual. Therefore, it is that individual who must come to understand his or her own spirituality and the nature of it, in order to recognize a sign when it is revealed. Each of us must develop a personal understanding and relationship with "GOD." We must recognize that the guiding energy that passes through the pathway of the soul, which connects us to "GOD," is manifested as feelings, thoughts, impressions, intuition, instinct, and the like. "GOD" is within us as well as all around us, so we have to be "in tune" with our surroundings in a spiritual sense, as well as in a physical sense. This will enable us to "feel" a sign manifested from within us and "see," "hear," "smell," or "taste" a sign manifested in the exterior of our space when it is presented.

Truly, a sign of divinity can be manifested in any dimension, in any form, and within any context. An example of this is the occurrence of "coincidence." A coincidence is defined as a sequence of events that although accidental, seems to have been planned or arranged. An individual's subjective interpretation categorizes a circumstance as being "accidental." The Holy Scriptures indicate that all divine truths (revelations) will be verified to those who perceive them. By dissecting the truth of the word "coincidence," what is truly had is "co-incidence," two or "together" incidences that validate each other. This validation, or the recognition of the "coincidence," is only evident to the individual(s) who find that particular circumstance relevant or significant to that moment of their life. With an open mind, one can reconcile the relevance and significance of a coincidence relative to its spiritual implications. A sign of divinity is intended for the individual, so if the individual is aware, it will meet their understanding so that they will recognize it. Each of us must seek to interpret the moments before us more fully.

A difficulty with interpreting "signs" within our spirituality we create for ourselves. This creation clouds our ability to distinguish a true spiritual sign from other stimuli. This difficulty is derived from the images and sounds we expose ourselves to as a form of entertainment. The signs of divinity we are meant to interpret occur such that they can be perceived by one of our five senses. If we "bombard" any one of these senses with an excessive amount of stimuli, we desensitize that sense. Consequently, this dulls an individual's ability to interpret reality relative to that sense. As well, that sense perceives stimulation less acutely. Moreover, the stimulus that is used to desensitize that sense becomes the guiding factor in determining that individual's direction. This is because it is a natural part of our being to have "signs" lead us. Therefore, our subconscious interprets this stimulus as the "sign" it needs to guide it. The source of the stimuli that a person is excessively exposed to replaces the true sign this sense is meant to perceive. What we watch on television, at the movie theater, in the video games, and in music videos influences our actions. What we listen to relative to music and other forms of entertainment also influences our actions. The same is true of what we taste, smell, and otherwise sense. The truth in this is exemplified by the millions of dollars spent to acquire "seconds" of television airtime for advertising. When our actions are predominantly influenced by outside stimuli, the subtle influences of intuition, of our innermost feelings are pushed aside. Wherever an individual dwells or lives is his or her "natural" environment. We must make for ourselves serene, quiet moments within our natural environment. Within this time, we must begin to listen to ourselves more deeply. We must become more in tune with our surroundings and ourselves.

Signs are manifested in very subtle ways. Either we misinterpret their meaning, or we miss their meaning altogether. In opening our mind to these truths, each of us must embrace the reality that simply because we do not recognize the existence of signs of divinity does not mean they are not there. To employ the soul as the divine guidance system requires trust in oneself and faith in the positive direction derived from the Divine Energy of Life. To believe in any system, whether it is GODs' plan, the Divine System of Nature, the system of American society, or the system of positive action, one must surrender to that belief. When one surrenders to GODs' plan or divine destiny by allowing their soul to guide their conscious existence, there are certain steps they must take. Individuals must begin to hone their ability to channel the positive energy within them and around them effectively. This is done by moving in a positive way, thinking in a positive way, and surrounding oneself with positive things. By embracing the positive elements of one's existence, persons can create the circumstances within which "GOD" intended each human being to dwell.

As individuals, we are always trying to figure out what it is that we want to have, and what it is that we want to do. More often than not, these questions go unanswered because with all of the opportunities inherent to life itself, we cannot truly figure out in our minds what is completely right or wrong for us as individuals. Within our soul is where we can find the knowledge that will enlighten us to what it is we truly want to have and what it is we truly want to do. The components of our soul will guide us in the direction in which we are supposed to move. However, this is only true if with our free will we choose positive action over negative action. Sometimes a person may think that they want to do something, but it does not "feel" completely right to them. This "feeling" is a spiritual manifestation of that person's divine guidance system. If in these instances, that person will heed the revelation of their "intuition," they will find that things will work out for the best. When persons surrender themselves to faith, they are releasing themselves to what is right and what is righteous, which makes the road to salvation and perfection an easy one to follow. It is our "inner being," our "heart," or our "soul," which keeps us from taking a wrong turn along the journey of life.

Learning to better interpret signs of divinity is relative to the pursuit of perfecting the function of the soul in a spiritual sense. How does one go about perfecting their soul in a worldly sense? With goodness of heart, a person is to act morally and ethically. "Moral" is defined as being of or related to conduct or character from the point of view of right and wrong. It is to be concerned with the goodness and badness of an action or character. It is to be concerned with the establishment of principles of right and wrong, and their application. "Ethics" is the study and philosophy of human conduct, with emphasis on the determination of right and wrong. Ethics are the principles of right conduct applied to the circumstance of life. Both moral and ethical refer to human behavior as it relates to what is right or wrong. Within the context of our spirituality, right is positive and wrong is negative. To disregard the impact morality and ethics are to have on our behavior is to deny the truth. This truth is that ethics and morality are the worldly labels for the parameters of behavior within which "GOD" intended each of us to natural act.

People are supposed to do their best to do the right or righteous thing, always. Right is defined as being in accordance with what is good, true, proper, or just. While being in conformity with fact, it is what is fitting or appropriate, as well as being suitable, genuine, and authentic. By definition, it is clear that to "do the right thing" is the natural direction of a human's action, were it being true to reality. Righteous(ness) is found more in biblical language than present-day language. Perfect righteousness, or purely positive action (i.e. energy) is found only in "GOD" (the Divine Energy of Life). As "GOD" created the human in "his" image, the human also has a sense of righteousness. When the human is in touch with itself and its spirituality, it knows what direction behavior should take. Each human is to have a set of standards that define its personal behavior. Collectively, those standards must conform to the principles of morality and ethics. This keeps our energy flowing in the positive direction in accordance with Nature's divine system.

Following the doctrine behind morality and ethics is how we pursue the perfection of the soul in a worldly sense. Understanding the truth of ourselves as well as following the positive direction our feelings and perceptions lead us in, is how we pursue the perfection of the soul in a spiritual sense. I do not seek to explain what morality and ethics are, that is for each individual to discern during his or her pursuit of knowledge. My concern is to emphasize the importance of our conduct and behaviors occurring within the parameters provided by these terms. From a spiritual standpoint, these written doctrines define the unwritten principles naturally inherent within the human species. They are based on the truth that as the human is created in the image of "GOD," its character (the foundation from which our actions are launched) should reflect the goodness within the Divine Energy of Life. As we respond to the moments of our lives (both good and bad) with positive, right (eous) actions, what we learn from these circumstances allows us to develop and solidify the ethical and moral fiber of our character. Having an ethical and moral character is not a purely private matter. The values derived from the individual character of members of a civilized society have a direct effect on the affairs of that society. Therefore, without an ethical and moral character, our social structure is doomed to suffer. Written laws can cope with the actions that affect our society. However, they cannot deal with the attitudes from which those actions are derived. Those attitudes are based upon an individual's values, and the foundation of our values is our character.

To truly put our spirituality in context, each of us must recognize the relevance and significance of our actions and the vibrations those actions create. Every movement creates a vibration that reverberates through the atmosphere that can be associated with a certain frequency. The air around us is a physical, electrified element that brings more to our lives than what is considered as physically required. Our atmosphere is the electromagnetic field that allows the flow of divine energy to take place. By understanding the connection between the flow of our movements to the flow of electric energy through a parallel circuit, we are better able to place into context the truth that acting rightly is a physical requirement of the system that keeps us alive. The choices we make must satisfy our physical, or worldly reality. Yet, the actions that result from the choices we make are to be (must be) guided by our innate spiritual awareness to do the positive thing(s). The polarity of the energy that is generated by the vibrations of our movements through the "field of force," positive or negative, is a part of the system of our Earth. Our actions or behaviors are directly connected to what occurs around us that is produced by the forces of Nature.

We must allow ourselves to get "in touch" with our surroundings and with Nature. Individuals must allow themselves to feel the "vibrations" around them. Each of us can "feel" the electric force we breathe. If each of us does good and right(eous) things, we will feel the positive electric current as it flows through those circumstances. It is a truly joyous experience. Personally, I can reach out and touch the positive energy around me sometimes because it is so strong. It is as though I can touch a true part of "GOD," because I can touch and feel the Divine Energy of Life. I touch "him" because I know of all the goodness that is around me that is created by living things. I can see the goodness, I can touch the goodness, and I can be within that goodness. If it is alive, I feel as though I can relate (or communicate) with it, in essence I can "connect" with it. An example of this "connection" would be the truth in the circumstance of people growing better plants by being in a good mood and talking pleasantly with the plants. This is the result of a positive "electrical connection" having been established between two living things. The two entities are on like "frequencies," and exchanging positive energy in a very real sense. We must make positive sounds just as we must do good deeds. If we exude goodness, everything around us flourishes. If every living being were doing that, we would all flourish. We all give off energy that is part of the field of force. We all are joined by that field of force. We all are separated by that field of force. Everything for the living being is derived from that field of force, the air we breathe, the atmosphere within which we exist. The air is derived from the planet. Therefore, we are connected to the planet. We must recognize all these things together in earnest.

Each of us must re-connect with Nature and become "in tune" with our surroundings. Spending time in the open air, which is the naturally electrified "field of force" of the planetary circuitry energizes the vibrations within us and sharpens our ability to interpret and understand ourselves from within. As animals, we need to be outside in the fresh air, under the sun, exerting energy. As animals, we must embrace the benefits of natural surroundings. We must do the things that are inherent to animals in Nature and to our species in our natural surroundings if we are to reach our full spiritual potential and get into the path of positive flowing energy. Communing with Nature is not a joke. We can "re-connect" ourselves to Nature by spending time deep within her grasp (the woods, the shore, etc.). In these surroundings, we can develop important aspects of our mind and our soul. In the throngs of Nature, we can learn about ourselves by paying attention to what "makes us tick." There we can listen to ourselves and develop our intuition. These are the things each of us needs to do to find the nature and speed of our individual "divine energy flow." When a person has synchronized his or her being with the positive flowing energy in the world around them, that person feels good and positive inside. as well, the people around that person are happy as a result of being near them, and things in that person's life happen the right(eous) way.

It is both our interpretation of reality together with the understanding and perspective created from our interpretation, which makes it all too difficult for each of us to understand our true spirituality. Words like "supernatural," "astrology," "numerology," and the like, are really disciplines of thought that are misinterpreted or not completely understood within their proper contexts. As the human always fears what it does not understand, we disregard the prospect of there being any true practical value in endeavoring to embrace these areas of thought relative to the truth of our existence. Take astrology for example. Astrology does have relevance to our existence because it defines the frequency at which each of us exists. The alignment of the planets is relevant to us as individuals. All movement creates a vibration that has a frequency.

Everything that contains movement, which is every event, moment, tangible element of reality, animal, and vegetable has a frequency. All living things receive energy from the Divine Energy of Life. For humans, this energy is received by receptors along our spinal cord and transmitted throughout the body by way of our nerves. Because each individual's neural network is unique to him or her. This makes everyone's "spiritual frequency" is different. The "frequency" (psychic or spiritual) upon which our individuality is based with regard to our relationship to the Divine Energy of Life is determined by the position of all of the heavenly bodies of the Universe at the moment of our birth. If we are objective enough to see it, this explains why we as individuals cannot share with another person our personal connection to "GOD." It is because no one else can experience it or relate to it but the individual himself or herself. For most of us, if we were to share with others some of the things we personally believe "link" us to "GOD," we would be labeled loony. Each individual has to seek "GOD" for himself or herself. In effect, we find our frequency by "tuning in" to "GOD." Each of us must create for ourselves a personal relationship with the Divine Energy of Life. Astrology and other philosophies of the human analysis help guide us to the insight of who we truly are as we examine ourselves as individuals.

We consider dreams, the occult, the super-natural, <u>extra</u>-sensory perception, intuition, instinct, gut feelings, hunches, astrology, numerology, Nature, spirituality, etc., to "perhaps" exist on one plane of reality. These are <u>naturally</u> occurring phenomenon. We resist fully embracing the value of naturally occurring phenomenon that we do not fully understand because of thinking of ourselves as beings outside of Nature. We consider human reasoning, intellect, "animal" instinct, psychology, the sciences, etc., to occupy a more significant, certain plane of reality. The "truth" is there is only one reality, and therefore only one plane of existence. It is divine in nature, because "GOD" (the Divine Energy of Life) created it. Even if an individual cannot embrace the concept of "GOD," they must accept the fact that reality is the result of one occurrence, the spinning of the planet. Therefore, everything that occurs on this planet can be connected to this fact. This makes those things interconnected themselves. The laws of Nature, the laws of physics, the laws of mathematics, and the laws of science, are all a part of our "spiritual" reality. The right interpretation of reality must include all that we know of, while having consideration for all that we do not. This means that we must always have an open mind that is receptive to new information. Whether we choose to recognize it or not, reality is spiritual or divine in nature and origin. All of existence owes its actuality to "GOD" (the Divine Energy of Life) first. We humans, through our subjectively perceived superiority, are in fact, merely minute parts of the larger divine ecosystem.

In understanding the pathway through which the Earth transmits energy to animals, we need to realize that we have given a number of labels to aspects of our being that we interpret to be separate from each other. Labels like "consciousness," "spirituality," "intuition," "psychic energy," "ESP.," "gut feelings," etc., all identify a single circumstance of existence, divided into many interpretations. That single circumstance is the flow of divine energy, and these labels actually identify different levels or frequencies of this energy transmission. Together these terms represent the humans' recognition of the connective pathway through which the Earth gives us the Divine Energy of Life, and the manifestation of that energy and knowledge within us. The fact that all of these terms are dealt with in segregated contexts is an example of the limited understanding that is a characteristic of the subjective state of mind. It will not allow the truth to manifest itself. All of these labels exist because we needed to identify something of which we are consciously aware.

The consciousness, or rightly put, our nervous system and brain constitute the physical pathway through which energy flows. The only right interpretation we have made about our consciousness and the nature of this pathway is that they are truly God-given senses. This is in addition to the five we readily acknowledge. Part of the human's misconception of reality is the need to keep separate the physical, scientific knowledge we have come to learn of, and the spiritual knowledge of which we have been made aware.

These philosophies seem like opposing theories that can be compared to the opposing poles of a single bar magnet. A single metal bar provides for a very good analogy, because these two fields of thought, as with the poles of a bar magnet, are naturally connected. If the analogy is to be realistic, there must be a reason that the bar becomes magnetized by energy. This will require movement. since the principles implied by a philosophy require active measures to be manifested into reality, the analogous bar becomes a magnet by virtue of it having opposing ends, and being energized by the movement or action required to implement the doctrine of each respective philosophy. It is true that magnetically speaking, only opposites attract. If the opposite poles of a single (one) bar magnet were connected, a circle would be formed. These two subjective fields of thought, spirituality and science, as a circle would suggest, make up one, whole reality.

From the realities of the system of Nature and the truths of the system of human spirituality, we can derive a set of required actions or responsibilities. Based on the realities of the system of Nature, each of us is to move in a positive direction. Individuals are to think positive. We are to all supposed to move in ways that aid in our own survival. This is work. As well, each of us is to grow in body, mind, and soul. Based on the truths of the system of human spirituality, each of us is to obey authority. We are to resolve the moments we pass through in positive ways while seeking balance and avoiding excess. We are to act in a civilized manner. Each of us is to help those around us by making it easier for them to move and by sharing what we derive from the Divine System of Nature. Lastly, every one of us is to pursue our positive wants/desires while moving in positive ways.

By following the positive direction derived from knowing one's true self and trusting the positive indicators of one's own feelings, an individual will ultimately be led to discover their individual God-given gifts and blessings that take the form of personal abilities. In these gifts lies that person's destiny. Therein lies the need for the individual to allow his or her soul to guide the actions of that person's life. This element of our being contains the "details" of each individual's relevance to "GODs" plan." It is a sort of "road map" of an individual's journey through the adventure of existing. The "spirit" and "heart," or the "soul," can direct a person through the righteous moments of his or her life. We must live through the heart or soul, rather than living through the mind alone.

We must also recognize and embrace the importance of what is common between members of our species. If all humans existed within the same controlled environment and were exposed to the same circumstances and stimuli, each individual would start to exhibit the same thoughts and behaviors. From this, each of us must understand that our differences are truly superficial. As a species, we cannot afford to continue to allow these differences to come between us. We must embrace the kinship that binds us together, and enjoy the enrichment that difference can bring to our individual lives. We can come to understand ourselves better by embracing the truths within our nature. We are to use these things to steer ourselves onto a positive course of life and away from a negative one.

The Spiritual Nature of Responsibility

Romans 13:1-2, "let every soul be subject unto the higher powers. For there is no power but of GOD: the powers that be are ordained of GOD. Whosoever therefore resisteth the power, resisteth the ordinance of GOD: and they that resist shall receive to themselves damnation."

What "GOD" said to do is "his" will. These are the actions that are required of each living thing that has the divine energy of "GOD" flowing through it. These are our responsibilities. To successfully negotiate the "end times" and be delivered into "GODs" kingdom, the human species must acquire the ability to differentiate between the Will of "GOD" and the Will of the human. This ability is within each of us. Unfortunately, our species has collectively suppressed it because of immaturity, selfishness, and greed. A large part of our evolution as a species relies upon our embracing truth and accepting the challenges presented by it. For the human consciousness to evolve to the next stage of awareness, our species must collectively experience "GOD." The Divine Energy of Life is within each of us. How do individuals experience "GOD?" The answer is through divine truth. Each of us must look for the higher (spiritual) meaning of the actions that take place around us as we move through life. As each person has an experience, each must objectively examine the elements that compose it. What will be revealed are things that our subjectivity shielded from us. as individuals begin to see all the inherent truths as well as their connections to each other, each will begin to see how truly awesome the Divine Energy of Life is for having created existence. This will awaken in us all a joy and appreciation for the opportunity of being alive.

There is "GODs" will interpreted within the context of the worldly reality. As well, there is "GODs" will interpreted within the context of the spiritual reality. However, there is a term that spans both interpretations, and adequately represents what "GOD" would have each of us do. That term is "responsibility." The required actions of our worldly reality and our spiritual reality are our responsibilities. Each of us must live up to our responsibilities. Each of us must aspire to having responsibilities. In essence, what "GOD" said to do is "be responsible." We are to be responsible to the truth. Each of us is to act according to the truth, whatever that truth may be.

What we must recognize is that what GODs' Will created was life, and a positive condition within which it would grow and perpetuate itself. We are truly animals that are a single part of one large group.

This large group is composed of everything living thing upon our Earth, and within the Universe. We are connected to everything that lives, including our living Earth. Because of these physical realities and the truths they support, each of us must do what is right. Each of us must do what is positive. Of all we do not know about "GOD," we do know that this has been the intended direction for human action from the very beginning. Spiritually speaking, all humans were expected to move (or act) in the positive, right direction. This direction would have us do not only the positive, right things for us as individuals, but also the positive, right things for all that exists. We must do this not only because of some religious doctrine, but because it is a physical requirement of the divine system "GOD" created to sustain and perpetuate life. It is our responsibility to choose to move this way. Right(eous) action is what we must perform to satisfy our responsibility to the Divine System of Nature.

Whether the label for it is "Nature," "Mother Nature," or the "Divine System of Nature," on some level we humans think of ourselves as being outside of it. Each of us must come to understand that the basis of the Divine System of Nature is positive action leading to growth. In being a true part of this system as the human species is, we too must have positive action and growth. What are we to grow into being? For us, "GOD" is the example. By example, we are to work first, before we rest, not the other way around. "GOD" worked for six days to create growth, then "He" rested on the seventh.

We are to create by doing. This is each of us moving. This movement must have a direction, that direction right or positive. We are to create growth by doing what is right or positive. We are to create the most perfect (best) living condition by doing what is right or positive. We are to create cleanliness by doing what is right or positive. We are to create sustenance by doing what is right or positive. We are to create our families and communities by doing what is right or positive. We are to create happiness and enjoyment by doing what is right or positive. We are to create balance by doing what is right or positive. We must first work to accomplish what is necessary for our lives, before we relax. Each of us must fulfill our responsibilities. In our pursuit of self-gratification, there are a lot of us that give rest and leisure more of a priority than work. This is contrary to the Divine System of Nature. It is contrary to the way "GOD" created. It is contrary to the cycle of the day. It is contrary to the cycle of the season. We must try to become a part of the Divine System of Nature by doing what is right. What is right is what is positive. This is our natural responsibility. We must consciously choose it, because we consciously choose our actions.

Existence is the result of a "system," an orderly body of methods. It is a complex scheme or plan. This system is a combination of things or parts that together form a unitary "whole." Think of this unitary whole as one "body." Every system within this body is supposed to do something. Each is supposed to move or function rightly, and in unison with the other systems of the body to keep it alive and healthy. Metabolism, reproduction, and growth are the result of movement, or action. Everything that lives, plants and animals, will do something. It will move or have action. This holds true for even the "amoebae," a one-celled animal. It is a naked mass of protoplasm that is constantly changing in shape as it moves and engulfs food. All life within this system moves with a purpose. There is no single living organism of note that does not do something or have movement directed towards the perpetuation of its own existence. Doing, i.e. having action or movement, is an inherent part of the system of existence. The elements of the Atom move within the context of the system that sustains it, i.e. its correct or right body function. The elements within the body of a plant move within the context of the system that sustains it, i.e. its correct or right body function. The elements within the body of an animal also move within the context of the system that sustains it. Again, this movement occurs in the way that rightly maintains the body's function.

As the Earth is a living organism or a body, the living things of the Earth constitute the moving elements that make up the system that sustains it. Therefore, our movements or actions must occur within the context that is right to perpetuate Nature's entire system and our Earth itself. As it relates to the worldly aspect of reality, we readily recognize that we must do things or have movement to survive in this worldly reality. We recognize that actions are required of us as beings. We must all face the truth that as it relates to the spiritual aspect of our existence, we must also do "things" related to this part of reality as well. Here too, there are actions that are required of us. The right direction for this and every human action is positive. To do nothing is to not live. We must continue to do, even though we do not completely understand. The human has the ability to think while it is doing, and we are supposed to utilize this gift. We must recognize the importance of doing the positive action first, knowing that we can come to an understanding of the circumstance "while" or "after" the necessary action(s). It is not necessary to have a full understanding of what we are doing prior to doing it. It is the positive action itself that is most important. Determine what that is and pursue it. Then, while or after it is done, come to an understanding of the meaning and benefit of that direction. Each of us must act and react positively before and whether or not we come to a complete understanding of a given circumstance. As well, each of us must act and react positively regardless of our subjective feelings. These choices are our responsibility. Responsibility is the divine label for the "required action" of living organisms, the required actions that produce a positive living condition, i.e. a place to grow.

All of GODs' socialized beings perform some action that supports themselves as individuals within the context of the collective community. Each individual member of a socialized species also performs some action that supports the perpetuation of the group or community to which they belong. Being a part of a socialized species means each individual is a dependent member of the larger group. Examples of socialized species are certain bees, ants, butterflies, fish, primates, and the like. Entomologists label bees and such as "eusocial insects" or "truly" social insects. Included in this classification are ants and termites, as well as highly organized bees and wasps. Truly, our lives are no different from any of the other creatures that are characterized as socialized. To whatever degree, we are all community oriented, with some phase of the work we perform being done for the collective. Using the insects as an example, most would agree that their actions are instinctive and intuitive, pretty much a reflex of their Nature. Since the animal kingdom encompasses insects and humans, and as we are both "socialized," one could argue we have the same instinctive inclinations. As a part of a bee's action or activity aimed at supporting the individual and the community, they collect nectar from flowers. It is used to produce food (honey). This food is stored in the hive, to be consumed by the individual and the collective. During the process of helping itself and its species group, the individual bee also performs a natural task that aids in the perpetuation of the life around it. It is the process of pollination. Collecting nectar and spreading pollen is what bees do. These are their naturally required actions, their responsibilities to the Divine System of Nature.

As a socialized species, humans are no different. We too have "naturally required actions" that we perform during the course of our lives. However, our existence is more complex because of our higher level of development and the intellect associated with the conscious mind. The part of human action or behavior that supports the individual and the collective is commerce. For the most part, it is the making and spending of money. As farfetched as this may sound, within a civilized social structure, this is the "natural" action that humans perform within the context of their species group to support the individual and the collective. If a comparison between the efforts of making money to the activity of ants is made, striking similarities become apparent. For example, the individual ant leaves the immediate home and goes out into the world in search of the necessities of its life. Within the context of human existence, those necessities require payment of some sort. When the ant has found that reward it deems beneficial to the group, it "works" at bringing it home. Humans work and bring home the reward for their effort, money. Some ants bring home larger portions than other ants. This is also true of humans relative to this circumstance. Whatever rewards each individual ant has returned with is utilized by itself and the collective to enrich their lives. When the individual human spends the money it has earned, that person enriches both his or her own existence, and that of the person from whom they have bought. Within the confines of our social system, each individual's effort enriches not only that person's own life, but also the lives of all the members of the social system. Within human circumstances that do not contain the element of "money," the members of that group find other assets to exchange for mutual benefit. This is called "bartering."

In addition to the beneficial efforts related to the species group, humans are supposed to naturally "do" things to perpetuate the life that exists around it by using knowledge and energy (effort) together to benefit the natural system of existence. Like the bee carrying pollen from flower to flower, the human has a responsibility to the life that exists around it. As well, this responsibility or required action is mandated by our having dominion over the living planet. As a group of conscious beings with dominion over the planet, it is our responsibility to apply our mental energy (intelligence) and physical energy (effort) to the task of creating a more perfect world for the existence of all living things. Both working and thinking are natural, positive, divine responsibilities. These things are supposed to be a reflex of our nature. I have said that our existence is more complex than other socialized species. This is partly due to our ability to conceive of and produce sensation, as well as manufacture enjoyment.

While sensation and enjoyment are primary human concerns, they are truly secondary to perpetuating the existence of life. In facing and dealing with reality, we must accept and embrace the revelation that we must first satisfy all our divine responsibilities, before we can use our energies to pursue self-serving pleasures.

Human society is a mirror of the combined characteristics and social structures of other socialized species. Within these structures, there are drones, or workers, factions, and leaders. Humans must recognize the natural occurrence of these roles. Related to individuals, if we are not leaders then we are workers. As conscious workers, we eke out whatever pleasures we can get out of life while we carry out the responsibilities related to the positions that we hold within the social structure. Whatever position that is, the nature of the work that an individual performs must not only aid the furtherance toward that individual's goals, but also the common goals of the group. As we define our individual goals, this is a subjective interpretation of our direction. If individuals examined these goals, comparing them to the goals of other individuals within our social structure, each of us would see that objectively speaking, our individual pursuits are actually goals common to us all. Everyone generally wants to live well and enjoy life. Living well and enjoying life within a group forms a social structure. The truth is, social structure by any name is simply <u>organized</u> mutual benefit. Another label that could be used to identify this "organized mutual benefit" is <u>help</u>. Therefore, as prescribed by the laws of Nature and of the human, we are supposed to help each other; help each other to live well and enjoy life. For Americans, this effort by definition occurs within the context of "civility." Help is simply to aid another such that their movements are made easier. It could involve anything from staying out of another's way, to holding a door open, to lifting a package, to mowing another's grass, to giving another a monetary contribution, to attentively listening to another. Help is simply to aid another such that their movements are made easier.

If we serve (or help) each other, we serve "GOD" by making the Divine System of Nature work right(eously). Within the Holy Scripture at Galatians 5:13, those words yield the following interpretation for Americans and all of humanity: "you, my brothers, were called to be free. But do not use your freedom to indulge the sinful Nature; rather, serve one another in love." The entire edict is summed up in a single command: "love your neighbor as yourself." It continues, "But if you bite and devour one another, take heed that you be not consumed one of another." Truly, within the context of spirituality, the meaning of the term "neighbor" is not limited to the nearest human. It means to live near or be near. Hence, the term itself is inclusive of all living things. We fit into Nature's ecosystem with all of GODs' living creatures. This planet is not here for only us. It is here to support life in a much broader sense. Though it may or may not be very good for us, we eat cows, sheep, chickens, and some fish. Yet, there exists a large variety of beings that we do not consume. Just as we cultivate the existence of the life that we need for our own sustenance, we must seek to provide for all living things a safe, natural habitat in which to coexist with other members of the life cycle. The living things that we do not devour as a part of our survival are those with which we must coexist. We were meant to share our knowledge and energy to benefit ourselves, as well as what exists around us.

Helping one another is supporting one another's existence. This is an inherent characteristic of a socialized species. Supporting each other uplifts the individual spirit. Each of us must appreciate the people with whom we are fortunate enough to interact. Within our understanding of the realities of life, we must recognize that individual life is finite. This fact makes every individual life significantly relevant to the time within which it occurs. With this in mind, each person should truly enjoy the interactions they have with other people and other living things. This is because every person or living thing that is interacted with brings new experience to one's life. Each person should be as helpful as possible relative to aiding the existence of another living thing.

There is benefit for each of us in every act of goodness (positive) we produce. For every bit of goodness he or she can produce, there is goodness that will be returned to that person (action/reaction). This is true whether it occurs immediately, or in the moments to come. Individuals can generally assume they are going to be on our planet for 70 years. If help is given to someone today, as long as that "return" comes during the period of the "helpers" life, which it will, that is just one more advantage to look forward as the days pass. In truth, the planet is small enough that, if an individual chooses to be mean spirited towards another person (or another living thing), there is a good possibility that person could be encountered by that individual again. As well, that person can easily become negative, hostile, or offensive, and release those feelings in their next encounter. Maybe it will not happen, but what if it does? Life is a series of opportunities and/or chances. To increase one's chances for success and prosperity, each of us relies on the odds (of) being good.

One of the most important laws of physics is newton's third law of motion. It states that for every action there is an equal and opposite reaction. This is a much broader reality that governs our entire living condition. Stemming from this law there is a clear inference of the principle of "reciprocity." Interpreted in spiritual terms, this principle indicates that actions aimed at giving or sharing are reciprocated such that one's own position or prosperity is never lost, if the "aided" makes an effort to "return the favor." The principle states that if one pushes down on part (a) of a complicated system and observes that part (b) moves to the left, then surely by pushing (b) to the right will make (a) move up. Expressed more spiritually, if an equal effort is made in the direction that constitutes "giving back," the original position of those who give aid (a) is never lost. Hence, no ground is lost, and balance is restored. This is true because the complicated system is intended to work this way. The transference of energy and deeds travels transversely within the complicated human system of existence if the intent is there. Therefore, to expend energy for the benefit of another does not decrease one's own resources if those who benefit intend to repay their debt, or give "back" an equivalent effort, energy, or deed. It is not terribly relevant whom the energy, effort, or deed is directed at, if we are all working as a unitary system. The words that tell the story of human spirituality, i.e. the holy books of our species, infer that our actions are to be positive, righteous, and good. Moreover, if our actions are such, righteous blessing will be our reward. The revelation here is humankind must recognize its responsibility to the truth in these words. We must face this reality because it is a part of our existence. We must incorporate this understanding into our perspective so that it affects every choice we make, and every action we take, and everything that we do. As individuals open their minds and acknowledge that none of us knows all there is to know, this perspective must be taken into consideration.

What each of us does is relevant and significant within the context of our spiritual Nature. Whatever we do as individuals is a natural part of our existence. No matter what an individual's perception of their daily actions is, what humans do is a "natural" occurrence, a part of our "natural" existence. It is a closed-minded, self-absorbed perspective that keeps this from being seen clearly. Movement is a required action or responsibility within the context of being alive. What humans do is our contribution to the pattern or system of Nature, just as what ants and bees do is their spiritual, natural contribution to Nature's system. The divine truth is that just as the other creatures of our planet go about the routine of their lives, what humans "do" is the routine of their lives. Examined relative to what is considered normal or status quo, we all do the same thing, though with slight variations. We are all born the same way, just into different circumstances. Most all work, except the job differs. We all seek recreation and pleasure, etc. Generally speaking, we all think the same things. It is our interpretations and the resulting perspectives that differ. The reason one person can lead many is because the "core" of our being, i.e. our innermost thoughts, are relatively the same. This allows others to "speak" for us. Our daily activities, no matter how individualized or mundane, are spiritually relevant to our existence.

To be truthful to our spirituality, our reality, and to Nature, we must seek to do what is good, or move in a positive way. This is because good is positive, and positive is the direction that energy is to flow to perpetuate the life-giving circuitry of our planet. The route of the energy flow is circular and traveling in one direction (as the Earth spins). for us to get the most out of the Divine System of Nature, or to have the Divine System of Nature work as best it can for the living things on our planet, our species must be of the correct polarity to fit right(eously) into our Earth's living circuitry. The divine truth is that the energy that we as individuals feel when we help a living thing to survive or help another's movement, as well as what we feel when we perform an act of goodness or when we do the right(eous) thing, is accurately deemed positive (energy). These motions are the ones that help produce growth and that help perpetuate existence.

As the world around us changes, our minds, our consciousness, our understanding, our way of thinking, everything about our being alive must also change. Within the context of Nature, this process of change is called "evolution." Our species has reached the point in our existence where we must "think" our way to our own evolution. It is a profound matter, and we should deal with our collective future within that context. We must change our way of thinking so that we may all embrace the major element of our evolution. It is the recognition of the divine relationship between the energy that we feel inside of us that gives us life, and the energy of the planet as defined by the combination of every law and principle known to the human species. This relationship is the essence of spirituality. Divinity has domain over our existence because it is from where our living bodies came. As well, it is where our existence continues to get the energy to move forward. We must recognize the truthful implications of what we all perceive as reality <u>together</u>. The truth is that none of us would have any of what we have if it were not for the system of existence itself. This system <u>is</u> the planet. It is the Divine System of Nature. It is our society. It is America. It is truly <u>every</u> individual system of existence working "rightly" together as one. We must have a common understanding of what our collective future holds, and what actions we must all have together to go forth, i.e. to move forward into that future.

There are things that we know to be right, things we desire, things about ourselves that we want to change. More often than not, these are things that we only think about and do not act upon. One of the reasons we do not move to make these changes is because our daily lives are so consumed by the actions that satisfy the requirements of our physical reality, and our never-ending pursuit of self-gratification. The time has come for us to bring the repressed aspects of our being into reality. As a collective group of individuals, it is time to make our righteousness and our goodness, as well as our dreams and aspirations, apparent for the entire world to see and share in. We accomplish this by manifesting our positive thoughts into reality. We accomplish this by doing what is necessary, step-by-step (systematically), to bring about betterment in our lives, in our reality, and in ourselves. We do this to make the earthly existence the best it can possibly be for all living things. We do this to manifest the change that will bring about both salvation and prosperity. Each of us must recognize the importance of understanding the role of energy with regard to all the areas relevant to human existence. These are the areas relevant to the body (movement and action), the mind (discipline and control), and the soul (positive direction). In addition, each of us must recognize the importance of understanding the influence polarity has upon energy in these areas, i.e. positive or negative. Every defined action occurs within a span of time that has a beginning and an end, or conclusion. It could be sweeping the floor, driving to the store, or pursuing a college degree. To direct one's actions through these spans of time in hopes of achieving positive results is to seek "positive (perfect) resolution" of the circumstances of reality that are being faced.

During our systematic pursuit of positive (perfect) resolution, an individual may not always receive <u>immediate</u> self-gratification, but each individual will always receive <u>long-term</u> gratification. We must accept the sacrifice of immediate self-gratification in the interest of mutual satisfaction and balance. If our entire species pursued positive (perfect) resolution in an objective manner, our resulting state of existence would be utopian. We must draw conclusions in an effort to make decisions that bring about positive resolution. These conclusions must be based on objective reality. They cannot be based on subjective fantasy. We cannot "create" reality in our minds. It must be a part of time and space. So as we draw conclusions in the moments of reality, those conclusions must be based on the facts of that reality, not subjective fantasy. We must stop placing the truth of our personal needs and desires above the other truths of our reality. We must act or react positively upon the words of truth related to what objectively exists, before we act or react to the words of truth that relate to us subjectively as individuals. We must first be objective, before we indulge our subjectivity. We must make judgments based on the facts, not what we choose to believe or what we make up to believe. Our decisions must be based on conclusions drawn from the truth, i.e. the realities that relate to those particular moments. This is what it means to recognize and deal with reality.

Each of us must recognize that as free-willed beings, our will unfortunately differs from that of "GOD." This has allowed the human to change the nature of the existence "GOD" had planned for all living things. Every time the human allowed his or her will to supersede that of "GOD," the human altered the intent of "GOD." "GOD" intended all living things to coexist in peace and harmony. "GOD" also intended all living things to pursue perfection (betterment) through creation and growth. Within the Holy Scripture at the book of genesis, it says that, in order, "GOD" created the Earth, the water, the light, and dry land. These are all the essential or most nearly perfect elements for natural growth. With these elements in place, "GOD" then brought forth grass, the herb yielding seed, and the fruit tree yielding fruit and its seed as well. The grass "He" intended to grow within the conditions "He" created, as was the intent for the tree. The seeds of those creations were intended to perpetuate the existence of those original creations. "GOD" then created the cycle of day and night. The light of day was meant to facilitate the activity of growth, and the darkness of night was meant for rest and regeneration. This original cycle also was to grow. It was to grow into the cycle of seasons. Then, "GOD" brought forth from the sea, the moving creature that had life, and fowl that could fly above the Earth. "GOD" then blessed them, saying, be fruitful, and multiply (create and grow). It was after all this that "GOD" created the male human, followed by the female and allowed them to have dominion over all things of the Earth. "GOD" blessed them also. "GOD" said unto them, "be fruitful, and multiply (create and grow), and replenish the Earth, and subdue it..." "...and "GOD" said, behold, I have given you every herb bearing seed, which is upon the face of all the Earth, and every tree, in which is the fruit of a tree yielding seed; to you it shall be for meat. And to every beast of the Earth, and to every fowl of the air, and to everything that creepeth upon the Earth, wherein there is life, I have given every green herb for meat…"

One can conclude from the writings of the Holy Scripture that "GOD" created the living condition, and then created things to grow within it. This was GODs' Will. This condition of existence is a positive one, as opposed to a negative one, and it is the most perfect condition for positive change. In a natural or divine sense, this positive change is growth. To grow is to gain by natural development. Growth is the development from a simpler to a more complex stage of existence. Growth is a building process. It is a process whereupon progress is made, based on the foundation upon which it is built. The act of "adding" or "increasing," of "gaining," or of "growing," are all movements in a positive direction. Regardless of what our species may think the purpose of our existence serves, or whatever GODs' ultimate plan is, what humans are supposed to do is clear. "GOD" gave each of us the ability to create. Each of us must use that ability to perpetuate the original creation, that being the most nearly perfect condition for positive change or growth. As we live our lives within the confines of this condition of existence, we must do what is expected of living things. We must grow.

To gain a better understanding of the true nature of our existence, as well as what GODs' intent was regarding the human species, it is necessary to examine the beginning of human life. The renowned writings that deal with conscious human action relative to that period are the Holy Scriptures. An objective examination of the Holy Scriptures reveals three conditions of human existence that are directly attributed to GODs' Will. The first is the condition of the physical environment. This environment was "Eden." Eden was the first and only utopia. The second condition dealt with the authority (or dominion) over the physical environment. That authority was bestowed upon the human by the "supreme authority," i.e. "GOD" (the Divine Energy of Life). The third condition dealt with the authority to which the human would be held accountable. That authority was "GOD" (the Divine Energy of Life). GODs' Will was to have the human exist in a utopian environment set in motion by the Divine Energy of Life. The human was to have the freedom to do whatever it chose to do as long as it satisfied two conditions. The first was to accept the responsibility of dominion over utopia. The second was to be obedient to GODs' Will. The current state of human existence is the result of the human species inability to uphold the mandates of "GOD" (the Divine Energy of Life).

Our Utopia

…The lord GOD planted a garden eastward in Eden; and there he put the man whom he had formed.

The lord GOD took the man, and put him into the Garden of Eden to dress it and to keep it.

…The lord GOD said, it is not good that the man should be alone.

…The lord GOD caused a deep sleep to fall upon Adam, and he slept: and he took one of his ribs, and closed up the flesh instead thereof; and the rib, which the lord GOD had taken from man, made he a woman, and brought her unto the man. And Adam said, this is now bone of my bones, and flesh of my flesh: she shall be called woman, because she was taken out of man.

There is a spiritual mandate requiring all humans to work together toward maintaining a perfect living condition. "GOD" created Eden as the utopian place within which Adam and Eve were to grow. As they both grew, Eden was supposed to grow as well. As Adam and Eve populated our Earth, their offspring were also supposed to live within the utopian Eden. Human existence was to be as Eden was, and Eden was utopia. Therefore, based upon this, human existence was truly supposed to be nearly perfect, if our actions had followed the Will of "GOD." Eden was to grow to encompass all humanity within its utopian framework. Before they ate of the fruit of knowledge, Adam and Eve were completely in tune with "GOD" and "his" will. They lived according to their spirituality. Not respecting GODs' authority and partaking of the fruit of knowledge caused Adam and Eve to recognize "GOD" as being separate from their state of existence. This event changed the way they perceived their spirituality. It was the first human action to alter the direction of human existence from what "GOD" had intended. It altered the way "GOD" had intended things to be. It was not of GODs' Will, but of the humans' will.

All the other significant human actions that were contrary to what "GOD" would have had us do have had the same effect. We have been fruitful and we have multiplied. Yet, we must recognize that we have grown "through" the experiences of past transgressions, to arrive at the point where we presently are. Relying simply upon our knowledge, instinct, intuition, resourcefulness, and drive toward self-satisfaction, some members (but not all) of the human species may very well continue to reap prosperous benefit. However, the almighty intended the living condition of all humanity to grow into a "civilized utopia." That would have been GODs' Will. The humans' will altered that original intent. The result is the living condition that the human finds itself living within now. Until we collectively recognize "GOD" (the Divine Energy of Life) and the authority thereof, we can never regenerate the conditions within which "GOD" intended life to exist. Each of us must embrace the connection between our spirituality and our everyday lives. Collective satisfaction for all humanity is truly divine in nature. To create utopia, each of us must understand and embrace this revelation.

Utopia can be created by each human recognizing their responsibility to both worldly and spiritual reality, through the acceptance of the need to act upon what can be labeled "positive truths." The only utopia that ever existed was Eden. We must recognize the significance of the fact that spirituality was the context within which that reality occurred. Our understanding of the concept of utopia must be spiritual, and it must occur within the context of our understanding of reality. In a realistic utopian existence, an individual must have an understanding of the importance of every living thing. A relationship with the source of our creation must exist to the degree that at the very least, individuals consciously recognize how the systems of existence work together as a whole unit to allow for the perpetuation of living things.

Though all humans are bound by the authority of "GOD," within utopia each would have <u>nearly</u> everything they needed and be allowed to do <u>nearly</u> whatever they wanted, as long as their actions stayed within positive parameters and within the limits of the social system. In this state of existence, there would be happiness, satisfaction, and harmony. The only way to manifest this is for each individual to conduct themselves within the confines of a code of behavior that protects others from having their individual rights, privileges, or space infringed upon. There must also be a minimum standard of living created by the sharing of the prosperity of nations.

To achieve this, each of us must first acknowledge the fact that reality is divine in nature. Relative to this, human existence here on our Earth is the result of a spiritual process or system of actions. The design for the operation of each individual system is based upon the Atom. It is a group of like elements revolving around a positive central point, altogether producing energy through positive action. We must look at our existence as though it consisted of a multitude of various, similarly constructed systems that were to operate the same way. As such, humans were meant to fulfill minor roles within one, larger system of which every living thing was a part. The goal of each individual action within each system is to perpetuate the conditions for growth. We must come to understand that everything is a part of the Divine System of Nature, and each of us must perform the necessary deeds that make the entire system work rightly. There are circumstances inherent to human existence that require our actions simply because we breathe air. We must recognize and accept these commitments and responsibilities that we have to the cycle of life, if for no other reason than because we are alive and breathing.

These more spiritual responsibilities must be accepted along with our personal and social responsibilities. It may seem like a complex task, but we must embrace these things because they are required of us as conscious, living beings. Every living thing on this circle or planet performs productive activity to sustain its existence, and the human is no different. We must embrace the basic reality of work and the opportunity it provides for us. We must also embrace the revelation that life is a gift. We start by not taking the moments of our lives for granted. By this I mean, we must stop living as though there are things in life that are owed to us, simply because we occupy space in time. We must stop living as though time does not matter because we all have an infinite amount of it. In reality, time is the only true human possession and for each individual it is very limited. We must all seek to use it wisely and positively. In addition, each of us must accept the responsibility that results from our being alive. Simply put, we must work to perform the required actions of our reality.

This effort or work must have a reward. That reward may take one of many forms. In a worldly sense, it could be monetary or physical compensation. In a spiritual sense, it could be the positive energy produced by the good feeling generated from positive efforts. On the other hand, it could be just the gift of life itself. Whatever the case, each of us must be rewarded for the work we do. Everyone expects to be rewarded for his or her work, and each individual will be because it is a natural part of the Divine System of Nature. What is the reward for the collective effort or work related to the pursuit of perfection? It is the realization of utopia and perpetual motion. Utopia and perpetual motion are thought of as unattainable conditions that exist only in theory. This conclusion is due in part to the misunderstanding of what these two labels represent. For one thing, they are interconnected, as is all knowledge. For utopia to exist there must be perpetual motion. The inverse is also true, for perpetual motion to exist there must be utopia.

Utopia is a condition within which life exists in a state that is nearly perfect for growth. Utopia is the state of near perfect spiritual manifestation, where all of the systems of existence work together in nearly perfect harmony with each other. Most think of utopia as an ideal "place," when it is more an ideal state of existence. It is a state within which creation and growth flourish. Think of utopia as a "stress-free," positive existence. In very simple terms, that is all it is. Utopia is a vision, an image, a structural concept. Therefore, it is related to "thinking" in a positive manner. Utopia identifies the condition of existence that can be produced by consistent, thought of a positive Nature.

This conscious thought of a positive Nature will lead to a utopian restructuring of our living conditions. This will provide the most nearly perfect conditions for positive change or growth. In coming to this understanding, recognize that enjoyment is an individual interpretation. As a kindred species, there are activities that are common to most all of us, like movies, vacations, horseback riding, or whatever. However, enjoyment _is_ the result of individual interpretation. Therefore, utopia is not something that can be constructed, because its blueprint would be limited to the conception of the individual doing the constructing. In application and practice, the "state" of utopia is a stress-free, full existence. It is a reality where all of our positive needs and desires are met, and we have no paramount worries or grave concerns. To have no grave concerns means that, by and large, when an individual thinks of something, they can manifest it without question or bother.

Perpetual motion is the condition of continuous movement in which energy would be inexhaustible or constantly replenished. Perpetual motion is "life." It is the movement derived from being alive. For utopia to exist there must be life. For life to continue to exist on this planet, we must reach a state of utopia or humans will destroy themselves, as well as the planet itself and the life upon it. Perpetual motion is a mechanical concept. Therefore, it is related to "doing" in a positive manner. Perpetual motion identifies the movement that results from the condition of existence that is produced by consistent action in a positive direction. This consistent action in a positive direction will facilitate the most nearly perfect conditions for indefinite procreation, which is the continued existence of life. We must seek to perpetuate life by growing into the likeness of that from which we are created. Just as a child aspires to be an adult, the human must aspire to be like the entity that created it. That entity is "GOD" (the Divine Energy of Life). What does this mean? Well, the Divine Energy of Life is positive in polarity, and manifests a state of supreme perfection. "GOD" created everything, so "He" is the standard; "He" is perfect and positive. Not one of us is "GOD," so not one of us can be perfect. However, since we are created in "his" image, we should always seek to be improving ourselves to become as near perfect as is possible. In doing this, each of us must move such that our actions are positive, and we must seek to bring forth the creativity that exists within each of us.

How we achieve all of this is through the word of "GOD." These positive words will lead us to the right, positive actions that will result in our salvation. Our salvation lies within our ability to reach a state of near spiritual perfection. It is within the power of the human to destroy all life. It is within the responsibility of the human to see that life exists forever. This is accomplished by endeavoring to become a positive part of our earthly existence, to sustain the inherent balance within the Divine System of Nature on a daily, continuous basis, seven days a week, three hundred and sixty-five days a year.

Being of the flesh, our physical impulses lead us to temptations. This, together with our inherent lack of understanding, makes betterment something that cannot be attained without making a conscious commitment to search for it. Our search needs to be tempered with perseverance and sacrifice. This endeavor requires that each of us exercise self-discipline. We must monitor ourselves and consciously right ourselves when we err, in our never-ending endeavor. The search will never end for the individual. This is because of the negative aspect of one's being that is a part of human Nature. Knowledge of this must not be allowed to hinder the individual pursuit of betterment or perfection. The task is accomplished through a conscious effort that occurs in our mind while we are going about our day-to-day activities. This should awaken the average person to the revelation that not one of us can simply "mosey" through life without thinking and planning.

Understanding spiritual perfection and trying to achieve it within the context of human existence is a way of life. It is a way of approaching the moments of individual existence that allows one's actions to correspond to the balanced system of Nature. As each person seeks to be the best he or she can be, this effort must be directed at every aspect of oneself. This means that each person must seek to better the body, mind, and soul.

Seeking betterment is a step-by-step (systematic) process that occurs over time. One must recognize this and take it one day at a time. As individuals go through each day, if they are seeking to be the best that they can be, they are doing things. They are "working" towards that goal. Even if what is being done is simply reading something, effort is being made somehow. Seeking knowledge is experiencing things. It is moving around. As a person seeks to achieve balance by avoiding excesses, this understanding keeps that person from lying around "too" much. It keeps that person from eating "too" much. It keeps that person from indulging in anything "too" much, because "too" much is excessive and leads to an imbalance within our world.

As this relates to the truth of "GOD," the fourth commandment is, "remember the Sabbath day, to keep it holy. six days shalt thou labour, and do all thy work: but the seventh day is the Sabbath of the lord thy "GOD": in it thou shalt not do any work." the implication of this commandment leads to the inference that each person is <u>supposed</u> to do some degree of work every one of the other six days of the week. Within the context of this "work," one should be exercising their entire being, i.e. the body, the mind, and the soul. One would be exercising the body by moving around and doing things. One would be exercising the mind because the mind would be actively generating thoughts that direct the body as things are being done. In addition, there would be movement and activity in the mind as a person seeks to absorb knowledge and better themselves. One would be exercising the soul if that person were living true to themselves. This is because the soul would constantly be engaged or deferred to for guidance in the right (or righteous) direction. The part of a person labeled the "soul" can indicate what is right and wrong for that individual. This is how each individual is to exercise all three elements of his or her being.

We were to live in utopia. This state of utopia was to be an outgrowth of Eden. It was to have been the most perfect conditions for growth for all living things. Over time, this growth would have been characterized as evolution. Like all the other livings things, the humans' growth and evolution was to encompass all elements of its being. The humans' body, mind, and soul were to all grow and evolve.

Within this framework, there was to be plentiful resources for the human to utilize to sustain and satisfy its body so that it would become the best it could possibly be at generating and conducting positive energy. There was to be immense opportunities for the human to experience new things and learn from them so that its mind would become the best it could possibly be at creating, attracting, and emanating positive energy. There was also to be an outpouring communal love and joy so that the human soul would become the best it could possibly be at leading the mind and body in the positive direction. This is the Will of "GOD" (the Divine Energy of Life).

We were given the
Responsibility of Dominion

…GOD said, let us make man in our image, after our likeness: and let them have dominion over the fish of the sea, and over the fowl of the air, and over the cattle, and over all the Earth, and over every creeping thing that creepeth upon the Earth. So GOD created man in his own image, in the image of GOD created he him; male and female created he them. …GOD blessed them, and GOD said unto them, be fruitful, and multiply, and replenish the Earth, and subdue it: and have dominion over the fish of the sea, and over the fowl of the air, and over every living thing that moveth upon the Earth.

The human was made in the image of "GOD" for a reason. Individually and collectively, we are the manifestation of "GOD" into the physical realm. That part of us that is in the image of "GOD" is our conscious awareness and our ability to generate creations. The responsibility of our dominion is to use these powers to perpetuate what "GOD" started. What "GOD" started was life. Our responsibility both individually and collectively is to oversee GODs' creations, and to create the conditions that perpetuate the existence of those creations. Dominion is the power or right of governing and controlling. It is sovereign authority. Having dominion as a species means that each individual is charged with the <u>responsibility</u> to oversee or govern. We are therefore <u>naturally</u> required to act responsibly with regard to the respective dominions we oversee. This is true whether that dominion is a household, a classroom, a workplace, a community, the wilds of Nature, anywhere within our nation, or any place on our planet. If the human species wishes to maintain its position and its existence, then its actions must be directed toward that end. Each human must continue to grow. Humans must work to be the best that they can be, following Nature's rule that the strong survive.

As animals, this means that our bodies must be strong to deal with the challenges of our earthly existence. We understand this within the context of being in the wilds of Nature. While civilization is not in the "wilds of Nature," this does not mean that Nature's rules or laws do not apply to our civilized existence. As a species group, our bodies must be strong for our species to survive. The rigors of civilized existence take a toll on the human body. The better shape we are in, the more prepared we are to meet any challenge. The stronger our bodies are, the more effective our metabolic and reproductive systems can be. As a species, our individual bodies must be strong in these areas for us all to continue to exist. As divine beings, our understanding must also be strong. Each of us must have a strong understanding of the elements and systems we govern. This is accomplished through learning and experiencing. We must study and know the words that define the nature of our existence and the actions thereof. Each of us must know the words of science. Each of us must know the words of mathematics (numbers). Each of us must know the words of philosophy, of sociology and psychology, of history and of current events. We know this to be true, which is why we have structured education systems. Each of us must study those words so that we know the dogma. Parents must teach the words that explain the need for responsible behavior to their offspring, because those children will inherit dominion from the elders of our planet as the young replace the old.

With our body and mind strong, we must move or act. In application, being civilized is characterized by actions that convey manners, class, intellect, and the like. Therefore, we must be strong in these areas. The rules of civility lie within the parameters of harmony, balance, ethics, morality, and truth. These labels characterized the parameters within which our conscious actions are to remain. Human life is not given substance simply by the words that define its existence, but by the actions of each individual. Therefore, each of us must take the words that define our existence, and manifest them through our actions. The words that define our reality are what we must work to accomplish. They are positive words like civilized, strong, moral, and ethical.

Not words like wild, weak, savage, and brutal. To give our acts direction, our soul must be strong. Our soul is made strong by faith, first in "GOD," and then in ourselves. This is so that our works or actions follow the right, common direction. That direction is positive. The essence of faith is "trust." Having faith in "GOD" is to trust that moving in a positive, right(eous) manner will make the systems of existence work as they should. Having faith in ourselves is to not only trust in oneself, but also to trust in each other. The only way to achieve this level of collective trust is if each individual commits to moving in a positive manner relative to the objective truth, rather than acting such that only doing what is positive for oneself is sought. To have the position of dominion means that each of us must act upon what is in the best interest of what we oversee and govern before doing what serves ourselves. Because our individual authority covers our entire planet, this means all our movements must be absent of selfishness and greed. As each of us manifests the best of our ability, we manifest "GOD" into our reality.

Throughout time, the human species has exercised its rights to the benefits derived from having dominion. We have collectively done so without having given full consideration to the long-term effects our actions would have on what exists around us. The approach to this consumption has been one characterized by a disregard for the finite nature of the resources of our planet and the frailty of the life upon it. We have now reached the point in human existence when we must collectively face the realities before us all. The position of having dominion that our species holds mandates that we all work together to perpetuate the existence of all living things. We must all learn to live in harmony with what exists around us, so that we too might continue to live. The human species is responsible for what happens to the life on our Earth. This is true regardless of whether or not individuals accept this as fact. The existence of our species is truly dependent upon a flourishing system of Nature, of which all living things are a part. Each of us must accept our individual responsibility for what happens on this planet. While huge groups of humans are governed by other humans, this in no way relieves individuals of their responsibility as defined by their collective position of having dominion. This is the Will of "GOD" (the Divine Energy of Life).

We were to be Obedient to Authority

…Out of the ground made the lord GOD to grow every tree that is pleasant to the sight, and good for food; the tree of life also in the midst of the garden, and the tree of knowledge of good and evil.

…The lord GOD commanded the man, saying, of every tree of the garden thou mayest freely eat: but of the tree of the knowledge of good and evil, thou shalt not eat of it: for in the day that thou eatest thereof thou shalt surely die.

…Now the serpent was more subtle than any beast of the field which the lord GOD had made. And he said unto the woman, yea, hath GOD said, ye shall not eat of every tree of the garden? And the woman said unto the serpent, we may eat of the fruit of the trees of the garden: but of the fruit of the tree which is in the midst of the garden, GOD hath said, ye shall not eat of it, neither shall ye touch it, lest ye die. And the serpent said unto the woman, ye shall not surely die: for GOD doth know that in the day ye eat thereof, then your eyes shall be opened, and ye shall be as GODs", knowing good and evil. And when the woman saw that the tree was good for food, and that it was pleasant to the eyes, and a tree to be desired to make one wise, she took of the fruit thereof, and did eat, and gave also unto her husband with her; and he did eat. And the eyes of them both were opened, and they knew that they were naked; and they sewed fig leaves together, and made themselves aprons.

Though our species has dominion over the elements of our Earth, our authority is not absolute. Each of us is a part of a system and subject to the authority of the system within which we move. In addition, each of us is subject to a supreme authority, that of "GOD" (the Divine Energy of Life). Within every system of existence there is a central "governing" point or entity around which the elements of that system revolve or function. This central point or nucleus is the centerpiece of each system and its controlling factor. It is the "authority" at the center of action and the elements related to that authority "revolve" around it. For each system of our existence to work rightly, each of us must recognize that there is, by Nature, a hierarchy within the structure of each system. This hierarchy leads to the development of a controlling influence, or an "authority figure(s)" related to a given system. "GOD" is the authority figure within the system of the Universe, and the elements of that system <u>revolve</u>

around this entity. The president is the authority figure within a system of government or a business, and the elements of these systems <u>revolve</u> around this entity. A teacher is the authority figure within a classroom, and the elements of that system <u>revolve</u> around that entity. The parents (which when married form one unit) are the authority figures of the family, and the elements of that system <u>revolve</u> around these entities. The human mind is the authority figure of the system of the human body, and the elements of the body <u>revolve</u> around it. These figures of authority are charged with the responsibility of establishing the patterns of movement, i.e. the rules, codes, and laws that govern the actions of the elements within the systems these figures influence. The entities of authority for the major systems of human existence are "GOD" (the Divine System of Nature), country (i.e. society and civilization), family (of which friends and community are a part), and self (in that order).

What does it mean to revolve around? Our first perception is the obvious truth related to circular motion. However, the earmark of civilized communication within the context of the English language is the ability to interchange words of similar meanings, and meanings of similar words. With this fact in mind, there is a more profound interpretation to be derived from a fuller interpretation of the word "revolve." Like many words within the English language, "revolve" has more than one meaning. "Revolve" also means to ponder and reflect. It means to consider carefully and at length.

It means to deliberate, to celebrate, to contemplate, to entertain, to excogitate, to meditate, to muse, to ponder, to pore over, to reflect, to ruminate, to study, to turn over, to weigh, to chew over, to cogitate, to mull, or to think through. In essence, each of us must understand that to revolve around something also means to think about that which each of us revolves around. As our thoughts lead to our actions, those actions will be impacted by the contemplation of that which each of us revolves around. That which we revolve around becomes the example by which our behavior or motion is patterned after.

Reflect upon this truth within our reality. Do we not embrace a pattern of movement or action that is influenced by the behavior of certain people with whom we interact? these are persons we "think about," i.e. friends, family members, teachers or other mentors, public or political figures, actors or sports figures, etc. Each of us <u>naturally</u> aspires to move or act such that we are likened to those we obey, respect, and about whom we think. In essence, we want and/or desire to have the same "system" of movement or action as that entity. That entity becomes the authority of our individual system of action, by establishing the pattern our movements follow. When we truly embrace the authority of the system of "GOD" (the Divine Energy of Life), we think about the nature of that system and its workings. Because of our thoughts of this entity, as well as our aspirations to be likened to it, we are led to have the same movements or actions that rightly associate us with this system. When we truly embrace the authority of the system of our country, we think about the nature of that system and its workings. Because of our thoughts of this entity, as well as our aspirations to be likened to it, we are led to have the movements or actions that rightly associate us with this system. The same pattern of exists when either the system of the family or that of the self is at the center of our minds.

Being obedient to the "governing" entity of a circumstance (or yielding to the authority thereof) is how living things are <u>guided</u> to work together to make each system work right(eous)ly. The recognition of, acceptance of, and obedience to authority is a crucial part of our spirituality and the Divine System of Nature. It is the factor of existence that makes all systems function correctly, positively, and/or right(eous)ly. Examining the natural occurrences (actions/movements) around each of us, it is easy to see that obedience of authority is the dominating factor of a correctly, right(eous)ly, or positively functioning system. When our Earth spins in only one direction, it is obeying the authority of Nature. When a tree sways in the wind, it is obeying the authority of Nature. When a bee completes the process of pollination, it is obeying the authority of Nature. When tidal water rises, it is obeying the authority of Nature. When a dog chases a cat, it is obeying the authority of Nature. Obedience to authority is simply having a pattern of movement (acting) within the rules, codes, and laws set forth by the authoritative entity. As conscious, free-willed beings, each of us must choose obedience over disregard if we are to right the ills of our current existence, as well as perpetuate our individual lives along with our species as a whole.

Choice is the significant and relevant element of free will that we must all place into the proper context of understanding. Each of us makes choices that we will be held accountable for during our "final judgment." Relative to GODs' judgment, we are not held accountable for what goes on in our minds, because this is where the choices are made. Think of the mind as a grand pool or reservoir of thoughts, both positive and negative. At any given moment, we select one or more thoughts from that pool to act on. As we must choose the positive thoughts to act upon, we must accept that the negative ones are still there. Because of this ability to "choose," each individual human being is clearly responsible for the actions of his or her body, as well as the circumstances that those actions create. It is the nature of our hearts and the direction of our actions upon which we will be judged. We must allow the positive aspects of our existence, both physical and spiritual, to guide us toward the right(eous) choices. We cannot eliminate all that is negative from our thoughts, and some of those thoughts will lead to negative actions. This is a defined element of spiritual reality, "the human will never be without sin." Yet, we must seek to overcome the negatives within our lives, and minimize the effect negative has on our reality. We must seek to be the best we can become.

There are examples of how the human species has failed the test of choice, i.e. whether or not we would be obedient and freely choose GODs' Will over human will. There was the instance that occurred in Eden. There was a "sign of divinity," an obvious message from "GOD" to humanity that gave warning of the impending peril that would result from choosing the wrong, incorrect, negative path. Within Eden is where "GOD" instructed the human(s) to obey "his" will. The sign was ignored, and the human failed this test. The choice made was to place the humans' will above that of GODs' Will. The human chose the direction opposite that of the Divine Energy of Life. As the Divine Energy of Life is wholly positive, the human(s) had chosen to have their energy follow the negative path. Choosing the negative path had a negative result, i.e. having to leave the utopia of old. After this, "GOD" allowed the human species to choose its own path, to see what its' will would be. It was to see if we would freely choose to obey "his" will by having movement in a positive way and producing positive energy. Left to our own devices, our species choose human will. We chose wickedness, evil, corruption, and violence. This again was the negative path for our energy, and it had a negative result. The period during which Noah built his ark was the "sign of divinity" indicating the impending peril that would result from choosing the wrong, incorrect, negative path. The sign was ignored, and the human failed this test. After Noah built the ark, the waters cleansed our Earth of its ills.

There was the instance of Jesus Christ. This time "GOD" let us <u>hear</u> that we should obey "his" will from one of our own species, another human being. Jesus Christ himself was a sign of divinity. To understand how what happened with Jesus Christ relative to GODs' Will vs. human will, one must truly open their mind beyond the influence of religion and embrace the positive energy generated by truth. By this I mean, each of us can feel within ourselves what is truly right(eous). As these words are digested, be objective and allow the inherent power of the soul to be the guide to what is positive and true. As an exercise in feeling what is right, positive, or truthful from within oneself, let us objectively examine the connection between two stories each of us should already know, the story of Moses and that of Jesus Christ. For these moments, forget what is taught about these occurrences, and forget what most believe about these happenings. Digest these words as though they were being experienced for the first time. Do so with an open mind. Interpret these words objectively, rather than with subjective bias and prejudgment. Let us set the standard for this examination by agreeing on the declaration that, regarding one's interpretation of GODs' actions, "GOD" is perfect, without flaw, incapable of error or hypocrisy. Hypocrisy is imperfect. It is an error, and it is a flaw.

Objectively speaking, it is easy to believe that a man was born so that at some point in his life, "GOD" would open "himself" up to this one man. With this revelation, this man was to save his people from the subjugation of human aggression that was manifested from uncontrolled selfishness and greed. It is easy to believe Moses was given Ten Commandments, divinely natural laws regarding a human's conduct. These Commandments were to establish the parameters of human interaction. They applied either to interaction with "GOD," or with other humans. It is here that this story becomes harder to believe if one is objective and feels the truth carried by the Divine Energy of Life.

One of those Commandments was "thou shalt not murder." Objectively speaking, how likely is it that our perfect lord, the Almighty "GOD," would specifically indicate that the human was not to murder another, then have the human, as a part of its destiny, brutally murder GODs' first recognized divine human gift to this species as a way of achieving absolution? I truly believe Jesus Christ was our savior, sent to us by our "GOD." However, my objectivity and divine cognition (inner truth) will not allow me to subscribe to the notion that our "GOD" sent us "his" most nearly perfect creation, the teacher to humanity, with the intent of humans murdering him as a way "cleansing" itself of sin. Particularly in light of the fact that one of "his" Commandments is, "thou shall do no murder" (the word "murder" is a more accurate translation of Exodus 20:13 in the original Hebrew). This murder was the humans' will. It was not GODs' Will. As I objectively examined the collection of words related to that circumstance of time, my understanding of the actions and the results led me to another interpretation of those events.

Since there are only Ten Commandments, it would seem very likely that each was critical to our approach to coexistence. Within the context of the system of Nature, death is a natural occurrence. For a human to die at the hands of another is not a natural death. I will not believe that "GOD" would instruct the human not to murder another, then have it do so to somehow "cleanse" itself of wrongdoing. The <u>only</u> way the human has ever been forgiven for sin is by GODs' grace. This salvation of ourselves is received through faith alone. Within the context of our understanding of reality, Jesus Christ was put to death, murdered at the hands of the romans. It was not justly done. It was not a sacrifice. The circumstances surrounding the crucifixion are not consistent with the ritual of sacrifice that existed at that time. The romans were the dominant empire of the time. Jesus Christ threatened the foundation of that empire, because people were hearing GODs' words and following Jesus Christ to "Him." Ergo, it was the romans who chose to eliminate or murder Jesus Christ with the help of treachery from some Hebrews. Could this truly be the <u>only</u> reason for the execution of Jesus Christ, a killing that resulted from the ignorance, selfishness, and greed of a few humans? In an effort to arrive at the truth, this is something one must consider.

"GOD" did send us Jesus Christ to be our savior. He was our savior within the context of him being born to teach us how "GOD" wanted us to live. He was to bear the burden of our sin. Through the misinterpretation and the manipulation of the truth, humanity has embraced the misconception that Jesus Christ died on the cross for only our sins. The validity of this misconception is rooted in the understanding that he was on the cross dying, and it was then that he gave us the message about him bearing our sins upon his death. The death of Jesus Christ was to strengthen the conscious link between ourselves and "GOD." This is because Jesus Christ was known to be real. Relative to our most pronounced physical senses, he was seen, touched, heard, and smelled (and tasted in some fashion). He also had the incredible power "GOD" had bestowed upon him, proving the Divine Energy of Life was real. Upon his death, as he (his energy) returned to "the father," our sensory recollection of Jesus Christ would strengthen and maintain our connection to "GOD" and "his" way of moving or living. In essence, upon his death, Jesus Christ was to become our link to "GOD."

However, with an open mind, one can easily infer what the series of events would have been had Jesus Christ lived a normal lifespan. The circumstances surrounding his death and the message about him bearing our sins was to be delivered in an entirely different way. As with all living things within the system of Nature, the intent of Jesus Christ's existence was indeed to live a normal lifespan. Jesus Christ was to live a long life. Had he done so, he would have established GODs' kingdom on Earth. During his life, he was to teach us many, many, many glorious things. In doing so, he would create for us an entire outlook of truth, before concluding with that which is considered the most important. Perhaps in some other moments before his passing, like on his death bed, he would have told us that although the path through righteousness is a difficult path to follow, we all must do so for as many years as each of us lives. In light of the reality that the human individual will never be without sin, we must maintain a vigilante, disciplined pursuit of righteousness during the course of your lives.

In addition, we must always have the goodness of "GOD" in our hearts, and act in a righteous (positive) manner while exercising good or right(eous) judgment. We must follow this path always. In those moments when the direction of our actions veered from this path toward sin and transgression, we must responsibly recognize our weakness. We must recognize our steps as "moments" of imperfection (perfection being the destination of our journey through life). As it is true that a few steps do not comprise an entire journey, we must not allow a trek down the wrong path or the burden of having taken those misdirected steps to slow or destroy our pursuit of betterment and perfection. Heaven forbid we should act in sin, but should our weakness allow it to occur, we must responsibly recognize what we have done. With humility in our hearts, we must pray for forgiveness. After this, we must then release the burden of that sin or transgression to Jesus Christ. After doing so, we must continue along the path of righteousness. It was Jesus Christ's intent to have us understand that we must "unburden" ourselves of the baggage that results from wrong by humbly asking for forgiveness in prayer and that we must repent in earnest. In doing this, we must look to him, Jesus Christ, as the bearer of the burden of our sin as he ascends to the father. The burdens were guilt and remorse, worry, self-pity, and the like. This is one of the most important aspects of our spirituality, and it is one of the things that Jesus Christ wanted us to learn. It was intended to give humanity the understanding of how it is to pursue perfection, knowing it can never attain it. How we are to grow into the best we can possibly be, without letting our weakness hamper or derail this process.

Anyone having been nailed to a cross, including Jesus Christ, would realize that the end of his or her time with on Earth was fast approaching. It was in those moments that Jesus Christ made the choice to impart to us what he thought was most important for us to know. It was something that he was supposed to teach us at some point later in his life. It was a divine truth given to us in haste, by a condemned "man." He did not have the luxury of time to place fully what he said in a proper perspective. Hence, it was interpreted literally. Through prophecy, Jesus Christ and others foretold of his death, and that he was to be the bearer of the burden of the sins of humanity. However, prophecy is not destiny. It is a vision of the future that is not based upon whether or not the future event is right or correct, just that it will happen. Anyone can change the moments of a circumstance that lies before him or her if there were knowledge of those events beforehand. This is because humans have a free will that allows each of us the opportunity to choose how we will react to the moments that we are confronted with. There is a choice as to whether or not one should be at a certain place at a certain time, dealing with a certain happenstance. Because of this, we cannot infer that because the murder of Jesus Christ was foretold, it was the "right" thing to have happen, or that it was what "GOD" intended. By allowing himself to be crucified, Jesus Christ perhaps intended to teach us all that each individual must accept the responsibility that is created by his or her actions. As well, each must be prepared to deal with the ramifications of the specific choices we make. As each of us performs the action of choosing, each of us has to deal with the reaction to our choice. That is the essence of the lesson we all were to learn from the crucifixion.

As each of us is aware of our own actions, we should be aware of the direction of those actions and be prepared for the reactions to them. If our action is to throw a ball in a straight line against a wall, the reaction of that is the ball will come back at the thrower. Because the person knows they threw the ball in the first place, they are mindful of its return to them and they can catch it, bringing the event full circle and to a positive conclusion. If in this circumstance that person decided to abandon the flow of reality and use their free will to choose an action that is contrary to the objective, positive action, they would disrupt not only their existence, but also the realities around them. If when that ball returned, that person did not follow the natural flow of the circumstance by catching it and they ducked, if there were another person behind them, the ball would hit that person. Not being aware of the throwers intent or actions, they would not be prepared for the reaction. The ball would strike them, possibly harming them, and definitely distracting them from their preparation for the reaction to their own actions. By not being responsible for our own actions and by not pursuing a positive resolution to them, we throw existence into chaos. As Jesus Christ chose to preach the positive words of the gospel (an action), he allowed himself to be crucified because that was the responsibility that resulted from his positive actions (the reaction). The crucifixion of Jesus Christ was the result of human will, and it changed GODs' origin intent for Jesus Christ. With all the divine knowledge given to Jesus Christ to impart to us, imagine how humanity would have developed had Jesus Christ been allowed to live a normal lifespan.

Using the power of inference, what would have happened was that Jesus Christ would have taught us all to live in harmony and peace. From him we would have learned to coexistence through compromise and tolerance. We would have learned to accept each other's differences and use them to better our collective existence. Jesus Christ was to lay the groundwork for the true kingdom of "GOD," i.e. another utopia. Utopia is the state of existence within which "GOD" would have the human and all other living things dwell. Inference will yield the state of existence that would have developed from the growth of Eden. Apply this same reasoning to the development of human existence had Jesus Christ lived an entire lifespan and been able to teach us the ways of love and kinship. The resulting condition of human existence would have been utopian. In both instances, this was the Will of "GOD." What destroyed both conditions was the humans' freedom to be selfish and greedy. The condition of existence that "GOD" has sought to create on our Earth has been the most nearly perfect condition for positive change. This positive change is growth. We must accept the responsibility of manifesting GODs' Will by creating this condition ourselves. We are the tools to facilitate positive change on this planet. No other animal species has the ability to change the conditions of this entire planet for the betterment of all living things. Only the human has this ability. "GOD" gave it to us for this purpose. This is the Will of "GOD" (the Divine Energy of Life). If we choose to work at this task, the rewards would be positively overwhelming.

"GOD" (the Divine Energy of Life) is perfect, good, right (eous), and wholly positive in nature. "His" will is characterized as such as well. None of the murders of the world committed in GODs' name was actually GODs' Will. It was the humans' will committed using the label for "GOD." None of the (holy) wars of the world committed in GODs' name was actually GODs' Will. It was the humans' will committed using the label for "GOD." There are those that would have us believe that the terrorist attacks of September 11, 2001, were "GOD" telling us to embrace "Him." This is not the truth. The Divine Energy of Life would not direct or lead a single human being to kill thousands of people to get the attention of humanity {however, this unfortunate happenstance is a "sign of divinity." It marks the place along the journey of humanity where the fork in the road begins}. None of the racist or otherwise bias acts of the world committed in GODs' name was actually GODs' Will. It was the humans' will committed using the label for "GOD." None of the rapes, thefts, abuses, or any of the like of this world committed in GODs' name was actually GODs' Will. It was all the result of the humans' will committed using the label for "GOD." In essence, none of the trials of the world is GODs' Will. All these acts, many done "in the name of "GOD"," are the result of the human placing its will above that of "GOD." Knowing the truth that these acts were wrong from deep within themselves, these perpetrators used the label for "GOD" to convince themselves and those around them that they were acting right(eous)ly. The tribulations of the world that occur as the result of Nature are not GODs' Will either. "Negative" is a manifestation of the Divine System of Nature. It is not a part of "GOD" (the Divine Energy of Life). It is a naturally occurring part of the system of existence. It is generated by the electrical circuitry related to the laws of magnetism, all of which are produced by the spinning action of our planet. It cannot be eliminated or avoided. Negative happenings are a naturally occurring part of our earthly existence.

The authoritative entities within our existence establish the parameters within which our actions and movements are to occur. These codes, rules, and laws form the system of actions that make up existence. Rules and laws govern the system of actions that occur within the entire Universe. There are laws of general science, laws of mathematics, laws of physics, laws of electromagnetic energy, laws of motion, laws of Nature, laws of philosophy, laws of the community and society, laws of family, and this list is not even complete. Because of this, we must recognize that our daily lives can be no different in that each of us must seek to obey the authority of the system within which we are functioning. All our actions must conform to the codes, rules, and laws of these authorities.

The system of actions that compose our daily lives must abide by codes, rules, and laws whether those actions occur relative to the authority of "GOD," our country, our families, or ourselves. The rules and/or laws of "GOD" take precedence over all others. Each of us must leave our selfishness and greed behind and do good works to ensure that we are a positive part of the Divine System of Nature. The rules and/or laws of our society (i.e. country) take precedence over those of the family and the self. Why must we consider the authority of our country after that of "GOD"? It is because it is truly within our nature as the members of a socialized species to consider the collective before individual concerns in an objective circumstance. The rules and/or laws of the family take precedence over those of the self. The family is the nucleus of a society. Without the family, the individual (self) would not exist within a socialized species.

From Eden, "GOD" expected humanity would grow as it satisfied its immediate needs. Each being was then to embrace every living thing it interacted with in a loving manner. Each was then to establish a "sense of self" by learning new things. This education was to be combined with individual creativity in such a way as to allow that individual to become "productive." Within GODs' Divine System of Nature, the reaction to the action of productivity is the reward of satisfaction. Once all this is accomplished, "GOD" knew "his" creation called "human" would have grown to "full-bloom," not unlike what happens within the kingdom of vegetation. The living condition becomes utopian when everything is in full bloom. Utopia is not an abstract concept. It is the label for the reality or living condition within which "GOD" intend humanity and all other living things to dwell.

As the human learned, became productive (i.e. creative), and blossomed, the species was to collectively assume the responsibilities of governing the elements of our Earth. The human was to govern over the creations of "GOD." This is the responsibility of each individual member of our species working collectively, because a bit of "GOD" is within each of us. It is only by working together that we can fully manifest the power of the Divine Energy of Life within the physical realm of existence. As the tool of "GOD," the human species was to use its abilities to create the conditions that would perpetuate the utopian living conditions that "GOD" established on our Earth at the beginning.

To be a positive part of the system that "GOD" created to generate life, the human was to obey the system of creation by respecting and yielding to authority. Within the divine chain of command related to the earthly existence, the human species holds the third position of authority behind that of the supreme authority of "GOD" (the Divine Energy of Life) and that of the Divine System of Nature. To believe in "GOD" is to recognize that the Divine Energy of Life generates the (positive) energy, or has the (positive) action, or moves in such a way as to have created the Universe and our Earth within it. To not want to acknowledge this, and yet, still subscribe to the truth of there being a system of creation, is to recognize that the Divine System of Nature generates the (positive) energy, or has the (positive) action, or moves in such a way as to have created the earthly systems of existence. The human species is to generate the (positive) energy, or have the (positive) action, or move in such a way as to create the systems to support the perpetuation of "GODs'"/Nature's original creation. To create a utopian living condition, the human species must commit their individual efforts to obeying the rules, codes, and laws of "GOD," their countries, their families, and their own code of (moral, ethical, or positive) behavior. If we are to sustain our commitment, we must also ensure that our social system supports us in our efforts. Evolution is a radical change in form. It is a gradual process within which something changes into a different and usually more complex, better form. As individuals, each of us must embrace this truth and do what is necessary to achieve this end because it is a natural element of the system of living. The human species, along with the social system that supports them, must evolve along with its technology to wield the power within both technology and the human effectively.

The human species must open its collective mind to embrace the divine truth of GODs' Will relative to the laws, rules, and codes of our earthly existence. Each of us must recognize the revelation that spiritual reality has sovereign authority over any other interpretation of existence the human creates within its mind. The parameters of spiritual reality are defined by the laws of Nature. The laws of Nature are a direct result of, and therefore based upon what happened after the Divine Energy of Life sent our Earth spinning upon its axis. Were this spinning action every to cease, everything the human recognizes as real would no longer exist. Therefore, <u>everything</u> of earthly existence is subject to interpretation relative to GODs' Will. This includes all the knowledge of which the human species has come to learn. It also includes the human species itself, along with its manufactured laws, rules, and codes of conduct. What this means is that the mandate of obedience to authority is all-inclusive. It encompasses all the systems of existence.

According to the Holy Scriptures, "GOD" physically gave the human species 10 Commandments to follow during its time of living. These Commandments govern the interactions between the human species and "GOD," as well as interactions with each other. There are only 10 of them. Therefore, each must have a profound significance. To have all human beings living within the parameters defined by the Ten Commandments forges the foundation for our mutual trust and respect. When an individual need not fear that those he or she interacts with will murder them or steal from them, that person can trust. When that person can be sure that others will not lie on them or seek intimacy with their spouse, that individual can trust. When one knows that they share with those around them a love of "GOD" and Nature, that person can truly respect others without apprehension. One of the most profound elements of a utopian existence is harmonious movement and interaction. To create this living condition for ourselves, each of us must live within the parameters of the Ten Commandments. It is not very hard at all. From any spot upon our Earth, at any point in time, an individual has at least 2,160 ways in which that person can choose to move. That person can choose to turn to any one of the 360 degrees (of a circle) from their original position. At any degree of that circular turn, that person has at least 6 more ways in which they can choose to move. That individual can move forward or backward, up or down, left or right. Not even taking distance of movement into account, at any moment in one's life, with at least 2,160 movements to choose from, to choose to move in such a way as to not break one of the Ten Commandments is not an impossible task. Moving within the parameters of the Ten Commandments is the Will of "GOD" (the Divine Energy of Life).

The Divine Energy of Life created Nature's system. It is the system that sustains all living things upon our Earth. The physical characteristics of the Divine System of Nature are balance, harmony (rhythm), and positive movement. The key element within the Divine System of Nature is positive energy. This positive energy is combined with the elements of Nature's system and those of the mineral kingdom to produce a specific positive movement within the animal and vegetable kingdoms. The positive direction of this movement is both upward and forward. It is growth. This growth ultimately leads to evolution and betterment. All living things are a part of the Divine System of Nature, and they each have a function they must contribute to make the system work rightly. The contribution of each living thing also helps to keep the system perpetually moving in a positive direction. Each of us must embrace our required actions, i.e. our responsibilities. Every individual must try to achieve balance between themselves and the world around them. The only way one can achieve a balance is to avoid excess. Each of us must move in harmony with what exists around us. In doing so, compromise and tolerance must be used to avoid conflict. Each of us must also be a positive part of Nature's system by moving in positive ways rather than negative ones. Our obedience to "GOD" requires that each of us do what is physically necessary to make this system work as it was intended. This is the Will of "GOD" (the Divine Energy of Life).

Civilization is an outgrowth of Nature. It is a part of the Divine System of Nature because the human species is a part of this system. Civilization is derived from the natural growth of the human species. As our species grew, our evolutionary actions lead to the creation of this system of existence. Every socialized species develops a system within which they all coexist and help each other. The civilized social system provides the structure that its members need to satisfy each individual fairly while growth continues to occur for all. If the human species is to continue to grow and evolve, civilization must evolve and continue to thrive as well. The civilized social system requires that individuals work for themselves and the collective. As well, it requires that members adhere to a pattern of behavior that produces harmony and fairness within its collective. Each of us must realize that to be a positive part of Nature's system, we must also be a positive part of our social system. This is the Will of "GOD" (the Divine Energy of Life).

For the human, moving in a good, right, and righteous way is key. If we interact and work together as the term "socialized (species)" implies, we can have our cake and eat it too. By following in the footsteps of Jesus Christ, i.e. living our lives with only goodness (towards life) in our hearts and accepting the responsibilities of life's mandates, we can manifest for ourselves many personal rewards. There are many great things derived from embracing spirituality and goodness, as well as from obeying authority and making a full commitment to having faith in "GOD" (the Divine Energy of Life). One great thing is that living in truth allows for some measure (not excessive) of self-serving, self-indulgent behavior on the part of individuals to satisfy the desires related to the flesh and the senses. One cannot say they are being truthful if they have no concern for pleasing themselves. This can be done while still satisfying our responsibilities to the Divine System of Nature. In Job 36:11, these words will be found: "if they obey and serve him, they shall spend their days in prosperity, and their years in pleasures." This is the Will of "GOD" (the Divine Energy of Life).

Satisfaction is GODs' Motivator

For "GOD" to put "his" plan into action, "He" had to cause living things to move on "his" behalf. "GOD" needed something to motivate living things to move in certain ways. To satisfy this need, "GOD" created a system for action on our Earth. The human, like all other living beings of our planet, need and/or desire to be satisfied. This is what motivates us to move. For living things to become what "GOD" would have them be, each entity has to seek satisfaction while moving in the same direction as does the Divine Energy of Life. That direction is positive. Each individual must understand their satisfaction from within the right(eous) perspective. The interpretation that is relevant to worldly reality must be combined with the interpretation relevant to spiritual reality. This must yield one perspective of understanding with regard to individual motivation. Our wants and desires are a manifestation of our fleshy existence. They are indulgences within our worldly reality. Our needs are a spiritual and/or natural manifestation. They are requirements of our spiritual reality. With the satisfaction of our needs, every part of our being is supposed to grow (body, mind, and soul). Satisfying our needs will lead to the development of the individual "GOD" intended each of us to become. What "GOD" would have us become is determined by the satisfaction of our true needs. However, this is only true if all our movements are in a positive direction or of a positive Nature. Therefore, to be right relative to the system of spirituality or the system of Nature, the satisfaction of our needs, as well as our wants/desires, cannot be attained through negative action.

In America, there are a number of different "sub-systems" that together make up the whole system of existence we call "American life." Two paramount sub-systems are the system of democracy, and the system of capitalism. Our capitalist economic system supports our ability to be a democratically free society. The driving principle of our economy is "supply and demand." The foundation of "supply and demand" is the need to satisfy ourselves. This is not a coincidence. It is a part of "GODs" plan." It is believed by most that have faith in the existence of our creator that there is a "plan." It is also believed that within the context of this plan, "GOD" controls or directs our actions. This revelation can be understood if placed within the context of understanding that attributes all of creation to "GOD". If "GOD" created the individual and wanted that person to do something, the way to accomplish getting him or her to do it would be to have that person want or need to do it. This would be a natural occurrence, reflective of our being a part of the Divine System of Nature. It is our positive needs, as well as our wants/desires, that lead us to what "GOD" would have us do.

Each of us must distinguish the satisfaction of our needs from the satisfaction of our wants/desires. The satisfaction of our needs is necessary. Each of us must have these things, as is a part of the Divine System of Nature. These needs are common throughout our species. The satisfaction of our wants/desires is not necessary to our existence, but satisfying them produces positive stimulation within each of us. Our wants/desires lead each of us down the path of our lives. By satisfying our needs, we do our part to perpetuate the Divine System of Nature. By satisfying our truly positive wants/desires, we make ourselves feel good while becoming what "GOD" intended each of us to become. Without water, food, shelter, or clothing, individuals would die unnatural deaths, and the life force of those individuals would no longer contribute to the Divine System of Nature. To satisfy the need for these things, one must work. Hence, working is a natural, spiritual action. Working is an action that is a part of Nature's system. This holds true for the actions that lead to the satisfaction of our other needs as well.

Relative to our wants/desires, each of us has goals that are specific to us. These become the basis for our personal values. Some people want to be mothers, doctors, comedians, or bankers, and some want a job that just pays the bills. Some people want to travel the world, and some just want to hang out with friends. If a woman did not <u>want</u> or <u>desire</u> to be a mother, we would have no mothers. If a person did not <u>want</u> or <u>desire</u> to be a doctor, we would have no doctors. If a person did not <u>want</u> or <u>desire</u> to be a comedian, we would have no comedians. Each one of these groups of individuals adds something significant and relevant to our system of existence. Our wants/desires determine the direction of the course of our individual lives. Each of us must come to a true understanding of what we truly wants/desires. The direction of our lives is not to be determined by what anyone else wants for us, but by what each of us truly wants for ourselves. Does an individual truly want to rob a bank? Or is it the money that person desires? Does an individual truly want to commit a carjacking? Or is it the vehicle that person desires? Does an individual truly want to rape someone? Or is it the sex that person desires? People must ask these questions of themselves. Each individual must exercise the strength to control themselves so that they can do the positive things to manifest their true desires. Each of us must determine from within ourselves what it is we truly want and/or desire, and pursue it with position action. Within these moments, each of us is seeking divine perfection.

By Nature, wants and desires drive our actions. However, some of us are taking shortcuts around the positive path by using a negative path to arrive at what is a positive destination for ourselves. This is not only wrong from a philosophical or moral standpoint. It is physically wrong relative to the Divine System of Nature. By having action or energy flow in a direction that is opposite of the direction that makes the Divine System of Nature function right(eous)ly, we are weakening the power of the Nature's system as a whole. This creates polarity conflicts within our Earth's electromagnetic field of force, affecting the system of Nature, our Earth and others around us. Negative action generates negative flowing energy that is released into the "field of force," or the air around us. The energy our Earth's system needs to perpetuate its positive (circular) direction must flow from a positive direction. Our negative actions and the resulting energy those actions generate are in conflict with the Divine System of Nature.

Because of the physical properties of our spirituality as defined by the laws of electromagnetism, the head of an individual is supposed to be positive. This is because the base of the spine is negative and attached (by a conductor running to the feet) to the neutral ground surrounding a huge positive core. Being good, right(eous), correct, and positive creates the necessary positive polarity within that individual's head. This allows that individual to fit into the systems to which his or her actions are applied in a natural way. Each of us is supposed to satisfy our respective wants/desires to fulfill our roles within "GODs" plan." However, we are supposed to do this in a positive manner while pursuing the perfection or betterment of ourselves. This will lead to what is called "self-actualization." Seeking the perfection of ourselves is working at being the best we could possibly be. "Best" is relative to the individual. To achieve it, individuals must combine discipline, patience, perseverance and sacrifice to the task of controlling the actions they direct at satisfying their wants/desires. This is the way Nature planned it.

More than likely, most have all heard the phrase "silence is golden." one reason this is true is because those quiet moments provide a "golden" opportunity for the human to discern the truth of itself as an individual, as well as what exists around him or her. To understand oneself requires that each of us search for an understanding of what lies within our being. Each of us must actually explore the inside of our bodies and our minds, listening for what is true about ourselves. In those quiet moments when an individual is alone with their thoughts and something random comes to mind, that person should ask themselves, "Where does that thought come from?"

Other good questions to ask are, "What is the real truth of who I am?"; "What is it I really want?"; "What makes me happy and content?"; "What makes me the most comfortable?"; "What really motivations me to do what I do?"; "Why do I do this or that?" What it means to listen to oneself is to ask these questions and <u>wait for an answer</u>. Once each of us comes to a "working" understanding of ourselves, each individual comes up with a set of parameters within which their actions are to adhere. This set of parameters is labeled the "value system" of that individual. Once that person defines their desires and motivations, they can determine a long-range path for their actions to follow.

No individual should ever forget that there are guidelines or parameters within which our actions are to occur as we go about satisfying ourselves. These guidelines or parameters are consistent with those that define the system of Nature. One could easily consider these the "primary set of values." All other sets of values are secondary and subordinate to these values. The label for this set of values is our "spiritual values." They are based upon the mandate to move in a positive direction or way to generate positive flowing energy, rather than moving in a negative direction or way and generating negative flowing energy. By applying this simple truth in our reasoning process and allowing it to determine the direction of our actions, we can begin to make strides toward our collective satisfaction while building a utopian existence for not only humankind, but for all living things upon our planet.

Truly, human existence is a most magnanimous gift. Following the Universe and our Earth, the human body is the next greatest creation generated from the Divine Energy of Life. It is the humans' conscious awareness and ability to infer that give it the capacity to <u>seek</u> the indulgence of its five to seven discernable senses in the pleasurable acts that generate sensation and satisfaction. Knowing that these acts and the resulting sensations and satisfactions can occur produces temptations for these experiences. Temptation is the result of the humans' weakness in the face of the perceived joy of stimulating sensation. There are three categories of temptation that lead our species to transgress. They are the lust of the flesh, the lust of the eyes, and the pride of life. "Lust" is the label for a passionate or overmastering (excessive) desire. The lust of the flesh is the overpowering (excessive) desire to stimulate the senses of the body. When the lust of the flesh is externalized, the desired stimulation is satisfied through touch, chiefly by sexual means. When the lust of the flesh is internalized, the desired stimulation is satisfied through the ingestion of substances that produce stimulation. These substances could be anything from food, to alcohol, to drugs. The lust of the eyes is the overwhelming (excessive) desire to stimulate the senses of the body by the acquisition of that which titillates the sense of sight. When this lust is externalized, the desired stimulation is satisfied through tangible possession. When internalized, the desired stimulation is satisfied through ingestion. The pride of life leads the individual human to believe itself greater (excessive) than another. Recognized or not, pride is the placing of oneself first above other humans, then above GOD, by the manifestation of thoughts that are self-glorifying. A braggart would exemplify the externalized exhibition of the stimulation associated with indulging in pride. Snobbery would exemplify the internalized manifestation of the stimulation associated with such indulgence.

Regardless of the strength of our will, it is undermined by the weaknesses of our being. Our physical existence is easily dominated by sensation. Resisting temptation should be looked upon as a test of the strength of human will and resolve. Dealing with the temptations that surround us in a positive, balanced manner serves to strengthen our character. Because of the length of our lives and the humans flawed Nature, each of us will sometimes give in to our desire for stimulating sensation. Each of us must look beyond the fault of our indulgence and learn about ourselves from our moments of weakness. As we grow through those experiences, we must learn about our weaknesses so as to avoid allowing them to lead us away from the positive path of our lives. The first time human Will leads to a happening, it is an experience and a lesson. The second time human Will leads to the same thing happening, it is a mistake. Each of us will make mistakes within our lifetimes. Each of us must strive to resolve our trespasses with positive actions.

Vice

As humans have common characteristics and behaviors relative to being of the same species, there are many individuals within our group that succumb to the same earthly temptations. The English-speaking family of our species has a label for these common temptations. They are called "vices." From a puritanical standpoint, a vice is a fault, a shortcoming, or an imperfection within one's behavior pattern. A vice is a "not so nice" habit based upon the views of a segment of our society. It is generally an act of indulgence, relative to one's personal weakness in the face of earthly temptation. Our collective society must accept the flaws and frailties that exist within our group when faced with temptation. While doing so, each individual that succumbs to temptation must humbly understand that a balance must be struck between personal indulgence and harmful action relative to what the collective interprets as being negative in nature. If an objective examination is made of what has been deemed negative in nature, regardless of what it is, one will ultimately find that it is based upon some degree of excess leading to imbalance. Each of us must be made cognizant of the ramifications of exceeding the limits of a balanced exist. This balance relates to our understanding of everything from work and play (body) to competition and fairness (mind), to movement and Nature (soul). The importance of seeking balance with one's actions must be taught in the home. It must be a part of the curriculum within our schools. It must be a message contained within the expressions of our media systems. It is so important that our society must be exposed to this divine truth as often as possible.

It is true that there are those within our social system that indulge themselves in vices. They do so because for them it is a positive choice. In some way, those individuals are stimulated and satisfied. It is also true that most all within our society are aware of the harm produced by those that abuse the elements of our existence. A balance must be sought such that those that responsibly and peacefully partake of self-indulgence are not criminalized for doing so. If something produces little public harm and is desired by many, outlawing that something because it is deemed unacceptable by others is not universally effective. That means it is a flawed approach to solving the problem, not a more perfect one. Not one of us can fully experience and learn from something by denying its existence. For a species that is naturally compelled to stimulate and satisfy itself, this stance of denying our innate desire to indulge in vice will only lead to conflict. Controlling the exposure to that which exists is a more balanced way of dealing with the reality of anything. Seeing lions and tigers roamed about is a pleasurable experience. Yet, they are also deemed harmful to human existence. We do not outlaw them and try to eliminate them from the face of our Earth. Instead, we control our exposure to them such that some sort of balance between their existence, our enjoyment of their existence, and the possible harm they pose to our existence is achieved (at least this is the aim). With regard to the indulgence in vice, individuals need to exert control over themselves by using the positive energy from within to command their bodies to react correctly and rightly. As well, societies must make allowances for such indulgences.

As our social system evolves, we must collectively accept the perpetual existence of vice. Activities that fall into this category have been around since the beginning of the humans' existence. As well, they can be expected to remain a part of the humans' future. The human will never be without flaw. We all must reconcile ourselves to the reality that certain transgressions have become a part of human existence because of this fact. These are things like gambling, prostitution (and pornography), non-destructive perversion (i.e. consensual deviate sex, homosexuality, etc.), and self-medicating with what are now considered illicit drugs. By accepting these things as a part of the human living condition, our collective in no way condones neither them nor harmful acts in general.

Simply, we would be incorporating our non-destructive weaknesses into a restructured, controllable behavioral pattern. In doing this, we would be providing an outlet for these desires as the social collective continues to work to get beyond succumbing to the temptations that lead to abusive behaviors. The word of "GOD" (the Divine Energy of Life) is intended to be applied to the factuality of the present moment. We must apply biblical teachings to the realities of our time, and make the necessary adjustments and allowances so that what has been learned is accurately applied to the system or pattern of circumstances within which we exist as a part of Nature. Those adjustments and allowances will be few if each and every one of us allows the goodness within our hearts to come forth. The nature of a human being exhibiting such goodness of heart is that his or her actions are positive and good. In this state, a person's few transgressions are generally related to their personal indulgence rather than being committed against others. Considering vice from a spiritual standpoint, the significant and relevant question to be answered is whether or not vice and/or self-indulgence is sinful. An objective examination of the Ten Commandments yields a divine truth that sheds tremendous light upon the answer that is hidden in plain view. Examine these Ten Commandments:

THE TEN COMMANDMENTS

And GOD said all these words, saying, I am the lord thy GOD,

(1) Thou shalt have no other GODs before me.

(2) Thou shalt not make unto thee any graven image, or any likeness of anything that is in heaven above, or that is in the Earth beneath, or that is in the water under the Earth. Thou shalt not bow down thyself to them, nor serve them.

(3) Thou shalt not take the name of the lord thy GOD in vain; for the lord will not hold him guiltless that taketh his name in vain.

(4) Remember the Sabbath day, to keep it holy.

(5) Honor thy father and thy mother.

(6) Thou shalt not (murder).

(7) Thou shalt not commit adultery.

(8) Thou shalt not steal.

(9) Thou shalt not bear false witness against thy neighbor.

(10) Thou shalt not covet thy neighbor's house; thou shalt not covet thy neighbor's wife, nor his manservant, nor his maidservant, nor anything that is thy neighbor's.

Each commandment refers to an act of transgression either against "GOD" or against another human being. None of the Ten Commandments relate to an individual committing a sin against themselves. In light of this, it is a stretch of the truth to declare that it is sinful for an individual to seek to stimulate his or her God-given senses. As well, the same applies to the indulgence in an experience that produces satisfaction while not causing harm to another life. Human harm from self-indulgence is usually the result of the abuse of a given element of existence. It is at this point, where most any action enters the realm of being transgressive. This is because the basis of all sin is excess. The element of existence we call a "gun" is neither harmful nor sinful because it exists. Harm and sin are manifested when a gun is used in an excessive or extreme manner. Because of the humans' degree of awareness, it is required to manifest the control and the discipline necessary to confine its "use of things" to the limits of responsible action. This is rather than indulging in the undisciplined, irresponsible behavior that is characteristic of excess.

This must be done by each individual as a matter of self-control. We cannot fully legislate human action. Self-discipline cannot be established through the creation of laws. Not one of us can relinquish the responsibility of controlling our individual actions to an entity outside of our own bodies. Once this happens, we cease to be free. To have a truly complete acceptance of "GOD" and the corresponding spiritual doctrine, one must "conquer" the flesh, i.e. the senses of the body. It truly becomes mind over matter. This "mind over matter," or control of the body, is manifested by the human in the form of patience and perseverance, sacrifice and discipline. This is not to say that individuals will not still succumb to the temptation of stimulation and sensation. We all will at some point in time. However, when one does give in to temptation in any form, he or she needs to have an understanding of what their actions will lead. Individuals must focus on rising above their personal weaknesses that have resulted in their transgressions, rather than focusing on the pursuit of personal satisfaction. If we as a society accept our "weaknesses" as a true part of us, i.e. a reality, and provide controlled outlets for the indulgences of individuals, we will have all our behavioral bases covered. The main characteristics that each person needs to manifest are patience and perseverance, as well as sacrifice and discipline.

Each of us must recognize the necessity of balance and repentance, as opposed to excessive indulgence and disregard. Sometimes there will be negative energy present that keeps one from doing something positive. It very well may be negative energy in the form of negative thought. In dealing with this, come to realize the basis for the need to release oneself of the burden of negative energy. Negative thoughts lead to acting in the wrong direction, and will lead to a negative circumstance in our reality created by the individual with those thoughts. In an extreme instance, this is the basis of sin.

If an individual gives in to that thought, that person must recognize that this is weakness. Each of us has weakness. Each of us must work to strengthen ourselves against weakness. If a person allows their mind to keep recognizing what that negative thought caused them to do, it keeps that person from getting back on the positive path. If the burden of negative thought and sin are not consciously released, it remains within the mind, consciously and subconsciously. There, the negative mental energy conflicts with the inherent positive energy, causing internal turmoil. Once a person consciously recognizes their transgression, and excises it with repentance and penance, that person can resume their positive pursuit. Repenting in earnest allows each of us the opportunity to move on without restriction and with a clear conscious. Paying penance replaces the positive energy lost because of such an act. As long as individuals resume their positive course of action, the proper direction can be regained. The greater one's degree of positive thought, the greater one's ability to produce positive action. The more an individual expends positive energy, the more positive energy that individual will draw to himself or herself. This is because polarized energy within a circuit (and more specifically the earthly circuit) travels in one direction, individuals are conductors within this divine circuitry.

An objective examination of the truths we know of infer that if there truly is a spiritual purpose for living things, it is to experience "being" in an effort to acquire and transmit knowledge back to the source of our creation. From this, it can also be stated that to avoid an experience is contrary to this effort. Some experiences are more difficult to withstand than others are. To facilitate the circumstances where those that were strong and capable enough to do so were positioned to experience the difficult elements of our reality, the Divine System of Nature was created such that the distribution of experiences is based upon a formula of wants, desires, effort, will, and random occurrence. To ensure that every possible perception of experience is attained, the elements of tribulation, success, and failure are injected into the equation of circumstances. To keep each of us pursuing experience and/or knowledge, a reward is placed within the equation.

An individual's reward manifests itself in the form of gratification, as experienced through the pleasurable stimulation of any number of the senses within that individual's body. This is true whether the actual reward takes the form of joy and happiness, or a new car. The reward is still manifested as a feeling or sensation. Sensation and stimulation are natural, divine parts of the system within which we live, i.e. the Divine System of Nature. To deny or deprive our senses has been shown to be futile, and in many cases torturous. To control them is what "GOD" demands, and therefore, control is what we must demand of ourselves. The truth of this is exemplified within the context of the very nature of our being. It is manifested in the form of our inherent need to exert self-control and/or self-discipline.

One could argue that this declaration implies that murder and rape, along with other human atrocities can be justified by this interpretation of reality because these things too need to be experienced. No one can justify doing such negative, harmful things. However, regardless of how positive and utopian human existence becomes, there are going to be those that commit deviate, criminal acts. If all acquired knowledge does in fact return to a single, common source, then it is not necessary for every human to have the same experiences. Therefore, relative to there being a physical experience for every circumstance of reality, every possible experience is had as long as some individual has one of every experience. The deviant, harmful experiences of our existence are, however unfortunate, naturally accounted for as a part of the Divine System of Nature.

The human species is born into sin, and it will never be without sin. This in itself explains the need for constant repentance. If our species is to evolve as a group of civilized societies, we must all reconcile ourselves to the truth that certain transgressions have become a part of human Nature. Again, these are things like gambling, prostitution (and pornography), non-destructive perversion (i.e. consensual deviate sex, homosexuality, etc.), and self-medicating with what are now considered illicit drugs. It is written that we are to be judged on "judgment day." Upon what are we to be judged? The divine test is whether the human can exert discipline and control over the awesome power that lies within itself, or not. This power is the result of the human having been created in the image of "GOD." We must have control of the mind to overcome the temptations to give into the stimulation of the senses of the body, and discipline ourselves so that we consistently choose the path of righteousness. If the human can accomplish that, the reward is not only complete awakening to the truth, but a near perfect utopian existence. If the American population embraced goodness and positive energy as "GOD" intended, each of us would be "reborn." With unified focus and effort, the American family can use the information superhighway together with our economic, social, and political power to realize our spiritual destiny. By doing this, we can avoid many of the chaotic episodes of this new millennium.

What we must also reconcile ourselves to is that as individuals, each indulgence of our wants and/or desires is an important part of our mandate to experience. As each individual indulges themselves in the pleasures being alive offers us, each must remember the parameters within which our movements must remain. Each of us must move in a positive direction. Each of us must balance our movements and avoid excess. Our individual movements must not harm or endanger any living being around us outside of the laws of Nature. As well, each of our movements must contribute to our overall growth and the perpetuation of life. Through the pursuit of our wants/desires is how each of us is to arrive at the destination of our existence. As a species, we can no longer hide the truth about ourselves from each other. Utopia is a state of existence where truth, happiness, and liberty reign. It is not a state of existence where denial, sorrow, and persecution flourish.

The More Perfect Union

The first human (Adam), was the most perfect creation of "GOD." That human was composed of the union of the body, mind, and soul. Over time, each element of his being was to grow and become better, or more perfect. His body was to get better and grow in strength as he worked at providing for his needs and played as he desired. His mind was to get better and grow as he learned from the perceptions derived from the senses of his body as he experienced each and every moment of his earthly life. His soul was to get better and grow as he became insightful and wise. He was to use his body, mind, and soul to understand how to guide himself in the positive direction. He was to live in harmony with the other life around him, and learn how to produce (create) positive actions that would help to sustain and perpetuate all those living things. Adam was to become a better person, as a more perfect union of his elements developed.

However, being alone was not ideal for him. So "GOD" created a female (eve) to partner with him and make his existence more perfect. She, like her male partner, was to become a more perfect individual. This was to enhance their partnership, making it a more perfect union. As they grew and got better at living in harmony with what existed around them, together with their giving aid to the perpetuation of the living things they encountered, they would form a more perfect union with their environment. They were to have offspring, leading to the formation of a human family. Each individual member was to grow and become better through more perfect unions. All those individuals were to work together to enhance their all-inclusive existence by forming more perfect unions. Had the human followed GODs' Will, the condition of existence for all of humanity would be utopian because of the continual process or system of growth, betterment, and the formation of more perfect unions.

That was then. This is now. Within the "now," America is in crisis. Our social system has problems that must be addressed if we are to maintain our current standard of living and go into this new millennium with stable progression. We can all feel in our hearts that the morality and code of ethics that we need to govern ourselves during the countless hours of our lives is faltering. As a society, we are headed for the same catastrophic upheaval as beset the ancient cities of Sodom and Gomorra, and for the same basic reasons, the spiritual and moral degradation of society. We cannot allow ourselves to be indifferent to each other and our society. America is our home and our country, and it is in crisis.

Our social system is losing the order upon which it was built. We see the rampant abuses of people, places, and things. American society is dividing and self-destructing. We look upon difference with uncompromising intolerance. Racial and bias crimes have become increasingly more prevalent. Our cities are unruly to say the least, and they are occupied by a largely uneducated, poor population that is made up of mostly minority individuals. White America is building a more affluent, suburban existence. Yet, the problems they are running away from are slowing creeping into their respective communities. This translates into social decay in both our urban and rural communities. Violence occurs in our midst as though it is a part of civilization, and it is not. Violent acts occur so frequently that often only the more horrendous of acts move us to react.

The nucleus of our nation, the American family system, has all but fallen apart. Our spiritual and family values are almost non-existent. There are men fathering children without concern for the wellbeing of their creation. Parents of "Baby-Busters" and "Generation Xers" are having to repeat their child-rearing experiences with their grandchildren because their single-parent offspring are overwhelmed by their responsibilities as well as for other more unfortunate reasons. There are parents who are killing their children, and children who are killing their parents.

There are children having children. Without the guidance they need, many children have developed their own set of values based upon a child's immature, superficial view of life. These children are turning to each other to provide the value system and support they are not getting at home. They are coming together in the form of "gangs," with the intent of attaining the food, shelter, clothing and other materials that support the shortsighted value system their immature minds have constructed. The rebellion of our youth is partly the result of the frustration and lack of hope that they experience when they mentally project themselves into some future circumstance of existence. Within their minds, they do not see a clear path that leads them where they want to be, and it appears as though their world has an end. If their dream were sleeping on a beach in Hawaii, they do not see the prospects before them that will provide that opportunity, and they doubt they will live long enough to attain it anyway. Because of poor parenting, social chaos, poverty, pollution, terrorism, war and many of our society's other ills, they do not see living as a prosperous and sustainable happening.

With no inner sense of self-worth or value, both children and adults act in desperation to achieve respect and short-term gratification. The adolescents of our society, who will lead our nation in the years to come when they are elders, are not arming themselves with the academic or social skills necessary for this task. Nor do they have the ethical, moral, or spiritual values necessary to lead a people. They have no motivation or hope of creating anything unique and positive, because their vision of the future is unstable and without focus. Adults are supposed to teach the young a spiritual, moral, and ethical value system upon which to build the foundation of their character. Without a foundation for character, our children act in ways that are not true to themselves, doing what is not really in their "hearts" to do. Without this foundation, they are unprepared to select the proper direction for their actions. It is like taking a child and placing them in the wilderness, and briefly describing their destination to them and telling them to go find it. From that point, they are not supplied for the journey. They have no idea which direction to go in, because it is not merely north, south, east, or west; at that point that child is dealing with the degrees of a circle. There are also numerous dangers out there, both known and unknown. What must be done in this circumstance is the same thing that must be done to prepare our offspring for their journey through life within a civilized society. We must supply the child with the wears it will need to survive. We must teach him or her a sense of direction. We must provide them with a "map" that will lead them to the destination that is their future. To ensure their safety, we must be there to provide protection and guidance.

The cost of living in America is on the rise, and incomes are going down. Children are either not leaving home when they become adults, or they are returning numerous times for economic reasons. This increases the financial burden on the parent(s), and does little for the maturing process of the child. The opportunities within the job market have become more dependent upon communication skills and intellectual ability. For those who are unprepared for this change, income levels are declining to a point where the dollars received fall far short of what is needed to provide individual independence. Long-term employment with one company is almost a thing of the past. Promotions take much longer to earn. Poverty and homelessness are two missed paychecks away for a vast number of Americans. To compound these problems, the economy is not structured so that it meets the needs of all members of our society. We can see that the policies of the corporations and the politicians are aimed at profit and control. The system that supports our lives is driven by a union between business and government that serves those in control of resources. This control of resources gives them power. The true power of this nation is in the hands of its people. However, the people need access to resources. Therefore, if one controls access to resources, one controls the people and the power. Our government, which is supposedly "for the people, by the people," tends to yield to those in control of the power, seemingly only those with resources and position.

Within all civilized societies both past and present, there have been activities that are deemed to be in conflict with the standards of that society. These activities are usually judged immoral and/or evil. We have labeled these activities "vices." Some of these "immoral" and "evil" activities are prostitution, gambling, drinking and using drugs. This list can go on a bit depending upon to whom one is speaking. Our abuse of such activities is what is decaying the spiritual and moral fiber of our social system. Many members of our society have exalted indulgence and excess to a position of esteem greater than that of "GOD." For the most part, individual and collective human behavior is out of control.

Our country is physically falling apart and in need of repair. Many of the buildings in our cities are deteriorating, and the housing there is dilapidated. Our nation's roads and bridges must be enhanced to bear the burden of ever-increasing amounts of volume and weight. We are polluting all the areas of our Earth's remaining natural environment in the name of progress. Blind selfishness and greed driven by profit is leading to uncalculated destruction of our Earth's natural resources in the face of the realization that we need the air, the water, and the soil to survive. We are recklessly destroying the trees that produce the air when need to survive, and the forests that stabilize our weather patterns. We are polluting the oceans as though we will never need them as a source of food and water. In the name of expansion and progress, we have used asphalt and concrete to "shield" us from the barbaric practice of walking on and living on the bare ground. This has led to the elimination of huge areas of natural habitat. in addition to this, through nuclear testing and mining we have poisoned vast areas of the soil to such a degree that, not only can no edible food be grown in it, but it is also dangerous to live in proximity to such contaminated areas. The rampant destruction of our environment is almost out of control.

There are terrorist groups made up of foreign nationals originating from outside of our nations border who are bent upon destroying our nation for fanatical reasons. There are terrorist groups made up of American citizens originating from within our nations border who are bent upon destroying our nation for fanatical reasons. Utilizing the very liberties America was founded on, these groups strike out at innocent people to satisfy their skewed desires. The list of problems plaguing our nation goes on and on. We see all these realities around us, but we ignore these realities because we know in our hearts that to acknowledge our recognition of these things means that we must react to them. It would mean that we would have to do what was right(eous) to correct the wrongs we see. Rather than expend our limited energy doing what is right, objectively speaking, we would rather use our energy to satisfy ourselves, subjectively speaking. To react to reality in this manner is to deny the truth. That truth is that each and every one of us is responsible for the circumstances that exist in this country. Additionally, it is the citizenry of this great land called "America" that must actively right the wrongs of our living condition. This is true whether those wrongs occur within our homes, our communities, or our nation as a whole.

During the humans' existence, the cultures of four long ago civilizations made great contributions to current-day civilization, they were Mesopotamia, ancient Egypt, Greece, and Rome. Mesopotamia gave us writing, metallurgy, law, and such basic inventions as the wheel, the razor, the frying pan, and the sixty-minute hour. Ancient Egypt developed great technical skill in art, mathematics, and construction. Ancient Egypt is from where scholarship arose. Greece was a laboratory of democracy. Rome gave us Catholicism and the basis for modern civil law among other things. These once great civilizations no longer exist. America is in the same league as these four, and it may not exist for as long as most think. As john underwood once wrote in the Boston globe, "civilizations do not give out, they give in. In a society where anything goes, eventually, everything will." Look at this quote with regard to our own society and the way that it has progressed. We have gone from a society that was capable of utter outrage at the use of dogs and water cannons on human beings, to one that is now able to justify the acquittal of police officers videotaped violently beating a human being into submission with clubs.

Though each of the aforementioned great societies had its own reason for collapse, one thing is clear. Whatever the reason, history tells us that large-scale chaos precludes the destruction of a civilization. They do not disappear without considerable pain to the immediate populous.

We, as Americans, are headed for a chaotic and turbulent future as the result of many things. One of which is that we have been progressively relinquishing responsibility for our wellbeing to other people. These other people are mean political parties, civic organizations, welfare administrators, teachers, salesman, police departments, employers, the media, drug dealers and other criminals. The rat race has caused us as individuals to think only in terms of ourselves, and maybe our families. As long as we have the liberty to pursue our self-serving sources of enjoyment, or more precisely put, personal stimulation, we will tolerate most anything as long as we do not feel pain. This selfish approach to living will ultimately lead to our own social chaos. This is true because selfishness is contrary to our very Nature as a socialized species.

In essence, people are lost. They are confused to the degree that they are unable to make any real sense of human existence and their place in it. The sheer magnitude and number of our nation's problems require the unified effort of all Americans if we are to solve them to our collective satisfaction.

In 1915, former president teddy Roosevelt gave a speech in New York. In it, he criticized U.S. citizens who identified themselves by dual nationalities. He said, "There is no room in this country for 'hyphenated Americanism'." in essence this means that if one is born on American soil, or are otherwise a legal American citizen, they are a member of this group we call "nation." As such, each of us has a responsibility to the group, i.e. the collective. It is plain and simple. A major obstacle to our successfully addressing the destructive issues that we face as a citizenry is our attitudes as individual Americans. We must change our way of thinking as well as our frame of mind.

There is a distinct difference in thinking "for" yourself, and thinking "of" yourself. So many of us are afraid or are otherwise unable to take responsibility for our being and the actions we produce as individuals. This is because of an inherent fear of the power an individual truly has, and the innate knowledge that it must be wielded responsibly. We are not sure what to think, how to act, or what to do with our lives, so we look to the media, public opinion, and others to define our existence for us. We want them to tell us what we should be thinking, and what we should be doing, and what we should be feeling. It is very easy to fall into this trap. The reason is that by letting others think for us, we are left with the time and energy desired to submerge ourselves in thoughts "of" ourselves. This is wrong because in doing this, we are giving away our inherent individual power. A person must think "for" themselves to maintain control over themselves and to wield the influence of their power effectively within the context of what exists around them.

In thinking for oneself, an individual must respond to a circumstance in a way that is right for them. This can only be truly determined by the individuals themselves. This determination is to lead to positive or perfect resolution, in a manner of action that remains within the parameters of what is positive and right(eous). These parameters should naturally correspond with both spiritual and civil codes, rules, and laws. While thinking for oneself, an inherent element of our being becomes prevalent. That is the natural tendency to help others of the human community, as is consistent with the behavior of members of a socialized species. This must be done while always being guided by intellect, instinct, intuition, and righteousness. It is not positive or perfect resolution if the conclusion to a circumstance has a negative impact upon an entity involved that one is aware of, and it could be avoided through the use of compromise and tolerance. Thinking for oneself and doing what is right for ourselves as individuals we can all feel is the right direction for our actions if we listen to our innermost thoughts.

There is another reason individuals must seek to perpetuate independent thought. It has to do with the issue of creativity. There are nearly always different ways of doing "one" thing. No one person thinks exactly the same way as another, so no one person can figure out all the ways of doing.

Being focused on thinking "for" oneself generates the individually unique thoughts that are the foundation of creativity. Each and every one of us as an individual has something to contribute somewhere within our collective existence. Our contributions are something unique derived only from ourselves, something specific to the individual. The basis for unique creative ability cannot be manifested within the mind of a person focused on thinking "of" oneself. When this is the case, that person is not freely examining the objective circumstances before him or her. That person's thought process is not aimed at figuring out a "more perfect" or better way of doing. Being focused on oneself and the stimulation of the primary (5) senses thereof allows a person to be easily led. To be told what to think, what to feel, and how to act stifles an individual's ability to manifest creative thought.

We must all strive together to produce a collective living condition that will reduce stress. Selfishness, greed, and the stress that results from these elements of our lives cause all of the problems in our society. Because of the competitive complexities of the situations in our lives, we feel we do not have the time to sit down and analyze the ramifications of the choices and events we face on a day-to-day basis. If each of us had the time to sit down in a completely relaxed environment and analyze the circumstances we face, we would inevitably ask ourselves the questions that will lead to better solutions. To reach this point, which all of us are capable of, we must come together to reduce the stresses in our collective lives. To do this, we must mature, we must trust, and we must be responsible. As an individual, a man, a woman, a boy, or a girl, we may be able to rationalize the behavior we choose. However, as a citizen of this country, we must act responsibly with respect to the collective to fully exercise our citizenship and form a more perfect union.

It is easy for any individual to wonder why the citizens of the greatest nation in the history of humankind do not make a greater effort to correct the problems we face. It is because individuals are so caught up in the circumstances of their day-to-day existence that they think their priority is to worry about their immediate situation and let our government deal with correcting our societal problems. The intent here is not to say that this way of thinking is wrong, but that it is too limited. We do (and should) expect our government to contribute revenue, resources, and management to the betterment of our collective being (or existence). However, we as citizens are never absolved of our responsibilities as laid out within the constitution. Scholars of all disciplines tell us that we do not use the full capacity of our brainpower. Well, how can we if we continue to place limits and restrictions on our concept of reality and our thought processes? We need to open our minds and raise our level of consciousness so that we are able to understand that our personal lives are just one aspect of our being. An aspect to which we could fully devote our energies if we lived in a vacuum, but none of us does. Because of the nature of community life and the fact that we are sentient, social beings, we must interact to survive. As well, the solutions to most of our society's problems must come from the collective. "The collective," put in more familiar terms, is "we the people."

Over the last forty years, our society has seen some significant changes in our value system.

In an effort to ensure that our population does not lose any freedoms, we as a whole became more tolerant in our acceptance of degrading, vulgar, barbaric, violent behavior and the depiction of violent expression, regardless of how offensive and destructive our interpretations of these realities may have seemed at the time. This liberal acceptance of negative expression together with the misconception of the American dream to be the pursuit of immediate self-gratification gotten through whatever means, has led to a level of street violence that defames the word civilized. These acts should be characterized as domestic terrorism. At present, we do not have a common set of values to serve as an adhesive to hold our social structure together. In the future, the American society of today could very well be looked upon as just another great civilization that no longer exists. Should this be our fate, it will truly be a travesty because of our technological and social development, and we will have no one to blame but ourselves.

Values are what perpetuate nations. Having values allows the individual to function positively in a given situation. A positive set of values strengthens an individual's character and resolve. Values are contagious to the degree that, the positive action of a person with a strong sense of values as well as their approach to life, gives others the strength they need to work toward their goals through example. "Work" being the operative word. I once heard someone say something simple that I found very profound, "the only place success comes before work is in the dictionary." One must understand that everything is the result of effort or work. Imagine the reality of a circumstance in which birth was just a process by which we floated down to our Earth as five-year-old, with no parents assigned to be responsible for us. To survive on the planet regardless of what form society took, we would have to do things, put forth effort, or work to ensure our survival. Consciously apply this realization to life's present circumstance. The truth in it is no different. Childbirth is definitely a different experience, but beyond that, the facts differ very little. Our social structure dictates that our parents be responsible for us for only the first eighteen or so years of our lives. This is the formative, preliminary period of human life. It is to be utilized to prepare oneself for the challenge of surviving within our society. It is work that one performs in school to get an education. It is work that one performs later in life to get a paycheck. Looking at life from the perspective that someone in America or American society as a whole owes an individual a livelihood simply because that person physically exists is a narrow, selfish, immature approach to life.

If our species matures to the next level of human understanding and fully embraces the true context of our existence as expressed by the term "spirituality," we will have chosen the right path for the course of human existence. By working towards goodness and righteousness, and by utilizing the opportunities and resources before us for the benefit of all of humanity rather than for the satisfaction of the selfishness and greed of individuals or small groups, we will receive the gift of everlasting existence as a species. If we choose the wrong path for the journey of our lives, we will destroy ourselves. We cannot allow negative behavior to erode the liberties upon which this country was founded. This will happen if we continue to require and rely on others to legislate and enforce a code of conduct that we should "freely" adhere to as part of a natural, spiritual, and intellectual understanding and application of truth. What we must be concerned about is that as we ask lawmakers to legislate our lives, we are giving them power to tell us how to move. This is because to apply those laws is to enforce them, and this means armed "enforcers." These enforcers, in the form of police or soldiers, will begin to restrict and dictate our movements, i.e. our actions and reactions. This will inevitably lead to a deterioration of liberty, and eventual hidden tyranny.

What we in America must awaken to is the truth. A part of the truth is the oncoming need for martial law and strict, structural rule through local enforcement. It will very likely include police or military occupation. Does this appear to be something not likely to happen? The truth is, police departments across our country, both large and small, are arming themselves to the teeth with weapons provided by the pentagon. There are small-town police departments with arsenals that go far beyond the needs of the municipalities that are to "protect." It is in the small southern towns where the air support is stored in the form of helicopters and small planes. These arms and support are military style. What war are they to be used to fight? The question is, "why is it that a small town needs a helicopter gun-ship?" With the attacks of September 11, 2001, it is easy to say this provides a good reason for such arming. However, this was in place long before these attacks occurred. We can avoid the need to have such measures instituted by simply changing our behavior. We must control our individual actions and reactions, before we force the ruling powers of this nation to do that for us.

It is up to the citizens of the United States of America to bring humanity into a utopian experience in this new millennium. If we ignore the realities before us, we will have set in motion the circumstances that will bring about damnation for all humankind. Our reality could be perceived objectively as occurring at random. It could also be perceived as a scripted divine screenplay that will play itself out, with the ending being determined by the "ad-libbed" influence of the human species or living things in general. On the other hand, it could be perceived as a battle between good and evil that includes an organized conspiracy of evil whose agenda will be met using negative action to reach its desired end. Whatever perception individuals may choose to subscribe to, the reality is that we are headed for damnation as a species. This will happen only if we allow our behavior to continue to follow the direction that is producing the negative results that are the current human condition. Selfishness and greed are causing the minority group we could label the "haves" to separate themselves from the majority group we could call the "have nots." The "haves" are building walls and gates around their communities. They are hiring "enforcers" to keep out "undesirable" people. We must deal with the cause of this reaction to bring about positive resolution for everyone's benefit.

If we do not do this, gang violence will continue as youth from all racial backgrounds become swallowed up by subcultures that give them the stability their households, their perception of the future, and their interpretation of "mainstream America" is not providing. An undercurrent of elitism/racism exists within segments of the political system, and the policies that are brought forth from this faction will erode the last pillars that support the entire underclass, whether the intent is aimed at undermining the minority and poor communities specifically or not. under the guise of what we all know are much needed changes to our governmental support systems, things like entitlement programs in general, welfare aid, Medicare/Medicaid, public education, community health services and the like will be all but eliminated. This will perpetuate the circumstances that create "haves" and "have nots." As the gap between these two groups widens, the existing separatists and white supremacists that have been lying in wait will use the anger and despair of the "have nots" to fuel their racist propaganda machine. Our competitive economic challenges will then be distorted into racial biases. With hatred at the root of these biases, Americans will blame each other for their woes, as is now the case. This will pit countrymen against countrymen, brother against brother, and sister against sister.

The Holy Scriptures state that the borders of our nations, and the lineage of our families define us as a people. This, together with what our reality indicates is true, it can be said that if an individual is a legal citizen within American borders, or that person's family is made up of Americans, that individual is American. When an individual walks down the street in a foreign country, more often than not that individual can spot a person not native to that land. This is because that person's physical characteristics and/or appearance differs from that of the indigenous population. This is not true in America. On any street in America, one cannot look at another person's physical appearance and tell whether he or she is an American or not. Therefore, it is impractical, unrealistic, and detrimental to our national unity to categorize and discriminate based upon superficial physical characteristics. This is because America truly is an ethnic "melting pot." America is a nation built upon the strengths of nearly all the ethnic groups of our planet. Americans are supposed to be united members of a nation of states. "Nation" is defined as "a body of persons having a common origin and language," as with a family. The infighting going on between American citizens of different ethnic backgrounds is, in reality, brother against brother, and sister against sister. This escalating infighting will lead to domestic violence, and/or civil war. In the beginning, it will seem like a race war, because racists will have initiated it. However, close examination of the realities of the circumstance will reveal it to be a "class" war. This will guarantee the inclusion of Caucasians on either side of the conflict, polarizing their own communities, which will lead to total confusion and chaos. Internal violence will weaken America from within, making her visibly vulnerable to her enemies that exist outside her borders. They will seize the opportunity to strike.

Meanwhile, our actions are affecting an element of our collective existence that we do not fully understand or embrace. It is contained within the context of "spiritual reality." This spiritual reality is a physical manifestation of our divine connection to each other and our Earth. Our thoughts and actions produce a divine energy that is polarized and transmitted between ourselves and our planet, as well as all other living things. This is a characteristic of the divine relationship between the life upon this circle and the circle itself. The divine truth is that the chaos we are allowing, and the negative flowing energy directly related to it, has and will continue to lead to catastrophic climatic and geographic "reactions" from our Earth. This will compound the destructive effects of our behavior. If we do not recognize our responsibility to direct our actions toward the positive resolution of the moments existence places before each of us, the aspect of our reality that is supposed to be positive will continue to be wrongly polarized. This is the energy produced by us that is flowing from us, whose polarity is determined by positive or negative thought. It is also the energy that results from the movement produced by those thoughts, whose polarity is determined by the nature of the result of those actions, positive or negative.

Over the course of the human's existence, each individual has contributed to an accumulation of negative flowing energy created by negative human actions. This is causing our living Earth to strike back at us, in much the same way the human faith reacts to eliminate problem circumstances that dwell within it. Within the human body, "antibodies" exist in harmony with the rest of the body's systems. Much like the weather and our Earth, until something wrong or negative is detected. These antibodies then "localize" themselves in the vicinity of the problem and release their destructive force upon that which is causing the problem in an all-out effort to eradicate it. Our Earth has and will continue to react the same way to us with its "immune system," the forces of Nature. This must be understood within the context of the elements of the planet. The elements that give life on this planet are the Earth, the wind, the fire, and the water.

If the "natural body" of our Earth would react to us, it would be with these elements. The element Earth would be contained within the earthquakes and volcanic activity. The element of fire would be contained within the lightning and volcanic activity. The element of water would be contained within the rainstorms and other phenomenon that produce floods. The element of wind would be contained within the storms we call hurricanes, cyclones, and typhoons. Within the context of our Earth as a living body, these are the forces of Nature that it has as antibodies. It is not adversarial to the degree that our Earth is literally "striking" out at us. Rather, this is the "natural" reaction of every living body system to protect and perpetuate itself. This reaction is the result of our contributing negative flowing energy to the Earth's system when we are naturally supposed to be contributing positive flowing energy to it. Satisfying our responsibility to produce and contribute positive flowing energy to the system around us will lead to near utopian weather patterns. Within this context, it is truly our positive actions that will bring about a utopian living condition. This is a "more perfect" living condition. otherwise, natural disasters like devastating floods, earthquakes, and destructive weather patterns, will further the demise of this country and all humankind, through loss of life, panic, despair, geographic change, and economic depression. These are the factors of damnation.

We cannot continue to exhibit irresponsible behavior. If we do, our society will soon deteriorate to the degree that we will be forced to act violently against each other. Once that occurs, it will set off a chain of events, i.e. a cycle of negative actions and reactions that we may not be able to stop. If we are fortunate enough to stop it, many will have suffered and died. We must consciously control our individual actions. We must take responsibility for ourselves and not expect others, i.e. the legislature, the government, the police, or the military, to control society for us. If we allow laws to be passed aimed at controlling the behaviors we should be controlling ourselves, those laws will apply to everyone, and we will begin losing our individual liberties. We must start controlling ourselves before it is necessary to legislate our behavior. Once our governing bodies start using legislation to replace person discipline, adulthood will no longer have any meaning. As well, legislation requires enforcement. To enforce restrictions on individual movement requires power. Within this context, "power" actually refers to the ability to force (guns). This is reality. It is right before us, and we must open our eyes along with our minds so that we see it and deal with it. We must recognize the direction of our actions, and take control of ourselves so that we direct our actions rightly.

Humans look for so much out of life, while not seeing what the true gift of existence really is. This gift is life itself. It is the opportunity to experience. It is up to the individual to make those experiences either positive or negative. Human beings are all the same in a basic sense. We think the same basic things, but our thoughts differ relative to time and individual circumstance. We desire the same things, but the specifics of those desires are individualized relative to time and circumstance. However, we must recognize our common concerns and respond accordingly. If an individual wants to be praised and recognized for what they do, he or she must accept that others want that as well. If an individual wants things that make their life comfortable, he or she must accept that others want that as well. If an individual wants everything to go their way, he or she must accept that others want that as well and they are just as entitled. If an individual wants their rights and property respected, he or she must accept that others want that as well. Therefore, to have happiness and comfort for oneself, individuals must recognize that others are equally entitled, and each must respect the other's position of existence. This requires compromise and tolerance. As balance is the most profound factor of creation, compromise and tolerance are essential elements necessary to achieving balance. Each of us must accept our responsibility to utilize these elements to manifest the natural balances required for the perpetuation of ourselves and of all other living things.

What we have lost sight of as individuals and as a nation is that the liberties that we have to express our attitudes, our selfishness, our greed, and our rebellion, are only allowable because of the very nature of the American social system. In other countries, individuals do not have the freedom of expression that we have in this country. Each of us must patriotically support this system with our very lives. This is true if for no other reason than it is <u>this</u> nation that allows us to be who we are as individuals. The complexities and pressures of our daily lives along with our selfishness and greed cause us to forget basic facts. We are forgetting the essence of our existence and the nature of our direction. Each of us must have our memories refreshed. The only way for all of us to do this together is to rally around what our nation stands for, life, liberty, and the pursuit of happiness. This nation is the one thing that all Americans have in common. As well, it is the one thing we must have for our desired existence.

For reasons that are both spiritual and practical, we as Americans must pull together as a nation for the betterment of all individual citizens. This will allow us all to take advantage of the opportunities the future holds for us. To do this successfully we must become aware, involved, and organized. The key to a progressive society is the contribution from each individual member, even if that only means being personally productive. This system is set up so that it helps its citizenry with providing for the needs of individual existence. Yet, these helpful programs are meant only as an aid to prosperity rather than the gift of it. When these resources are the sole means of support for a large number of people, it places a drain on the system. This is because people are drawing on the resources of the system longer than was intended, while not contributing to or replenishing those resources.

Each individual must develop the self-reliance and fortitude to not allow life's circumstances to undermine their existence in society. This is done by making a commitment to be responsible for oneself, and to those around us. Within this context, each of us must pursue what is <u>truly</u> desired by utilizing the natural abilities that our system has helped each of us to develop. Our system of existence, i.e. our social structure, is in place to aid us as we seek to better ourselves, so that we may pursue our positive desires. "What is truly desired" does not mean going after what others have. It means to use the element of solitude to listen for the true wishes of oneself. The individual must determine what would make them happy on the inside. It may be a nice car, a big house, and lots of money. Alternatively, it may be a comfortable existence and a happy family that includes these things. Nevertheless, let it be what is really wanted. One must seek to live within the truth.

We as human beings, as Americans, have no choice except to evolve to a higher level of human understanding. The information superhighway places humanity at the fork in the road of its journey through time. The choice of which direction to go in must be a collective one. America, as the leading nation of the planet, must be the first to make the choice. The rest of the Earth's nations, i.e. the rest of humanity, will then have to make their choice. One direction is positive, and moving in that way will lead to human evolution and prosperity. The other direction is negative, and it will lead to regression and destruction. The information superhighway will give each of us access to volumes of words that humanity has already developed. As the human species reviews all words from its collective existence, the principles, doctrines, codes, philosophies, and structure of human existence will be re-evaluated. Within this sea of information lie the answers to all our problems. One reason why a person finds a movie slightly more entertaining the more times it is seen is because each time the movie is (re)viewed, an individual is able to observe more detail because he or she doesn't have to focus their attention on the more obvious things of which they are already aware. For us to take full advantage of the technology that comprises the "computer age," we must first come to understand ourselves in a way we all strive towards, but rarely come close. We must understand what drives and motivates us. What satisfies and brings us true pleasure? What occupations are we capable of and what skills do we possess? We must "get in touch" with ourselves. Each of us must be able to answer the question, "what is the desire of my heart?" The answer to this question is derived from a deep understanding of what makes oneself move.

We must all examine our character and personality. We must look deeper into the truth of what we really want. This is not a reference to one's immediate desires, it is a reference to what a person wants out of their existence, this is the direction that person wants the journey of their life to take, no matter what that is. When one has an understanding of what their true desires are, it gives that person a visual image upon which they can focus. That focus will bring a certain amount of definition, intensity, benefit, and serenity to that person's life in that they will come to know who they truly are, not what others want them to be. It gives one a perception of themselves and their ability that they can focus on, work on, and refine. That is a benefit of recognizing the moments of time for what they truly are, i.e. facing reality. Many of us think of life as being so complex that we do not try to understand it. Truly, it is our personal existence that each of us is really trying to place into context. Individuals are trying to answer the question of how they personally fit into reality. Whatever conclusion one comes to when asking themselves this question, being a living, breathing, human individual truly is not a negative thing. Therefore, the expression of individuality should not have a negative effect on society.

As each of us comes to understand ourselves as individuals, we must not forget that relative to Nature and science, humans are an animal species. Every animal aids its own survival, so each of us must recognize our responsibility to do the same. Each individual must seek to understand the principles of our society, our system, and our structured existence so that we are all able to function in harmony with them. Spiritually speaking, one must do the same for the system of Nature.

The individual has to adapt to those rules so that they are benefited and aided in the pursuit of a successful existence. One must work to provide for their existence within the confines of the social structure, because whether or not any of us wants to believe it, each of us is a lifelong member of an interdependent socialized species. It cannot be looked at it any other way. The system that supports American life is set up to aid its "working parts" in the lawfully free pursuit of prosperity. It is here to aid each of us as we progress through our lives. We have labeled the reward of this pursuit the "American dream." This dream consists of life, liberty, and the pursuit of happiness. As each of us pursues our version of the American dream, we must seek to make our own way through life so that we need as little aid as possible. This defines our success as adults in our society. The laws are set up to establish the parameters or boundaries within which our behavior is to remain. Laws do not control us. We control ourselves and we choose to obey rules and laws. This is what we must do. This is our responsibility. Each of us is to make the right, positive choices for our actions. If we continue to allow our individual thoughts and actions to lead us in the direction we are all currently headed in, this will ultimately lead to the destruction and extinction of the human species.

The citizens of this country need the American social structure. It provides the environment of existence we must have to survive and successfully reach the next level of human evolution. Because of our social structure, our economy, our liberty, our social development, our lifestyle, and our military strength, we are in the position to accept the role of leadership of the human family that is our destiny as a nation. We are a nation built on the efforts of people from all segments of the world. We must accept the responsibility that goes along with being American. We must lead by example, showing the strength of our character, of our spirituality, and of our humanity. Our lifestyle is at stake. We do not want to live like the Japanese, the Irish, the Indians, or the Africans. We want to live like Americans, and to do that we must commit ourselves to responsibly protecting our way of life.

This may sound like a lot of patriotic "mumbo jumbo." However, our need for patriotism and commitment to this nation is a real one. Each of us must truly understand what this truly means. This nation is formed by its citizenry. Therefore, the commitment to the nation is truly a commitment to each other. It is one made to each individual citizen by every other citizen. To embrace this on a national level is not an easy task. We will need something more profound than national brotherhood and patriotic love to bind us together. It has to be strong enough to hold us together through very difficult and desperate times. As a matter of course, this nation faces worldly events that serve as a rallying point around which we come together. At those times, if we perceive our entire system to be threatened, we are forced to look at the essence of our existence. That essence being the truth that America is one unit. We are individuals belonging to a group of "united" states. Exterior pressures like communism, nuclear threats, economic interference like oil embargoes, international and domestic terrorism, and the like force us to come together as a nation to head-off any possible harm to our way of life. During these times, we are distracted from our personal despair because we recognize that without the structure of our nation, we will not have the personal lives to which we have grown accustomed. When these exterior factors are not a part of our daily existence, we lose our national focus, and we begin to look more closely at our own despair and the troubles within our lives. We start to wallow in our troubles and feel sorry for ourselves. These worries lead to feelings of resentment. We begin to project that resentment onto each other, blaming each other for the difficulties of our personal existence. We look at the benefits others seem to be "given" by the system, and it produces feelings of anger, which manifests itself in the form of hatred. It is hatred for the people who receive "special" consideration in the form of these benefits, as well as for the system that gives it to them.

This is the result of a personally subjective interpretation of existence, not a realistic look at all the facts. This way of interpreting things becomes our reality, because reality is existence subjected to human interpretation. We do not lose the capability of seeing the truth, but hatred is fueled by emotion, and our feelings have a stronger influence on our attitude than does our conscious intellect. That is one of the joys of our makeup, but also one of the hindrances of our humanity. The truth be told, there are privileges set aside for whites, blacks, obese people, handicap people, defectors, immigrants, politicians, business executives, homeless persons, children, adults, civil servants, senior citizens, etc. An individual should maximize and utilize all the advantages available to them, and minimize any obstacles or hindrances. To question and challenge the existence of aid to people who may or may not need it is not one of the issues that require our concern. The issues of concern are opportunity, balance, and harmony. The reality we must embrace is that "GOD" has given each and every one of us a "gift" to share with humanity to enrich our collective existence, along with a set of trials and tribulations to work through during our lifetime. We must experience both the "good" and the "bad" with a smile on our faces and with goodness in our hearts because that is our destiny. What we need to bind us together and clear our minds so that we may see revelation is the elevation of our spiritual Nature. We have reached a point in our human evolution where to enjoy the treasures of our existence more fully, we must embrace our attributes as an animal species within Nature and as spiritual beings. However, we must not think and act as though we are individual GODs'.

In America, our civilized society is built on the foundation of every nation of our Earth, as evidenced by its history and its multinational make up. This "melting pot" of human culture is what makes America the great country that it is, and to deny this is to deny reality. There is so much insight and wisdom to be gained from recognizing all of humanity as an animal species, while embracing our humanhood within the context of ethnic and individual difference. Each culture and each individual has gifts to add to the "melting pot" of humanity that we call "America." It is the destiny of this nation to be the melting pot. It is within this pot that the combined elements of ethnic diversity and individual difference within the makeup of our population are blended to exhibit the best characteristics of all of us. To do this we must manifest the goodness that is within each of us as individuals, so that we can reap the benefits of our energy as a collective. Each of us needs to do and be the best we can for ourselves as individuals, to be able to contribute positively to the collective unit. To help oneself in a positive manner while being part of a society is to help the collective social unit. This connection between positive action and benefit (or blessing) is the most profound element of spiritual reality. The greatness and joy of embracing this revelation is that one does not have to give up the experience of individual satisfaction because it is a necessary element of collective satisfaction. It is a part of the Divine System of Nature.

Americans have not been dealing with the realities of their existence in a wholly positive manner because of the selfishness that exists within all humans, and the pressures that exist in our society. We need faith to deal with our selfishness, and we need hope to deal with the social pressures. Faith will result from our acceptance of the realities of "GOD" and of human spirituality. Hope will require a lot of structural reform, along with the mature elevation of our intellectual and spiritual understanding. We need a strong value system that is embraced by us all as was once the case. There was a time when all in our society embraced the concept of our working together to create a country for us all to live in. The goal then was to create a place to live comfortably and raise our families. Other smaller countries with fewer resources than we have are nearly besting us economically, and it is all in the pursuit of the standard of living that we take for granted. They are doing it because they are working <u>together</u> with a common goal. We have to recapture this same focus. It is that spirit that helped our forefathers build this nation. To say that it cannot be done is a lie and a cop-out because we all know that in times of war and disaster, our countrymen and women have proven they can respond as a united, patriotic team. Our goal and focus as a nation has to be the perpetuation of the greatness of America to preserve and improve our way of life for ourselves, and the generations that will follow us.

We must collectively embrace the truth that we must modify our social system by restructuring the controls and objectives of our government, in conjunction with modifying our personal behavior to deal with our future in a positive manner. This is mandated by our social situation, coupled with our being engulfed within the computer age. We have to restructure to evolve. That is what Nature requires within the context of any evolutionary process. Our current system was created to deal with a set of circumstances. We must create a new set of guidelines for our new set of circumstances. Restructuring is a natural part of evolution, and we must all embrace it.

It is the responsibility of every American citizen to help save this country. Being a part of the system of America is like working for a business or corporation. You may not own the business, but you recognize the stake you have in its success. By working in the interest of the company, you enrich your own life. Some of the company's employees you like and some you do not. Nevertheless, you keep that to yourself, you do not run around expressing your inner feelings because they are not relevant to the company, and they are counterproductive to the work environment. You take care of your responsibilities, irrespective of anyone else, as does everyone else. You are all a part of the same group, the company; you are all a team. If everyone fulfills their role and does their job, the company runs smoothly. The better individuals of the company do their jobs, the better the company is able to function or perform. Once this happens, each individual member of the company will become enriched. There are roles, or jobs to be filled. You accept the job you are qualified to do. If you want to move up, you learn the skill that will afford you that opportunity. It is the same way within our society.

As a part of our belief system, we must believe in America. The reality is that as human beings, we need a system of existence, a structure like America to provide us with the opportunity to pursue and achieve. This country provides each of us with the opportunity to live as we desire as individuals. This is why America exists. As human beings, our lives in America are the epitome of what we as conscious, civilized animals can achieve in terms of cooperative interaction on a grand scale. We must <u>all</u> accept the fact that life must exist within the context of a system. Therefore, humans must act and react within the constraints or parameters of that system. We must live by rules. To live out GODs' plan, the human needs to be free to express every element of its being. Freedom of expression is a part of the foundation of America. We as American citizens have the greatest opportunities before us that humankind has ever known.

"We, the people of the United States, in order to form a <u>more perfect union</u>, establish justice, insure domestic tranquility, provide for the common defense, promote the general welfare, and secure the blessings of liberty to ourselves and our posterity, do ordain and establish this constitution of the United States of America." The most important part of the preamble to our constitution is at the beginning. Note that it does not state that "We, the government of…." it says, "We, the people of…." the citizenry of our nation are charged with the responsibility of forming a more perfect union. If we are to save our nation from crisis, we must come together and form a more perfect union. "More perfect" implies that no matter how good something is, it can still always be better. From this, each American must recognize that for every day of our lives, we are not unlike pioneers forging ahead into future moments creating betterment for ourselves, those that are with us, and those that will follow us. Each and every one of us must be forever working at building more perfect unions. This is true with regard to making better the individual, the family, the community, the state, the nation, and the entire human species.

In dealing with the truth of our collective existence, each of us must come to understand that "forming a more perfect union" is a mandate. It is not the mandate of this nation relative to the Will of man. It is more importantly the mandate of our species relative to the Will of "GOD" (the Divine Energy of Life). The natural progression towards growth and betterment are elements of the divine mandate to pursue perfection. Each of us is to seek it in all areas of our lives within the context of the rules and laws of our systems of living, which are all a part of the one divine system. Every individual system of life is a "sub-system" of this one larger system. We must continually work to make the individual's system better, the family system better, the educational system better, the occupational system better, the community system better, the governmental system better, and the ecological system better. This is so that we can make our total system of existence better. If one is not comfortable calling it a "divine" system, our "system of existence" can truthfully be referred to as "Nature." Whether it is considered divine or natural, earthly existence is very simple in that every system related to living things can be likened to a simple machine with separate parts working together for one purpose as a unit.

Each human being must interpret their respective society within the context of worldly reality. Within this context, that society is the body within which individuals apply their effort toward satisfying their needs while existing within a group, as is the nature of a socialized species. Each human being must also interpret their respective society within the context of spiritual reality. Individuals must see each society as a spiritual manifestation. Within the context of spiritual reality, society is the body within which individuals contribute their effort toward helping each other satisfy their needs. This is also within the nature of a socialized species. It is accomplished with many different movements that directly and indirectly help others move easier. The American social system is a place where each individual can satisfy its needs while having the freedom to become the person "GOD" intended. For this reason alone, though there are many more, each individual member of our society must do all that they can to ensure the safe and prosperous perpetuation of our nation.

Creating Utopia

If we are to return to GODs' way, we must recreate "Eden," i.e. the kingdom of "GOD." in other words, we must create for living things a state of existence that affords <u>near</u> perfect (only "GOD," the Divine Energy of Life is perfect) harmony as well as a balanced coexistence within and between the animal kingdom, the vegetable kingdom, and the mineral kingdom. This will be the manifestation of GODs' kingdom. We have labeled this "utopia." Truly, utopia is the evolution of our current living condition. There are two major elements of utopia. The first is having all our needs met. The second is to be afforded the liberty to pursue our wants/desires. Given a choice, most all of us would readily choose to do what we <u>want</u> and/or <u>desire</u>. This is because of the satisfying stimulation we would feel as a result. The prospect of this positive stimulation makes moving toward or doing what we want and/or desire to do an easy endeavor. Moving toward or doing what is needed is not always easy. Yet, it is necessary to perpetuate a positive condition of living. Because of this, doing what we <u>need</u> to do is just as satisfying.

What each human being craves is satisfaction. Each of us must embrace the revelation that our satisfaction comes as much from what we need to do as what we want and/or desire to do. We must make the choice to do what must be done to satisfy our needs or "responsibilities" before we seek self-stimulation. In the early stages of life, many of us are allowed to do most of what we want and/or desire. This is because someone else has taken on the required actions (responsibilities) necessary to sustain us. During this time, we are permitted to pursue our joy and happiness without having to put forth the effort that supports it. This makes childhood a very pleasant time. From this experience, one may begin to think that receiving stimulation is paramount in one's life. To some degree, this is true. However, by Nature, each living organism must move in ways that aid its own survival. Our species is no different. Doing only what one wants and/or desires to do will serve only that individual. As each of us chooses to use the limited amount of energy within our lives, we must direct our efforts toward activities that produce positive results in for ourselves and for our environment (the area around us). This is so that we benefit as individuals and as a collective. Yes, we must be true to ourselves as individuals. We must seek to work towards our wants/desires with positive actions as we grow from them. However, each of us must first produce the positive actions that satisfy our responsibilities before we endeavor to seek self-serving stimulation. As well, individuals need to revel in the stimulating satisfaction derived from the knowledge that doing what needs to be done serves reality beyond individual interest.

Our true needs are common within our species specifically, and the animal kingdom in general. These needs are basic to our existence. Each of us must first satisfy our most basic needs before we can give effort to satisfying our wants/desires. We must satisfy our basic needs before we can begin to grow and aspire. Being living animals, we have needs that take priority over others. Our most basic needs are air, water, food, and shelter. We take breathing for granted, because oxygen is all around us and it is free. We Americans also take having water for granted because here in our country, water is generally a plentiful commodity. However, the reality is that if we were deprived of water, our thirst would preoccupy our thoughts. The actions that we would generate from those thoughts would be aimed at satisfying our need for water. If deprived of air, our thoughts of thirst would disappear, and the acquisition of air would dominate our thoughts to the degree that we would think of nothing else. The actions we would generate from those thoughts would be focused on satisfying our need for air to breathe. This is a system of actions, and it applies to all our needs. This is also the system of actions utilized with respect to our wants/desires. All our actions are aimed at the satisfaction of our needs, wants and/or desires.

As our Earth spins and time passes, things happen. Circumstances change and adaptations must be made. Through it all, it is possible that any individual person can achieve what "GOD" would have for them against any odds. However, just as with the rest of existence, "GOD" created a system of actions that would lead each individual along the path of life "He" would have them travel. If we are to fulfill GODs' Will as a species, each of us must follow the step-by-step (systematic) process, i.e. the positive system of actions in place to facilitate our reaching whatever goal is before us. Psychologist Abraham h. Maslow deciphered the sequence of positive actions pertaining to the system that leads to human actualization. He illustrated quite well the priority attached to our basic needs by developing a "hierarchy of needs." The most basic needs are related to our physiology, i.e. water, food, and shelter (clothing for warmth is a human need, not one common within the animal kingdom). Because of the thoughts generated by our need for these things, our actions will be directly focused on satisfying these needs first. It is only after these needs are met, that we are compelled to pursue others. Our next basic need is for safety. These four basic needs are profoundly common among members of the animal kingdom. Once they are satisfied, the pursuit of the next set of needs begins. According to Dr. Maslow, the list goes on to include (in order of pursuit) the need to give and receive love. This includes the need to belong and to be accepted to avoid loneliness and alienation. There are then needs he labels "esteem needs." They are the need for self-esteem, achievement, competence, and independence, which tie in with the need for recognition and respect from others. Finally, there are what he deems the highest of needs, what he has labeled the "self-actualization needs." This is the need to live up to one's fullest and unique potential. Achieving satisfaction of the preceding needs relieves the stress upon the body and mind of the individual. This allows one's true self to emerge. This leads to self-actualization. Once each of us has successfully satisfied ourselves to the degree that we are content and comfortable with our lives as well as ourselves, we begin to direct our energies toward producing the actions that would facilitate our individual God-given gift being recognized and utilized. Reaching this point in one's life is from where the benefit to others flows. The structure of Dr. Maslow's analysis is not etched in stone. However, it does provide a clear understanding of the priority assigned to human action based upon our primal motivation.

if we use Dr. Maslow's hierarchy of needs as a guideline to understanding the basis for our primal motivations, then it is the acquisition of food, water, shelter, and clothing that the individual would first move or have action towards. Having a sustainable supply of water, food, shelter, and clothing provides the conditions for the stable perpetuation of one's life. Every element of our composition will become involved in the pursuit of these needs until they are met (the body, mind, and soul). Each of us must use our cognitive power to create for ourselves a plan or system of positive action to satisfy our need for water, food, shelter, and clothing on a continuous basis. The system of actions associated with this plan must be positive when interpreted within the context of worldly reality. When considered alone, this interpretation should be objective and correspond with what is right. The system of actions associated with this plan must be positive when interpreted within the context of spiritual reality as well. When considered alone, this interpretation should be subjective and correspond to what is righteous. These two interpretations need to be combined so that the one individual has one perspective within which they understand their actions. This one perspective is the right (eous) perspective.

To satisfy one's need for water, food, shelter, and clothing on a continuous basis, the individual must develop a system of actions. To fit into the civilized system of existence rightly, the movements within that system should be positive. When those movements are interpreted objectively, they should correspond with what is right as defined by the parameters of the civilized system. This system of actions would allow an individual to continually live with some degree of comfort without negatively affecting what exists around that person.

As if instinctively, the human body will move to satisfy the need for water, food, shelter, and clothing. Were humans a less developed form of animal life, there would be little to know beyond our acting upon our impulses to satisfy ourselves. Just as a wild animal would do, individuals would scavenge about, putting moisture and food into their mouths from whatever sources they found. If a source were plentiful, individual animals would gorge themselves to the point of satisfaction. If it were not, individuals would take in all that was available and continue searching for more. If a source of satisfaction could not be found, desperation would set in. Individuals would then act as any wild, desperate animals would act. They would do whatever it would take to satisfy their need for water and food. For shelter, individuals would seek refuge wherever their strength would allow them to be. The stronger ones would have better shelter than those that were weaker. As for clothing, these items would be fashioned from whatever could be found. These would be impulsive and instinctive actions that the body would take were it not guided by consciousness.

Humans are sentient, aware beings that have become civilized. As such, the way in which we go about satisfying ourselves must reflect these facts. As a being that is aware of the reality that surrounds it, each of us must recognize that the physical effort we produce in order to make gains is a responsibility we have labeled "work." Using this term, every person must "work" to contribute to his or her own livelihood. An uncivilized animal would have to work to attain water, food, shelter, and clothing. This truth does not change once an individual becomes a part of a civilized system. An uncivilized animal with the strength of a human would employ aggression and brute force as a means to an end. Civilized animals, i.e. humans, have developed a system of actions that allows the weak and the strong equal opportunities to work toward gaining what it is they need. Because of this balanced system of action, the individual is ultimately responsible for making the positive movements that will gain for them these needs. Our individual prosperity is based on our individual efforts, not the efforts of the social system. Every living thing produces some sort of self-sustaining action, and the human is no different. It is the perspective within which we interpret those actions that differs from other animals. Some humans conclude that because of their "GOD-like" feeling of superiority, they can choose to do nothing. This is not true. Each of us must work to produce for ourselves.

As an aware civilized being, each of us must make the choice to continually act or move in a positive way within the social system. Being civilized and not barbaric, the system of actions by which we seek to attain water, food, shelter, and clothing must be influenced by the characteristics inherent to civility. These characteristics are civil, orderly, and lawful, rather than rude, chaotic, and criminal. Our social system is composed of each and every one of us as individuals. The way in which it is to function is much like a machine. The "system" of a machine is not the structure that houses the parts of the machine, but the sum total of the efforts of the "parts" within the housing. Our social system is the housing and each of us is a functioning or moving part. For each of us to have our basic needs met on a continuous basis, we must continually <u>do</u> things. These things are required actions. They are individual <u>responsibilities</u>, and they make our social system work. Each individual must identify which movements or actions are positive and which are negative relative to the satisfaction of these needs. One must then choose to move in the way that is positive and right to gain these needs. To sustain oneself within our social system on a continuous basis, each individual must arm themselves with the tools they will need to survive in the ever-changing world within which we live. Knowledge is the key to this survival. As the world is changing and growing, each individual must change and grow to keep in pace with it. Individuals must rely upon themselves to provide for their survival within the confines of this asphalt and concrete jungle. If a person has a skill and it becomes outdated, then that person will have to acquire a new skill. If a person has knowledge and it becomes outdated, then that person will have to acquire new knowledge.

During the moments of each person's life, there will come times when the choices one must make will not be apparent. It is within such a moment that each individual must employ trust and faith. When the choice one is to make is not readily apparent, the human mind shifts its cognitive efforts toward deciphering one's internal feelings regarding what must be decided. Each of us can truly feel what is right and wrong for us as individuals. Each of us can feel what is positive and is negative. Individuals must trust what they feel. They must also have faith that the outcome of those moments will truly be what is right for them. By trusting ourselves and having faith in what we feel, each of us is guided along the right path through our lives.

To satisfy one's need for water, food, shelter, and clothing on a continuous basis, the individual has developed a system of actions. To fit into the Divine System of Nature rightly, the movements within that system should be positive. When those movements are interpreted subjectively, they should correspond with what is righteous as defined by the parameters of the system of human spirituality and/or the Divine System of Nature. As well, individuals should understand that their pursuit of the satisfaction of these needs has more meaning than is readily apparent. What is the more meaningful and/or spiritual reason to satisfy these needs? It is to generate the growth of our species. There are reasons why each human being must embrace a righteous system of actions that would allow that individual to help others continually live with some degree of comfort without negatively affecting the world around them. One reason is our position of having dominion on our Earth. The other is the definition of our nature as a socialized species. Humans are a socialized species that has an awareness of the spiritual, systematic foundation of existence, and that gives us dominion on our Earth. As such, the way in which we go about satisfying ourselves must reflect these facts as well. The worldly realities each of us interprets must not be allowed to become the full basis for our understanding of all that objectively exists. Every one of us must embrace the revelation that there is more to our existence than just what we see, hear, taste, smell, and touch. Each of us must derive an understanding of the context within which our individual daily actions relate to a more spiritual or "Nature-based" system of existence. This is an understanding of our actions subjectively speaking relative to spiritual reality and our soul. As each of us moves through the course of our lives, we must embrace a profound part of ourselves that we know to be there, but do not fully understand or trust. The English-speaking family of the human species has created labels that identify elementary interpretations of what is truly one manifestation, that of our soul. The labels are instinct, conscience, feeling (i.e. hunch, first impression, gut, etc.), intuition, and the like. Each of us must learn to embrace these sensory perceptions so that we can trust them to guide us to the positive resolution of the moments we face. If we act upon the positive impressions derived from within our individual bodies, each of us will be guided toward positive action, balance, and personal enrichment/satisfaction as individuals grow into their respective destinies.

Each person must accept their responsibility to continually fulfill their role within the divine or natural system of existence. The perpetual motion of this Divine System of Nature is dependent upon one element of earthly existence helping or contributing to the positive movement of another. Because of this, together with the nature of our species and our position of having dominion on our Earth, every individual must embrace their responsibility to our socialized species group. one's actions must be influenced by the characteristics associated with their interdependence on all that surrounds them, and their kinship to the world on which we all live. Every individual will be met with opportunities to help and to share as they move through their life. Some opportunities are right for that person, and some are not. Each individual must sense and feel what the right(eous) move to make or action to take is relative to each moment they go through. One must identify the righteous movements to make to help others satisfy their needs when possible. Every person is guided to this end by the impulses they receive through their body's senses during the course of their movements and/or actions. These impulses include spiritual impressions each of us derives from our instincts, intuitions, gut feelings, and first impressions, as well as that positive voice from within that has been labeled the "conscience." This is utilizing the element of our being we have labeled the "soul."

As an aware spiritual being, no individual should move in such a way as to violate any of the Ten Commandments to satisfy their need for water, food, shelter, and clothing. As a spiritual being, each of us must embrace the regal nature of our bodies. Through it the Divine Energy of Life flows. Each of us must seek to move in the way that this energy would have us. We must move in a positive manner seeking balance as we gain what it is we need. To perpetuate the existence of the human species and to fulfill our role within the Divine System of Nature, the human collective must work to make the systems of existence function correctly, right(eous)ly, or positively.

As an aware being of Nature relative to membership in a socialized species, each of us must recognize the spiritual responsibility to work in order to make gains. As a member of an interdependent species, every person must make an effort to contribute not only to his or her own livelihood, but also to that of the collective. To aid the collective effort, each of us must share our resources when possible, and help others meet their need for these things when possible. Each individual must understand how our species fits into the Divine System of Nature. As a socialized animal species, the interpretation of the nature of our general characteristics and the explanation of our daily activity has to correspond with that of other socialized species for that interpretation to be considered right. For example, it is true that members of a socialized species "naturally" come together to form communities. We humans do that too. Our species may believe our reason for doing so is derived from our thought process and this very well may be true. However, we must also relate to the divine truth that socialized species without our complex thought process do the same thing. Therefore, perhaps we are driven by more spiritual directives, and our perspective of understanding is simply our way of explaining the outcome to ourselves.

As exhibited by the socialized species of less complexity than ourselves, there is the common work effort that binds communities together. Each individual member works, and the whole community benefits from each individual's efforts. A bee or an ant goes out and works to collect sustenance and return it to the community coffer for equitable distribution among the collective. We humans do that too. However, again, our way of understanding it is how we explain it to ourselves. In an average American community, the same thing happens in a more complex way, as we are beings that are more complex. Individual members go out and "work" to collect sustenance. What is more complex is that rather than collecting the sustenance itself, we collect "vouchers" for the sustenance, i.e. money. Our personal employment is the work effort that we are to contribute to our communities. As well, it binds the individual to the collective because each separate job is a factor of the social system. There is an occurrence of interaction within the communities of other socialized species, wherein the distribution of the collected sustenance takes place. We humans have this occurrence of interaction and distribution as well. It is the spending of money. As this is all true, these facts indicate that "money-making" businesses and corporations, have a more significant role within the human communities. The Divine System of Nature is a balanced system. Excess destroys balance. Because of this, at the very least, profit (excessive by Nature) making entities have a responsibility to financially aid human communities by returning to them some of those profits.

As each individual member of a socialized species works to survive, Nature creates a system to support their individual efforts by combining them with the efforts of the collective group to which they belong, i.e. the social system. The first group whose efforts are naturally combined for a system of support is the family. There is a system of naturally combined effort that supports the family. That group is the community. It is the responsibility of the immediate community to aid the individual and the family structure. Each community has to understand that as a socialized species, each individual member has a responsibility to aid another individual or family that is trying to help themselves.

This is from where charity and volunteerism arose. Yet, irrespective of human compassion and a social commitment to each other, each of us must expend energy towards the efforts of our own survival before the community can come to our aid. If people are not helping themselves, it then becomes a hardship for the community to help them. We all must "pull our own weight" so that the structure of the system is maintained. In this way, the benefits we receive from the social structure are greater because everyone is contributing. If and/or when an individual is not pulling their own weight and providing for the needs of their own existence, that person's strain on society is doubled. This is because not only are the expected contributions of that person non-existent, but now the social machine must slowdown and expend energy in areas where social energy and resources should not be required.

As we move into our future, we must consciously evolve as a species. Social structures are going to need to radically change as well, to keep pace with the changes that occur within our species. These changes are inevitable because of our technological development. Technology will liberate us from the burdensome tasks (movements) of our daily lives, while bringing knowledge of our entire world to our fingertips. Every contributing member of our society will have the opportunity to explore his or her potential and desires more fully, via the knowledge and aid that can be derived from the computer and the information superhighway. As machines take over the more laborious tasks within our industrial systems, each of us will find ourselves with more time to focus on bettering ourselves. People interested in attaining knowledge within a given discipline will be smarter in that area because of a wider availability of information to utilize in the learning process, and the ease with which it can be accessed. Life will become more intensely competitive because of the evolution of our species and our social structures brought on by the computer age. Access to a computer and the internet will define an individual's worth within our new millennium. If one does not understand the fundamentals of pc operation and the keyboard itself, that person's worth as a commodity and their access to the social system will be greatly restricted. As the trends related to our evolution continue, there will be a large group or subculture of people who will not evolve into the computer age. This group will include those who are homeless and/or poverty-stricken, along with those who are caught up in unhealthy and negative addictions and activities. These people will be unable to establish an environment for growth and radical change.

Within the coming years, not only will it be necessary for each person to own a computer system, but it will also be necessary to maintain an environment to support it. The computer system must have a roof over it, and it must have a telephone or cable line to link it to the outside world. Therefore, individuals must first be able to put a roof over their own heads, and they must be able to maintain it. Within this condition of existence, all of the basic necessities must be met before persons can think about acquiring what are considered luxury items, i.e. a telephone/cable line and a computer system. What good is a computer if one is starving? A person must be clothed, fed, and without the stress produced by worrying about their basic day-to-day existence, so they can fully embrace the opportunity for growth. The essence of this is that for our society to evolve into this new millennium as a unit, our standard of living as a nation must actually increase beyond current levels. This is not the responsibility of the government to produce this circumstance of existence. It is up to each individual to produce the means by which they become part of what is considered "mainstream" America. However, because of the finite nature of our Earth's resources, social structures are going to have to evolve so that social systems can better manage and distribute resources for consumption.

The human animal is under certain stresses because of its existence. Our current state of mind is the result of our reaction to those stresses. To evolve physically and mentally, our existence most become stable to the degree that we no longer feel stress with regard to our basic existence. For an individual to better himself or herself, they must focus their mind on this task. This focus is very difficult if that person is hungry, thirsty, cold, or feeling unsafe.

Our basic necessities like food, shelter, and clothing must be provided for if we are to focus our energies on becoming better human beings. Once there is no stress attached to basic survival, a person can begin to focus on growth. For all Americans to embrace and pursue the American dream in earnest, we must reach a point where we are physiologically prepared to aspire. This point in human existence is achieved after basic needs have been satisfied.

"Abundance" is defined as an extremely plentiful or over-sufficient quantity or supply. "Excess" is defined as <u>super</u>abundance. As the use of the word "abundance" appears within the Holy Scriptures, it more often than not has a positive connotation to it. With regard to the use of the word "excess" within the Holy Scriptures, every use of it is in a negative context. In seeking balance, we must accept the existence of abundance. Within the confines of a free-enterprise system, there are those who work harder than others do. As well, there are those who are presented with more opportunities than others are. Thusly, there are those that have abundantly greater gains than those of other people. However, when this "abundance" reaches excessive proportions, the result is negative and contrary to the Divine System of Nature. If it is contrary to the Divine System of Nature, it can only produce problems and conflicts that result from the manifestation of imbalance.

Within this context, how can "superabundance" or "excessive proportion" be determined? Well, if a person has one of something, they have enough to take care of the need that they have for it. If that person has two of that something, this brings security because if they used all of one up or something happens to one, that person has another to replace it. If that person has three of that something, this provides satisfaction because that person can share and still be well supplied and secure. To have four of something means that person has reached the level of abundance, the divine reward for positive, constructive effort. From this perspective, to have one more than four of that something can be considered superabundance, i.e. the point of excess. To balance the limited resources of our planet with the need to share those resources among the masses for collective survival, a formula of equation based upon this concept of satisfaction can be derived, aimed at achieving a fair distribution of resources.

Each of us should have one system of actions that is interpreted within the context of worldly reality and spiritual reality. These two interpretations are combined into one, right(eous) perspective. When developing a system of actions, each of us must remember that we are a part of the circuitry of our Earth's electrical system. As a circuit, the energy within this system travels in a circle. There are two choices of direction for the energy to travel. One is positive, and the other is negative. Following the circular path of energy flow, if positive energy is emitted from the source, it will return to the source as positive energy. This is as it should be. Hence, if each individual does good deeds, good deeds will be done for each individual. "Do unto others as you would have others do unto you."

Objective speaking, the right system of actions is derived from the fact that one knows that they must have water, food, shelter, and clothing to survive. Since all living organisms move in ways that are self-sustaining, each individual is by Nature required to put forth effort/work to satisfy these needs. Each of us must work for what we must have to sustain ourselves. The system of actions that one chooses to satisfy these needs must be positive. For example, we must not steal what we need to survive. We must not do anything negative to attain what we need. Subjective speaking, the righteous system of actions is derived from the fact that each of us is a conscious human being. Because of this, each person must use their ability to understand in an effort to aid their acceptance of their responsibility to truth. Each of us is a member of a socialized species. Therefore, individuals must use some of their energy to help others satisfy these needs as well. The system of actions that one chooses to use to help others satisfy these needs must be positive. For example, not one of us should hoard what is produced from our efforts. This would be contrary to the truth of a socialized being. Each of us must use a part of our energy to help others when it is possible. Within the context of living in a society, this is to support the social system's efforts to aid the collective as it gives aid to each of us.

Our social system is made up of many communities. There is the neighborhood community, the municipal community, the state community, and so on. All these communities added together equal our nation, the United States of America. Government is the system by which communities are directed and serviced. By virtue of the authoritative position that government has in our lives, it has a responsibility to ensure that those under its authority are aided in their pursuit of survival. Its role in this capacity is to promote the general welfare of the citizenry. This is done by using resources collected from the efforts of its members to provide <u>secondary</u> livelihood support through aid and services. As one of the wealthiest, "free" civilized nations on our planet, we must utilize our resources to promote the general welfare. The general welfare refers to the basic needs of all Americans. The need for air, water, food, shelter, clothing (and safety) have to be satisfied if the nation as a whole is to progress in unison. These needs are essential to civilized human existence. These needs cannot be replaced with options, substitutes, or alternative elements. Our social system is bound by definition to sustain all those that actively contribute individual work efforts. This must be done for humanitarian reasons relative to human rights. As well, it must be done because the next level of personal development is built upon the satisfaction of these needs. If we as a nation restructure and refocus our policies and programs, we can derive a more perfect distribution of the resources available to us.

This is not to say that individuals are not required to take care of themselves. However, by definition (which is truth), as interdependent members of a socialized species existing in a civilized living condition, we must care for and help each other to survive. As a socialized species, our existence is naturally structured such that our individual work efforts benefit both the individual and the collective. Though the individual does not always directly provide for the other members of the collective, it is the social structure within which the individual works that is to collect and redistribute the benefits from that effort throughout the collective. For both poor and wealthy Americans, our social system has support built into it to aid those in pursuit of a fruitful existence. However, this support is based on the premise that each of us is making an effort to produce ourselves. We must make the effort to produce ourselves, and take advantage of our support system to the greatest degree, before this support is eliminated. The elements of comfort, enjoyment, and stable retirement are individual pursuits. The successful satisfaction of which depends upon the drive and specifications of the individual. Related to the definition of a socialized species, there is a naturally occurring activity that each member has that benefits not only the individual member of the group, but also the group as a whole. For the members of industrialized societies, it is the combination of individual employment and the spending of the money earned. Because of this, all members of the social system must consider our individual and collective existence within the context of economics. Each of us must participate by contributing in positive ways.

Funding a More Perfect
Living Condition

Our government's role in supporting the collective effort to survive relates to the redistribution of collected resources generated by our individual efforts. This translates into funding for domestic policies and programs. There are three ways of funding the changes needed within our social system. While they are radical when pondered, they have precedents that have generated positive results within stages of human existence. They are viable options when applied correctly and right(eous)ly by a people exhibiting the characteristics associated with being "civilized." These changes are aimed at shifting the funding of our system of existence from the backs of the working Americans to other elements of our social structure where the gains from our efforts are collected. One involves shifting some of the financial responsibilities of society to the corporations that are supported by the dollars we work for and spend. Another involves the participation of our government in the free enterprise system. The last involves an area of free enterprise from which the government can profit. The 3 ways of funding our evolved, restructured, more perfect social system are through **"Corporate Aid,"** very limited and specific **"Nationalization,"** and the **"Legalization of Vice."**

Regarding the use of corporate aid to fund the restructuring of our social system, each individual member of our system must recognize this fact. It is that though each of us is an individual, we are still members or parts of all the earthly systems of our existence. It could be the system of Nature, of the family, of a church, of a business, of patrons of a park, of people walking a street, of patrons to a laundromat, etc. Regardless of the type of system in question, when we have actions that are relevant to that system, we become a part of that system. As a result, that system has a stake in us, and we in turn have a stake in that system. That system needs us around for it to function optimally, and we need that system around for us to function optimally. Each working member of our society is a functioning part of this nation's economic system. Applying the aforementioned rationale to our economic system, it has a stake in the consuming public, and likewise, we the consuming public have a stake in the economic system.

This is nothing new. There is an entire field of thought related to this called "social economics." There is also a blossoming concept in business that is having a profound impact on how business decisions are made. This concept is called "Stakeholderism or Stakeholder Capitalism." In simplest terms, stakeholders are employees, customers, and communities. They are the individuals and groups that have a stake in the activities and actions undertaken by a corporation in addition to stockholders and corporate leaders. The concept of Stakeholder Capitalism is based upon the conclusion that corporate decisions should take into account the impact business decisions will have on those that are most affected by the activities and actions of that corporation. Stakeholder capitalism is a real consideration. It is an accepted business principle in places like Germany, Japan, and Britain. In the early 1990s, such states as Pennsylvania, Ohio, and Indiana even incorporated stakeholder rights into some of their business-related statutes. What we must recognize here in America is that the systems that sustain our lives need to evolve just as individuals must evolve. Stakeholder Capitalism is a limited acknowledgment that large businesses understand that they must start aiding our existence rather than only taking from it. We stakeholders have the power, and each of us must now exercise it in unison with others of our national collective to effect changes aimed directly at benefiting "we the people." The paying consumers of an economic system <u>are</u> the economic system. From this perspective, it is not hard to understand how those doing the spending can desire an economic direction that is in the best interests of themselves. Producers and consumers alike have a common goal. It is not simply to make and spend money. It is to live comfortable lives.

By utilizing resources to provide minimal, basic standards of living comfort to all American individuals, we will not substantially reduce the levels of comfort experienced by those in the positions controlling our resources. In fact, the level of comfort for everyone will increase. This is because at the very foundation of most of the crime and chaos within our society, is the gap that exists between those that have what they need and desire, and those that have not. If we set aside for a moment the perspectives we have derived from the influences of selfishness and greed, we will see that it is in the best interest of producers, marketers, and consumers, to distribute the enrichments derived from our planet more equitably. There should be no poor, and there should be no super-rich. "Super-rich" is having wealth beyond ones need to consume it, and this translates into the hoarding of resources. It is becoming clear to many that we must start taking into consideration the welfare of all Americans before we are too distinctly separated into a group that "has," and a group that "has not."

Here in America, the entity in control of our economic welfare is the Federal Reserve. One of the reserves responsibilities is to set policy that affects interest rates and economic growth. The name of this entity would lead one to believe that it is controlled and/or run by our federal government. If this were true, one could easily conclude that the decision-making process would be reflective of the best interests of the people that the government serves. However, the Federal Reserve is not an institution of the government. It is a private corporation owned by stockholders. People buy stock to make money, and corporations are interested in profit. Neither group is interested in simply "breaking even." Therefore, it is safe to assume that the entity that controls our economy is not wholly interested in the welfare of the people who use its money. Rather, it is concerned with profit margin and longevity. As the destiny of our economic system is in the hands of a private corporation, we must recognize the reality that the decisions made by this body are reflective of the decisions made by any other business organization. Those decisions are based upon the continued existence of the business, not the continued existence of humanity. While this may adequately serve and support the system of "man," it does not adequately serve and support the system of "GOD," i.e. the Divine System of Nature.

Our economic system works, this is true. However, the expenses and revenues derived from this system working now need to be more evenly distributed as the resources of our planet lessen and become more costly to retrieve. Like our government system, our economic system remains structured and continues to function within the same parameters as at its inception. Circumstances have changed, and the systems that govern those circumstances must change as well. To this degree, corporations must take a more active role in supporting our social infrastructure. Most of them are already willing to do so, and they are making an effort to do this. However, these decisions are being made by businesspersons, not saviors. As with any investment, they want to receive a beneficial return on the dollars they invest in us. This is in keeping with the right(eous)ly functioning Divine System of Nature. The beneficial returns are encompassed within our becoming a safer, more productive society. This is accomplished by us all having more positive actions, by us moving in more positive ways. These beneficial returns are derived from the increased productivity that will ultimately result from there being less chaos, less criminal activity, less property destruction (not destroying and defacing what they build for us), more schooling, more work, and more cleanliness. To sum it up, our society will have more <u>civility</u>.

If one truthfully compares the content and nature of human societies with that of any other socialized species, the responsibility that a profiting entity like a corporation has to the collective community is a clear one. However, beyond this comparison, why should corporations help the communities from which they profit? Well, according to information gotten from the internal revenue service, during the fiscal year of 1999, there were four major categories of income for our government. The government received the majority of its income, a whopping 82%, from taxes imposed on individual taxpayers. This figure is broken up into two categories. Personal income taxes comprised 48%, while the remaining 34% came from social security, Medicare, unemployment, and other retirement taxes. Corporate income taxes comprised a meager 10% of our governments' income. The remaining 8% came from excise, customs, estate, gift, and other miscellaneous taxes. While individuals are burdened with paying the expenses of our social system, corporations are reaping "excessive" revenues. These revenues are exemplified by CEO salaries, which are in the millions of dollars (and so are their contract buyout and retirement packages).

The welfare programs that aid individuals do have to be restructured. However, the entire welfare system needs an overhaul, not just the entitlement programs that aid those with little or no monetary income. According to a breakdown of the spending of the income our government receives, 17% of it is spent on social programs. Of that amount, 12% was split between Medicaid, supplemental security income, food stamps, temporary assistance for needy families, and other related programs. It was reported that in the mid-1990s, our federal government spent roughly $40 billion on both food stamps and aid to individuals and families with dependent children. Yet in contrast, there was a little over $104 billion spent on "corporate welfare." There was $51 billion spent as direct subsidies to businesses, and another $53.3 billion was lost because of tax breaks given to corporations, this was according to the office of management and budget and the joint committee on taxation. Our government is supposed to be looking out more for the interests of the citizens of our nation, rather than the interests of the corporations.

It is true that changes must be made in the area of government expenditure related to aid to individuals and families with dependent children. One of the biggest changes has to occur within the minds of both those receiving this aid and the minds of those paying for it. Those receiving the aid must embrace the divine truth that the responsibility for their comfort rests solely upon their own efforts. All must recognize that there is no stigma attached to doing any kind of work, as long as that working person has a comfortable life and the dignity they need to satisfy their own self-esteem. Each of these individuals must understand that if they choose to do nothing positive to aid in their own support, then they can expect to have no comforts. This is a naturally created reality relative to the nature of living things.

The fact that members of a socialized species naturally support each other's efforts to survive must remain incorporated into our social system's application. With regard to those that are unskilled, those people have to know that as long as they are willing to make a continual effort toward betterment, their basic necessities will be met whether by their own accomplishment or through outside aid. Those paying for the aid must let go of the notion that there is a large percentage of the populous beyond a point where they can contribute and/or benefit from any sort of social reform. It must be remembered that jobs within the service industries and in other lesser skilled, laborious occupations will always need to be performed. American citizens that have, as well as those that have not, must work as a unit. All this positive effort, together with a more efficient use of the resources we are capable of producing as a nation, would surely provide for our entire nation a more perfect future. We can restructure our social system such that the overwhelming percentage of our nation's "lost generation" can make positive contributions to help generate more perfect living conditions. In doing this, we all can create for ourselves a comfortable, stable standard of living while reaping the positive benefits of each other's positive actions.

It is also true that changes must be made in the area of government expenditure related to business subsidies and tax breaks. The tax laws of our nation have created a "corporate welfare system." An example of this would be the granting of tax breaks as a means of "creating" jobs. Tax breaks are given to businesses as a way of creating jobs, without any stipulations. The assertion is that a company will reinvest those dollars in their business. This is risky speculation. These businesses are not being forced to expand or hire. Therefore, if these decision-makers choose to look at this money as profit, this is their prerogative. These "tax breaks" then become income for business, and this places the taxpayer in a worse scenario because not only has there been no improvement in the employment situation, but the individual taxpayer will eventually be held responsible for the revenue lost from those tax breaks.

Another example of the "corporate welfare system" in action is in the area of non-profit companies. I am not talking about charitable organizations. I am talking about entities like the PGA Tour Inc., the national football league, and the American bankers association. It was reported in October of 1995 that the PGA Tour Inc. grosses $180 million a year from sponsoring professional golf tours for men. In the article, it reported that in the two years prior, the PGA had paid $4.2 million dollars to its retired commissioner. The ability to make such lofty retirement payments was attributed in part to the fact that the PGA tour is a nonprofit corporation. This means it does not have to pay federal tax on its tour operations. Many of today's nonprofit organizations do not resemble charities in any way.

A good example would be the major professional sports leagues. How much money is earned by one of these teams if it can pay one of its employees (a player) $16 million a year, along with all the other lofty salaries? There are thousands of American corporations that are exempt from paying taxes. The reason is they are classified as "non-profit." However, they are making money or profit, and using these funds in ways that are contrary to the definition of "non-profit." The "heads" of these organizations are also earning salaries in the millions of dollars.

I have read much literature related to defining and explaining the system of taxation in America. It is so cumbersome and confusing that I would not dare endeavor to address the specifics of how this system is applied. There are nearly 500 different tax forms, and nearly 300 pages of documentation to explain how to use these different forms. One thing is evident, however. For our system of taxation to be fair, it must be aimed at supporting individuals and their families. for the graphic details of what is wrong with our tax system, there is a very informative book written by Donald L. Barlett and James B. Steele called "America: who pays the taxes?." This is suggested reading if one needs to be shocked into becoming the informed, involved, active American citizen each of us is supposed to be. a few of the other points of detriment these gentlemen found within our system of taxation are that the poor pay a greater percentage of taxes than the rich do; that there are many tax abuses; and that there are many tax "cheats." This all points to a need to reevaluate and restructure the way our social system is financed.

A corporations' aid to a community does not have to be a huge investment. A better effort can be made to distribute some of the money that they have already earmarked for communities as a matter of public relations. The compensation some workers receive could be restructured so that their basic needs are assuredly met. Take the issue of minimum wage for example. Ideally, the minimum wage should be based upon the average income necessary for one individual to survival independent of another. However, the cost of such would be very high indeed. That cost is perhaps more than could be paid for without undue hardship on the businesses within our economic system. Nevertheless, establishing the foundation for this minimum standard of living could be accomplished by one or more corporations paying a "tax" that would go directly to the production of "credit" housing for working individuals (building these facilities also creates jobs and tax revenues as a byproduct). Within this housing complex, individuals could live free of charge as a general benefit for being registered as working for someone who pays this tax. These would obviously be modest accommodations, like efficiency or one-bedroom abodes, and the residents would need to agree to maintain the quality of the facility. Some of the money could even go to a fund that would go to supermarkets to pay for "credits" an individual could cash in, sort of like food stamps, but paid for by corporations. In this way, the minimum wage could be calculated in accordance with what would be deemed the difference between the practical costs of independence, minus the cost of subsidized living.

Another possibility would involve a partnership between corporations and our government. Instead of providing independent monetary assistance to families in need of assistance, perhaps "assistance" dormitories could be built (creating construction jobs and tax revenues) where people on assistance could live. In addition to housing and food, these facilities could provide in-house daycare (more jobs) to aid parents while they attend mandatory in-house job training programs.

Another approach could be a corporate sponsored program aimed at neighborhood cleanup. A manned storefront of some sort (more jobs and tax revenue) could be set up so that any person could walk in off the street and sign up for a day (working on a day-to-day basis) to work under supervision cleaning up a community. this could easily be expanded into community work centers where the homeless can go to sign up for work on a day-to-day basis, doing work like painting, cleaning abandon lots, or street sweeping.

Corporations could band together to rescue our nation from scholastic decay by adopting a school or a school district. In doing this, the corporation would agree to become a supporting resource for that individual school or district. They would become a source that can be drawn from to supplement the process of upgrading the public school system. Because of the resources associated with the computer, corporations could monitor individual student progress and achievement in hopes of identifying a student with abilities and interests that would make them desirable prospects for future employment. They could then adopt that student. They could fund that student's educational experience in return for a termed commitment of employment.

There are many ways for there to be increased corporate involvement in the giving of aid to support our social infrastructure yet to be explored. The only way to get corporations and our government to consider such measures would be each individual citizen's active participation in the "administration" of our system. We do this by voting and letting our representatives know what it is we want. As an example, it was in the late 1970s that the American people revolted against high taxes and voiced their collective concern. Those actions forced local and state governments to cut tax rates dramatically. In turn, those on Capitol Hill had to respond to the voice of the people. The result was that in 1981, politicians enacted the largest tax cut in American history. The citizens of this nation have the power to effect positive changes. We must collectively exercise that power.

Our basic needs serve as the foundation upon which the American dream is built. We are members of a social system that has a number of responsibilities to its "contributing" members that require funding. The changes to our social structure that will stabilize our lives and bring about mutual satisfaction will have a high price tag. To produce the revenue our nation will need to evolve, the answer is not as simple as making some changes to the corporate tax (welfare) system and seeking more corporate dollars and sponsorship. Many more dollars are going to be needed to build a more perfect present and future living condition for the American citizenry. We must consider nationalizing certain strategically vital industries that are already heavily subsidies by taxpayer dollars. These dollars are used to support the ability of these industries to profit. Very limited nationalization can directly offset the burden of funding our social system through roughly five months of work each year by each productive individual in American. Perhaps then we could eliminate personal income tax altogether. If need be, it could be replaced with a consumption tax. This would be collecting tax revenue from households as they purchase goods and services.

The governing body of the social system that supports the American collective is the United States government. It must have money to accomplish what we ask of it. At present, most of that money is provided through taxation. The government will need additional sources of funding to aid our citizenry in making improvements to our living conditions. These funds <u>cannot</u> be expected to come from already overburdened taxpayers.

With the difficulty that already exists for the average Joe and Josette in this competitive free enterprise system, we must seek to reduce the tax burden on citizens struggling to survive. Most politicians have acknowledged the fact that America needs "reforms" in its government structure. However, the "reforms" they propose and enact are not radical enough to affect the changes that are necessary to produce mutual satisfaction for the entire cross-section of American society. These changes will keep us just barely ahead of the status quo. We need true, effective, radical changes to our current system. We the people need changes that balance the needs of the citizenry with the needs of business. First, we must identify our common desires and our goals as a nation of individuals. We must then look at our current existence and relate those goals to reality in an effort to make our desires realistic. Then, we define the steps, the path, or the general direction of our actions that will lead us to these goals. We then manifest our plan into reality by taking action, or moving in the right or positive direction.

Regarding our government's participation in the free enterprise system, each of us must realize that this is all that nationalization is truly. Nationalization is a label that describes the circumstance of bringing industries and/or land under the control or ownership of the nation. This is good for our citizenry because it is "we the people" that own the assets of our nation. With all the wealth of our nation, our domestic support programs, i.e. the ones aimed at aiding individual American citizens, are always being reduced or eliminated because of a lack of funding. In addition, corporate cutbacks and layoffs aimed at generating greater company profits are creating hardships for working consumers. Limited, specifically targeted nationalization is a way of providing the funds needed for our domestic support programs. As well, this resource will provide our government with a way of directly providing employment. This will provide a stability producing option for those affected by cutbacks and layoffs. Through nationalization, our government will have control over not only another source of revenue, but also a source of employment. It can apply this resource to the task of consistently reducing unemployment. Nationalizing certain vital industries will provide our government with another financial resource. It can be used to lessen the burden of taxation placed upon our general population. It can also aid in providing more support for our collective livelihood and a more perfect existence for our citizenry. The wealth derived from the resources of our nation needs to be more equitably distributed to our citizenry because the resources of our nation belong to all of us. There should be no reason for the individuals of our society to go without the necessities of food, shelter, and clothing, when corporations are reaping huge profits that are the result of the efforts of each productive individual member of our society. Terms like "nationalism" are simply labels that identify the system by which wealth redistribution can occur. Nothing actually changes except the government takes over the operation of key industries and returns those profits to the working class through the internal workings of the social system.

Some people believe that our citizenry will get better services through privatization because of the pressure and leverage that result from competition. They also believe that these same services will be cheaper because of competitive pricing. This thinking led to deregulation within the airline industry. However, instead of producing the 20 or so strong airline companies as expected, four or five major airlines emerge to dominate the market. Ultimately, this theory of cost reduction based upon competition is not without flaw. One of the ways these "private sector" companies maintain high profits while lowering prices to consumers is by cutting into the wage and benefit packages of its workers. This in turn reduces the standard of living for the individual worker and his/her family. As well, it reduces the income of the community they reside in because of the decrease in the respective family's ability to spend. Through privatization, all you are truly changing is the administration of the service, and one set of problems for another. The system under which a business is run can be the same for a government agency, if that is how the system is set up. Therefore, rather than penalize the workers through these changes, those who administer the system that should be held accountable. An example would be the notion that municipal workers are lazy, and it takes many to do the job of one.

The thinking is that if those "lazy" workers were replaced by private industry employees, their efforts and energies would be more fully utilized. Ask yourself, "What is the true difference in this circumstance?" Is the private industry worker naturally more productive? No, it has nothing at all to do with Nature. The administrators in private industry do not allow this sort of thing to happen. If the municipal worker makes more than the same worker does in private industry, why is that? It is because the system allows that to occur. It is then the system itself that needs to be changed.

Let us use the example of snow removal. After a snowfall, taxpayers expect their streets to be cleaned. Is there any citizen that truly wants to have to wake up in the morning and call someone to do this? No, most all of us want it done automatically. Either way, this service must still be paid for by the taxpayer. If it can be shown that a private company can pay their workers less for the same job, this does not mean the taxpayer will save money. In the private sector, every business is set up to make money. Whatever the workers are being paid, the company they work for must still make a profit. Who is to say any savings created by privatizing are going to be passed on to the public? A better solution would be to restructure the pay scale of the municipal worker to reflect that of his or her private industry counterpart. The excess funds that would normally be considered "profit," are still in the pockets of the taxpayers. Costs could actually drop because the intent of the operating policy is to provide good service and stable employment on a continual basis. As long as the influx of dollars provides the income necessary to meet these objectives adequately, the operation is successful. The cost of services affect would be structured around this principle. This is a true saving. We need to restructure government by making it more efficient and responsible to our citizenry. We do not need to allow corporations to control our lives. We need to make changes to our social system and how it is administered, and not change who profits from it.

The U.S. postal service is reportedly a profitable business under the operation of the United States government that employs over 700,000 individuals. In an article from the associated press in May of 1998, it was reported that the independent postal rate commission said that the U.S. postal service had been making profits of over $1 billion a year since 1995. The postal service is a nationalized business, and it has not discouraged or eliminated competition in this industry. Nor has its existence led to communism, dictatorship, or tyranny. Our social system must evolve to support our individual evolution. Within the context of this effort, we must nationalize certain vital industries to provide the revenue that our government says it does not have. The industries to nationalize are vital to the success of our society, and they are businesses with national markets and networks. It makes sense to nationalize them because they must always exist. The need for their continued existence is the founding philosophy behind our federal subsidy programs. Most of the industries that should be nationalized are already heavily subsidies by citizenry tax dollars. Our system of government is involved up to its proverbial "ears" in the free enterprise system. To say that our government should stay out of the areas of ownership and control is not truly practical when one faces the fact that we rely on our government to provide funds to localities for this and that, and to subsidies the ability of businesses to profit. What we need to do is provide our government with another source of revenue so that it can adequately provide services for us, while aiding it in the production and maintenance of balanced federal budgets. With limited nationalization, a streamlining of government and better financial management, we the people, working together, can meet the challenges the future has in store for us.

There are those in our society that believe it is in the best interest of our social system to make our government smaller. Government provides the structure of a social system, and it is where the interests of the people are represented in an organized manner. Government is the structured system through which the people derive and maintain mutual benefit and protection. Corporations represent the interests of individuals or small groups who act in their own best interests. They are primarily concerned with their own profit and gain.

By making our government smaller, the representation of we the people is made smaller. This concentrates the control of both resources and livelihoods within the hands of the individuals inside these corporations, which use their profits to influence those in positions of administration. We should not be afraid of large government because it is merely a conception created by the label we give it. To one degree or another, we should actually pursue a larger government. This is because we want and expect our government to provide as many of the necessary services that we need free of charge, so that we do not have to spend our limited financial resources for those things. This in turn frees some of our limited finances, which can then be spent on things more to our liking and desire. This will elevate our standard of living.

Five industries within the American social system should be nationalized. Doing this will generate greater benefits for our citizenry. One of those to nationalize is the healthcare and health service industry. A nationalized healthcare system would provide the sort of universal health coverage the American citizenry needs and deserves. When an individual is working steady and has a good healthcare plan, it is very easy to dismiss the need for universal healthcare because that person thinks such a plan is aimed at caring only for the poor. yet, if that same person were to find himself or herself caught in the layoff scheme of a company that is downsizing and they lost their health benefits, the need for such a plan would become all too apparent. Aside from this, our society has a number of difficulties lying in wait within our collective future. Human life expectancy is getting longer with each passing year. Poverty is preventing an enormous number of people from getting very basic medical service. These are things like prenatal care, dental care, physical examinations, and preventive care. To add to the problem, the cost of medical care and medicines are skyrocketing. In November of 1998, an article printed in a newspaper said that one of the big questions facing the American citizenry was "how a smaller working-age population (would) find the resources needed to support (older Americans) in retirement and provide the healthcare services they (will) need."

Hospitals already receive taxpayer money, as they are heavily subsidies. There are laws on the books that require hospitals to provide care for anyone that needs it. There are also such laws aimed directly at medical care for children, and pregnant women. The intent of such laws is to ensure that those without medical insurance receive medical treatment. The state then reimburses (subsidizing) the hospitals for the cost of this care, and these subsidies alone total in the hundreds of millions of dollars.

Asking corporations to aid communities truly would add additional costs to their operating budgets. However, if we stop placing the burden of our nation's healthcare on the backs of employers, the revenue for their aid to communities will be more easily parted with. The average business pays between $5000 and $7000 per year (depending upon the type of plan) to provide an employee with healthcare coverage. Once small business and large corporate employers are released from the financial constraints of providing healthcare coverage to employees, some of the resources needed to aid communities will be recovered without significantly reducing the profits of normal business activity.

Nationalizing healthcare is not a new concept relative to American consideration. While congress has been debating the healthcare issue, the notion of nationalizing the healthcare system has come up more than once in various forms (for example, the McDermott/Wellstone bill). Great Britain, New Zealand, and Canada are examples of countries that have national healthcare systems. One of the arguments against a national healthcare system here in America is that the quality of care will go down because of it. however, according to a world health organization analysis report, while the United States spends more per person on healthcare, it ranks 37th in the world in overall quality of care given. This ranking is below that of Great Britain (18th), and Canada (30th).

Medical care in America has become a big business, and it is being driven by profit gain rather than concern for providing care to all Americans. In a report attributed to the census bureau in November of 2001, the revenues for the healthcare and social assistance industries were a combined $1.06 trillion dollars. Of this amount, hospitals alone had revenues of $430 billion dollars.

Hospitals are merging to compete for business. They are being bought up and restructured such that their facilities are aimed at giving care to specific individuals and their ailments as a way of increasing profit. Through the nationalization of healthcare and related services, our nation can provide basic medical coverage for all Americans. This will increase our collective standard of living, our national health, and help to create a more perfect living condition for us all.

Movement is the essence of living, and the public transportation of consumers is an essential part of most civilized societies. Our public transportation systems make our social infrastructure work by aiding in the facilitation of the movement of citizens to and from the areas in which their efforts are aimed. Without these transportation systems, our society would cease to function properly. For this reason, we should nationalize public transportation systems, i.e. buses, trains, subways, and airlines (yes, the airline industry should also be included in this group.). These transportation systems are privately owned companies receiving large monetary subsidies and grants from local, state, and federal government agencies. Our federal and state governments subsidize these businesses because they are vital to our social system. Bus lines, subway systems, railway systems, and airlines should be owned and operated by the social system. The profits from these services should then be used to enhance and perpetuate their existence. Any leftover profits could be pumped into a general social fund to reduce the amount of taxes paid by our citizenry.

Again, these are not new concepts. Amtrak is one of our nation's railway companies. It began servicing the public on May 1, 1971, and has been receiving government subsidies for about 30 years, pretty much all of its entire existence. Regarding our nation's entire railway system, Amtrak alone has been given more than $23 billion dollars in subsidy money. This calculates to over $766 million dollars per year since its inception. It was reported in July of 2001 that Amtrak's revenue for the year 2000 from passenger trains and other ventures totaled nearly $2.09 billion dollars. Because of operating expense (which include lofty executive salaries) and high debt with interest, it had an operating loss of $944 million dollars. Do the math. Only the nation itself can operate a business on a "break even" principle because its ultimate objective is to provide the populous with the service, rather than making a profit. Because a national railway system is vital to commerce, in March of 2001, the Amtrak reform council suggested establishing a new government corporation to own and operate a national rail system. Originally, the government ran the railways anyway, as it is in most other countries. The government built this business, and then turned it over to private interests. The same thing is about to happen again. The government used taxpayer dollars to build the space shuttle program. Now, NASA is seriously considering turning over the operating of the four space shuttles to a private company. Who truly profits from this exchange?

Most countries operate their own airline systems. The United States airline system is a $135 billion dollar industry. Yet, the American public has no idea of the degree to which this industry is subsidized by our federal government. In addition to the monetary support, a good number of the employees that make the system work are federal employees like air traffic controllers, the FAA, etc. Now add to this group the National Guard and a federal security force. As well, airport construction is heavily subsidized, if not completely paid for with our tax dollars.

To solidify our nationalization program and ensure its continued profitability, we should nationalize continental and intercontinental tourism. Tourism and travel are our nation's third largest retail industry while generating over $582 billion in revenue. In nationalizing tourism, we can nurture ethnic diversity and cultural difference to produce environments to be toured and shared by all. States and local municipalities already make trips abroad to set up tourism networks.

Funds can be granted to neighborhoods to enhance them, so that tourists desire to visit them as a part of the vacation experience. In this way, we will see that there is truly nothing wrong with ethnic communities. We can eliminate bigotry and discrimination without destroying ethnic unity. The national tourism system can be supported by the national transportation system with discounts and vacation packages.

Our government must ensure the safety of our citizenry within United States borders, as well as that of our citizens when they travel abroad on this hostile orb. It is the responsibility of a society to protect its members. Because of the awakening that occurred because of the attacks on September 11, 2001, the areas of concern regarding public safety need to be broadened. For these reasons, we should nationalize public safety services. These are police departments, fire departments, emergency rescue squads, and the like. The entities that provide these services should never be without adequate funding. As well, additional branches of security will need to be established aimed at specific areas of concern. One of which will be the protection of American citizens as they travel abroad. Protecting our citizens who travel abroad should be a priority for our armed forces. With the proper training and an emphasis on professionalism, our armed forces and/or security forces can become a viable, honorable, and prestigious employment option for our youth.

The human species must always have food. There can never be "enough" food. If America were to reach a point where there was an adequate supply for ourselves after having eliminated hunger within our borders, the need for food supplies around the world is never-ending. For this reason, we should nationalize farming. Farming is a subsidized industry with many faults and abuses. Our government has attempted to support crop prices by controlling how acreage is planted. This has been done partly with acreage "set-asides" and some other land-idling schemes affecting some 60 million acres annually. The effect these programs have had on prices is minimal because global competitors take advantage of our cutbacks and reap the profits we "set aside." All the while this manipulation of supply and pricing has been going on, there is starvation occurring in nearly every part of our world. We are blindly allowing the rain forests of our planet to be destroyed in the name of progress. This is done in part to allow farming of those areas to feed the indigenous population, and for commercial development. We are allowing this to happen even though the oxygen we breathe and the weather systems that sustain us are derived by these types of areas. We must place a moratorium on commercial development in these areas. However, the necessity of feeding the peoples of these areas still exists. To deal with this, we must again look at reality. In this country, we are paying farmers not to grow food. Why not pay them to grow all the food they can. This would lower our monthly food bill, and create a surplus. This surplus could be used to feed those in need, both here and abroad. By doing this, we would be eliminating hunger as a human concern.

Farming is the human being joining with Nature in the birthing of new plant life. The farmer should be a pampered individual in our society. It is a special person who loves this craft and who wants to commit himself or herself to farming. It is a valued and much-needed craft.

We must aid and pamper our farmers because farming is an art that must not be allowed to die out. It must be nurtured and encouraged at every opportunity. The small farmer should be afforded every possible aid. To facilitate this aid, a nationalized farming system should consist primarily of a marketing and distribution system. Private farmers should continue to own their land and control their operations. Within this structure, individual farmers should be encouraged to produce as much food as possible. They should receive payment for everything they produce. Our government should then market these commodities domestically and abroad. In truth, we should be able to reduce some of our monetary foreign aid packages by replacing the dollars with a steady, quality food supply. (This saving should again be put into a general social fund to offset taxes paid by the citizenry.)

One might question what the repercussions would be of providing food for a country rather than having them farm and produce it themselves. In many third world countries, the soil and geography does not lend itself to plentiful farming and food production. Here in America, we have a farming industry that is profitable and very much capable of growth. Though many of the third world countries are poor and under-developed, there can still be an equitable exchange negotiated. It would be mutually beneficial to export an entire industry to another country to replace the uselessness of the land they inhabit. One such industry is the housing of prison inmates. In exchange for food, we can locate our prisons in these countries. This will actually create an industry that does not need the support of the area's natural resources. This will bring economic stability to the region, and the money necessary to bring about a slow, constructive approach to the utilization of the natural resources present to produce a thriving, stable economy that is not raping the land. These prisons will create construction jobs, support jobs (i.e. food services, medical, laundry, etc.), and businesses around the prisons will be generated. We could also start locating some of our prisons in underdeveloped countries that receive foreign aid money from us. This "industry exportation" would accomplish a number of things. For one, it would be a way of reducing the amount of money involved in a particular foreign aid package. By "contracting out" the prison system, these indigenous people would be working for the money they receive from us. We would be providing them with additional jobs. Another benefit would be that the United States would actually be receiving some return on its "investment" in these other countries. In addition, we would remove the criminal from familiar turf here in America. This adds a greater psychological burden to the convicted criminal. If he/she should successfully escape, where would they go? In many cases, this would serve as a greater deterrent to crime than the death penalty.

Another goods and service exchange could be land rights structured as leasing packages. We could provide poor localities with food in exchange for land rights to be utilized to build vacation resorts. These resorts could be built with a combination of American and regional workers, creating jobs for both. It would be another offering for our national tourism program. It would be supported by our national transportation system. Moreover, it would be kept secure with a branch of our national security units. This all generates more employment opportunities for our citizenry.

These five industries should be nationalized under the reformation of our social system. Our free enterprise system should remain as it is, and there should be no consideration given to expanding nationalization beyond these five industries. All this would be labeled by some as "socialism." Socialism is a system of social organization that advocates the vesting of the ownership and control of the means of production, capital, land, etc., within the community as a whole. In this case, "community" refers to government. The fear here is that, according to Karl Marx, socialism is the stage of social organization that follows capitalism, and precedes communism. In theory, this may seem true. However, if we are to take his definition to heart, we must embrace it in its entirety. He went on to say that socialism is characterized by the <u>imperfect</u> implementation of collective principles. In truth, this means there is a right and wrong way to create a system of financing government so that it may better serve the interests of those that are governed. A purely socialist system in its formative years is all-consuming in terms of material wealth. This suffocates and extinguishes the most vital resources of a nation. Those resources are the creativity, motivation, and revenue produced by individual entrepreneurship. our way of life has already instilled in us these characteristics as the foundation of our lives, at least to the degree that we can allow our system to evolve in a way that is more beneficial to the common populous, without destroying our basic ideology and motivation.

There are those who would argue that embracing nationalization would indeed be changing our form of government. It is not. Nationalization is a part of the social system of many democratic, industrialized countries. The airline system in France and the healthcare system in Canada are excellent examples. This sort of reform is beneficial to the citizens of this country. Who cares what label it has? Ants are called "tiny socialists" because their actions are reflective of what characterizes them as a socialized species. Is it not a denial of reality to think that humans are any different as a socialized species? Nationalization is the government providing its citizenry with national services. There is concern that our government does not become socialist in nature, yet the truth is that it is already riddled with social programs. Are social programs not a form of socialism? Establishing certain so-called socialistic programs or approaches to solving our social problems does not detract from our commitment to democracy or its doctrine. As a part of our conscious evolution, each of us must reach a level of maturity that would have us embrace the opportunities that all the knowledge available to us provides. With every piece of information that is derived from past human experiences, structured or otherwise, there is a benefit for us. We have to be inspired enough and innovative enough to find it and utilize it such that we are able to foresee any possible harm. Our executive and legislative branches of government should be up to the challenge of amending our system in a way that will sustain our successors for 200 years, just as the original constitution has served us. This country was founded on the pioneering spirit. The foundation of this nation lies in the bravery it takes to go in new directions and blaze new trails. Our survival and progress as a nation is the result of our ability to be innovative. We must continue to discover new methods of doing things as well as implement new ideas that may seem radical if not viewed with an open mind. During the height of the debate on healthcare reform, the issue of whether or not nationalization was the solution came up in congress. Why is that? It is because the idea of "limited" nationalization as a way of producing service and revenue has considerable merit.

There is a political doctrine labeled "Democratic-Socialism." However, in no way am I suggesting we consider the changing of our form of government as an option. What I am saying is the same thing everyone else is saying. We need to reform our current system. The game of football is radically different from the art of ballet. Yet there have been football players who have benefited greatly from elements of ballet training because of a "crossover" benefit. Such is true of all knowledge. The truth contains benefits that can be applied across a very wide range of circumstances, if an objective examination of it is done. We must mature to the degree that we can understand that our perpetuation as a species is what is all-important, so that our children and their children will have a place to live out their term of the living cycle. We must make whatever decisions are necessary to ensure our future as a nation and to protect our way of life. Limited nationalization is a benefit we can have without destroying our form of government or the philosophies that sustain us. Limited nationalization is a matter of social security. It is a move that is necessary for the stability of our future. Our politicians have been discussing the merits of nationalization for some time. This is by no means beyond the parameters of our social system.

The arguments that say nationalization is a part of socialism are arguments derived from a narrow viewpoint. Our society started out with democracy and free enterprise. We have grown to the point where our system is established, and yet still ailing to a degree. The excuse we hear most often when government agrees it should supply us as we think it should is "how do we pay for it?" In no way am I saying we should do away with democracy or free enterprise. All I am saying is we have reached a point where we need to look for other ways to fund the needs of our social system. Realistically, the need for nationalization was created out of a lack of ethics and responsibility for our lives and our destinies. We have let our social decay escalate to the degree that we need drastic measures or reforms to reestablish the necessary collective continuity need within our everyday existence, and that takes dollars. Because of the magnitude of our social problems, we need and rightly expect the help of our federal government. However, our government is already facing financial despair such that it is terribly difficult to find dollars for our current needs. The citizenry is already heavily burdened with taxes as it is, and everyone is looking for ways to reduce taxes.

We need to reduce spending, wasteful and otherwise, by our government. We must seek to get the most out of the dollars spent, and we need another source of revenue for our government. We need this limited nationalization to help provide that income. Our system of government and our economy have grown to the degree that it can withstand the type of reforms that would include these so-called "socialist programs."

To resolve a circumstance or condition with a solution that is "socialistic" in nature does not detract from our democratic ideals or our commitment to them. It is a mature perspective that allows us to understand that we must embrace the opportunities and benefits that all knowledge available to us provides. Every piece of information that exists is to be utilized to aid in our prosperity, regardless of what category it falls in. If fears exist, we must anticipate and analyze them, then adapt to them or overcome them. The U.S. Constitution has safeguards, in the form of checks and balances that see to it certain limits are not exceeded. The government has to be restructured to the degree that in some areas, it will have to exert greater control and in other areas, it will have to limit its control. We the people of this society have to look at the big picture.

Examining all this, it may seem as though this is an expansion of the size of our government. That is not necessarily true. However, the size of our government is not the issue to be concerned with at this juncture of our national survival. What we really need to be concerned with is the power of our government. While the overall size of our government may increase with these reforms, this increase in size will in turn create jobs. When our citizenry becomes more involved in our political system, the power of this nation will be where it is supposed to be. It will be in the hands of "we the people." Then there will be no need to be concerned with the size of our government. It is necessary for us as a nation to be more focused in our direction. This will require a strong system of support for communities and states to meet their future needs. This is a primary function of government.

As citizens of this country, for "we the people" to reap these benefits, we must meet our responsibilities. We do this by electing individuals to represent us within our political structure, and then monitoring those for whom we have voted. We do this by working to produce stable settings for raising and nurturing our children. We the people must clean up our neighborhoods. We the people must eliminate the difficulties associated with ethnic difference. We the people must stop the violence in our communities. We the people must stop the abuse of drugs. We the people must work to strengthen the American economy. We the people must establish the conditions that eliminate the need for our government to restrict the liberties we enjoy in our individual communities. We the people must perform the required actions that keep America strong and free. True, this will definitely be a challenge. However, if our forefathers could create a document that has held our society together for more than 226 years, surely we in this day and age are equal to that task. We the people must form a more perfect union.

Whatever becomes manifested into our reality will be recognized and experienced. This recognition and experience, in effect, sets a precedent. A "precedent" is an act or instance capable of being used as a guide or standard in evaluating and determining future actions. Once a precedent is set, we cannot ignore it and expect the truth within that instance to go away. It is up to us to use the knowledge derived from that precedent in a positive manner. If we are truly recognizing reality, then we must face the significance and relevance of every precedent, as well as what it means to have that precedent set. Once something exists, truth demands that we recognize it, and it is our responsibility to gain something positive from the fact that it exists. Everything that exists was created by "GOD" for us to gain knowledge and benefit from. This is done by experiencing everything we are faced with in a positive way during the course of our daily actions.

The success of having corporations give financial support to communities has precedents, and can therefore be right(eous)ly applied within our social system in a positive way. The success of nationalization has precedents, and can therefore be right(eous)ly applied within our social system in a positive way. The success of legalized "vice" has precedents as well, and can therefore be right(eous)ly applied within our social system in a positive way.

The principles upon which our United States were built are based upon the right to individual liberty. While not producing harm, an individual should be able to spend their hard-earned money any way they desire. As well, if an individual is not in complete control of his or her own body, then that person has no true liberty. If a system of government dictates how its citizens spend their own money or use their own bodies, by definition, that system of government is not a full democracy. It is, at least in part, a dictatorship. A dictatorship is a system of government that exercises overbearing control over its citizenry. Legalizing the most prevalent vices of our society recognizes that true liberty requires that mature, responsible adults have the freedom to indulge as they see fit, as long as they are not harming or imposing their will upon another. If we are to produce a utopian living condition and protect individual liberty, consenting adults must be allowed to do anything that is peaceful in nature within private places.

To say that we have individual liberty while our social system dictates our peaceful actions is hypocrisy. While our social system is structured around high moral and ethical standards, as a collective we are practicing hypocrites. It is hypocrisy to make things like gambling, prostitution and marijuana use illegal. Bingo is a form of gambling that has been indulged in by social groups and some churches for "GOD" only knows how long. This is hypocrisy in action. To allow prostitution to be legal in some states of the union, while making it illegal elsewhere is hypocrisy. For the United States government to grow marijuana for use by individuals it has decided need the drug, while making it illegal for others is hypocrisy. To be aware of all the opium dens within the "Chinatowns" of some of the cities in America, as some police departments are (ex. San Francisco), and not shut down every single one of them, is hypocrisy. Hypocrisy is a lie. It is a denial of reality. We must truly recognize the realities of our existence and deal with them in a truly positive manner in the hope of achieving a balanced, harmonious living condition. We do this by exercising discipline, compromise, and tolerance. The harm with most anything that exists is not the use of it, but rather the abuse of it. The problem within our society is not indulgence itself. The problem is the behavior that results from the abuse and excess of indulgence. To correct this wrong, the human must make a conscious choice to do what is right(eous). The social system cannot make this choice for any individual.

The legalization of vices would be a positive action within the context of both our worldly reality and spiritual reality. It would be of positive benefit to the body, mind, and soul of our society. It would give order to the systems of our lives and put an end to the hypocrisies we have created. Vice legalization would broaden our social system's economic base. As well, it would replace some of the entrepreneurial opportunities lost through nationalization. The profiting from and/or taxing of various vices would supplement, if not completely supply the revenue needed to facilitate the reformation of our nation's education, recreation, and healthcare systems. We must act responsibly so that we can use everything available to us in a positive way. We must use the elements of existence, not abuse them. As each of us moves through our lives, we must explore the positive uses of every element available to us. We must derive from these elements the benefit to be realized from their use or movement. Our society must evolve in consciousness, not regress. It is time for us to face the realities before us maturely. Vice is not going to go away. We are not lowering our moral standards by legalizing the most prevalent vices that exist within our society. Something that is legal according to civil law can still be morally wrong. We cannot legislate our behavior into the realm of morality. Each of us must responsibly choose the moral path for ourselves. So let us incorporate the outlet of vice into our social system such that it has a positive impact upon our collective existence. In this way, we will create for ourselves a more perfect living condition.

Gambling is the wagering of money or other things of value on an uncertain event. Humans have gambled throughout history. Evidence of games of chance has been found by anthropologists. In our present, gambling occurs in almost all nations of the planet in many different forms. Here within our united states, the act of wagering is considered a destructive activity that is for the most part illegal. Yet, some segments of our society have found it prudent to legalize it in "zoned" areas. Some of our states have even begun to indulge in gambling as a way of producing revenue to the degree that it is a major industry in some u's cities. Gambling was legalized in Las Vegas and Reno in 1931, and in Atlantic City in 1978. With certain limitations, gambling is legal in South Dakota. There are gambling casinos in Minnesota, Mississippi, and Louisiana. In 1990, the gross revenue from state and local lotteries exceeded $20 billion. Since then, many Indian reservations and tribes have been permitted to build and operate gambling establishments. Washington, Montana, North Carolina, Florida, Connecticut, Arizona, Idaho, and New York are a few of the states that have American Indian-run casino gambling establishments. Iowa revived riverboat gambling in 1991. There are the resort casinos in places like Monte Carlo. There are the betting offices in Britain. As well, there are systems in the United States like the off-track betting (OTB) system in New York City established in 1971. In New York City, the objective of the legalization of the vice called "gambling" was to raise revenue and <u>discourage illegal gambling</u>. It is estimated that there is $100 billion dollars spent illegally on gambling each year. The existence of legalized gambling in America has set a precedent. Let us now apply the positive things we have learned from it, together with compromise and tolerance, to achieve harmony and balance within a more perfect union. We must face the hypocrisies of our existence and apply our faculties such that all the elements of our world aid and enhance our lives. To this degree, all states should have some form of legalized gambling, with the proceeds used to, among other things, aid the aging population of America.

Prostitution has been a part of human existence since ancient times. There are references to prostitution within the Bible, as early as the book of genesis. It currently exists in both civilized and primitive societies. Prostitution even occurs in animal species other than humans. In some ancient societies, prostitution had religious connotations. In ancient Greece, prostitutes were women of high social position. In contrast, the prostitutes of Rome were women of low social position. In the Middle Ages, legally licensed brothels were a revenue source for municipalities. In the 16th century, an epidemic of sexually transmitted diseases led to Europe's efforts to control the prostitution trade. Those efforts to control prostitution included the closing of establishments where prostitution occurred, and strict punishment for those caught engaging in the sex trade. Yet, these efforts proved ineffective at stopping prostitution. Europe's efforts were then redirected toward regulating prostitution to curb the spread of sexually transmitted diseases.

At one time, prostitution flourished here in the United States. It was not until the early 1900's that legal efforts were made to negatively impact the sex trade in America. Now, most states have laws forbidding prostitution. However, there are exceptions. In our present-day society, just as in societies past, there is a need for "red-light districts," strip shows, prostitution, etc. In looking to restructure our social system, because we can do nothing to eliminate the desire for these things, we need to recognize the need for these outlets for the "sexually indulgent." They should be made a legal part of the economy so that people have this choice as an outlet and an indulgence. For one, they provide economic sustenance for those involved in that sort of trade.

Secondly, they are an outlet for those who succumb to the temptations of the flesh. The human cannot eliminate temptation. It must resist it. Succumbing to temptation is either an individual choice, or an individual weakness. Therefore, it is up to the individual to gain perspective from their weaknesses, and to understand the motivation behind their choices. That person must reconcile their acts within the context of their life to the degree that he or she remains positive in nature. As long as that person does not cause harm to another, the rest of us must understand that person consciously deals with the ramifications of their deeds, and is judged only by the system of "GOD."

To give in to physical temptation while having a commitment and love for "GOD" in one's heart is personally humiliating. That person must reconcile their behavior within the context of their oneness with the Divine Energy of Life. We others cannot judge this person's morality. We can only create a moral environment within which persons can dwell. However, each of us must accept the truth that the human will not be without sin as is stated within the Holy Scriptures. Alternatively said in scientific terms, the human cannot eliminate all that is negative from its existence because of the magnetic foundation of all living things. Interpreted either way, each of us must recognize and allow for each other's weakness in places of "limited immorality," so that we can realistically separate and deal with both morality and immorality in a positive manner. In this way, our society will be exercising compromise and tolerance to achieve harmony and balance. It is not positive to deprive a person of the indulgence of their flesh. As well, it is not positive to allow that person to impose their will upon, or otherwise harm another. Therefore, we must make allowance for that person's need to experience while seeking to control it. This attitude is necessary for the betterment and evolution of our civilization.

Thirdly, the occurrence of these things serves as an example of a weakness of character and moral fiber prevalent within the human species. These happenings are an example to those who understand the negative ramifications of this type of indulgence. Someone once said, "without darkness, how will we know the light?" For the individual who gives in to his or her physical nature and partakes of the sins of the flesh, it is up to them to gain perspective on their transgression. It is up to the individual to gain an understanding of the magnitude of the ramifications related to their actions. An individual must reconcile their actions with their spiritual or secular belief system, their commitment to right(eous)ness, and the path the journey of their life is to take. The rest of us cannot and should not judge, condemn, or deprive that person of their self-indulgent desire. This is true in so long as that person does not inflict harm or impose their desires upon another who does not concur. While not imposing our individual will upon another, as a collective, we must respect one another's desire for such indulgence.

Sexual indulgence has a major role within human existence. Just as the human must seek to control all of its other behavior while experiencing life in all its fullness, the human must apply this same conscious rationale to the area of sexuality. An example of how a social system applied civilized rationale to the legalization of prostitution exists in a British parliamentary act of 1959. This act made solicitation by "streetwalking" prostitutes illegal. However, it permitted women to engage in prostitution within the privacy of their own homes. There were provisions made for those wishing to get out of the life of prostitution. They were to be given training to develop commercial or technical skills.

Other European and Asian countries have policies aimed at dealing with the realities of prostitution, as opposed to the unrealistic efforts to eliminate it. In Amsterdam, Netherlands, there is the red-light district. Prostitution is legal there for those over the age of 18. There is a thriving sex industry in Japan. Prostitution was legal there until 1956. Yet, having a law against it has had little effect on the trade itself. It is a multi-billion-dollar industry that is very open, caters to every desire, and enjoys very little police interference.

In Windsor, Canada, prostitution is legal when the business is conducted within the confines of escort services. The availability of sex-for-hire and/or pornography has not destroyed the social structure of any of these countries, as is always the implication. We must face the hypocrisies of our existence and apply our faculties such that all the elements of existence aid and enhance our lives.

Pornography also should be "zoned." This is already the case in some municipalities. In an article dated Nov. 4, 1996, it was reported that the council of one New Jersey town approved an ordinance that designated a part of its industrial section as the official "porn district." This was done in an effort to localize all these businesses into a single, out-of-the-way, identifiable vicinity. The council's intent was not an "open invitation" to the sex industry. Rather, it was an attempt to deal with the issues related to an individual's right to indulge themselves in the offerings of the sex industry without harming the community at large. In 1998, the mayor of New York City began to initiate a plan to "zone" sex-oriented businesses. By "zoning" the activities related to prostitution and pornography, we localize and separate it from our everyday existence. If it is necessary to look at this truth as an issue of good vs. evil, the zoning of these vices still makes sense. Right now, good and evil exist together within our social system. Evil is all around us. Some of us live next door to it. It is in our communities, and we cannot identify it. What we must do is separate good behavior from bad behavior. We must localize the unsavory elements of our society in a place that we can more easily "choose" to stay away from, while we in turn respect another's desire for such indulgence.

Another possible benefit of legalizing prostitution has to do with the control of the destructive nature of the pedophile. There are many pedophiles within our midst. Many more than one might believe. Most pedophiles suppress their deviant desires because they know that those desires are morally and socially wrong. Sometimes the suppression and/or denial of these impulses can go on for years. All the while, they are building in intensity. It is almost inevitable that an individual with this problem will lose control at some point during the course of their life. Most often than not, it will be when that person is confronted with the combination of great opportunity and great temptation. When this occurs, these desires will erupt with a vengeance, and cause great harm to some very innocent members of our human community. Examples of this very occurrence are all too present within our society. The legalization of prostitution could aid our society in dealing with this hidden threat. Many individuals that go into this "line of work" have very adolescent features, while actually being legal adults. These persons could "dress up" and provide an outlet for the pedophile that is largely successful at suppressing his or her desires. Having the option of occasionally releasing the stress created from not being able to indulge in their desire, individuals with this problem may never pose a threat to the public. This also affords that individual the opportunity to keep their perversion private, which goes a long way in allowing them to remain a positive, contributing member of our social system. This is because a pedophile can come from many walks of life. They could be a priest, a doctor, a nurse, a teacher, or any number of respected individuals. By having a legal way of indulging their deviant desires and releasing their pinned-up impulses, society increases its chances of never being confronted with the aftermath of what happens when that person erupts in the midst of our nation's most innocent.

Legalizing and zoning these elements of our existence is not condoning the activities themselves. Rather, the social system is applying a more realistic approach to dealing with their existence. According to some interpretations of GODs' law, divorce and/or abortion are not to be condoned. Yet, they are legal within defined parameters. This was done because certain human realities could not be ignored. One of our systems of existence found it necessary to apply compromise and tolerance to the problems of unwanted marriages and births. This led to solutions that, while perhaps contrary to morality and/ or spiritual doctrine, were incorporated into our social structure to satisfy those in need. Our social system must apply this rationale to a great many of our social problems. If we are going to create a more perfect union, we must collectively open our minds and apply all the knowledge at our disposal to the task of building a living condition within which we all can thrive.

Another of the vices that needs to be legalized is the recreational use of illicit drugs. To some it is very difficult to rationalize the notion of legalizing the use of what are currently illicit drugs. To understand this, it is truly necessary to open one's mind and let the truth come in. It is also necessary to understand the need for compromise and tolerance in an effort to make more perfect our entire living condition. There are a great many people, from all walks of life, that practice "self-medication." We collectively accept an individual's right to take an aspirin, or cough medicine, or any other drug purchased from the "drug store." The same principles that are the foundation of this acceptance apply to an individual's right to utilize other drugs as well. Mental health is considered an important element of one's overall wellbeing. Recreational drug use does provide some individuals with the capacity to relax and explore themselves. If this activity is helpful and satisfying to them, it is a contributing factor to their mental wellbeing.

The social system claims to be after a "drug-free America." However, the descriptive term "drugs" includes aspirin and other drugs that have a positive effect on society when used properly and not abuse. So too the use of what are now illicit drugs can have a positive effect upon our society if they are not abused. The declaration regarding a drug-free America is not a true one. It is hypocrisy. One of the largest industries within the American economic picture is the pharmaceutical industry. It has been estimated that 98% of the human population will have taken some form of drug before death is reached. To be truthful, what some members of our society seek is an "illicit drug-free America." In examining this, we find that the drugs we are trying to get rid of are judged to be negative for a segment of our society based upon the behavior of individuals that abuse them. The mature "use" of these given substances can have a positive effect upon the individual using them. If that individual positively functions within the parameters of society and they are not harming or violating another, then that person should be allowed to do whatever peaceful thing satisfies them. If we were truly seeking to protect our society from harm and violation, our nation would be focusing closer on the drug companies that are flooding our society with drugs that are at least as harmful. Take a focused look at a commercial for one of these new drugs. For the sake of example, say it is advertised as a way to get rid of migraine headaches. Yet, the side effects are stomach cramps, diarrhea, and nausea, along with possible liver and kidney damage. What needs to be recognized here is that these drugs are being allowed to go to market before the research on them is complete. Because the side effects have been identified, they are allowed to market the drug as long as the consumer is made aware of those side effects.

What are the bigger questions? Why has the drug company not been required to modify the drug so that it does not cause those side effects? What damage to the body is being done, such that the body responds to the ingestion of said drug with the side effects mentioned? Why are these questions not being asked and answered? The answer is related to selfishness and greed. For one, the American public is not paying close enough attention because of the complexities of their day-to-day existence. For the drug producers, it is time-consuming and costly to completely research all the effects of a drug. If in the long run the drug is found to be harmful, then the expense of the research is lost.

If the FDA, drug companies, and the medical establishment are allowed to medicate us while knowing they could be harming us, why then can't we self-medicate if we so choose, knowing as they do? We must face the hypocrisies of our existence and apply our faculties such that all the elements of existence aid and enhance our lives. What must be done is each of us must learn to produce the correct, right(eous), positive behavior. Our nation must not seek to restrict our liberties by legislating our personal choices. Our "GOD" gave us dominion over the elements around us to allow us to become more perfect. By denying individuals the right to exercise personal freedom and self-control, the social system is placing stress upon those that make up the fabric of society. This is a contributing factor to the tensions within our society, whether or not individuals and/or the collective can face the truth long enough to admit it.

It is contrary to the positive state of society to imply that a responsible, knowledgeable individual cannot make the choice to "self-medicate" with what are currently illicit drugs. People who have earned great community respect with their positive actions are forced to indulge themselves in secret and risk criminal charges if they are caught. All the while society is routinely self-medicating with so-called "over-the-counter" drugs. If an individual's daily life is composed of positive, moral, and ethical actions, what right does the society that benefits from those actions have to not allow that individual to use earthly chemicals to create stimulation and satisfaction within their own body in their personal time, for the purposes of relaxation and recreation? This should be true especially in a society so heavily dependent upon chemical ingestion as a means of survival. Individuals should be trusted to use illicit drugs for relaxation and recreation responsibly, just as they are trusted to use over-the-counter and prescription drugs.

Drugs have been utilized by humankind since the beginning of its existence. There are cultures, past and present, within which psychoactive substance use is an acceptable part of the system of living. The method of ingesting them varies according to the form of the drug itself. Tobacco and cocaine have been found in the mummies of ancient Egypt. The oldest books of the Arab culture contain mention of the poppy plant. Extracts from the poppy plant have been used on almost every continent. Use of an LSD-like drug produced by Amazonian Indians from a mixture of jungle vines and leaves dates back to prehistoric times. It is made into a tea, and its use is said to give individuals access to the divine, as well as strengthening community cohesion and social bonding. This same drug is now used in modern urban Brazilian communities that are equally comparable to Middle America. There is a Christian church referred to as the "UDV" present in many Brazilian cities. As a part of the congregation's ritual, they drink this tea twice a month. After each member drinks the tea, these individuals take a seat and remain in the church for up to 4 hours. Some talk, some listen, some close their eyes, and some stare. In the end, this psychedelic drug leads each user on a journey within themselves that answers the questions of how to become more perfect individuals. During the period between the rituals, these individuals are clearer about what they need to do to become better doctors, lawyers, teachers, husbands, wives, and parents. Because of their use of this psychedelic drug, they drink no alcohol and use no other drugs. Some doctors who have studied these people believe that this mixture can be made into a vaccine that will eliminate drug abuse.

In America, at around the turn of the century, one of the leading aspirin products sold to the public contained heroin. Cocaine was once hailed as a miracle drug. Physicians prescribed it for the treatment of exhaustion, depression, and morphine addiction. It was an ingredient in many patented medicines. Some wines and soda pops had either coca leaves or cocaine as an ingredient.

LSD was originally found to have useful qualities related to psychotherapy when administered in small doses. It was being formulated as a way to treat addictions. It was also found to enhance the creativity of individuals with PH.D.'s that were being studied as a part of a research project. LSD became harmful when it started making its way into society in a way that allowed it to be abused. The fact that it caused harm when it was abused did not erase the facts of its usefulness.

Yet, because of the limited understanding that the human species has of itself and its abilities, the "powers that be" took the easiest way out. That was to disregard the clinical evidence that this substance, when used properly, held potentially profound advantages for human application. Instead, it was outlawed. Now, there is an effort underway to have the FDA allow LSD to again be legal to administer and/or used, in a controlled setting of course.

In an associated press news article run in November of 1996, it was reported that the United States government itself supplies marijuana to eight people under the government's long-standing "compassionate use" program, paid for with taxpayer's dollars. According to the article, this program was started in the 1970s and was reportedly run by the same health and drug agencies that condemn marijuana as part of the national drug policy. Involved in this program are the department of health and human services, the food and drug administration, the national institute on drug abuse, and the drug enforcement agency. At the time, the government crop was located on a 7.5-acre pot farm at the research institute of pharmaceutical sciences at the University of Mississippi. The cost of this program was $200,000 per year. The article also pointed out that at that time, 20 states had laws allowing the medical use of marijuana, but they were rendered ineffective as long as the federal government continued its ban on its use.

While our government spends billions of dollars waging its war on drugs, government agents purchase close to 1,750 kilos of coca leaves per year for a cocaine plant in Maywood, NJ. The plant produces two products, cocaine and the extract that goes into the making of Coca-Cola. The making of the cocaine is done under the direction of several federal agencies. It is sold to hospitals where it is generally used as an anesthetic. What is the major point to recognize from this? It is the fact that our government having supplied United States citizens and companies with an illicit drug has set a precedent. It is unrealistic to maintain the belief that illicit drug use has a negative impact on human existence, and that our social system cannot effectively dispense these substances.

Drug enforcement agency administrative law judge was quoted as having declared in 1988 that, marijuana is possibly "one of the safest therapeutically active substances known to man." Cannabis or marijuana use has not been shown to be the factor of a single death. As well, there is mounting evidence of the medical benefits of the use of this plant. Marijuana has been shown to help people with glaucoma, aids, cancer, and other terminal illnesses. It helps glaucoma patients by helping to relieve the pressure in their eyes. It helps aids suffers by enhancing their appetite, thereby helping them fight weight loss and the weakness that results from it. Cancer patients are helped because marijuana use counters the waves of nausea that result from chemotherapy. It has also been shown to help those with multiple sclerosis, arthritis, and other pains. It has been reported by both doctors and nurses that cannabis eases pain, relaxes muscles, and reduces anxiety. In Britain, there is widespread support that includes top doctors and nurses there, for cannabis to be available on prescription. In an article dated May 6, 1994, it was reported that the chief constable of west Yorkshire was quoted as having said he could foresee a time when possession of cannabis would no longer be a crime. Nearly a year before that, a physician was acquitted by a Liverpool court of supplying marijuana to her daughter. She admitted doing this, and said it was done to help alleviate the symptoms of a "serious and intractable illness." In California, there have been efforts made to deal with the realities of our existence with regard to illicit drugs. In 1996, voters passed proposition 215, an initiative aimed at legalizing of marijuana use for medicinal purposes. In response to that initiative, officials in San Mateo County had begun the establishment of a first-of-its-kind, government-run program to distribute marijuana confiscated from drug offenders to the sick. This was to be administered under very tightly controlled conditions that include testing for freshness and contamination. Many states have laws on the books allowing the medical use of marijuana, but the federal ban blocks such plans to do so.

In October of 2002, it was reported that citizens in Nevada had organized a group called the Nevadans for responsible law enforcement. One of their goals was campaigning for the decriminalization of marijuana use by responsible adults. This group was not made up of hippies and dope-heads. These were otherwise law-abiding citizens that believed responsible adult individuals should not continue to go to jail for wanting to relax with a bit of marijuana after a hard day at the office. The University of Nevada conducted a study of the financial benefits of such a move. It found that the state would reap $28 million dollars a year in tax revenue alone.

Outlawing the use of a substance is not the answer, which is evidenced by human history. Alcohol use was banned by prohibition in 1919. The 18th amendment to the constitution, prohibiting the manufacture, sale, and use of alcohol, had the same effect on alcohol distribution and use that our current stance on illicit drug use has had. Both created huge profits for those who dispense these products via the black market, while being the catalyst for large organized crime elements to be established. Some 14 years later, after much consideration, pressure, and having wasted millions on the enforcement of prohibition, it was repealed. What's more, it has now been found that moderate alcohol consumption decreases the risk of death by as much as 20 percent. This knowledge resulted from a study by the American cancer society that is considered the biggest study of alcohol's effects on health ever conducted. The problems associated with alcohol consumption are the result of "abuse," not "use." Likewise, the destructive behavior attributed to illicit drug "use" is actually committed by those individuals that abuse these illicit substances.

The drug war in America is not what it seems. There is a lot of rhetoric associated with the effort of eliminating illicit drug use in our society. If this country truly wanted to stop the influx of these substances across our borders, it has the resources and the ability to do so. It could be accomplished in much the same way as when this country placed a blockade around Cuba. There could be such a thing done along our coastal areas. There would be a necessary increase in manpower needed, but this could come from any number of sources, because we truly do have the resources. We have DEA agents on the ground in other countries, while the U.S. air force, navy, coast guard roam the skies and the seas. U.S. customs agents staff our borders, and we have the manpower of the U.S. Army and the National Guard at our disposal. Yet, drug abuse remains a problem for our country. It has been estimated that there is nearly $100 million dollars spent per day on the American war against drugs. Yet, with all the taxpayer dollars being spent, there still has been little or no impact made on the availability or quality of any of illicit drugs.

While the drug control budget for fiscal year 2002 is $19.2 billion (up from $18.1 billion for the fiscal year 2001), it is estimated there is at least $50 billion per year actually spent battling drug use with the criminal justice system. According to an annual report from the bureau of justice statistics, our nation spent a staggering $112,868,448,000 on the federal, state, and local justice systems. The cost to house an inmate was $25,071 per inmate. However, the total cost of sending that individual through the justice system was $71,184 per inmate, when the judicial, legal, and police costs were added in. Statistics indicate that for 1999, persons sentenced to federal prison for drug offenses was 61% of the total number sentenced. On the state level, statistics for 1999 indicate that drug law violators made up 21% of adults in state prisons.

Let us do some math with rough estimates. Taking a percentage of the inmate population made up of those sentenced for drug offenses in 1999, about 25%, it cost $23 billion dollars (give or take some millions) to arrest, convict, and incarcerate them. It is estimated that the dollar amount of the money spent to purchase illicit drugs is nearly $55 billion per year. It has been reported that the monetary cost to our social system related to drug abuse was estimated at $140 billion in 1988!

Taking this outdated figure, together with these other numbers, this adds up to more than $218 billion dollars of resource funding for a given years spending, give or take a few billion. That is, if these drugs were legalized and dispensed by the social system. The budget signed into law for the state of New Jersey in June of 2001 was $22.9 billion dollars. In comparison, the resource attributed to the legalization of these substances is more than 9.5 times the amount of money needed to run a state. These figures are by no means etched in stone. However, they are indicative of the viability attached to considering the legalization of recreational drug use as a way of funding our nation's progression into the future. These funds could be used in a number of ways aimed at reducing drug abuse and the problems associated with drug addiction.

We need funding to increase the implementation of educational programs that effectively explain the impact of the use of any and all drugs, not only those deemed not right(eous). These programs should provide individuals with an understanding that will have them make responsible choices regarding the elements of their being, i.e. their bodies, minds, and souls. People should be shown that during the time that many illicit drugs are being abused, the abuser's life is stagnate and in peril. In addition to the physical dangers, there is usually no forward progression toward the betterment of the abuser's being or their living condition. Once the period of drug abuse is over, the body must then recuperate. This again produces a considerable period where there is no forward progression of that person's life. In a competitive society such as our own, an individual not doing positive things will quickly fall behind others who are growing beyond the level the stagnant one has attained. If this abusive course of action continues, the loss of growth within one's body, mind, and soul can be very detrimental to one's existence. Allowing this behavior to get out of control, one may never be able to produce a stable level of comfort for themselves. This ultimately leads to the stagnant one to becoming a liability for society. This is one of the realities of abuse, and it should be expressed within social awareness programs that need funding to be produced.

A study done by rand, a California research organization, found that one dollar's worth of drug treatment is worth seven dollars spent on the most successful law-enforcement efforts to curb the use of cocaine. They advocate cutting twenty-five percent of the federal, state and local money spent on combating cocaine producers and the like, and instead spending the funds on the treatment of drug abusers. To aid in the treatment of drug abusers, some of the funds reaped from the legalization program could be used to build residential rehabilitation centers. These centers work better than outpatient care facilities because they remove the abuser from the environment where the abuse takes place. Not only are we then helping the drug abuser, but also, building these rehab centers creates construction jobs. Support staffing also creates a source of employment. The reasons for taking a realistic approach to deal with the realities of drug use and abuse is not only because it is better for those that use these substances, it is better for the whole of society. By taking control of this situation, we reduce crime, welfare costs, healthcare costs, and the costs associated with the legal system. It is time for another approach to this social problem. One that takes the truths we have come to know of into consideration, and is formulated from the lessons of set precedents.

The legalization of recreational drug use, if done rightly, will eliminate the street dealer, which in turn will decrease street-level crime and violence. In an article dated June 13, 1994, a 42-year-old drug dealer in Colombia was quoted as saying how he "earned a lot more when the drug was outlawed." Colombia's constitutional court recently struck down laws against the use and possession of small amounts of cocaine, marijuana, hashish, and hallucinogens. Realistically speaking, how can one honestly expect to eliminate cocaine when countries like Columbia exist? This country relies on the coca plant to provide an economic base. It is also a major part of the culture there. To eliminate this plant as a major "crop" realistically, one must first recognize the truth of these circumstances. These individuals have a right to their own cultural Nature. Taking our war on drugs to their nation has profound cultural implications.

In addition, these people are "farmers," a very special element of our species. Their "crop" has a vast market. To immediately eliminate the crop is truly not right(eous) for many reasons. An effective approach would be to allow the production and sale of this crop during a transitional period. Over this period, the profits from these sales could be utilized to stabilize the country, allow the culture to become more progressive, and make better the living conditions there. Our government could buy the cocaine directly from the Colombians (at a substantially reduced cost) and dispense it through pharmaceutical channels. While this is going on, other alternative crops can be introduced to the region. Over time, the culture there may or may not continue to revolve around the coca plant. This is truly not for Americans to decide. The country's economic dependence could be shifted from the reliance on coca plants to crops that are more useful. Under such a plan, cocaine production would be under control. As well, world hunger would be helped to become a thing of the past.

It is time for America to rethink its stance on illicit drug use. Prohibition has not worked. Our future as a productive nation of free individuals depends upon our constructively dealing with the problems that threaten to erode the foundation these United States were built upon. What we need to do now is apply what has been learned from human history, and what currently is working in other countries. Italy, Spain, and Holland generally ignore the use of small amounts of drugs. Holland, with its liberal drug policy, has 60% less drug use than does the United States. In a newspaper article dated sept. 4, 1996, it told of what was happening in Bussum, Netherlands, a small town near Amsterdam. This town, in an effort to keep marijuana smokers off the street and away from hard drug dealers, decided to take control of the marijuana trade by going in the business and selling it themselves. Marijuana is sold legally elsewhere in the Netherlands in privately own coffee shops. In the Netherlands, they make a distinction between soft drugs, and hard drugs. Marijuana is considered a soft drug, because it is less addictive than a hard drug, like cocaine or heroin. Canada's stance on marijuana use has led to the opening of a restaurant in Vancouver called the "Cannabis Café." Marijuana smoking takes place right in the restaurant. Switzerland has a heroin maintenance program that has been successful in reducing the crime related to this particular drug's abuse. In addition, relative to precedents that have already been set, let us not forget that England once sold opium to China as a part of the trade between the two countries. Britain's control of Hong Kong was the result of an opium war fought over the 1839 confiscation and burning of the British shipments of opium by the Chinese authorities. America and France were also involved in the trade of opium with China.

Many knowledgeable and respected people within our society that agree it is time for our nation to look for more realistic alternatives for dealing with substance abuse. A former surgeon general agrees with many others that we can reduce the crime rate by legalizing drug use. She estimated that "60 percent of most of our violent crimes are associated with alcohol and drug abuse." There is the minister at the church the Clintons attended while Mr. Clinton was president. The reverend said that legalizing drug use would "make a safer environment for all of us." After the reverend was quoted as saying, "I'm not encouraging recreational use of drugs, (but) all society needs to reexamine the economic base for our use of drugs."

Then republican governor of New Mexico, Gary Johnson, spoke in April of 2001 at the NORML (National Organization for the Reform of Marijuana Laws) 2001 conference. He gave a very compelling speech regarding the legalization of illicit drugs. One of the points that he made was that there are surprisingly around 8,000 deaths per year from cocaine and heroin abuse. This is low when viewed in comparison to the 100,000 or so deaths from "legal" prescription drug abuse. He pointed out that it is drug prohibition that is responsible for most drug (overdose) deaths. Also, that the most harmful drugs in our society are tobacco and alcohol. Both of which are legal. Cigarettes have been shown to be one of the most addictive products ever used. However, because the distribution of this product is legal, there is little or no crime associated with obtaining them. The governor, like many others, believes this nation needs to focus on establishing what Governor Johnson labeled a "harm reduction policy."

A most comprehensive analysis of the illicit drug situation in America can be found in piece published by rolling stone magazine, issue #681, dated May 5, 1994. It was a special issue entitled, "drugs in America: the phony war, the real crisis." Inside was a series of articles done on the different issues and perspectives related to illicit drugs, and the war against them. There is a piece within the editorial section of the article that I think sums up the reality of drug use/abuse, and Americas' "war" against it. It says, "What it all adds up to is a contemporary variant of the crusades; a war to purge America of illicit drugs and anyone who makes, sells, or uses them. Forget compromise. Forget tolerance. In addition, for that matter, forget any attempt at cost-benefiting analysis. Forget as well the fact that virtually all societies in the history of human civilization have used psychoactive substances, whether it's marijuana or wine..."

The report in rolling stones magazine goes on to outline facts and possible solutions to the drug crisis we face here in America. For an in-depth understanding of this whole picture, individuals should order and read this report. For many reasons, our current approaches to dealing with the problems that result from drug abuse in this nation are not geared toward any realistically achievable goal. If success is to be had, the goal of an endeavor must be attainable. The elimination of illicit drug use is not an attainable goal. So, we must make compromises and be tolerant, to achieve harmony within our existence. Many of the ideas and programs that are suggested here are already in practice in Europe and other countries. They have yielded effective, positive results. it is our attitudes about right and wrong, as well as our lack of personal responsibility as adults of a civilized society that must be dealt with if we are to correct what is not right about our living conditions here in America. Quoting the rolling stones expose' again, these ideas are "already happening in many European cities." None of it is revolutionary. In fact, quite the opposite, virtually everything that is proposed here in this entire work, "can be considered evolutionary." It goes on to say that "any good non-prohibitionist drug policy has to contain three central ingredients. First, possession of small amounts of any drug for personal use has to be legal. Second, there have to be legal means by which adults can obtain drugs of certified quality, purity and quantity. These can vary from state to state and town to town, with the food and drug administration playing a supervisory role in controlling quality, providing information and assuring truth in advertising. And third, citizens have to be empowered in their decisions about drugs."

One of the most compelling works written on the subject of the legalization of certain illicit drugs is by a professor of criminology from the University of Missouri. This person was also with the Los Angeles police department in the 1980s. The title of the book is "after prohibition: an adult approach to drug policies in the 21st century." While he started his police career believing in the strict enforcement of drug laws, by the end of his stay with the LAPD his views had changed. At first, he supported the drug war and believed that enforcing the existing drug laws should be a top priority. His beliefs changed soon after he got close enough to the circumstances to experience the truth. He saw that because jail space was being filled with nonviolent drug offenders, violent criminals were allowed to remain amongst us. He saw that the drug war had no effect on the availability of drugs. It did not affect the price of drugs. Nor did it affect the usage rates. As well, the horrid impact upon the lives associated with chronic abuse continued to rise. Eventually, he concluded from his experiences that the United States should legalize illicit drugs. Taking a quote from his book, he "started to view most people involved with drugs either as broken souls who made self-destructive choices, or as harmless people who indulged their appetites in moderation, (but) not as crooks who needed to be punished." He accepted the truth that adults make poor choices. He also recognized that our nation cannot use the "force of law" to protect adults from the consequences of their choices. A very strong declaration regarding our nation's drug policy within this book is, "in a free society, negative consequences befall people who use their freedom to do foolish things. Victimless, self-destructive behavior is its own punishment, (and) not the business of the legal system."

We need to stop demonizing illicit-drug users and remind ourselves that these individuals are both citizens and human beings. We need to stop filling our prisons with petty dealers and unlucky users and focus our criminal justice resources on those who commit violent and predatory crimes. We need to stop believing that abstinence is the sole solution to the problems of drug abuse. There are advantages to the legalization of what are now illicit drugs. This legalization would generate an incredible amount of revenue for use in making our nation's living conditions more perfect. With those funds, our social system could provide adequate rehabilitative support services and facilities for drug abusers. We could expand school curriculums to include programs that better educate our youth on matters of health and instructions related to becoming productive citizens. We could build more recreation and activity centers to give our youth safe havens, while providing constructive outlets for their energy and time. Some of those funds could be steered toward our healthcare system to strengthen its ability to make healthy our nation's citizenry. This legalization gives our nation a better opportunity to protect our citizenry from the criminal happenings brought about by chronic drug abuse. Because of regulated distribution, there is an increased opportunity to monitor and control both the arena of usage and the behavior of the abuser. The legalization of illicit drug use is the only clear-cut way to eliminate drug abuse. As well as providing the necessary funds to provide for adequate and lasting recovery, it will remove some of the stigma attached to being addicted to a drug. This will create a more receptive and supportive environment for the addict to seek help in. This can truly lead to the full elimination of drug abuse. The problems of our society are specifically the result of drug abuse, not drug use.

There is a standard of perfection, goodness, or right(eous)ness that each of us is to aspire to for our individual and collective betterment. What our species has learned about the spiritual doctrine behind this standard acknowledges the divine truth that individual living beings will never be without fault (sin). Therefore, no individual life will ever be perfect. Perfection and perfect righteousness is found in "GOD" alone. This can be more easily understood relative to physical science. Interpret it such that the Divine Energy of Life is of a polarity that is wholly positive in nature. If the human being is reflective of the Divine Energy of Life (made in this image), then there are two characteristics that are naturally inherent to each of us. These characteristics must consciously be embraced within the right(eous) context. One is that, like the Divine Energy of Life, there is an enormous amount of creative ability within each individual. It is derived from each of us being composed of both consciousness and electromagnetic energy. Electromagnetic energy is the essence of creation, while our consciousness makes the ability to create more pronounced. Our creative abilities are exemplified by the expressions of human thought (mind), by the expressions of human physical strength (body), and by the expressions of human will (soul).

Second, the wholly positive polarity of the Divine Energy of Life is indicative of the singular direction this divine energy moves in. It moves in the positive, or right(eous) direction needed for the system of our Earth to function rightly. Because of this, each living being has an innate sense of right(eous)ness that manifests itself as a sensation within that being. It is crucial that we recognize and embrace this part of ourselves because human existence occurs in a dimension where both positive and negative flowing energy exists. Because of the physical properties of this dimension of existence, the elements that produce negative thoughts and negative actions will always be present. As our species continues to grow, we produce more avenues for our energy to travel. To discern the positive direction in which to move or the right(eous) actions to take, our species needs all the guidance it can muster.

Each of us must use our positive energy and our innate sense of right(eous) to propel us along a positive path. We must all recognize that neither physically nor philosophically can we eliminate all that constitutes "negative" from our existence. We must overcome the temptations of this easy way of moving and direct our thoughts as well as energies through whatever resistance we incur, so that we are moving in positive ways and towards positive things. This is not only a way of making our individual and collective lives consistently better, but also as a way of being true to the natural system of existence to which we belong. If an entity was created in the image of a fish, it should spend its existence swimming around, doing what is natural for fish to do. This is better for the entity than doing the more unnatural action of trying to swing in a tree like a primate or moo like a cow. This is also true of the human being. It was created in the image of the Divine Energy of Life. Therefore, each of us should spend the fair portion of our existence creating the most perfect conditions for all living things to exist within. As well, each of us should also be emanating positive energy and moving in a positive direction.

The truth that we individuals are not perfect does not absolve any of us of our divine responsibility as living beings within the Divine System of Nature. This is to continue to grow, to move in positive ways, and to strive for perfection. Perfection can otherwise be referred to as betterment. We must recognize that relative to ourselves, being perfect means to be the best we could possibly be. We humans must always seek perfection while recognizing that we will never achieve it. This innately causes us to "go after" or strive for something that is beyond our reach. Each of us must maturely reconcile ourselves to this fact. As Robert Browning once said, "Ah, but a man's reach should exceed his grasp, else, what's a heaven for?"

Once our nation has made these vices legal, how does this help to restore order to our system of living? Many say that gambling establishments exploit gamblers. Many say that prostitutes exploit their customers, and vice versa. Many say that drug dealers exploit drug users. This all may very well be true. However, the truth is that there are those within our social system that want to use and exploit. As well, there are those that want to be used and exploited. Are we to afford these citizens less liberty because of their victimless activities? In a broad sense, vice legalization will allow a more natural development of the elements we currently have within our society. The people that comprise these segments of our society will not be there because they were "forced" to be there. Gamblers will be such because they will have chosen that lifestyle. Prostitutes will be such because they will have chosen that lifestyle. Drug users will be such because they will have chosen that lifestyle. In creating a utopian living condition, we have to create a society where all our needs and desires are met. Within this context, each of us must be compromising and tolerant of the needs and desires of those around us.

The legalization of vices is a part of a program of change that includes a strong commitment to "GOD," country, and family. If we do not make these commitments as individuals, our citizenry will not be armed to endure the tribulations of change. If that change is difficult, it must not deter us from our pursuit of a positive outcome for our action. If we are to reap success from these radical changes to our social system, we must make all of these changes. We cannot legalize this vice and not that one. We cannot institute a nationalized healthcare system and not follow through with the other nationalizing or legalizing. Each and every one of these changes to our social system, instituted alone or with another one, would not have the overall effectiveness as would occur if all these radical changes were instituted together. Each of us must embrace what is true of positive action and positive outcome, of asset assessment and management, and of the need for an American infrastructure revitalization program that includes limited nationalization and the legalization of vices. These undertakings will lead our nation to create utopian living conditions, i.e. a more perfect union.

To create a more perfect union, we the people must effect change to our social system. To do this, each of us must exercise our power as a United States citizen. Each of us must vote. Each of us must monitor our elected officials. Each of us must make our individual and collective desires known to those that administer our social system. According to a UN report published in the early '90s, the central issue of our time is what is called "people's participation." The overwhelming majority of the world's people do not actively take part in the administrative events that shape their lives. However, according to the UN, there is good news on the horizon. Reality is forcing open many new windows of opportunity. The organization urges changes in priorities and approaches to emphasize the human aspect of human development. For example, ideas related to security must stress the security of people, not just nations. It is shameful that there are 8 times as many soldiers in poor nations as there are doctors, noted a top UN official. The report also emphasized that the world's nations must invest in human infrastructure like education, family planning, basic social services and the like, as well as in roads, electrical power, and other parts of the physical infrastructure. In addition, this UN report warns new forms of international cooperation must be developed that focus directly on the needs of people rather than on the preference of nations. Poverty is becoming internationalized without our knowing it. It travels across borders without a passport and threatens the disintegration of societies. This is the real threat to the world.

Our government is currently going through the process of being re-structured and modified for security reasons. We the people are not fully aware of, nor are we actively participating in the creation of the agenda this reorganization is based on. We the people must stand up and do what is necessary to maintain our personal liberty. Part of this is accomplished by acting in a responsible, positive manner. By allowing governing bodies to legislate our behavior, we are in effect, allowing them to control one of the most precious gifts derived from the Divine Energy of Life. This gift is our personal time. Each of us must recognize our responsibility to help make this country a better place. This is accomplished by all of us, we the people, becoming involved in the system of our society the way our forefathers intended.

Harmonious Movement +
Discipline = Collective Safety

According to Dr. Maslow's hierarchy of needs, an individual would focus his or her actions on the acquisition of safety after satisfying the need for water, food, shelter, and clothing. To be safe is to be secure from risk, danger, harm, or injury. Having safety releases the mind of the burden of concern one has for the events of their surroundings. This pursuit will involve every element of a person until the need for safety is met. Just as a wild animal will do, the human will move to satisfy the need for safety. Individuals would fight for their safety if they were strong enough. If they were not, they would be forced to run and hide wherever they could find safety. Those that were strong would be constantly fighting over resources and space, making their lives unsafe. Those that were weak would be subject to the whims of the strong and without ready access to resources and space, making their lives unsafe. The resulting living condition would be chaotic.

Humans are sentient, aware beings that have become civilized. As such, the way in which we go about satisfying ourselves must reflect these facts. As an aware civilized being, each of us must make the choice to continually act or move in a positive way within the social system. Being civilized and not barbaric, the system of actions by which we seek to attain safety must be influenced by the characteristics inherent to civility. Civilized individuals should move about harmoniously with others. This is accomplished by employing compromise and tolerance rather than aggression and brute force while moving toward the satisfaction of the need for safety.

To satisfy one's need for safety on a continuous basis, the individual must develop a system of actions. To fit into the civilized system of existence rightly, the movements within that system should be positive. When those movements are interpreted objectively, they should correspond with what is right as defined by the parameters of the civilized system. This system of actions would allow an individual to continually live without fear and/or the danger of harm caused by another without negatively affecting what exists around that person. For the most part, the civil issue of safety relates to the danger, harm, and injury that can result from interaction with another being. Our individual and collective safety is bound together by our participation within the society of America. The grouping together of individuals we have labeled "society" is partly due to the outgrowth of the individual need for safety. One of the reasons societies are formed is to furnish protection and security to its members. Society is defined as "the system of community life within which individuals form a <u>continuous</u> and <u>regulatory</u> association for their mutual benefit and protection." Therefore, by definition it is apparent that each individual within a civilized society has a responsibility to the collective to regulate himself or herself regarding interactive behavior by exercising self-control. Each individual member of a "society" relies upon the collective effort of the whole group to keep them all safe. Because of this, each individual member of the group also has an obligation to give effort towards ensuring the safety of those around them. This is done in an effort to ensure domestic tranquility.

Every "system" contains a series of actions that are required in order for that system to work rightly. If the rules that define the system are not adhered to, the system itself ceases to work rightly. This is true of every system of existence, and the American social system is no different. If the system in question is comprised of human action, then it is the "responsibility" of the human to adhere to the rules of the system. Within our society, the regulatory system that applies to human action has three areas of concern. These are the areas of natural law, civil law, and criminal law. <u>Civil law</u> is the set of rules that apply to the rights and privileges of private citizens. They are separate from those that apply to criminal, political, or military matters. They regulate the fairness of ordinary private matters related to individuals interacting with one another.

<u>Criminal law</u> is the set of rules dealing with criminals and their offenses. These laws are meant to regulate the conduct of individuals as they interact with others such that harm is reduced or eliminated. <u>Natural law</u> is the set of rules that apply to individual conduct. They are considered inherent in the humans' nature and discoverable by reason alone. Simply put, the "right" and "wrong" of natural law is determined by what is positive and what is negative.

When an individual is a part of a group, no matter if it is the society, the human species, the boy scouts, or a street gang, that person is never "free" in the truest sense of the word. To be truly free is to not be controlled, restricted, or hampered by external agents or influences. This is contrary to the nature of any organized system. As it relates to a society, individuals must give up some of their freedom to gain the protection of the social system. The codes of behavior, rules, and laws of our social system allow the system to work rightly, while each individual moves about harmoniously and safely. The regulatory nature of society, i.e. all the laws and rules of it, are geared toward and meant to allow members to coexist or move in harmony with one another. As a collective citizenry, all of us must understand the need for codes of behavior, rules, and laws. This is the nature of society by definition.

Within our society, what each individual member has is liberty. Liberty is independence. It is living without tyranny or foreign rule. As well, it is living without captivity, confinement, or physical restraint. To exercise the freedom derived from liberty, one needs to be continually safe. Otherwise, that person's actions are governed by fear, and they are held captive by fear. By definition, the freedom derived from liberty has limits. It is the responsibility of a mindful, aware being to recognize that everything that exists occurs within limits. Our time of living occurs within limits. Our abilities occur within limits. Our resources occur within limits. Our economy occurs within limits. Our earned money occurs within limits. Our entire existence occurs within limits. There are rules that keep our actions within limits so that there is a balanced, harmonious, system of coexistence. All of us must recognize why these rules exist, and we must discipline ourselves so that our actions remain within the parameters of these rules and conditions, regardless of how difficult they are perceived to be for us as individuals. The label "civilized" encompasses these rules and codes. Our behavior must reflect the definition of this term.

To become civilized is to be brought out of a state of savagery and into a state of civilization. This is the result of refinement and enlightenment. To act civilized is to move in accordance with the requirements of civilization. This is done by observing the recognized social amenities like being proper, polite, courteous, and mannerly. There is a wise saying, "good manners are the glue of society." Good manners and civil behavior are social ingredients that allow a large group of independent individuals to coexist within a confined space. Whether or not one is open-minded enough to see it, our country is a confined space, and so is our planet. The members of the human species dwelling in industrialized countries that have evolved to a level of existence identified by the label "civilized" are all bound as a group to exhibit the characteristics that define this state of existence. This truth bridges all sub-groups and sub-cultures within such a society.

Those functioning within the "mainstream" of America form the core of our civilized society. While the parameters of our social system are heavily influenced by the core or nucleus of our population, the other members or elements of "America" do still have liberty to move about without a high degree of restriction. Many subgroups and subcultures act in ways that are uncivilized as a form of rebellion against the mainstream group. However, they are actually limiting their own freedom to move by doing so. If one adheres to and moves within the parameters of the so-called mainstream, he or she is given access to all the advantages and benefits that go along with that level of participation within the social system.

This in turn provides a greater range of movement because that individual can choose to enter a subgroup or subculture at any time and have access to the advantages and benefits therein while still reaping the benefits of one's mainstream participation. To reject and/or have actions outside of the parameters of the so-called mainstream, one severs their access to its advantages and benefits. This greatly restricts that person's movements within the social system. This is but one of the disadvantages of antisocial, uncivilized behavior. Another disadvantage is that antisocial, uncivilized behavior by members of an interdependent, socialized species disrupts the harmonious movement of that collective. In effect, that wrongly directed behavior makes it harder for those around that individual to move. As movement is the essence of being alive, and living is spiritual in nature, antisocial, uncivilized behavior is contrary to not only the parameters of worldly societies, but also this behavior is contrary to our nature as spiritual, socialized beings.

Our intellectual and social development has led us out of the wilderness to create a place for human life called "civilization." As this characterizes us as being of a high level of intellectual and social development, our actions must reflect this development. This means each of us must exhibit the ability to learn and create. It means that we must exhibit the ability to move about in an organized, systematic fashion. Each of us must seek to be the best we can possibly be at whatever endeavor each of us finds ourselves engaging in. To be the best we could possibly be when going through the motions of our lives, we must become the best individuals we could possibly be. Our behavior must be thought out. We must act "responsibly." The reasons for this are not defined only by parameters set by humankind. They are also defined relative to the Divine System of Nature, the system of existence that supports our reality.

When an individual with liberty lives within close proximity to another with those same liberties, the need for tolerance, compromise, and self-control becomes apparent to all. To act freely and individually while coexisting and depending on others requires compromise and balance to achieve mutual satisfaction. This is one of the equations of human existence. Liberty + Compromise + Tolerance = Mutual Satisfaction. This is a country of liberty. However, our freedoms are only made real because our civilized social system affords us the opportunity to have them. Being free within this social structure does not mean that one is free to be uncivilized. It means that individuals can freely function within the parameters of the social system to pursue the personal ideals that will lead to their continued life, liberty, and happiness.

Collective safety starts with the individual. It is he or she conforming to some rule or code, while pursuing a positive end to the circumstances that are faced. In conforming to a civilized rule or code of behavior, one needs only to act within a positive, responsible, honest, moral, ethical, and right way while pursuing a prosperous lifestyle. The nature of society and the reason for the formation of it is to provide continual safety for its members. Because of this fact, each member of society must embrace his and her obligation to move in ways that do not cause conflict and imbalance. Those that create conflict and harm for others make their own lives unsafe. Individuals must identify which avenues of pursuit are positive and which are negative. Each must then choose to move in the way that is positive and right to produce and sustain safety.

As civilized individuals, each of us must exercise the self-control necessary to establish a pattern of behavior that falls within the parameters of being civilized. To act in any other way would be contrary to the truth, i.e. the definition of who and what we are as living beings. Civilization is the structure that provides us with every freedom and pleasure we experience in our lives. It was built with discipline, and it must be maintained with discipline. Self-control is not only a responsibility. It is the foundation of individual freedom. Each individual citizen of the United States of America must recognize the truth that surrounds us all. This is our civilization both individually and collectively.

Allow it to become unsafe, whether the cause is from within or without, and all that we take for granted will be destroyed.

To satisfy one's need for safety on a continuous basis, the individual has developed a system of actions. To fit into the Divine System of Nature rightly, the movements within that system should be positive. When those movements are interpreted subjectively, they should correspond with what is righteous as defined by the parameters of the system of human spirituality and/or the Divine System of Nature. As well, individuals should understand that their pursuit of the satisfaction of this need has more meaning than is readily apparent. What is the more meaningful and/or spiritual reason to satisfy the need for this state of being? It is to perpetuate the existence of living things, i.e. human beings. Each human being must embrace a righteous system of actions that would allow the individual to help others continually live without fear or the danger of harm caused by another, without negatively impacting what exists around that person. One reason is that it is a part of our responsibility related to our position of having dominion on our Earth. Another is that the definition of our nature as a socialized species related to community life is indicative of this fact as well.

The perpetual motion of this Divine System of Nature is dependent upon one element of earthly existence helping or contributing to the positive movement of another. Because of this, together with the inherent nature of our species, every individual must embrace their responsibility to humanity. Each of us must recognize that the <u>natural</u> response to help protect each other from harm is what led to the creation of societies. For natural and/or spiritual reasons, every person must make an effort to contribute not only to their own safety, but also to that of the group to which they belong. Each of us must help others meet the need for safety when possible. Each person making an effort to help another attain safety when possible is how safety is sustained for us all both individually and collectively. Every human being will be met with opportunities to help another attain safety as they move through their life. Some opportunities are right for that person, and some are not. Each individual must sense and feel what the right(eous) move to make or action to take is, relative to each moment they go through. One must identify the righteous movements to make to help others satisfy their needs when possible. Every person is guided to this end by the positive impulses they receive through their body's senses during the course of their movements and/or actions. These impulses include spiritual impressions each of us derives from our instincts, intuitions, gut feelings, and first impressions, as well as that positive voice from within that has been labeled the "conscience." This is utilizing the element of our being we have labeled the "soul."

Following the structural design of the Atom, as all systems do, there is a central source of radiant energy with its elements revolving around it. The central source of radiant energy, in essence, has influence over/has power over/has <u>authority</u> over those elements that revolve around it. How does this apply to the social system? Well, all the members of the social system are elements of the social system. The central source of radiant energy (power) is the governing body of the respective social system. The social system is made up of smaller sub-systems like that of the individual, the family, business, the community, and all the other systems created by its members. Each and every one of these systems has a "governing body." The activity or actions of each member and sub-system revolves (happens) around the governing body. Each member and sub-system relies upon the power and influence of the governing body for continued existence. Therefore, all members of the social structure are to yield to the authority of the governing body, as the members of society make up the "governed." Simply put, this means each of us is to obey the rules, codes, and laws that exist within the various governing systems of our society.

To have safety within our society, we must get our existence in "order." What is "order?" Within this context, "order" is the condition of methodical, harmonious arrangement. To have order in our lives means to have a harmonious method or system of approach that we apply to our actions. To achieve order takes discipline, and to have discipline takes order. To have social order means to have a harmonious method or system of approach that we apply to interpersonal interactions.

With regard to our lives and our society, disorder would be to act without reason or concern. It would be to behave as though nothing matters. Our consciousness is what separates us from wild animals. It is the <u>only</u> thing that separates us from wild animals. Disorder and disorganization lead to conflict, chaos, and social decay. If we are to eliminate conflict and chaos on the communal level, we must first restore order to our individual daily lives. We must restore order to our communities. Every change that is required of us, as a nation, must begin with each individual seeking to change and better themselves. The first step toward building a utopian condition of living is each individual accepting the personal responsibility created by the truth.

Recognized or not, the American social system is currently going through the first stages of breaking down. Social disorganization is the label for such a breakdown. It is another factor that makes our society unsafe. Social disorganization describes the breakdown of the organized system of actions that are crucial to the support of civilized existence. It is the breakdown of the structure of social relations and values resulting in the loss of social controls over individual and group behavior. It is the development of social isolation and conflict, and a sense of estrangement or alienation from the mainstream of one's culture. It is a natural occurrence to have sub-groups and sub-cultures exist within a larger group the size of our nation. It does not matter whether the smaller group is called family, friends, gang, community, ethnic group, or whatever. The formation of these groups is a natural occurrence. What must be realized is that "American culture" truly is the sum total of every system of actions developed by every existing group of American citizens. This truly means that "mainstream America" is not some exclusive club made up of the "well-to-do." The mainstream of America refers to the organized flow of systematic social actions that are participated in by the larger percentage of the citizenry. Therefore, mainstream America is the system by which our society functions as a whole, and each of us is a participant.

For the sake of the safety and mutual benefit of all, there must be an organized system to facilitate harmonious interaction between all groups. Otherwise, social isolation occurs. Social isolation is when persons, groups, or cultures lose or do not have communication or cooperation with one another. This often results in open conflict, making life for all unsafe. Our society uses social control as a solution to the problem of public safety. Social control is the enforcement of conformity by a society upon its members, either by law or by social pressure. Our society employs both social pressure and law as a mean of achieving some degree of conformity and harmonious movement. For a society to be safe, there must be social control.

If our rules, codes, and laws are to have any meaning, then they must be enforced. The most important element of this enforcement is discipline. Discipline is a learned factor for individual control. Discipline is self-control. With discipline, individuals can channel the awesome power they have into a positive manifestation within our physical dimension. Without discipline, this energy will move the individual in erratic directions. The magnitude of this (human) power will cause harm around it, in much the same way as fire does when it is not controlled. Discipline is taught to the individual by the authority figures that person associates with during their existence. It is the responsibility of the parents to impart the first stages of discipline to their offspring. It is within the family structure that individual values are to be taught and learned. What emerges from this process is a "value system," and within it is the understanding of right and wrong. Discipline is the self-control an individual is to exercise when directing their actions toward establishing a right, positive pattern of behavior. When self-discipline is nonexistent, and social pressure is not working either, the enforcement of law is the next line of defense against disorderly and undisciplined behavior that leads to open conflict. This behavior must then be dealt with by enforcing the rules and codes of social conduct to ensure domestic tranquility. The need for enforcement is the result of a lack of discipline and self-control by individuals or groups. This need has led to the establishment of "law enforcement officers."

The roots of the present-day law enforcement officer can be traced back to the year 1829, when Sir Robert peel secured approval from the English parliament of his bill for a "police." The English name for police, i.e. "Bobbies," was derived from "Robert." In the early eighteenth century, Sir John Fielding organized the bow street runners, a group of paid police officers who were very effective in the apprehension of hoodlums. As the effectiveness of the job these men were doing became clear, the English parliament was led to accept Sir Robert peel's proposals regarding a metropolitan police force. The degree of community involvement in law enforcement in the present-day versus 1829 has been lost through time, fear, and the lack of personal responsibility. We now accept the notion that police are paid to do what we as civilians are not supposed to do, or prefer not to do. Someone once wrote, "A police officer is someone who is paid to do what is every citizen's duty to do without pay." Having a police force does not relieve the members of a community of their responsibility to police themselves. The truth is that by definition, each of us is bound by our membership in this society to commit effort toward the ensuring of protection of our countrymen and women. Realistically speaking, every citizen is a police officer. It is from this truth, that members of our society derived their power to make a citizen's arrest. In the early stages of our society's development, every male was armed to one degree or another. When an alarm was sounded, every man within earshot came running, and joined in the pursuit of the offender. This was a standard required action, or responsibility owed to the community. Any able-bodied man that did not join in such a pursuit was thought of as neglectful of his duty to the community. Even as police were employed in communities, ordinary citizens still performed police functions. Citizens would pursue and apprehend offenders, then call upon the officer of the law to cart the offender off to jail. It was both the corruption of power and the growth of towns into cities that lead to a more structured approach to municipal policing. However, as individuals, not one of us is ever relieved of our responsibility for ourselves or our interests. The laws and law enforcement in general, are in place to serve and protect us, not to hamper our freedom.

There is a distinct definition of manhood. As well, there is a natural role for the human male within the natural order of a civilized society. If all human males lived by the truth of their manhood and their natural role within a civilized human community, there should be no crime ever committed against women or children. All men should be protecting both women and children, irrespective of whether or not they are a part of a person's immediate family. This is because we are all a part of the human family. This may not be so evident in the other socialized species of the world; this need to protect all women and children of the group. Nevertheless, as conscious, civilized beings, this is one of the human male's responsibilities. If the male human is to be the superior animal on the planet within the context of civilization, then each male must show restraint when physically dealing with animals of less strength. This applies particularly to those of its own species, i.e. women and children. Men brutalizing women is very wrong. Regardless of whether the abuse is physical, verbal, or emotional, the horror of the circumstance is the same. Men and women are different, and each has a defined role within the Divine System of Nature. We must come to recognize how crucial our understanding of this is to our harmonious coexistence. Human prosperity is derived from creating a positive system of actions aimed at achieving said prosperity. How can murder be interpreted as a positive system of actions? How can rape, disrespect, neglect, or abuse be interpreted as such?

In keeping with the analogous similarities between the Atom and the systems of existence, the family is truly the nucleus of a nation. The structure of the movements within the elements of a family is the same as those of the elements of an Atom. A number of families together then form a community, which expands into a city. A group of communities and cities then come together and form a state. Then, a group of states unite to form a nation, in our case, the **United States of America**. A unit is one entity, and to unite is the action of becoming a unit. There are things we must do to become united.

For individuals to come together and function as one unit, there must be a system in place. The rules of that system define the course of actions that make the system work rightly. In human terms, these would be rules of conduct. If our nation were ruled by a dictatorship, it would be up to the governing body of the system or the society, to enforce all the rules of conduct. However, since we are a system or society of individuals with liberty, it is up to each member to "enforce" (or discipline) themselves to allow the system to remain as free as it is. If the individuals of society are unable to control their conduct, and that control is necessary for the system to work, then someone other than the individual must enforce the rules of conduct. This erodes the freedom that each individual has.

Every system has a component(s) that leads it through the performance of its prescribed action. The Atom has the nucleus. Our Earth has its magma core. The individual person has the brain. The family has the father and mother. A company, community, city, state, or nation has a governing body. All of existence has the Divine Energy of Life. These "governing bodies" all have rules, codes, and laws that define the direction of the actions of the governed, as well as the parameters within which those actions are to occur. An individual that wishes to exercise the liberty to move as he or she wishes must possess the self-discipline necessary to yield to authority. Each person must exercise the self-discipline to control his or her actions to the degree that those actions remain within the parameters of the system to which they apply. This is true regardless of the system in question. It could be the system of the home, of the office, of the factory, of the community, of the city, of the state, of the nation, or of the more natural part of existence itself. It does not matter. Because all action occurs within the confines of a system, each individual must adhere to the rules of that system for it to work rightly.

There are only two ways to fix a system that is hampered by the actions of its parts. The respective part(s) must be fixed, i.e. made to perform, act, or move rightly within the rules of the system. Alternatively, the part(s) not performing, acting, or moving rightly can be removed and replaced it with one or more that does. Applying this to human conduct, the first option cannot be effectively performed because of the humans' free will. Others cannot force an individual with free will to adhere to the parameters of the social system. For individuals with free will, the only "force" that can be exerted upon them to conform to the parameters of the social system takes the form of discipline. Civilization is derived from discipline, and it cannot continue to exist without it. Discipline is the training of the mental, moral, and physical powers the human possess by instruction, control, and exercise. Discipline is the state of order and control that results from subjection to rule and authority. Discipline is a characteristic of the conscious mind. It is learned by the individual and applied by the individual. If an individual cannot gain the discipline to exert the self-control necessary to perform, act, or move rightly within the parameters of the systems of existence, then corrective measures must be taken. A part of the corrective measure related to rule or law enforcement is the penal or correction system. This leads to the second option that can be used to fix a part of a system that is not performing, acting, or moving rightly.

The second option is to remove the "defective" part from the system and replace it with a rightly working one. Applying this to human conduct, to remove an individual from the social system is to place them within the penal or corrections system. We look to this system as a means to restore order to our social system. Individuals who cannot function within the constraints of a lawful society should be separate from the populous so that the populous does not have to live in fear. Once an individual is convicted of committing a crime, they enter the "penal" system. Every definition of the word penal involves the word "punishment." As a society, we must all recognize this truth. Our current prison systems are not all reflective of this fact. Right now, for some, being in prison is an option to dealing with reality that seems easier. Reality is about effort. Each person must "find" a job, and "keep" it. Individuals must "provide" food, shelter, and clothing for themselves and their family. Everything must be "achieved." For some who cannot continually put forth the effort and/or exert the self-discipline having liberty requires, prison seems an easier way of living because everything one needs is given.

Within a prison, the only thing that must be worked for is survival, which is a natural instinct. Therefore, even survival could be considered easy because it is impulsive, and not necessarily work. Once it is recognized that prison is a "punishing" existence, people will realize it is easier and more beneficial to work in an environment of liberty. We must change the penal system so that it is not an attractive alternative to liberty, and it must include viable rehabilitation programs. Our social system must embrace the truth that an individual who commits a crime may have a problem that is a direct or indirect result of the circumstances created by to policies of our society. Therefore, our social system must take on the responsibility of providing workable rehabilitation as an initial aspect of incarceration. Placing a person behind bars and isolating them from society does not constitute rehabilitation. It must include psychoanalysis and therapy, reorientation on the structure and responsibilities of civilized society, and some sort of employment training. The successes of boot camps are a perfect example of how regimentation and discipline can produce rehabilitation. We are seeing the institution of the "three strikes rule" within the criminal justice system. After the commission of a certain type of crime for the third time, the individual is removed from society permanently. As a part of the "first" strike, that individual must be introduced to some sort of rehabilitation program. This must occur after the "second" strike as well. If you are going to remove an American citizen from society permanently, every effort must be made to give aid to that person before it is too late. There should be realistic, structure rehabilitation programs instituted at every prison. This also creates jobs for psychologists and the like, thereby energizing the job market for those who seek this occupation. We have a need for more of those trained in disciplines of the mind. Without job openings, people will shy away from these occupations, and we lose them as a resource. We need psychologists and psychiatrists just as much as we need medical doctors.

Once rehabilitation has failed, society must undertake the responsibility of humanely housing the criminal element. During the commission of a crime, something is taken from society. What is taken is either a commodity, a life, or security. Those convicted of a crime are indebted to the society because of this loss. There are many areas of our social existence where the labor of those indebted to the system could be applied. In an effort to repay that debt, prison populations should be utilized to augment the existing labor force. To benefit the society that has suffered the loss, those incarcerated within the penal system should do some form of productive labor, performed 10 hours a day. Each inmate should be required to work those hours within the industry that particular prison was designed to support. Alternatively, the work they perform should be profitable to the degree that the penal system itself becomes self-supporting. There should be no pay for this work, just minimal credits towards some very basic commodities. If an inmate wants to avoid the work detail, he should be allowed to pursue an education or skill. because this is at the expense of taxpayers, he should then be required to repay society for that advantage with some form of community service to repay not only the debt created by their actions against society, but also the cost of the education or training. A carrot should be dangled in front of prisoners who seek higher education in the form of perhaps an annual amnesty proceeding where that individual can petition a community of their choice to accept him or her as a resident in return for their service. In accepting the newly trained and rehabilitated person, that community becomes responsible for that person and that person has a commitment to that community. If the released violator commits a crime, it is against not only a new victim, but also that person's benefactors.

A program that allows the prison systems to become a productive resource would be of great benefit to society. This is a better alternative than prisons being a financial burden. The prisons in this country cost the American taxpayer somewhere around $20 billion dollars in the fiscal year of 1994. With the rise in the prison population, this figure has surely risen. Prisons are surely a costly burden. It is concluded by some who are knowledgeable on the subject that our prison systems cost almost twice as much as they should. Perhaps this is because of the "unnecessary" amenities afforded those who have no regard for the structure of our society.

Some prisons are better equipped than local schools and other recreational facilities. Inmates should have access to very limited recreation opportunities. Prisoners are provided with full, well-equipped weight training rooms. Weight rooms should be eliminated. What purpose does this sort of training serve? It is aimed at keeping inmates busy while they are behind bars. However, this training only makes that individual stronger, more menacing and dangerous, and more difficult for law enforcement to handle should he or she commit another crime. It is counterproductive to incarcerate an offender, then release him upon the public with the possibility offending again in a stronger physical condition than some police officers, and at the taxpayer's expense. There are more punitive ways to occupy the time of criminals. Some inmates have free access to full-sized basketball courts, handball areas, boxing gyms, volleyball and tennis courts, softball fields, golf courses, etc. All top quality and free. These facilities are nicer than what is usually found in the inner city that the youth enjoy. At Attica, the maximum-security prison in New York, there are three buildings where up to 18 inmates per week are permitted to have sex with their wives. These buildings are referred to as "the hotel." Some prisons have academic education budgets of nearly $50 million, and some have equally funded vocational training and employment budgets. With inmate-run TV stations and catering businesses, together with being allowed to attend banquets, where is the punitive aspect of incarceration? Those who are incarcerated for having been convicted of a crime against society should not be afforded the same luxuries in prison that they would have available to them as free, law-abiding citizens.

There is a distinct difference between human rights and civil rights. Human rights are inherent to us as a species. They must be respected because we are all human as opposed to being wild animals, and are therefore entitled to be treated humanely. Civil rights, i.e. the rights, immunities, and privileges of each citizen, are bestowed upon each of us by the social structure within which we live. They are earned and can therefore be lost. As Americans, we are bound by our citizenship to conform to the restrictions of our society. Those who choose to disregard this personal responsibility violate the terms of their citizenship (civil rights). Hence, they must be dealt with to whatever degree humanely necessary within the limits of the law to eradicate the problems they impose upon society. No human being can have their human rights taken away from them, and each must always be treated accordingly. However, once convicted of being a lawbreaker, constitutional or civil rights should be subject to restriction and possible forfeiture. This is to be applied to whatever degree, because of that individual's decision to disregard the laws that constitute the parameters of civilized society. Punishment that falls short of being "cruel and unusual" is not a violation of either human or civil rights. If we are to aid each other become safe, penal and/or corrections systems must be recognized as an element of providing that safety. This system must be structured such that it has a positive impact upon those it affects. These systems impact not only those incarcerated, but those that maintain their liberty.

Each of us must come to understand that "social order" is simply a label for our interpretation of the system within which humans move in collective harmony and safety. The system itself must be recognized objectively, rather than subjectively relative to the beliefs of individuals or subgroups within society. Each of us must accept that we have a role to play in making the system of social order work properly. That role is defined as our moving or acting in a positive, courteous, civil manner as we pursue individual, as well as collective growth and prosperity. Being orderly, civil, courteous, polite, and otherwise mannerly, makes it easier for each member of the social system to move about. These are some of the parameters of social order. One of the steps toward forming a more perfect union is all of us moving within the parameters set by our society. If one does not agree with a code, rule, or law, the mechanisms within our social system allow any single citizen to work at changing or amending a given statute. However, disagreement with the rules, codes, and laws of the social system is in no way a justification to disregard the parameters within which we are to move about.

To Give and Receive Love

According to Dr. Maslow's hierarchy of needs, the need to give and receive love is where we would focus our actions after attaining food, water, shelter, clothing, and safety. The need to give and receive love is the direct result of our desire to belong and to be accepted by a group. This is so that loneliness and alienation can be avoided. Giving and receiving love provides a sense of belonging while unifying the divine energy of living things into a single force. Individual members of our species are not met to exist in solitude. In general, each of us naturally longs to share the moments of our existence with others. This is the nature of being "socialized." Each of us feels the need to be a part of a group. The key element of becoming a part of a group is the forming of unions. Through these unions, humans are able to give and receive love. after our most basic needs are met, we begin to use a portion of our energy to produce action aimed at giving, in hopes of receiving; aimed at helping, in hopes of being helped; aimed at accepting, in hopes of being accepted; aimed at loving, in hopes of being loved.

To satisfy one's need to give and receive love on a continuous basis, the individual must develop a system of actions. To fit into the civilized system of existence rightly, the movements within that system should be positive. When those movements are interpreted objectively, they should correspond with what is right as defined by the parameters of the civilized system. This system of actions would allow an individual to continually move about more easily without negatively affecting what exists around that person. As an aware civilized being, it is no longer acceptable to force another into a subservient position in hopes of gaining respect and adoration. It is not necessary to discuss how an individual can go about receiving love. Our social system is an interdependent one where everyone is supposed to interact in a positive manner. If everyone within this system gives love to each other, then everyone within this system receives love. How does one "give" love? To answer this question, we must first differentiate between what it is to "care" and to "love." There is a true difference between caring and loving. A person can easily interpret a significant amount of caring as love. To care does not necessarily entail loving. Yet, to love does entail caring. We all know from the feelings experienced that love is much more. The "much more" is <u>responsibility</u>, the human label for required action. To "love" includes having to do things. To love is to do positive things that make it easier for the loved one to move. To "love" is to help, and to give help is to give love. At its very essence, helping another is to give aid in an effort to make it easier for that other to move about. What truly binds a group together is its ability to help each other. This is true whether it is a family, a group of friends, a gang, a street block, a classroom, a cellblock, a community, a city, a state, a country, or a mixed group of living beings. What binds a group together is its collective ability to aid each individual member of the group with their ability to move about.

The system by which we give and receive love is falling apart. The bonds within the family are being destroyed by the lack of male responsibility, divorce, and poor parenting. The lack of male responsibility leads to the creation of a disproportionate (unbalanced) number of single-parent homes. The high divorce rate not only helps to create single-parent homes, but also exemplifies the lack of commitment to the roles inherent to human gender. The poor parenting that has resulted from the breakdown of the family structure has led to the development of a generation of people without discipline or a common positive value system. Part of the problem that has befallen the American people in the past 30 years is related to our value system. Many of us have gravitated towards the prosperous aspects of our existence, but have tossed aside the adhesive principles, as well as the toil and work for which we are also responsible. In life, prosperity is a balanced package deal.

We have continued to value the pleasant, beneficial parts of prosperity and have embraced a disregard for the work, responsibility, compromise and tolerance that produces a stable, prosperous station. Those that aren't "legit," or legitimate, want all the material things, but they don't want to adhere to the laws and structure that provide the foundation and opportunity for such gains. This is due to a breakdown in their value system, which is a direct result of a breakdown of the family structure, where values are taught and learned. This is why a major solution to our collective problems is the re-establishment of the structured family. It is a blanket solution that is easier said than done. The simplicity of it is that, if we would just embrace the positive system of actions associated with giving and receiving love, everything would fall into place.

Family values give structure to the characteristics that identify the nature and direction of the efforts of the family. Unlike individual values, family values determine the nature and direction of the efforts of a group of people who work together as a unit. In this case, it is the family unit. Whenever there are separate parts working together as one unit, each separate part has its own purpose and function. Each separate part has an individual role that is clearly defined. Those roles must be filled, and the actions related to them must be performed for the system to operate rightly. When one part of a system designed to perform a specific function starts to perform in ways that are contrary to the rules of its specific function, the system falls apart. Within the family "system," there are parents, and children. Each has a role within the family system. The paramount role of parents is to instill in their children the characteristics that will lead them to develop the correct or right individual values.

To rebuild the family structure and strengthen it to last, our species must come to a better understanding of individuals, relative to sexual gender and the stages of human life. Both these factors of our lives determine which system of actions that each individual should apply within a given circumstance. Within our species in general and America specifically, men and women need to re-embrace the natural roles that create and support the balance required in the family-generating partnership. These natural roles form the foundation of the family unit. This partnership is at the center of our system of existence. As can be seen when examining any system of existence, the structure of the Atom provides the blueprint for the structure of the system. This structure is based upon elements of a system revolving around a central point, which is the nucleus or power that sustains the system. For the system of human existence, the partnership between the man and the woman is the nucleus that sustains this system, which we have labeled "society."

If we examine the definition of the word "human," we can clearly establish what this animal actually is. Biblically speaking, the first time this "being" is referred to, it is referred to as "man." Therefore, it would seem the term "Hu-man" has resulted from interpretation, rather than biblical text. "Hu-" refers to color, and "man" refers to the species of the being. Yet, human is defined as "of, belonging to, or characteristic of man." It refers also to woman and child. Within this definition, there is no specific reference to the implied significance of color. An examination of the peoples of the world yields no major physical difference in ethnic groups other than those that are superficial. A few of these superficial differences, like body type, skin color, and dialect can easily be explained to have directly resulted from the geography of the group in question. Another difference lies within the way they perform the actions of their lives, i.e. the nature of their motion. This is a difference of culture. The truly profound difference amongst people is one that was created at the beginning of human existence. It is a divine difference. It is the difference between man and woman. We humans concentrate too much of our energies dealing with superficial differences. We need to focus on coming to terms with the differences that are a manifestation of creation. Chiefly, we need to focus our energies on coming to terms with the difference between the sexes. This difference was created for a specific purpose. It is to satisfy specific roles within the Divine System of Nature.

Instead of wasting our time with superficial biases and hatred, we should be using our energies to try to come to a clearer understanding of the roles of men and women within our social structure. Within the wilds of Nature, males most often fulfill the role of leader, hunter, provider, and protector. The female fills the role of child-bearer, caregiver, nurturer, teacher, etc. As animals, we cannot abandon these roles, as they are a part of the Divine System of Nature. Women by themselves cannot completely usher boys into "manhood." As well, men by themselves cannot completely guide girls into "womanhood." This is because a part of the learning process for children is mimicking the behavior of those around them. Therefore, a child must have both a dominated male and female figure to relate to during their developmental years to acquire a sense of their true role within the social system. Humans have evolved much beyond wild animals. We are much more conscious, complex, and able. We have also structured our existence into a system we call "civilization." These factors must be taken into consideration as we re-examine the nature of our relationship to each other. However, we cannot escape reality. We must embrace it and the truth that goes along with it. We all have roles to play. These roles come with responsibilities or required actions that make our systems work rightly. We must endeavor to clearly define those roles, and determine who will play or act out what part. There are different characteristics that are inherent to each sex. There are behavioral differences. These differences are naturally occurring for reasons associated with achieving balance within Nature's systems. We cannot achieve some sort of "total" equality between the sexes because "GOD" did not create it as such. Every male and female member of the animal kingdom has a corresponding role within its respective species group. This all leads to the perpetual existence of life. We must bring the relationship of a man and woman back into its natural balance to maintain perpetual motion, which is the on-going creation of living things that move in a positive direction.

According to a UN report published in the early 1990s, not a single country treats women as well as it treats men. Relative to achieving balance within our species, each of us must embrace the truth that the "being" of man and woman are equal in importance to the Divine System of Nature. This makes them equal members of any and all social structures. Men cannot own or seek to control women, and vice versa. However, while the sexes are equal "in" Nature, they are not equal "by" Nature. Therefore, to define their natural roles in reality as such is not right(eous). In a very superficial sense, men are strong because they are muscular, and women are strong because they alone produce human life. This is an example of the divine balance inherent to creation. Another example of balance in nature's plan is that there are more women than there are men. If there were more men than women, males would be in constant conflict over women. In this scenario, civilization could never have transpired and humanity would have died or killed itself off. Existence is the result of a balanced system of actions, and we must consciously seek to achieve and maintain balance. Unfortunately, the long-term cumulative human action of a negative direction has caused a chaotic imbalance in nature. An example of this would be the action of destroying the food chain or the rain forests. Likewise, our actions aimed toward "equaling" the natural gender roles of the sexes have had the same effect.

Manhood is defined as the state of being a man or an adult male person while having manly qualities. Womanhood is defined as the state of being a woman or an adult female person while having womanly qualities. There is more to being a man or a woman than having the corresponding genitals identifying a person as being one or the other. For a man to want to be treated as a woman is not natural, and for a woman to want to be treated as a man is not natural (this is not accounting for homosexuality or other hormonal disorders). An employment scenario is a good example. It is true that if a woman does the same job as a man, she should be paid the same. However, it is also true that there are some jobs that are specific to men, as well as some to women.

Take for example, hard manual labor on a construction site. If the job requires that you carry 100-pound blocks from point A to point B, this is what must be done. In the interest of the efficient use of resources, a contractor must hire people capable of performing that specific task. If that contractor hires a person who cannot perform this task, it is not efficient to force them to keep that person on in that position. This has nothing to do with (sexual gender). Men are physically stronger than women are. Women have a "power" over men. These are realities we cannot close our eyes to in any given moment, if we are to maintain the "natural" balance created by "GOD" (the Divine Energy of Life).

Women are truly sacred beings. They are to be worshipped by men. They are gifts to us from "GOD." It is up to us as dominate males to disregard what women say about themselves and what they think about males. This is to have absolutely no impact on how we are to treat each and every woman, regardless of her age. We must love them. If to love is to do things, what is it that men must do regarding women? We must respect them, support them, protect them, encourage them, and satisfy them. Women are not here to compete with us. If they choose to compete with us, that is fine. However, during those competitive moments, we cannot treat them with the same disregard we would treat another man within those same circumstances. Women do not seek to rule, they wish to be free to rule. They wish to be engulfed in their womanhood, knowing they are free to pursue any avenue they choose as an equal member of the social system. Most men don't have any idea how profoundly wonderful that is for the males of our species.

Women are to be on a pedestal, and they must always remain there regardless of how much they resist. Women bring caring and compassion to every circumstance they encounter. By excluding them from any circumstance of our existence, we lose an element of humanity that brings balance to that reality. Women are here to support men and help them as they make the world a better place. It is the task of man to create utopia. A great minister once said, "The nature of a woman is to console a productive man." This is not to imply that within the world of single adulthood, women are supposed to be submissive to men. To the contrary, it is this period of life where <u>every</u> individual is to explore and develop themselves into strong, self-sustaining "individuals." However, regardless of what period of time we are referring to, reality never changes. One of those realities is that a man is a man, and a woman is a woman.

When a man and woman come together to form a union by marriage, they form the foundation for the structure of a family. Within this structure is where the gender roles are more profoundly defined. Man is the hunter, the provider, but recognition of reality indicates the fortitude and versatility of the human in that the woman can fill this role if necessary. However, the male should not abandon his role, nor relinquish his responsibility simply because females are capable of satisfying the circumstance. Bearing children is an ordained role given to women by "GOD." So, why is it so hard to subscribe to the notion that "GOD" also ordained a specific role for the men within the family structure? In Ephesians 5:21- 5:33, the prophet Paul explains the commitment that lies within these ordained roles. We are to submit ourselves to each other. There is an obvious implication that our interaction is to be balanced and equal. The husband is the "head" of the body of the family. The body follows the dictates of the head. The body supports the Will of the head. Within this union, every member has a role with responsibilities attached to it. Women are the central part, the heart of the family. The family starts with them, and it revolves around them. The mother is the nucleus of the family. This means women are the center of every civic group, from the community to the nation.

Within the context of "union," there are specific roles that emerge as a part of the Divine System of Nature. Those roles must be recognized, embraced, and fulfilled. A woman is equal to a man in that her life is as valuable as that of any human, but she must accept her role as defined by her femininity. This is a part of the Divine System of Nature. A man must accept the role that is inherent to him as defined by his masculinity.

Each of us must explore that avenue of our existence that deals with sexual gender while accepting the fact that racially we are one human family regardless of ethnicity. We must do this collectively if we are to progress or evolve as a species. The Divine Energy of Life created these roles for the purposes of maintaining a fruitful balance for the existence of life. Many of us use the strength derived from the ego to disregard the truth before us. This is to perpetuate selfish pursuits. By forcing a woman into the role of "father" in the single-family household, and by forsaking the role of provider, a man creates an imbalance that erodes the foundation of the family structure. By demanding to be treated as equal to a man in a circumstance where is untrue, and by resisting the efforts of males to maintain their role of protector and provider, a woman creates an imbalance that erodes the foundation of the family structure. Each of us must embrace the roles that are laid out for us physiologically, biblically, and historically. They occur naturally and are true. If the Bible is to be believed, man was created first, and woman was created of man and for him. The implication here for man is that he should see woman as a gift to him from "GOD." There is no implication or inference that she is unequal to him within the system of existence. Any gift from "GOD" is to be revered and cherished, and never taken for granted or abused. Women must willingly accept this adoration. Women must have behavior that corresponds to their feminine role, as men must have behavior that corresponds with their masculine role as well.

Some of the qualities each of us are to have as adults we are to be taught by our parents. These are things like maturity, honesty, strength, sensitivity, competence, decisiveness, moral character, fearlessness, intelligence, discipline and the like. Adults are to live without fright while exhibiting compassion as they move in the right, positive direction through their lives. They are to have a positive physical presence and good stature. Adulthood includes being sensual, stable, and strong. Manhood and womanhood occur during adulthood, which is after childhood. This is an extremely important point. The nature of adulthood is the acceptance of responsibility for oneself as an individual, as well as every aspect of reality related to that individual. Adulthood is recognizing truth, accepting truth, and living in truth. Adulthood is about having the strength to stand for honor and righteousness in the face of adversity and temptation. Adulthood is protecting and providing for all those in need that one encounters during the journey through life. Adulthood is helping to build and support the civilized social structure through having positively principled, constructive, moral, and ethical behavior. Each man and woman must pass into adulthood and accept the responsibilities attached to those positions within our social system.

There is more to being a father than being the source of the sperm, and there is more to being a mother than giving birth to a child. Giving love to a child entails certain responsibilities. not only are the adults of our society responsible for providing their offspring with stable living environments and continuing sustenance, but all adults must consciously make an effort to ensure that the experiences all children have are pleasant. This is a responsibility we as adults have to the children of our nation. We are allowing our children to grow up too fast. Life occurs in stages. We all must broaden our perspective to the degree that we recognize the importance and value of time. This is a reference to every second of human life. Our existence is broken up into time periods or stages of life. Therefore, we must not only be responsible to the moments we face, but we must recognize the necessity of consciously structuring our approach to daily life around the periods upon which our lives are based. We must live and function within the right sequence of our natural existence, if we are to make the systems of our existence function rightly. We must recognize the importance of this fact as we seek to make all the parts of the system function rightly. We cannot expect to have a tree, unless there is first growth from a seed. We cannot expect to have a bird, unless there is first growth from an egg. Likewise, we cannot expect to become adults, without first growing through childhood. We cannot live our lives out of sequence. Adults and parents must fulfill their divine responsibility to maintain order within the family structure. This "order" is maintained as we exchange love. The Divine System of Nature provides a period of existence for our offspring we have labeled "childhood." If we are doing the spiritually right thing, following the Divine System of Nature, our children must go through this period. They cannot by-pass it. They cannot go directly from birth to adulthood.

For example, in May of 1997, a New Jersey 13-year-old boy fatally shot himself with his father's rifle (this story was reported by a local newspaper). He was described by family members as an "expert" with a rifle. How could he be an "expert" at the young age of **13** years old? Adults around this boy were supporting this misconception of reality. In April of 1997, a playground "marriage" and "divorce" landed two fifth graders in <u>domestic violence court</u> in the state of New Mexico. The "minister" was a little girl who was a classmate. She also drew up the "divorce" because she decided she "liked" the groom herself. The little "groom" was **10** years old, and the little "bride" was **11** years old. The little boy's lawyer said the case belonged in children's court, but a special commissioner called for under the family violence protection act ruled that the <u>children</u> had a "continuing personal relationship" according to the definition of the law, and the little girl was "slapping" the little boy (this story was reported by the associated press). Adults around these children were supporting this misconception of reality.

There was the case of the little girl well under 10 years old that was allowed to fly an airplane. This incident ended in the fatal crash of that plane. There is the case where a well-known gymnast at the age of 17 years old was able to sue her parents. The case ended with her being allowed to be declared a "legal" adult. We have also allowed children to "divorce" their parents. Our children are becoming "parents" at an alarming rate. A study released in November of 1997 said, "Children born to teenage mothers are far more likely to drop out of high school live in poverty, and become teenage mothers themselves." The study goes on to say the offspring from the teen mothers are more likely to repeat this early pregnancy cycle than are offspring of older girls. The research suggests that older mothers are more mature and financially stable, so the children they raise are more likely to be successful because of this advantage. What is the bottom line here? Giving love to a child sometimes means that adults and parents must do what is necessary to instill in children their need to learn the ways of the world slowly. Children are children, and they must remain so until their time on our Earth (age) indicates otherwise.

Our nation is shocked by the viciousness and brutality of the crimes committed by our children. These crimes are committed by what seems more like predators, rather than pranksters as children are normally perceived. We are judging our children as we would adults for the crimes they are committing. Judging our children as though they were adults implies that there is little chance of rehabilitation. These children are then condemned to a life from which they could very well have been saved. We must get at the root of the problem. The answer is not judging our children as though they were adults. It is developing alternative penal and rehabilitation programs that address the needs of these youthful offenders. To stop juvenile crime, we must address what causes our youth to commit crime. To stop our youth from doing drugs, we must address the reasons behind their decision to do drugs. Experts say that some of the reasons our children are committing more crimes are because of family breakups; working parents with no time to take care of their kids; and also a general lack of understanding of personal responsibility. Parents must become more involved with their children. If giving love helps another move more easily, parents can give love to their offspring by better preparing them for the world we live in. Because our desired lifestyles dictate both parents must work, some parents compensate for their absence in their offspring's life by spoiling them. Giving a child a "thing" is no substitute for giving them love. We must never stop giving love to the children of our nation and the world.

Giving love requires doing things. Parents need to be directly involved in the education of their children. Where children attend school, their parents must revitalize their local PTA by the increased enrollment. They must attend school board meetings to have input in policymaking and on how money is spent. There is an incredible amount of research that shows a parent's involvement in a child's education greatly improves that child's academic and "real world" success. It is not up to the American school system, public or private, to teach our children values. It is the responsibility of the parent(s) to instill in their offspring the tools that will allow them to build a positive adulthood. With parental rights come parental responsibilities. There are too many "outside" agencies intruding on the inner workings of American families. However, these intrusions are the result of a need to do a job that the parents are not doing. Namely, that job is protecting the innocence and overall welfare of children. Parenting is unlikely any other job in that the "working hours" are midnight to midnight, 7 days a week. The results of a study released in February of 2000 show that proper parenting could stop a child's destructive behavior before it impacts the rest of their lives. The research tracked 40 children that were extremely unruly preschoolers and classified as severely emotionally disturbed. These were kids that had public tantrums and would hit their parents as well as their infant siblings. These children were expected to fail in school and become juvenile delinquents. Left unchecked, it was anticipated that these kids would surely commit adult crimes. To help these children, their parents entered and completed a training program that emphasized discipline. In following the progress of these children for 25 years, the researchers found that they all finished school and became well-adjusted adults. The professor from the university of Colorado said, "if (these types of children's) aggressive, antisocial behavior goes unchecked, (they) could end up costing the public billions to punish them in the criminal justice system." The entire study is very compelling. Ultimately, it says that our children can be taught to make good choices.

A professor from Temple University identified "traits" that lead individuals to achieve heroic success in their lives. These traits can be taught, and it is the responsibility of the parent to instill these in each of their offspring. By doing this, we are not guaranteeing that our children will become "heroes." However, we will be providing them with a firm foundation upon which they can develop into positive, contributing members of our civilized society. We must teach our children to have courage and be strong in standing up for what is right and positive while themselves behaving morally and ethically. The professor says that we must take responsibility for our own actions and not blame anyone else. In this way, we tackle problems we face head-on. We must teach our children that no matter what they may think, they have a gift or skill that they can become proficient and/or expert at. Each of us must find that "thing" we do well and work at developing and perfecting it.

We must teach our children to give love. In this way, they will receive love. We must teach our children the true purpose of generosity and concern. We are an "interdependent" group of individuals, and helping each other is how this interdependence is acted out. No single individual goes through their life without looking for and receiving "help" or "aid" for another individual outside of their family. To complete the cycle of interdependence, each of us must give, just as each of us receives. We must all support charities and volunteer our energies so that we ease the movements of those around us. We must teach our children the value and practicality of honesty. Being honest is simply a matter of not being afraid of facing reality. Finally, we must teach our children to seek adventure and experience different things. To do this, they must be willing to take risks. This is not to imply that individuals should be doing wild and crazy things. However, it is to imply that we must continually challenge ourselves if we are to continue to grow as individuals. We must seek out new and exciting experiences, whether that means trying different sorts of cuisine, participating in a variety of athletic challenges, learning a foreign language, or traveling to places one has never been before. Each new experience enriches us as individuals such that we are better equipped to enrich those around us.

As the American family structure falls apart, the opportunities to give and receive love are lessening. Gender roles and the stages of human life provide a structure within which the exchange of love can be perpetuated. The circumstance of family is a cycle of perpetual life support. It is faith and strength that hold the family together. In the immediate unit, the parents find each other and wed. They enjoy their own company for a while, and then the union begins to grow. They have children and they put their energy into raising and providing for them. They prepare them for productive and comfortable lives. There will come a time when the parents are no longer able to do for themselves. It is the responsibility of the offspring to give back to their parents the energies they had expended on the behalf of their children (energy travels in a circle, from the source and back to the source). From childhood to adulthood is generally 21 years (after college). The average lifespan is 75 years. Utilizing this average lifespan, the period from retirement to death is about 10 years. in a worst-case scenario, which is one or both the parents being unable to be responsible for themselves, the offspring could be responsible for "some" of their parent's existence for 10 years. Surely, that is equitable within the scope of the big picture.

Sisters and brothers, aunts and uncles, all just add support and enjoyment to the group because of the connection we identify as "family ties." We must embrace the reality and simplicity of the human existence. Each of us must commit our efforts to family, and those efforts must be supported by our social structure. Each mature individual has a responsibility to be a role model for other children of society. Our movements must generally correspond with the movements we want children to have. If we want our kids to enjoy reading, then we must show them we enjoy reading. We must read with them. If we want our children to exercise, we must set the example and standard for our offspring and the family unit. The adults of our society cannot afford to continue to live by the rule of "do as I say, not as I do."

To satisfy one's need to give and receive love on a continuous basis, the individual has developed a system of actions. To fit into the Divine System of Nature rightly, the movements within that system should be positive. When those movements are interpreted subjectively, they should correspond with what is righteous as defined by the parameters of the system of human spirituality and/or the Divine System of Nature. As well, individuals should understand that their pursuit of the satisfaction of this need has more meaning than is readily apparent. What is the more meaningful and/or spiritual reason to satisfy the need to pursue this exchange? The sharing of love is intended to unite the energy of all living things into one single "force," moving in the same direction. That direction is positive. Each human being must embrace a righteous system of actions that would allow an individual to help other living things move about more easily without negatively impacting what exists around that person. One reason is that it is a part of our responsibility related to our position of having dominion on our

Earth. Another is that the definition of our nature as a socialized species related to community life is indicative of this fact as well.

Giving and receiving love is a natural occurrence, and a key element of the Divine System of Nature. Love is the element of our existence that allows all of us to connect our positive energy together. The spiritual destiny of our reality is to have the energy of all living things become one force. The vehicle that is to make this happen is love. Exchanging love is sharing positive energy. Sharing positive energy makes it easier to move about. Deriving positive energy from a source outside of oneself makes a person's movements easier. This positive energy can come for a comedian, an actor, a singer, a musician, a clown, or any other performer. This positive energy also comes from interacting with polite, mannerly, caring people. Having food, water, and clothing makes it easier to move about. Having used a tool makes it easier to move about. Having gotten one's clothing dry-cleaned makes it easier to move about. Reading a newspaper makes it easier to move about. A garbage man makes it easier to move about. A banker makes it easier to move about. Every occupation from police officer, to firemen, to doctor, to store clerk, to gas attendant, to taxi driver, makes it easier to move about. The sharing of what we are and what we have is a way of exchanging love, and doing that makes it easier to move about. The essence of all interactions among living things is help, and help is at the foundation of our Earth's Divine System of Nature.

Helping another is the righteous thing to do relative to human spirituality. Helping another is the right thing to do relative to the Divine System of Nature. Helping another is giving love objectively, because it is the positive thing to do regardless of the interpretations. The subjective part of love is the deep caring, because whether or not an individual cares deeply depends upon their interpretations. Each of us must first be objective before we are subjective. Hence, each of us must help, whether we care or not. A man may have a woman in his life, and vice versa. One of these individuals may be of a mind to believe that their chosen one is the only living being they must give love too. Our spiritual reality is based upon balanced systems of action that are all-inclusive. Those two individuals do not live in a vacuum. They belong to various groups. Some of these groups are the family group, the community group, the social group, the species group, and the group of all living beings. To fulfill one's role within the Divine System of Nature, each individual must give love to the members of every group to which they belong. In this way, the individual will never feel alienated, they will never be alone, and they will always receive love in return. Giving and receiving love is how all our energy is to become connected into a single positive energy force.

It is easy to give love to one's family because the responsibility to family members is inherently understood. It is more difficult to give love to others, unless those others are considered "friends." Unfortunately, each individual's circle of friends is getting smaller as each of us trusts fewer and fewer people. With this, the opportunities to give and receive love are dwindling. A "friend" is not only a person attached to another by feelings of affection. The attachment can also be one of personal regard. A friend is a person that helps. Truly, by definition, within a civilized society, because each of us is to have respect for each other and we are to help each other, every individual we encounter could and should be considered a friend.

A key element of righting our collective problems is respect. "Respect" is the label for having regard and concern. It is to treat mannerly and with consideration. Treating others this way makes it easier for them to move about. Respect identifies the circumstance of recognition. To recognize others is to acknowledge that they existence. This recognition makes it easier for those others to move about. Hence, giving respect is another way of giving love. If having and giving respect were given rightful consideration, social order would be easily attained. Each of us must have respect for our bodies and the rights that it has been given, as well as respect for other people along with their rights and their property. In a civilized society, <u>liking</u> other people is a choice. However, <u>respecting</u> other people is an obligation. Some people use the excuse that they have the "right" to act any way they want because this is a "free" country. We live in a society. Therefore, we are bound by the rules that define it. Our "rights" are derived from this structured system. Therefore, they cannot exceed the parameters of the structure. In America, a person at home has the right to act as they wish. Once a person leaves the privacy of home and enters the public realm, that person enters the arena wherein everyone has the same rights of usage and access. Within this arena of movement, persons must exhibit courteous and restrained behavior. This is to allow everyone to exercise their right to have their being in public a pleasant experience. Exhibiting courteous and restrained behavior is a part of being civilized. Having positive personal conduct is each of us showing respect for the parameters of our society. A civilized person is a respectful person. Showing respect is giving love.

Love and Difference

Within our natural system of existence, when an entity is built upward on this Earth, the higher up it goes the more important the helpful support of that entity becomes. What helps to support that entity must be built up and made stronger along with the entity itself, or that entity is doomed to fall down. This is true of any physical structure that is upwardly built. The human is no different. As an individual seeks to build himself or herself up, the systems that help support that individual must be built up as well, or the progress will not last. When reference is made to the support systems contained within the system of American life, the issues regarding the division of people based upon their differences cannot be avoided. Relative to these issues, there are things that must be done differently on both sides of those issues if we are ever to reach a natural balance in our collective existence. This balance must be met because we all intend to continue existing. This coexistence must be built upon compromise and tolerance to achieve the balance necessary to produce mutual satisfaction. To compromise is to settle differences by mutual concessions. To tolerate something is to allow it to be or to allow something to be done without active opposition. It is our responsibility, i.e. our required action, to make positive choices with regard to what we do in our lives. Each of us must take into consideration the effect our actions will have on the reality around us.

Many of the truths of existence can be expressed through the use of mathematics. Mathematics is the systematic treatment of relationships between figures and forms, and relations between quantities expressed symbolically. The number two is the foundation of difference. This foundation is based upon the actions that add one different element to another different element. Difference and division are actions that occur because of addition. When these actions occur, they naturally develop an "equation." Equation is the act or process of achieving the balance that is inherent to the Divine System of Nature. Within the context of our reality, once there is more than one of something and the action of combining them occurs, an equation is formed that is to lead to the balanced coexistence of the factors of this combination. Every entity and element within our Earth's atmosphere is by definition "combined," by virtue of existing within the confines of our planet. Each individual element within our Earth's atmosphere is combined to produce one system of existence. That one system is the Divine System of Nature.

Once the action of addition, subtraction, multiplication, and division occurs, our earthly system requires that a balance result from such actions. The need for movements or actions to be equated and balanced is an inherent part of existence on our planet. Equation and balance are primary factors of reality. Each of us must understand that the acceptance of difference is a mandate derived from our existence upon this sphere. Though we humans may add, subtract, multiply, divide, and otherwise move in any number of ways relative to any combination of different elements, each of us must recognize that all that results from this is still a part of the whole Divine System of Nature. Therefore, balance must be sought relative to all our combined actions, both individually and collectively. When viewed objectively, a human's energy is to move that individual in the positive direction. When all human movements are combined, human action must have balance.

We must embrace the truth that difference is to always be combined to make up the (one) whole. It is the combination of different Atom s that make up one whole element of existence. It is the combination of different cells that make up one whole life form. It is the combination of different members of a species that makeup that one whole species. It is the combination of different members of a neighborhood that make up one whole community. It is the combination of different territories that make up one whole nation. Difference is an unavoidable, natural occurrence. Not to accept it and to resist the natural unity of all difference that is inherent to creation is contrary to the Divine System of Nature that "GOD" (the Divine Energy of Life) created.

Human females have keener perceptive senses than human males. Yet, most males are physically stronger than females. Combined, however, the differences support (help) each other, forming a more perfect unit from their union. People of different races possess different redeeming qualities. Combined, however, we can support and help each other, thereby forming a more perfect unit. The label or name for this unit is "species." We must first nurture elements of difference, then combine them with other elements of our reality to gain the best (nearly perfect) amount of benefit (blessing) for us all. As our species nurtures the elements of difference (Nature, animals, trees, everything that is different from another, i.e. all or everything), each separate element is benefited or helped. In essence, we give love to the elements, and we receive love from the elements. During the course of each of our lives, we utilize the different elements of reality to our benefit. This is true whether that benefit is aesthetic or physical. In essence, the elements help or give love to us. All difference is to be nurtured and combined for the benefit of the unit. That unit is labeled or named, "earth." We all must recognize reality and deal with it.

One of the keys to harmonious human interaction is the acceptance of the differences that exist, and the pursuit of balance through the use of compromise and tolerance. If someone in an American community were allergic to water, it would not be the choice of that community to send that individual off to a desert. Yet, that community cannot consciously expose that person to water as might happen with anyone else. That allergic individual must be allowed to exercise their liberty as defined by our constitution. Therefore, the community must make allowances. To coexist, we must all compromise and tolerate. "GOD" created all sorts of difference. What we humans have categorized as "oddities of Nature" are also GODs' creations. As we come to terms with the realities of human existence, we must recognize the extreme result of the negative action we label "discrimination." Discrimination is the act of making a distinction that works against a person or thing on the basis of the group, class, or category to which the person or thing belongs, rather than according to actual merit. Discriminatory actions make it harder for an entity to move about. In doing this, that which is discriminated against is not being given love. Surely, that entity will not give back love.

We discriminate against the differences naturally created by "GOD." We have discriminatory interactions related to the differences between men and women. We have discriminatory interactions related to the differences in skin color. We have discriminatory interactions related to differences in body type. We have discriminatory interactions related to the differences in sexual orientation. Most practicing homosexuals say their sexuality is a natural occurrence. There are those of us who are heterosexual that say this is not so. Without knowledge of all things, how can any of us make that judgment? Not one of us truly knows for sure, therefore, how can anyone of us say that this is not true? There is extreme difference within the Divine System of Nature, as there are people born with two sexual genitalia. What is their sexual orientation supposed to be? What difference does it make to the rest of us? What is important is the fact that they are alive and have divine energy flowing through them. Because of this fact, they must be allowed to coexist with the rest of us. Their existence must be tolerated, and a balance must be struck between the satisfaction of their needs, wants, and desires, and those of all other living beings, through the use of compromise and tolerance.

In reconciling ourselves to these and other differences, we must constantly remind ourselves that not a single one of us knows all of the truth about our existence. Not consistently recognizing this is one of the central problems of humankind. This truth is the source of much of the conflict experienced during personal interactions. It is what leads to a large percentage of us prejudging and discriminating. We seem unable to recognize that the differences that exist between us have occurred naturally. Because they occur naturally, they are a part of the Divine System of Nature. This means that they must be accepted as real and dealt with in a positive manner. We must begin to use positive flowing energy to produce the actions that are right for us as individuals and as a collective group.

In our interactions, we must seek to achieve harmony through our pursuit of balance by using compromise and tolerance in dealing with situations that involve elements of difference. In these interactions, we must do the positive, right thing regardless of what we subjectively feel. This is the way "GOD" intended us to conduct ourselves. This is how we are supposed to conduct ourselves relative to the word that describes our existence, which is "civilized." We must coexistence in harmony by pursuing the balance of our individual interests through the use of compromise and tolerance. As Americans specifically, and as an animal species in general, we must reconcile ourselves to the differences that exist between us. Our task is not to change creation, but to live our lives to the best of our ability within the framework of the opportunities creation has placed before us.

There will always be difference. It is a part of our existence. It produces the richness that is the human experience. To be biased and prejudging eliminates the possibility of enrichment each animal-to-animal interaction contains. To make distinctions and judgments based on those differences is to pre-judge, or be prejudiced. Relative to human interaction, this leads to discrimination, which leads to the manifestation of inequality. Within a social structure, this leads to conflict. To create conflict is to impede the harmony our systems need to function rightly. Our collective existence does not hinge on individuals "liking" each other. Our harmonious coexistence does, however, rely on our respecting each other. We must expand our way of thinking (i.e. open our minds) so that we are able to recognize the differences in race, culture, sexual orientation, and gender, and allow them to enrich our lives. With goodness of heart, we must interact in an unbiased manner. This can be accomplished through polite, mannerly behavior, which is positive action. It is exercising civility and tolerance. To act in any other way is to live a lie. This is because the term that defines our current state of existence is "<u>civil</u>-ized."

Because difference and division are inherent to Nature, we must be tolerant of both. We can manifest universal peace if **all** human action is directed toward positive, perfect resolution through tolerance and compromise. We can then accept the differences in each other along with whatever voluntary divisions occur within our populous. This acceptance will be derived from our not fearing these differences and divisions. We will not expect harm to occur, because we can anticipate individuals reacting positively, knowing they are prepared to tolerate and compromise. The need for tolerance does not mean that we must close our eyes to those actions that are negative and detrimental to the individual or the collective. We must establish a state of harmonious coexistence. To achieve this result, we must recognize that a state of coexistence means to acknowledge the right of all living things to inhibit this plane of reality.

To coexist harmoniously with others, we must trust that others will act accordingly. Trust of all within our society can be achieved if all members embrace some simple truths. Each human animal has a behavioral and psychological pattern that is common among the members of our species group. Individuals trust themselves. As well, they have an inherent need to interact. So they form groups, cliques, and gangs out of the need to have the same or common actions and attitude as others. In essence, they seek to "match-up" their behavioral or psychological patterns with others. This allows individuals of the group to trust each other. This is a naturally occurring phenomenon. from this, one can see that for humans to trust each other enough to come together as a species or to become one large community, its member's movements and perspectives need to be relatively the same. The smaller groupings will occur naturally. To become a part of the larger community, we must think in terms of being a part of that community. That "larger" community can be one's respective neighborhood, state, and country. As individuals, our conscious recognition of "self" has to be placed within the context of how each of us relates to and affects the populace around us. Our behaviors must be based upon the pattern set by the definition of the group and by the authority. The pattern set by definition is derived from the meaning of "civilized." The pattern set by authority has to be recognized relative to system structure. The hierarchy of authority within the human group is such that the highest authority is that of "GOD" (the Divine Energy of Life), or Nature. Divine authority is followed by the authority of the country. This includes all the authorities associated with the social structure, i.e. national, state, and municipal government. There is then the authority of the family. Finally, there is the authority of oneself.

As members of the same species, we share a multitude of similar psychological, sociological, and behavioral characteristics that are common elements of our shared existence, and they form a statistical pattern of behavior. Because this pattern of common characteristics has been identified, we all must conclude that we can collectively act within the parameters of a "social norm" while still satisfying our individual wants/desires. What is the "social norm?" Well, normal is defined as "conforming to or consisting of a pattern, process, or standard regarded as usual or typical, regular, or natural." Within this context, "social" is that which is of or pertaining to society or its structure. It is relating to persons as living in society or to the public as an aggregate body. So then, "social norm" refers to the standard of typical behavioral activity that occurs throughout the membership of a structured group experiencing a common existence. As the structure of the group is civilized, it is a high level of intellectual, social, and cultural development that characterizes the standards of this common existence. A high level of intellectual development manifested into reality would take the form of education. A high level of social development would take the form of the ability interact with anyone with courtesy, manners, and politeness. In our social setting, a high level of cultural development would be exhibited in two ways. There would be the recognition of the arts associated with American culture, which by Nature is all-inclusive. There would also be the merging of the differences that exist between various cultural groups of our land within the context of patterns built up and handed down from one generation to another. The social norm defines the parameters within which we are to pursue our individual betterment as we apply our energies in a positive direction. This in no way infringes upon a person's individuality. What conformity does in a free, civilized society is provide an atmosphere of harmony that allows every member of that society to indulge equally in the pursuit of peace, liberty, and happiness.

Accepting and relishing in ethnic difference or diversity enhances all our lives because each cultural group possesses something uniquely their own to add to the melting pot of American cultural life. Certain things are fated. Whatever the origin of the term "melting pot," but it seems destiny selected it to identify the American cultural circumstance. Our task as Americans is to mix together all the elements of our ethnic diversity. These elements are then "seasoned" with the similarities that will become inherently enhanced when pooled. The bond between us all will be strengthened as each of us recognizes how much we all have in common. These similarities will be apparent even through our cultural differences. What will result is the best, most beneficial blend. It will be the "brew" that is to be the true American culture. It is one that can be ingested and digested tolerably by us all. The commitment we must make to achieve this is that we as individuals, i.e. American individuals, must manifest and exhibit the goodness that we bury deep within ourselves. We must manifest this so that we can reap the benefits of our energies as a collective group. We must begin to conduct ourselves in the manner that embraces goodness with all our hearts. We must seek to have ourselves neither be a burden on each other, nor on our society. We must pursue with committed efforts, those avenues that not only allow us to satisfy our own selfish concept of a comfortable habitat and lifestyle, but also avenues of mutual benefit. We must consciously choose not to pursue avenues of endeavor that will tear at the fabric or at the foundation of our social structure.

Esteem and Achievement

According to Dr. Maslow's hierarchy of needs, the satisfaction of our esteem needs is where we would focus our actions after satisfying our need for food, water, shelter, clothing, safety, as well as the giving and receiving love. Achievement, competence, and independence are factors of the development of one's esteem. Gaining esteem is how persons build the foundation upon which they are to construct their individuality. Esteem is one of the primary factors of human creativity. It is affirmed by a person's belief in themselves and their abilities. Each of us has an ego and needs some degree of esteem. To satisfy one's need for esteem on a continuous basis, the individual must develop a system of actions. To fit into the civilized system of existence rightly, the movements within that system should be positive. When those movements are interpreted objectively, they should correspond with what is right as defined by the parameters of the civilized system. This system of actions would allow an individual to be continually competent and independent without negatively affecting what exists around that person. One gains esteem from improvement and growth. It can be gained from having a body that has grown. It can be gained from having a mind that has grown. It can also be gained from having a soul that has grown. Gaining esteem is a direct result of personal change. This change is a natural part of our individual growth. As each of us learns to create and generate, we gain esteem.

The body is the vessel that allows us to move. To move into our individual futures, each of us needs our bodies. To better that movement, our bodies need to be strong. The recognition of this strength would lead to a self-assured respect for ourselves. We have labeled this "self-esteem." The motivation behind improving one's body is almost always derived from a personal want or desire to be better physically. Our indoctrination into our social system instills in us the need to educate ourselves. American society makes the task of acquiring education easier by requiring children to attend school and providing a public education system. To pass through this system each of us is evaluated based upon our performance. This performance is aided by the fact that passing through this system is required, and it is monitored by figures of authority within the system. There are deadlines to meet, standards to match, and people to whom we answer. All of this becomes a factor in our motivation to excel. While it is true that an individual may personally want to learn, the motivation for this process is still partly based upon the obligation to perform. This is not true of our physical betterment. Our physical betterment is based more on an individual wanting and desiring to be more perfect. It is "creating" betterment for oneself. When the individuals examine this betterment of themselves, it generates esteem.

The evolution of the human species <u>requires</u> that we exercise our bodies to have them evolve. This is because evolution is supposed to make an organism better and more complex, and exercise is how we go about producing this physical change. Since movement is the essence of being alive, the physical form that increases our ability to move is better. Truly, there is nothing complex about fat. Muscle is more complex. If we become an obese species, we are simply "changing" for the worse. We are not evolving for the better. There is no esteem to be generated from that. We must actively pursue healthy forms of activity to work and develop the muscles of our bodies. During the times of our movement, we must strive to ensure that our bodies are supplied with the basic necessities required for the body to function properly. Once these minimums are met, we must continue to seek betterment for our bodies, which is good health and greater creature comfort. The betterment of the body includes the improvement of the conditions that support the body. The body must be exercised <u>and</u> comforted. We must actively pursue the surroundings that provide our bodies with comfort.

While it is instinct that will direct our actions towards things like food and shelter, it is awareness that makes us cognizant of the degrees in which these circumstances occur. Leaves, berries, and raw meat can sustain us, but our awareness leads us to tasty, processed foods. A pile of shrubbery or a cave could provide us with adequate shelter, but our awareness leads us toward a preference for a more comfortable, artificial environment. The label we have given to the requirements of our existence is "creature comforts." Our individual esteem is linked to our ability to enjoy such comfort.

The mind is the part of the brain muscle that allows us to be aware, to comprehend, and to interpret. With it, we are to figure out each positive system of actions within which our movements are to occur. An element of the growth and betterment of the human mind is to seek out a consistently positive attitude. With respect to the human, to have a positive direction or follow a positive path, one must produce positive action. One truth about positive action is that it is the result of the positive words of thought and speech. To this degree, "positive thought (or positive words) = positive action." For humans, positive action is the result of positive thought. Therefore, it can be said that it is <u>attitude</u> that humans must rely upon to produce the changes that lead to growth and prosperity. Attitude is the "state of mind," the condition of the mind at a given point in time. It is a matter of perspective. A major factor in determining what sort of attitude an individual will have is how that person interprets life. The state of mind is the result of the interpretation each human makes of his or her perceptions. From this, one can see that it is within the power of every healthy individual to control and/or change his or her attitude. An individual's attitude can be positive, or it can be negative. Every waking moment is a series of situations and circumstances. Each individual chooses how he or she will interpret the situations and circumstances that transpire during their lives. When one of those events is good in nature, one can easily choose to embrace the positive energy generated by it. When something bad happens, one can either choose to embrace the negative, i.e. by letting it become a downer, or dwelling on the negative impact of the event or circumstance. Or, the choice can be made to embrace the positive possibilities, the opportunity to learn from a mistake, or to help in some way.

Reality is not as harsh as it sometimes appears. The harshness is the result of the interpretation an individual makes of the circumstances he or she perceives. We are all aware that there are different ways of looking at things. We also know it is difficult to see the other side to things sometimes. The key to gaining the proper perspective lies in one's ability to be objective at the right time, and not subjective at the wrong time. We all have those days when nothing seems to go right. During those times, it is very difficult to be objective, especially when those days turn into weeks. Most have heard the phrase, "mind over matter." Within this context, recognize subjectivity as the matter. It is the result of the overpowering influence of "self," i.e. the body or our physical mass (matter). Relative to this, objectivity is the (state of) mind. Hence, interpreting reality within its proper context is truly mind over matter. It is true that being objective is very difficult to do sometimes. In truth, we all attempt to be objective most of the time, but sometimes it just seems impossible. The operative word here is "seems," which is indicative of the relevance one's interpretation has on one's perspective. Each of us must work and exercise the muscle of our minds (the brain) to maintain objectivity. The mind exists within the body and is connected to all the sensory receptors that exist within us. Without consistently exercising control over our mental state, the body wins the battle of influence by default.

Some might say, "Well, I guess my body wins sometimes." The truth is that an individual's mind must win all the time because that is what it is to be civilized. In wild animals, the body has the controlling influence over what actions it undertakes. It would seem that some of us are content to say, "Okay, so I'm wild." This response may sound humorous. However, in essence that person is subconsciously retreating from the effort it takes to exercise self-control always. This is partly because they already feel taxed and overwhelmed by their everyday life.

Each of us must embrace the truth that once through the effortful part, life opens up to unimaginable ease and beauty. Everyday life is very stressful, and it is difficult to maintain an objective point of view in the face of it. Each of us has days when it "seems" like the whole world is against us. This interpretation of the circumstances of our lives must be recognized as just that, an interpretation. It is not a positive one either.

Having a <u>positive</u> attitude is the natural state of mind. It is dependent upon the perspective that individuals regarding their relationship to the world around them. If individuals think in terms of having to relate to the world, they can be optimistic and positive because they recognize that they control their actions, so they can choose the positive path. When these individuals are not satisfied, they recognize that they can affect change to produce the desired result. To have a <u>negative</u> attitude is not a natural occurrence. A negative attitude is a very subjective state in that the mind is not open to all the possibilities that exist around it. It is limited by interpretations individuals make from the perspective of how the world relates to them. If their interpretations are self-centered to the degree that they perceive the world as having to relate to them, then a negative attitude will result from the great amount of disappointment they will experience as they meet with dissatisfaction. If individuals have a positive attitude, then their actions will be of a positive Nature. In a very natural sense, if individuals have the "right" attitude, then they will do the "right" thing.

Our attitude is the result of our state of mind. The "state of mind" is the perspective at a <u>specific</u> moment in time, whether that moment is one second or one year. Dealing with reality truthfully means to <u>maintain</u> an objective state of mind for the period of time in which reality occurs. This particular "period of time" is labeled "lifespan." A vital part of this process of maintaining an objective state of mind or an objective perspective, is the process of learning. Learning is a constant cycle of growth. It begins as if it were a seed. This seed is the original perspective. Then, as the seed is watered, or fed, it grows. As information is fed to us, or perceived by us, it must be interpreted. This interpretation occurs within the context of the state of mind at that time (the seed, i.e. the original perspective). Once our perceptions have been interpreted, they are translated into knowledge or truth. Once we derive truth, that truth is supposed to be "fed" or added to our original perspective so that our understanding grows. In other words, our understanding of reality expands. From this process, each of us should be constantly gaining a new perspective.

It is a closed mind that does not allow the perspective to grow from the truth. It is the closed-minded person that manipulates the truth to create a subjective, altered state of mind. Each of us has to embrace the totality of information available to us to make the choices that lead to positive or spiritually right actions. This will cause us to concentrate more. As well, we will have to become more open-minded and objective, examining all circumstances truthfully. It is truly a cognitive and intellectual evolution. It is maturing to a new, higher level of understanding of our reality, one that keeps the interpretation of reality within an objective context. We all must take this step together. That makes it a complex process, but it is a simple one to achieve because this understanding of reality is inherent to our spiritual Nature. This is true whether we are capable of recognizing it or not. We must accept reality objectively, because "time" is forcing us to do so. This is true in a spiritual sense, within the context of what is regarded as the "end times." It is true in a worldly sense, brought on by the circumstances of our present and future relative to the computer and the information superhighway. If we do not accept the obvious truth of our existence now, we are truly acting out the ways of the ostrich by sticking our proverbial heads in the sand. When an ostrich sticks its head in the sand, it does not see what is happening, but occurrence still takes place. That is what we must understand about reality, accepted or not, it still takes place.

A positive attitude results from an interpretation of specific moments in reality in a way that makes an individual feel good or right. How is one supposed to maintain a positive attitude when there are so many negative realities to interpret? The answer is "objectivity." Having faith, optimism, and hope is key to maintaining individual objectivity. "Faith" is belief that is not based upon proof. "Optimism" is the tendency to recognize the good or right side of happenings and anticipate the more favorable results. "Hope" is the feeling that events will turn out for the best. How does an individual embrace faith, optimism, and hope in such a way that it allows that person to maintain a positive attitude? It is through the objective interpretation and evaluation of the actions that occur within a span of time. Faith provides the opportunity to unburden the mind of concerns that are beyond one's control or understanding. Optimism provides the vision of positive possibilities. Hope provides the energy to persevere through adversity. We must look at the world and ourselves objectively, instead of subjectively. When we examine and judge ourselves, we must look at ourselves objectively to the degree that we measure ourselves by an objective standard of average people in our respective demographic group or circumstance. This, as opposed to subjectively judging ourselves by the standards we imagine for ourselves. This is how we maintain a positive attitude. When individuals look at themselves objectively, they can always find something good or positive. As harsh as this may sound, this is partly true because there are always others worse off. Another way of looking at it is to appreciate the truth that each of us has the opportunity to live through the challenge of adversity. The alternative to life is death.

As this truth relates to us as Americans, this nation can generate an incredible number of positive attitudes. This would be possible if everyone recognized that only in this country could each citizen say that no matter how troublesome their here may be, someone-somewhere has a more troublesome reality to deal with. Therefore, objectively speaking, everyone in America should have a positive outlook on life. A negative attitude sometimes comes from subjective comparisons we make of ourselves. Individuals get down on themselves when they compare themselves to others, basing their judgments on what they subjectively perceive as true. In many instances, they focus on a standard that is not reflective of reality. It is reflective of the standard they create from a perspective that cannot be true. It cannot be true because the standard is not derived from a complete picture. This is because they do not know all there is to know about those being used as the comparison. An example of what knowledge could be missing would be the effect of factors related to the psychological, sociological, economical, geographical, and other atypical circumstances that affect human development. By not considering relevant factors, individuals create a biased picture that more often than not, does not give a complete account of reality. Each of us must learn when to be objective, and when to be subjective.

Our efforts must be aimed at pursuing the perfection of ourselves as individuals first, ultimately leading to a more perfect union of our species. To maintain a consistently positive attitude in the face of the trials, tribulations, and disappointments that every one of us will face along the journey of our lives, each of us must understand something very important. The human can never be perfect. One, only "GOD" is perfect. Two, the Holy Scripture says the human will never be without sin. Three, "negative" can never be physically eliminated from our reality. Therefore, what we must understand is this: as we pursue perfection, we must be satisfied with being the best we could possibly be. We must accept the reality that we will falter along the journey to becoming the best we can become. Perfection is the standard. Best is the goal. We cannot let negative shortcomings and events undermine our positive efforts of pursuit. To stay on the positive path, we must manifest patience and perseverance, along with sacrifice and discipline.

As a part of our search for perfection, each of us must understand that <u>everything</u> we expect from another person, we must also expect that (same thing) from ourselves, <u>always</u>. If we expect another person to be patient with us, then we must be patient with others, always. If we expect another person to be nice to us, then we must be nice to others, always. If we expect not to have to deal with another person's ego, then we must keep our own egos in check, always. If we expect to be forgiven for our mistakes, then we must forgive others for their mistakes, always. Moreover, if another person falls short of our expectations, this in no way relieves us of our obligation to maintain that expectation of ourselves, because we must do it always. Not one of us will ever be without fault, according to the laws of Nature and the word of "GOD." This means that each of us is flawed. It means that each of us has shortcomings. Patience, courtesy, and forgiveness are elements of human character. Therefore, our actions should contain these elements always, not just when it benefits us.

Since the human being is composed of three elements, all three elements of the individual must evolve if the entire being is to be made better. This means that each human being must seek to better utilize the soul as well as their mind and body. Each of us can gain esteem through the growth of your soul. The soul is what lets an individual feel when something is right. The human soul is a very subtle part of our being. To have the soul evolve would be to have it become a more prominent element of our existence. The soul is the part of our being through which we experience our connection to the Divine Energy of Life and/or Nature. The evolution of our souls entails our functioning within the electromagnetic earthly system better. This means that the direction of our actions must become more positive. As well, our actions must become more reflective of our nature as a socialized species. In other words, each of us must become more positive {good, correct, right(eous), true}, and we must become more helpful. This "helpfulness" applies to the members of our species relative to definition, and it applies to all the life around us relative to the authority bestowed on us that resulted from our being given dominion over our planet.

To act correctly, rightly, or positively as an individual, each of us must trust ourselves relative to our true feelings, our intuition, and our impressions. These components of our being may seem confusing sometimes. Especially when they go against what everyone else tells us is the right thing to do. Each of us must learn to trust how we "naturally" interpret the world before the subjective part of our mind gets the information we perceive. Each of us is born alone. We are alone with our thoughts and feelings. Only the individual truly understands their personal relationship with "GOD." It is for these reasons and more that each individual must be the controlling influence in their own life. Each of us must use our minds to see the positive path and allow our bodies to lead us to the truth. In this way, each of us can better sustain the positive adaptation to the conditions under which we live. Our bodies are terribly important to directing our path through life. Within each individual's body is where that person experiences their feelings, intuitions, impressions and the like. These are all factors of our soul that are meant to guide us in the right, positive direction. The longer an individual moves in a right, positive direction, the more esteem that individual can gain.

To satisfy one's need for esteem on a continuous basis, the individual has developed a system of actions. To fit into the Divine System of Nature rightly, the movements within that system should be positive. When those movements are interpreted subjectively, they should correspond with what is righteous as defined by the parameters of the system of human spirituality and/or the Divine System of Nature. As well, individuals should understand that their pursuit of the satisfaction of this need has more meaning than is readily apparent. What is the more meaningful and/or spiritual reason to satisfy the need for esteem? It is to generate happiness and creativity from within the human collective.

Each human being must embrace a righteous system of actions that would not only build esteem for oneself, but also allow each of us to help others to become confident, competent, and independent, without negatively affecting what exists around us. This aid falls under the heading of "support." It would manifest itself into individual and collective happiness and creativity. One reason each of us must help others with their esteem is that it is a part of our responsibility related to our position of having dominion on our Earth. Another is that the definition of our nature as a socialized species related to community life is indicative of this fact as well.

Our civilized state is such because of the continued growth of our bodies, minds, and souls. As an animal species, while we continue to improve our living condition and degree of civility, we must not forget our responsibilities to the Divine System of Nature within which we live and grow. Persons are to use their strength to aid other living things in a positive way. Persons are to use their thoughts to aid other living things in a positive way. Persons are to use their positive energy to aid other living things in a positive way. Our value system has become skewed to the degree that we associate civilization with "worldly" possessions. We no longer consider the spiritual ramification of our actions relative to the nature of our civilized existence. Cooperation, helpfulness, civility, politeness, and mannerly behavior are truly the basis of a civilized society in a natural, spiritual sense relative to our humanity. These elements of human character make it easier for individuals within a group to move about. As we begin to move more easily, each of us will become better able to improve ourselves in a quest to discover that aspect of our being that was intended to be a blessing for what exists around us. That blessing is intended to aid in the perpetual flow of positive energy within this physical plane. One derives the greatest esteem from becoming what "GOD" would have us be.

Each of us must respect our body as though it were truly the temple of "GOD." The human body houses the two godliest manifestations. They are the human mind and the human soul. The essence of the message contained in this book is really about getting one's body into shape. Before experiencing revelations, I was originally going to call this book "with each rep." This was in part a reference to body "building" or "shaping." However, this phrase is truly relative to any conscious effort to work towards a goal consistently. The secret to positive change (or evolution) is "repetitive positive action." This is not merely a philosophical approach to life. It is a fundamental element of the Divine System of Nature. This positive effort produces a condition for growth. This positive effort needs to go beyond the limits of an individual's current efforts. It is a quest to better oneself by trying to manifest exceedingly greater movements. It is the pursuit of physical perfection that provides the stimulus that can bring about the spiritual understanding of our true power as "GOD-like" beings. It is related to pushing oneself beyond "known" limits in a way that requires and generates more energy than is normal for that individual.

Movement is the fundamental nature of living organisms. The strength of a living organism is what perpetuates its life. For complex living organisms, organic strength is derived from muscle mass. Again, thinking of the human relative to an analogous relationship to a complex computer system, the body would be the "hardware." As with our understanding and approach to computer construction, this "hardware" needs to be streamlined, not bulky. It must be as efficient as possible to handle everything to which it is exposed. This is also true of the human being. However, the human is an animal. As such, we can come to understand our place within the natural system better if we take what we know of ourselves and of animal life, and examine what is relevant and significant to both.

The human has dominion over the animal kingdom in both a worldly and spiritual sense. Within the natural animal environment, the hierarchy of the various animal species is defined by the strength of each animal. More often than not, the stronger animal is composed of a high percentage of muscle. "Muscle" is the primary component that is responsible for the manifestation of the elements of power within the animal kingdom, i.e. swiftness, physical power, and reasoning.

Running strength is the result of the muscle mass of the lower extremities. Lifting strength is the result of the muscle mass of the upper extremities. Reasoning strength is the result of the muscle mass of the brain. From this, we must conclude that to live up to our defined place within the animal kingdom, our physical composition must contain a high percentage of muscle tissue. We develop these muscles by exercising them.

It is the nervous system that receives the divine energy, and it is a biological fact that the muscle tissue nourishes the nerves. The human body receives the vibrations of the spiritual energy that brings us to life, and it is important to provide the best "receiver" for those vibrations. The nerves are the "receivers" and "transmitters" of the body. If it is movement that sustains life, then the more movement there is, the better that life will be. Therefore, in the interest of getting the best from our bodies in a physical and spiritual sense, we would need to be able to receive the greatest amount of energy to perpetuate as much movement as possible. For this, our nerves would need to be as healthy as is possible. Hence, we need as much muscle tissue as possible to provide the greatest amount of nourishment to our nerves. The more naturally produced muscle within the human body, the better its ability to move, function and generate.

To be the physically superior animal is to be composed of muscle, rather than fat. The individual metabolism is functioning with "full-movement" if it is composed of a high percentage of muscle. Fat tissue is storage tissue. Fat tissue is non-active mass, while muscle is active mass. This active mass is "moving" and "doing" what needs to be done to produce a positive effect. Looking at the anatomy of the body, the larger areas for mass muscle tissue are the head, the chest, the abdomen, and the legs. To produce the necessary muscle mass in light of the sedentary lifestyle of the American population, we need to embrace muscle-building and cardiovascular workouts. Making the human body highly muscular is from where the energy to accomplish what we need will come. Working our bodies to the point of them becoming strong is how we will generate the energy to do what must be done. The more of an individual's body mass that is muscle, the better the other organs in that body are able to function. The more efficient and tuned-up that body is, the more intense the energy that body is able to generate. The stronger an individual is, the stronger the energy they produce. Bodybuilding strengthens the body and produces muscle that enhances the body's physical circuitry to produce larger amounts of energy. The importance of physical activity is that it is the nature of life. The foundation of all life is energy, and energy is the result of motion. All that lives produces energy. Within this context of understanding, the human equivalent of energy producing motion is physical activity.

The two most "GOD-like" elements, the human mind and the human soul, are projected into the dimension within which we exist because of the human body. it is the proper functioning of the skeletal system, the muscular system, the nervous system, the circulatory system, the respiratory system, the digestive system, the reproductive system, all these systems and more, that bring the consciousness and the soul into this dimension. The stronger these systems are and the better they function, the stronger the manifestation of the awareness and direction. As the muscles nourish the nerves of the body, an individual with keen perception can actually feel the nerves receive the positive energy that is the Divine Energy of Life. The more muscle that is developed, the clearer things will become. Each repetition is a positive step, or action, towards the pursuit of betterment. Our existence is spiritual in nature, and our bodies are the link to understanding our place in it. It is through physical exercise that one can start to recognize how pursuing what is truly wanted and desired with positive action can produce prosperity and growth within one's life.

The evolution of our understanding requires us to open our minds up to new revelations. One of these revelations is that there is truly a purpose behind the existence of living things. Life is the extension of "GOD" into a physical dimension. As each living organism grows, it experiences the stimulation that occurs on its plane of existence. This stimulation produces knowledge of varying degrees. The knowledge acquired through the experiences of all living organisms is returned to the source via the electromagnetic circuit, and is added to the whole of divine knowledge. The knowledge gained by each individual that is interpreted both objectively and subjectively, becomes a part of the whole of divine knowledge. By endeavoring to satisfy ourselves through experiences, we will gain knowledge of the physical world to add to the one source of knowledge. Our experiences add to the knowledge and power of the Divine Energy of Life. As it relates to the human, it is to utilize its five senses to experience the world in which it exists. These senses are components of the body's composition. Strengthening the system of the body in turn strengthens our senses, thereby enhancing our ability to experience the world around us. If we allow ourselves to become a more obese populous, we limit our experiences. We also restrict the growth of our civilization. As we desire less movement, we restrict our growth as human beings. As our movement slows, so does our divine growth. Our divine growth is our growth as beings within the natural order or natural system. Thus, we become less spiritual and less "alive." Because computers and robotics are going to lessen our need for repetitive, mundane movement, we are going to have to seek movement out, i.e. exercise.

Personally, I have always sought out a personal relationship with the Divine Energy of Life. As well, I have always pursued the improvement of myself through education. It was not until I began to also pursue the perfection of my temple or body that I was awakened to the divine truth. This is when I began to experience "revelation." Exercise facilitates the positive separation of the body from the mind and soul during the pursuit of perfection. This is because as you work your body, the separate role the mind and soul have in directing your efforts is clearer. During most exercises, particularly related to activities like bodybuilding, bicycling, or jogging, you are telling your body to do a repetitive, energy-expending action. In the course of this "repetitive" action, at some point your mind is no longer fully involved in controlling the movements of your body because of the repetitive nature of what you are doing. It is here that the individual becomes acutely aware of their body and mind being separate functionally. The effort that individual has undertaken requires energy. The soul is the pathway through which we receive the divine energy that powers our bodies. It is wholly positive in nature. That individual starts to gain esteem as they feel good about themselves, as they feel stronger, and as they understand the positive nature of what they are doing. These thoughts and feelings allow them to "reach" for the energy they need to push themselves. This positive energy guides them in the right direction. If you doubt what I am saying, exercise and tax yourself and you will see the separation more clearly. Once you can see the separation, it becomes a simple matter of interpretation and understanding.

One could say that exercise led me closer to "GOD." Bodybuilding caused me to focus on the pursuit of perfection. During this pursuit, I found that exercise together with the pursuit of intellectual and spiritual reasoning led me to a better understanding of myself relative to the power and will within me as a physical being, and as a species of animal. I began to get a better understanding of myself relative to my being a part of Nature. As I worked through my bodybuilding/cardiovascular routines, I began to get a clearer understanding of the power and works of "GOD." As I used discipline to direct my thoughts, this allowed me to bring about positive change. In essence, my pursuit was facilitating the process of individual evolution. Our entire species must <u>consciously</u> pursue the betterment of ourselves relative to the composition of our being (the mind, body, and soul) for us to evolve as a group or collective.

As I worked out, I recognized and praised "GOD" for the energy that kept me going, and for the resulting benefits I received. As I did this, my energy and focus became stronger. As with any individual, once you start to receive these or any blessings, you must be conscious and thankful for what you receive and attain. This recognition is the foundation of the humility that is needed to stabilize the pursuit of betterment, and what it is to lead each of us to do within the context of our species. Everything, from the breath that keeps you alive, to the flower that grows in your yard, to the nickel in your pocket, is a gift. Individuals must be thankful to "GOD" for what is received because the Divine Energy of Life created the opportunity for everything. If a doctor in a hospital saves a person's life, that person must first be thankful to "GOD," because "GOD" (the Divine Energy of Life) that made the doctor and the hospital a reality. All of existence is made possible through the Divine Energy of Life. As I went through these moments of contemplation, the works of "GOD" became clearer to me.

When these words started flowing from me, I had been working out with the weights off and on for quite some time. I realized that I would never reach the level of perfection of a Lee Haney, or an Arnold Schwarzenegger. However, that was never my goal. My goal was to develop into the best that I could be. I was pursuing perfection and achieving betterment, which was the best my ability would allow. I measured my success not by the standard of others, but by what I believed I was capable of doing. My pursuit was a process in which each positive gain was built on the foundation of the last positive effort. It was work. As I worked to strengthen my body, it was necessary to strengthen my mind. Strengthening my body meant I had to eat the right things. I had to get the right amount of sleep. It meant I had to work out the right way. To affect positive change, I had to embrace a positive <u>system</u> of behavior. Behavior is the label for human action, and it is the human mind that produces human action. Therefore, my mind had to become stronger, if my body was to become stronger. However, I needed somewhere from which to draw the will and the energy for this pursuit. I had to push myself beyond what were my normal efforts. I needed some discipline of thought that would allow the power within me to emerge. I found that discipline where I have always found it, within the context of my relationship with "GOD" (the Divine Energy of Life).

In essence, this whole book is about Americas' fitness. There are comparisons to be made between the efforts that lead to success in body shaping and in life. For example, in body shaping, if you are not born with it, you have to work hard to get it. Once you get it, you have to work to keep it. It does not happen overnight, and the heights you reach are a direct reflection of the amount of work you have put into it. These same things are true with regard to human life. The path to the betterment of our individual and collective lives all starts with taking care of the human body, the true temple of "GOD." If we would just begin to respect and take care of our bodies, all the ills of society would go away. We would gain a better appreciation for the miracle of life and breath. It is our feelings and emotions, sensations that we feel and sense that allow us to determine the truth and what right truly is. Once individuals start to exercise, they focus on their body in a way that makes them a better being and gives them a clearer understanding of the power within themselves. They also focus on what is positive for themselves as well as what they truly want and desire from their time on our Earth. That individual can then look at his or her goals objectively, and plot the positive path to those goals. It must be a path that remains within the parameters set by the defining, governing element(s), i.e. the influential authority of the systems. The systems of our lives revolve around these entities. For the Divine System of Nature the authority is "GOD" (the Divine Energy of Life). For the system of our collective, harmonious interaction the authority the governing body of the social system, i.e. the government. For the system of our lineage, the authority is the head of the family. For the system of our individuality, the authority is the self.

In keeping with the analogous comparisons of the human being to a computer system, the mind is the central processing unit, the most ingenious part of the system. It makes everything work together. This component provides the system with the information necessary to perform its tasks relative to what is needed. The CPU determines the direction of the energy and knowledge fed into the system and decides what to do with both. The system is "pre-loaded" with basic information. This can be referred to as the "operating system." Then, other instructions (software) are loaded on top of this to allow the computer to perform a varied amount of tasks. This is also true of the human. Individuals have within themselves a basic amount of knowledge that will give them the ability to perform the tasks necessary to satisfy the most basic needs. One label we have given this knowledge is "instinct." The knowledge individuals acquire after that affords them the ability to pursue greater wants and desires. The label that describes our existence, "civilized," identifies the characteristics of our behavior that are derived from the knowledge we have "loaded" on top of our basic understanding. The nature of our civilized existence is to have raised us all from barbarism to an enlightened stage of development. It is to have brought us out of a primitive or savage state to where we are educated in matters of culture and refinement, making us more polished or sophisticated relative to what we do and how we act. This is how we define being civilized. What this indicates is that our minds, or the information put into our minds, is supposed to affect our behavior, as opposed to behaving recklessly and with wild abandon.

Our understanding of all that exists, as well as our consciousness, must evolve just as technology evolves. This evolution of our minds must cause us to get better and grow relative to the definition of our existence. As a "civilized" society, we are supposed to act with the high level of intellectual, social, and cultural development inherent to a civilized people. To continue to evolve or get better as civilized beings means to act with an even "high<u>er</u>" level of intellectual, social, and cultural development than our current standard, rather than less. Within this context, each individual must recognize his or her obligation to make a positive contribution to society. As our reality evolves, the nature and magnitude of that contribution evolves also. It is not enough to simply exist. Each of us must have purposeful, positive action. One must learn as much as they can, to be as prepared as they can be. The characteristics of humanhood are exemplified by such words as preparedness, trustworthiness, courtesy, kindness, honesty, and the like. Each of us must consciously seek to manifest these things when developing our character. It is the responsibility of each individual to develop his or her own personality and character as they seek to become who it is that person wants to be. Adolescents must undertake the personal task of evaluating themselves. Each person must answer the question, "what do I want out of life and who do I want to be?" Then each must look at the type of character that person should have and develop it for themselves.

As growth is a building process, for a person's mind to grow, that person must seek increase and build upon the knowledge already possessed. One's mind must be open to the degree that every newly experienced moment brings enlightenment, adding knowledge to be used to build towards a better understanding and perspective. Every single moment of time is a new bit of knowledge. We must first recognize what a moment of time truly is. To "recognize" is to place in reality. It is to <u>accept</u> as true within a <u>proper</u> context. All animals do this and it is simple. Humans have the unique ability to examine what is accepted as true. Objective examination is the essence of honor, respect, responsibility, and remaining truthful to oneself. To examine is to determine the meaning or truth in those moments. In effect, it is determining what is significant and relevant about that reality. Arriving at the truth requires the examination of both the relevant symbols of a circumstance, and the actions that those symbols produce. It is then time to discern the positive action that should {or must} result from what is learned. Each time an individual learns something, they are supposed to grow from it. They are supposed to grow because of the thoughts related to those relevant moments. Each moment is an opportunity for growth, and each of us chooses whether we grow from the circumstances we face. To grow would be to act and react positively. The alternative would be negative, which is not desirable, practical, correct, or right. No growth will yield no esteem.

We need to exercise our minds to build the brain muscle. Each of us needs to read, do crossword puzzles and mind teasers, anything that stimulates the mind. As the activity of exercise causes greater electrical activity, it expands into other areas of the brain. Think of it in terms of "storage" space in a computer. In a computer memory, the cell or file can become filled up. "Storage" space must then be added. As the human mind is the ultimate computer, it has vast reserves for memory storage and upgrades. Information, in the form of electrical current, travels the pathways of the brain. As this happens, it is stimulating and "turning on" the areas it passes through. The way to greater awareness, consciousness, and greater mental ability is through mental stimulation in the form of use. This is also the way to spiritual enlightenment and success. Granted, for improvement and understanding to take place in specific disciplines, one must do specific studies, but the principle is still the same. Use it or lose it.

There is a never-ending need for education. The more knowledge a person gains, the more of an understanding that person will have about the things of which that person is aware. By understanding how things are, whether it is an animal or a machine, this insight allows one to be objective about things because that person's understanding allows them to see other points of view. The larger a person's vocabulary and computation skills, the better that person's ability to understand, conceive, and infer. Being literate makes one better able to process the information to which they are exposed. This is the essence of why being literate is important. Literacy is about more than just being able to read. It is about improving the ability to think.

The soul of a human is a very prominent element of its being. It encompasses more than is thought. The soul is truly the connective pathway through which all living things are linked to each other and the Divine Energy of Life. The soul of an individual does not necessarily grow in the truest sense of the word. Individuals <u>improve</u> their ability to interpret and utilize the power derived through this pathway to guide their movements in the correct, right, or positive way. A person knowing that their behaviors (movements or actions) are truly correct, right, or positive is from where esteem can develop. With regard to one's soul, esteem translates into "peace of mind/peace of being."

By living outside of our true spirituality and not embracing our divine connection to the system of Nature, in effect, we have magnified that aspect of our perception that is the most pronounced. Those being the perceptions derived from our most obvious physical senses. The perceptions derived from physical senses are inherent to all animals. As well, other animals experience what we have labeled intuition, gut feeling, first impressions, and the like. Our ability to interpret those perceptions more fully separates us from other animal species. These interpretations were to be used to ensure our ability to perpetuate the right flow of divine energy through us and around us.

Each of us must begin to think positive. Each of us must move in positive ways, doing positive things. As well, to be sure that the journey of each individual's life follows the path that person truly wants and that was intended for that person, each of us must trust in ourselves. People must trust in what makes them feel good and positive. They must trust more in their instinct, intuition, first impressions, and gut feeling. Within the system of every living body, there is a source of radiant positive energy. For the Atom, it is the nucleus. For the Universe, it is the Divine Energy of Life. For the solar system, it is the sun. For our Earth, it is the molten lava at the core of our planet. For the human being, it is the brain. Each one of these bodies is alive because it has divine energy flowing through it. Unlike most other living bodies, the human brain allows it to do something unique with the divine energy it receives. Once the human receives the Divine Energy of Life, it is divided into two parts.

This is because from the Divine Energy of Life, not only does the human receive the positive energy necessary to sustain it and power its movements, but also, we receive knowledge through this pathway. The labels we have given this knowledge are instinct, intuition, first impression, gut feeling, extra-sensory perception, and the like. This is knowledge contained within ourselves, and it leads us to what "GOD" would have us do.

To clarify the understanding of this "pathway," it can be compared to a telephone line. Our divine energy flow can be more easily understood if discerned within the context of this electrical system. not only does that line (pathway) deliver or send the energy emitted from another source that rings the bell and powers the unit (that makes it "work"), but that pathway also delivers or sends the words (information) disseminated from another source that is meant to enlighten. The Divine Energy of Life not only transmits the positive energy necessary to produce existence and have it grow, but it transmits the knowledge or awareness that, for the human, produces the individual <u>creativity</u> necessary for the collective growth of our species. It is "collective" growth because words are the result of a need to communicate or share knowledge between individuals. The brain ultimately receives the positive energy from the Divine Energy of Life. Within this complex processor is where the energy it receives is divided into its respective parts. The electrical energy is utilized to power the human machine towards physical growth by keeping the heart muscle pumping. The radiant energy is used to guide the human machine in a positive direction towards mental growth.

With all this, each of us must embrace the truth that not every individual is meant to do magnanimous things. One's self-esteem can be derived from fulfilling one's natural role within to context of their existence. Some are meant to be presidents, and some are meant to be fathers and mothers. Some are meant to be movies stars, and some are meant to be husbands and wives. Some are meant to be priests or politicians, and some are meant to be friends. Each of us must fulfill the responsibilities that lie along the path of our lives. As individuals release themselves to the Will of "GOD," each must understand that they are still responsible to choose their actions. The choice is a simple one. Each of us must choose to do the correct, right(eous), or positive thing.

The issues related to esteem cannot be examined without addressing the elements of awe and humility. Awe is an overwhelming feeling of reverence and admiration, produced by that which is grand or extremely powerful. Awe is the highest expression of esteem. The fact that this word exists, means that the human is to have this feeling, because words are the result of the humans need to identify and communicate things of which it is consciously aware. Our species has supreme dominion over everything that exists on our planet. Therefore, in truth, the only entity the human can be in awe of is "GOD" (the Divine Energy of Life). A human is only to be in awe of "GOD," as expressed by one of the Ten Commandments. The human reaction to the action of feeling "in awe" is what we label "humility." To be humble is to recognize the truth that there is a power greater than any single human being, or the collective human species. To be humble is to have an understanding of the value of life and the actions derived from it. It is recognizing that all living things are precious and important. Each of us must face this aspect of our existence in light of the truth that not one of us truly understands the power that gives us life, and we have no control over it. Life is such a magnanimous blessing. Regardless of the difficulties each of us may face, we must appreciate the opportunity to exist. Therefore, each of us must reconcile ourselves to these facts in a manner that is positive relative to us as individuals.

The manifestation that results from this reconciliation is humility. Humility is supposed to be at the foundation of our enjoyment and appreciation of the gift living. It is the outward expression of our appreciation of existence, and of the things and beings around us. As we gain esteem, we must remain humble. Each of us must remain humble as we grow strong and tall. Each of us must remain humble, as we grow more skilled and intelligent. Each of us must remain humble as we grow and our positive energy produces prosperity around us.

The outward expression of our humility is to share the growth of our elements with the living beings around us. Esteem cannot be confused with pride. The harm of pride is that it takes us away from our spiritual roots. "Proud" and "pride" are terms that the human uses as it takes credit for what is produced by "GOD" (the Divine Energy of Life). Anything accomplished by an individual is something that person should be able to accomplish as one of GODs' greatest creations. So, the glory truly goes to "GOD" when we are able to achieve. Hence, we cannot be proud of what we do, because we are supposed to be able to do it. For every place these terms are used, they can easily be replaced with "happy" or "happiness" respectively. The feelings associated with what we have labeled as pride are simply feelings of happiness to have manifested whatever is done. That happiness should be experienced and indulged. It is a sensation of reward. However, not one of us should forget to be thankful to "GOD" (the Divine Energy of Life) for having created us, and given us the opportunity to live and do and feel. Being proud and filled with pride is indulging oneself in selfishness, greed, and arrogance. No good can come of this in the end, and neither can there be true esteem.

The American dream is about greater desire and aspiration than simply basic need. This dream assumes the satisfaction of basic need and aspires toward comfort and enjoyment for the individual, the family, and the community. It includes the desire for a stable retirement for those who have contributed a lifetime of good works. Adulthood in America means more than reaching a specific age, it means accepting certain responsibilities. The most basic of these responsibilities is providing for one's own creature comforts. Creature comforts stabilize an individual's existence such that they may continue to grow after having left the stability and security provided them by their parental figures. As we work and put our efforts toward making the world around us better, we make ourselves better in the process. In essence, this is the building of esteem. We must pursue personal education, we must exercise our bodies, and we must pursue a righteous, positive path for ourselves utilizing all the knowledge and energy manifested from within and around us. From this, each of us will grow.

Growth is a primary element of being alive. It occurs within the animal and vegetable kingdoms (it even occurs in the mineral kingdom). Life is the condition that distinguishes animals and plants from inorganic objects and dead organisms. Life is manifested by a system of growth through metabolism, reproduction, and the ability to adapt to the environment through <u>changes</u> originating internally. Like every aspect of existence, there is a system of actions behind every set of conditions, as well as the elements contained within those conditions. For plants, the internal <u>change</u> occurs such that all the parts of the plant are involved and affected. For the human animal, this internal <u>change</u> must also include all the parts of human composition. These are the elements of the body, mind, and soul. Adaptation is the process by which one changes to adjust to new conditions of existence. For the human animal, this includes the components of compromise and tolerance relevant to each individual area of human composition. Growth within the human animal is a system of movement aimed at changing to adjust to new conditions of existence, through internal changes that are physical and mental in nature. This is all a part of our spirituality. As it is the individual human's responsibility to direct their actions, each of us must therefore seek out or pursue the growth of our soul as well. Each of us gains esteem from our growth as individuals, and our adaptation to the conditions under which we live.

To awaken the full power within our spirituality, we must actively pursue betterment of all three elements of human composition simultaneously. As one expends energy toward this goal, they end up pushing themselves beyond their perceived limitations. The energy for this "extra" effort must come from somewhere. It comes from the divine energy source. The expenditure of energy by each individual increases his or her respective draw from this energy source. The increased energy flowing through that person in the positive, right(eous) direction carries with it additional knowledge and/or divine truths, i.e. revelations. as an individual feels themselves growing from this energy, this knowledge will allow that person to begin to understand not only how the humans' entire being is to work together as one, but also the nature of positive energy relative to "GOD." It is a part of GODs' divine plan to expose us to divine truth if we pursue a true likeness to "him," which is the perfection or betterment of all the elements of our <u>whole</u> being. Those elements are the body, mind, and soul.

Self-Actualization

According to Dr. Maslow's hierarchy of needs, the satisfaction of our need for self-actualization is where we would focus our actions after satisfying all our other needs. This is because satisfying all our other needs is to sustain us and strengthen us such that we are able to achieve our greatest potential. One's need for self-actualization is derived from an innate desire to live up to one's fullest and unique potential by reaching the most near perfect state of being. To actualize is to make real. Self-actualization is the manifestation of one's <u>true</u> "self," through the positive efforts guided by impulses and insights derived from within ourselves. This need is rarely satisfied. As well, it is rarely recognized within its proper context, even though it is pursued by us all to one degree or another. This state of being is most easily attained when an individual is free from pressure and overwhelming obligation. Self-actualization is the ultimate human experience. It is the realizing of what one's energy has the potential to produce. Self-actualization is a wholly spiritual accomplishment because it is how the Divine System of Nature is formed.

"GOD" created each of us to be near perfect. However, because our system of existence contains stages of growth, it is up to each individual to live up to or grow into their fullest potential. Translated, that is the best one can be if they only moved in a positive way. Each individual takes his or her place within the system, having the action or doing the job that needs to be done to satisfy the requirement/responsibility of that aspect of the whole system. "GOD" created a system of existence wherein each living element contributes to the perpetuation of the whole system by giving positive energy to it, by way of its individual movements. That is how everything needed to make our social systems to function correctly, right(eous)ly, or positively gets done. Each of us must recognize that there is more to the purpose of human life than mere existence and self-indulgence.

"GOD" created a most nearly perfect system of existence wherein every element of existence had a role to play. The goal was the perpetual existence of living things, so that the absorption of the knowledge derived from individual experience would be never-ending. Through the immensity and complexity of GODs' power and ability, each individual life had its own path to follow through the journey of its days and nights. This was true of the blade of grass, the tree, the ant, the horse, etc. Relative to the humans' journey through life, each individual path has purposeful significance because of the position of dominion held by our species. To support this authority, as well as to ease and enrich the life of the individual human, "GOD" gave each one or more "gifts" that would aid him or her as that person tried to reach their destination or goal. An individual's "gift" is something that will come out of them naturally.

Because of this, a person will ultimately share what was bestowed on them with those immediately around them. The most fruitful prosperity will come from sharing one's gift with masses of humanity in a positive, near perfect manner. The individual contribution each person is to make can be great or it can be small, but it must be positive. Humanity receives individual contributions from the likes of everyone from doctors to police officers, politicians to CEOs, and horse groomers to hamburger flippers. Individuals, through the efforts produced by their own energy, become what their will would have them. "GOD" created each of us to be a most near perfect living organism. Our individual potential is limit only by the positive energy output (i.e. positive movements) of the individual. It is up to each person to develop his or her individual ability fully, to utilize the awesome power that lies within. As one does reach self-actualization, there are positive experiences that produce sense stimulation (i.e. pleasure) there for that person to enjoy at the end of such a journey. Fully satisfying this need produces prosperity. Individuals need to find what it is they most skillfully enjoy. Each must then put all their positive energy into it, and prosperity (soul), wealth (body), and wisdom (mind) will be the reward. This is by GODs' Will.

Each of us must look for and embrace that unique aspect of individuality that makes us different from one another. For some individuals, it may seem as though there is nothing unique about them. This is not true. Every individual is as different from another as snowflakes are unalike. Our abilities and methods of expression likewise are just as different. Each of us has a unique path to follow as we move through the moments of our lives. Not a single one of us lives the exact same life as another. As well, the process of understanding that people go through is specific and distinctive to each individual, as are experiences and positions in life. So when exposed to the same stimuli, each individual's process of understanding will invariably take different paths. From this, different mechanics of a circumstances or doctrine may be realized that go undetected by others. All these differences provide each person with the opportunity to contribute some unique skill, interpretative expression, or bit of wisdom to the collective if those things are shared. This infers that not only is their truth for all to see, but there is also truth unseen by all but one, the individual. This is the essence of human creativity, and it must be nurtured and preserved. By the laws of Nature, we are obligated to share our truths amongst the collective of our species group. Our species is then to use these truths to achieve a balanced existence that pursues perfection for ourselves, and achieves mutual satisfaction for all living things.

An individual may not know what their particular mission in life is, and they may feel like they are floundering around like a chicken without its head. Most times, this is truly not to the case. More often than not, most of us live out our lives very close to the path we are to follow. We just do not understand it or place it within its proper context. As well, rarely do individuals allow themselves to reach the full height of their own potential. Some people were meant to aid masses of people, some were meant to be good parents, and some were simply meant to be a good friend to others. Does a person need a crystal ball to be able to see these things? In figurative terms, each of us does have that crystal ball, honest to goodness. It is within each of us. Our feelings, impressions, wants and desires, along with our intuitions, instincts and the like are there to guide us through our individual lives in the proper direction. Some of the misinterpretation that occurs when relying on oneself in this way may lead to some errors or misdirection of actions during the course of one's life. Placing these circumstances in the proper perspective is where this all gets a bit deep. Truly, to come to the proper perspective, each of us must awaken within ourselves the essence of human spirituality. This "essence" is the soul, through which our guiding energies flow. We readily accept the truth that we are to use our minds and our bodies. Each of us must now more significantly utilize the elements of the soul as a guide to one's lifetime goal. This will allow each individual to go forward "through" the fear generated by confusion and doubt.

We must cultivate our individuality while also embracing the common aspects of our reality, as defined within the context of an interdependent, interconnected group of like beings with like characteristics. We must pursue the perfection of our difference, i.e. our own individuality, to manifest into reality that special element each of us is to contribute to our surroundings. For the most part, our wants/desires are interpreted as a solely "human" choice. The truth is that some of those choices, the ones from deep inside of us like playing the piano, or writing a book, or playing football, or loving the wife and children, etc., are choices that are derived from a spiritual source. They define how each of us fits into reality in the way that is spiritually or naturally intended. as one strives to be the best that they can be, that person must listen to their inner being and come to understand himself or herself from the inside, outward. The words that are listened for come through the pathway we have labeled the "soul." Each of us must recognize the deeper things that make us individuals, not just the superficial things that make us humans. In <u>doing</u> the things that are required of us and that we enjoy, each of us can begin to develop the gifts that we have.

Individuals must embrace whatever it is they truly enjoy <u>doing</u>, and allow it to manifest itself fully. That is a major factor in the process of determining one's gift from "GOD." That gift is intended to enrich not only the existence of that individual, but also the existence of humanity, and in the process, all living things. Once a person's gifts reach the proper level of proficiency, that person will be rewarded for the skills that were naturally bestowed upon them. It is true that most people of great success or wealth have achieved that status by making the most of the abilities that came to them "naturally."

As one analyzes the progression of civilization, the evolution of thought and the way it is manifested are a perfect example of the unique individuality of human expression. There are things that were created during the history of mankind that were purely artistic. There are creations that were intellectual, and some that were structural. Through the understanding of human spirituality, one can come to see the relevance of our individuality to the collective species group. "GOD" created each of us to be different. Each of us was given something unique to contribute to the whole picture of existence. Within this context, when one examines a creation of another of GODs' children, that person should be filled with admiration rather that with envy and jealousy. Social systems must cultivate individual thought to perpetuate creation. Each human creation is representative of the greatness of "GOD." We as humans have a responsibility to ourselves, to our existence, and to the Divine System of Nature to evolve and excel. Our responsibility is to grow. We are created in the image of a perfect "GOD," so we must seek to progress as individuals in terms of that perfection. As a civilized being, this is characterized by awareness, intellect, and skill. There is greatness within each of us, because each person is in the image of perfection. Individuals must seek out that greatness, that betterment of themselves and share it with others. Greatness has no relevance to reality unless it is shared. Within the cycle of our spiritual reality, there are physical as well as mental rewards to be enjoyed for having reached a level of proficiency. The rewards are even greater with regard to the manifestation of our personal, God-given gift(s). This has always been a part of GODs' word, but we have never truly had enough faith in it and in ourselves to commit to it as a species, which is what we must do. While recognizing all that is relevant to spiritual reality in the proper context, it is only through our recognition of and commitment to faith in the Divine Energy of Life that we will reap salvation and enrichment. In this entire text, the most important word of all is **FAITH**.

Each of us is taught that we will be rewarded for our faith and commitment with the desires of our hearts. This is a spiritual reality. Each of us is also taught that the social system will reward individuals that possess proficient abilities. Those people who have guided us (parents, teachers, mentors, etc.) have been telling us this throughout our lives. This is a worldly reality. They have told us that when we are good to others, good things come to us. This is true. This corresponds with the truth that within an electrical circuit, energy (benefit) travels in a circle. When we create something that is beneficial to society, once it is accepted as such, we are rewarded with enrichment for our efforts. Enrichment is our reward for our contributions to humanity regardless of the perspective within which it is interpreted. In understanding this, it should be clear that no person should begrudge another for any success that other person might have. Why is that? For one thing, any of us is capable of producing the same thing. However, since it was another that did so and it was a positive accomplishment, it deserves the pat on the back. As well, that success is derived from having produced benefit for a mass of humans, perhaps even ourselves. This is positive for us. Another person's success should inspire us to look within ourselves for that gift "GOD" has given to us, for which we will be rewarded when we share it with humanity. Individuals must look within themselves to what their strengths are. They must then hone and develop them, so that they can be controlled or mastered. Individuals must learn what their weaknesses are. They must then seek to minimize or work around them.

As well, individuals must learn other things so that each has other advantages that can be utilized if need be. Then, when the opportunity for enrichment presents itself, and each individual is aware enough to see the opportunity that fits best, each can take it on and give it his or her all. The individual must believe in it and be committed to it. He or she must put positive energy into it. From this, each individual will be enriched.

As a species, an interdependent group of like beings, there is one principle each of us must embrace as a part of our natural existence or our spirituality. It is that to perpetuate the flow of spiritually right action, for every benefit that we receive (good action), we must make an effort to produce a benefit for another, or give something beneficial back to reality somewhere. From this truth is where words like "charity" and "volunteerism" were derived. With this awareness of the truth and our divine cognition giving us direction regarding what should be done, eventually everything required to produce a positive existence gets done. This is because everyone is thinking about doing something to benefit others, i.e. the collective. If each of us is consistently seeking to "help," the individual can choose when to expend energy in that way. It will be when that person has it to spare. That will save another person energy that they can use to help another. So it will go, around and around, in a mutually beneficial loop or circle. This will only be the result if we are all working together with a common goal. Working together and for the common good is the nature of most every socialized species on our planet. It is our conscious state of mind and our awareness derived through our senses that cause us to pursue self-serving interests.

We must embrace a more mature way of thinking. Each of us must understand that we can still pursue our personal agendas within the confines of a civilized, committed social structure. In doing this the right(eous) way, not only will there be a benefit for the one, there will be benefit for all. This may sound like a lot of work. However, this interpretation is truly a matter of perspective. Do not view work as a chore or task. Rather, look at it as simply movement. This perspective will allow individuals to embrace any effort as a form of exercise, for either the mind, body, or soul. This thereby allows each of us to give and get the most from our efforts. If a person wants to live a certain way, then that person must make that happen. If a person wants his or her environment to be clean, then that person has to clean it up. If persons want the material things in their lives to be of a certain quality, then they must work to provide for that. Each of us must work to make our life what we want it to be. The meaning of our individual lives is defined by the meaning that our movements or actions give to it, i.e. what that specific person wants his/her life to mean.

There is a song entitled "wakeup everybody." One line in the song goes, "the world won't get no better, if we all just let it be." It is time for humanity to wake up, now! We as individuals and as a collective must be prepared to take advantage of the opportunities before us. Each individual has needs and wants/desires, and it is up to the individual to satisfy those needs and wants/desires through positive endeavor. To accomplish anything requires energy and strength that we must somehow generate from within ourselves. This energy is confined within the body, mind, and soul. To get the most out of ourselves, we must allow the energy within each of these elements of our being to spew forth into our respective reality. Seeking to become a better person does this. It is done by working to make ourselves better than we already are. It is done by "pursuing perfection," or working to be the best we can be. To do this, people must focus the power or energy of their mind. Our motions are the result of the impulses generated by our thoughts. With all that is going on in our individual lives, one may wonder how to generate the addition energy needed for this effort. Each of us will be able to generate it by constantly telling ourselves, or more aptly phrased, produced the thought that says, **"I can."** The process of thinking produces energy, and the phrase itself provides the direction for the resulting actions. Repeating this phrase to oneself will produce the energy that the body will need for the efforts of positive endeavor.

What each of us does for pleasure, we do because we <u>can</u>. Whatever it is, whether it is harmful to us or not, whether it is legal or not. Spiritually speaking, that part of each individual, the "I can," is the manifestation of that person's inherent pursuit of perfection. It is each individual knowing that in the moments he or she truly needs, wants, and desires something, it can be gained, because the "self" <u>can</u> pursue and gain whatever satisfies it. In examining this truth, we will find a misinterpretation and/or lack of perceptual depth that has occurred on the part of our species. Humans fail to recognize that the laws of reality apply to every circumstance of existence. Each of us recognizes that we <u>can</u> gain what satisfies our personal whims in those moments when we are thinking only of ourselves. We go rent movie, or go to a party, or buy a car or a house, or commit rape, robbery, or murder because we feel we <u>can</u>. Each of us must realize that we <u>can</u> do anything we set our minds to accomplish. If we <u>do</u>, it is because we <u>can</u>. As each of us strives for perfection, whatever we do, i.e. our actions or movements, must have direction. Within the context of spirituality and natural science, this direction should be positive and aimed towards righteousness and goodness. The "can" must be applied with regard to all our efforts and actions, including the pursuit of a likeness to "GOD." This likeness is manifested as a standard of perfection. This perfection, understood within the proper context, is movement that is wholly positive.

Relative to individuals making a difference, each of us must accepted that we can do this as well. This is true to the degree that persons believe they can. Each person's belief in themselves will determine the amount of "energy" one will have to create the actions necessary to manifest the desired result. In essence, each day we all have to answer the question of what it is we can accomplish. It is true that everything is a part of a (one) system. What we must embrace is that our actions (i.e. what we do) are a part of what constitutes this system. We cannot believe that what we do as individuals has no effect on the reality around us. Being a part of the system of existence means that whatever we do or do not contribute within it is significant and relevant. If an individual recognizes something wrong with their neighborhood or with government, they cannot continue to ignore it, thinking somebody else or "the system" will take care of it. We are the system. If an individual does not become a legislator, a judge, a lawyer, a doctor, or a nurse, this by no means suggests that what that person becomes is not an intricate part of the system. Therefore, each of us must perform our required action, or do our part to make the system work rightly.

To reach self-actualization, one must create a workable system of actions to achieve what is by Nature a long-range life goal. In other words, one must create a plan. Creating a system of actions aimed at attaining long-range goals is itself a systematic process. Individuals must first experience things so that they learn about themselves. In conjunction with this, individuals must use these experiences to learn about what exists around them. Individuals must then learn how to take what they gain from their experiences, and use it to create. To learn is to have a relatively permanent change in behavior due to experience. This is one of the most important revelations of this book. It is truly a divine truth. It is a fundamental characteristic of all living things. What any living organism learns from its experience should cause it to change. This change is supposed to produce growth, which will benefit that organism's existence. Beyond this basic truth, there is one thing the human must learn. We must all learn to create. That is the "GOD-like" characteristic of being human. Within this context, "create" is synonymous with "generate." Each individual must seek to perfect his or her ability to create/generate by learning and doing. What is it we are seeking to create/generate? Collectively, it is the most perfect condition of existence for continued growth and the perpetuation of all living things. Individually, we must seek to create/generate what satisfies our needs as well as our wants/desires. We must first satisfy our basic needs before we can pursuit other wants/desires. Our reality is composed of not only tangible components of substance, but also intangible components we can label "circumstances."

Therefore, each person must recognize the need to create/generate more than tangible things. Each must seek to create/generate intangible situations. When these tangible and intangible components of existence are added together, what we will have created/generated is a system that produces opportunities for growth and/or gain. Whether we create/generate the opportunity to gain water, food, shelter, a Mercedes Benz, or a chance to see the sunrise over the Grand Canyon, we learn to create/generate the (positive) system of actions and circumstances that lead to that desired end.

Many of us go through life thinking that we know ourselves simply because our mind occupies our body. What we have to do is stop moving, relax, and literally go within ourselves. Persons must look for the reality of what would actually make each of us as individuals happy. We need to be happy with our lives in general, as well as with ourselves during the course of our entire lifespan. Stop and think about that, honestly. For 70 or so years, each individual has to be able to support "their own body," at least with housing, food, clothing, medical and utility costs to maintain their existence. To do this, each individual will have to create their own plan to meet life goals. However, some very basic elements of this plan are common among the members our society. For individuals within our social system, years 0 to 17 should be spent developing themselves by gaining an education, learning the customs of the society, and learning to function independently within the parameters of the society. Years 18 to 21 should be used to establish oneself within the society. This is done by utilizing the best array of opportunities available through the social structure, i.e. college, military, entrepreneurship, or employment. Moving away from one's parents, living alone and independently for a time, in the beginning stages of adulthood, is an important element of individual human development. Once adulthood is reached, and before getting married, individuals should experience a period of living alone. This is so individuals can indulge themselves, and more clearly define for themselves their aspirations, dreams, and direction. Individuals need to gain some "insight" or see inside themselves, to derive an understanding of their personal existence, i.e. their significance and relevance to their surroundings. This is so that he or she can move forward with confidence in a positive direction. This period gives each of us the opportunity to focus on ourselves, learning about ourselves as individuals, and planning for our journey through the moments of our time of living. Years 22 to 65, forty-three years, should be used for a great many things. Not the least of which is learning about ourselves and who we really are as individuals. each of us must determine what it is we really want out of life and take steps towards the goals we must set for ourselves to attain personal satisfaction.

It takes a long time to become proficient at something that requires an education or a skill, sometimes as long as 10 years depending on the application. Therefore, wasting time (truly our most valued commodity) is not a practical approach to living. The individual human's energy supply is limited to the period between birth and death, whatever that time period turns out to be. When an individual commits his or her actions to growth and change, it will become clear that there is no time or energy to waste on the pursuit of negative things. "Negative things" is not an all-encompassing reference to enjoyment and indulgence. Each of us must look at ourselves in terms of the reality of our individual circumstance. Each of us must recognize where we are, where we want to be, and what must be done to get there. Then, one must be satisfied with the destination to which his or her efforts deliver them. What must always be remembered is that within the Divine System of Nature, each living thing is responsible to produce the actions that will sustain it. Therefore, each individual must first do what is necessary to provide for their personal existence while moving in a positive direction. They must do this before they consider doing anything else with their life. In addition, those efforts should ultimately be aimed at acquiring the means to sustain one's physical existence during an extended period of non-employment. Civilized humans have labeled this period "retirement." The length of this period is undefined. It can last anywhere from one year to twenty years or more. The years after the age of 65 are meant to be filled with leisure activity, and each of us must prepare for that time.

Having done what is necessary to stabilize one's existence, there will still be energy and time to be utilized. If individuals could do anything that they could think of, and had everything that they could want, in the end all that would be left for them would be what they did with their existence. Therefore, it is what each of us chooses to do (our actions/our behavior) that determines the "meaning" of our life. As a matter of reality, there are some things that each of us must do, and individuals readily recognize this fact. These are required actions or responsibilities. Each of us must fulfill these actions as we pursue the perfection of ourselves through growth. As individuals begin to perfect themselves, each will begin to utilize the 24-hour day and the 7-day week efficiently. This will result in the <u>planning</u> and <u>organizing</u> of actions such that each will create/generate a system of existence for themselves. At some point during that process, each person will reach personal enlightenment, at which time the distinct path of his or her journey to enrichment will be revealed.

Because of the stress related to functioning in the highly competitive societies of the industrialized world, many people tend not to be concerned with planning what to do with leisure moments and resign themselves to taking things as they come. Our basic needs require us to work for what we must have to sustain ourselves. During these working hours, we generally focus on the work that we are doing, and the activity generated by the interactions involved. After we endeavor to satisfy our most basic needs, we expend energy to satisfy the needs of our personal environments. Once these needs are satisfied, we are left with a small amount of "leisure" time. These are our personal moments. They are likely the only opportunity an individual will have to work on personal goals of betterment and perfection. Recognizing how finite this group of moments is, one can easily see the need for planning and organizing one's time. Without goals, we are left to focus on whatever else is on our minds. As physical beings, our focus shifts to what we feel. Why is this? Because we do not have to work for that, it just happens to be there in the forefront. As we focus on what we feel, our priority becomes stimulating "sensation." This is how we lose our objectivity and become subjective, opening the door for selfishness and greed to cloud our perspective. To escape from this trap, we must prioritize to the degree that our focus or main objective is to achieve some goal. The overall goal should be to better ourselves as we provide ourselves with the necessary creature comforts, and work towards that end. Then, with the stress of these concerns eliminated, we are better equipped to function on an interpersonal level.

From an individual perspective, each of us is to recognize that every moment in time has a meaning. It would be irrational and egotistical to think one could determine the meaning within each and every moment. Therefore, an individual must seek to single out and understand those moments that are relevant and significant to one's own existence. The problem humans face with interpretation is one of ego coupled with impatience. In our haste to have answers quickly, we draw conclusions we consider to be based on the whole truth, while not recognizing that arriving at a point of understanding is a time-consuming process. Unfortunately, humans need to understand everything as soon as possible, not always allowing for the moments needed to reflect upon reality to determine the truth that is inherent to it. Many humans usually hurry to draw conclusions so the "individual" can determine his or her course of action or necessary response, which is most often predicated on the desire for personal stimulation and gratification. The response is more often than not, behavior motivated by what that person feels is in his or her best interests, not the best interests of the circumstance. In essence, that person is making his or her own will more of a priority than GODs' Will. Balancing one's own personal interests with all those to be affected by a given moment would satisfy all those with a stake in that circumstance. This is using compromise and tolerance to achieve positive resolution. This would be the way of Nature and of what we consider divinity.

To accept these realities, in a spiritual sense, is an exercise in being humble before "GOD." We must act out our own reality based on what feels right and positive <u>to</u> us, not <u>for</u> us. It is true that we must follow our own personal, individual feelings. However, as we go about this task, we must do the right, positive things relative to the moments we pass through. Understanding our true feelings enlightens us to how we fit into the picture of reality. This will lead each of us to the gift(s) that "GOD" has given to us, which we are to share with humanity. As we follow our feelings, we <u>must</u> move in a positive direction. This is what it means to be righteous. Moving can be made easier by each of us having the goodness of heart, which ensures our actions will be of a positive or neutral Nature. This will decrease the mental effort that goes into directing behavioral movements. This is because individuals can then trust their instinctive, intuitive reactions. Then, the mental energy that would normally be required to direct behavioral movements can be diverted to more pressing matters. One of those pressing matters is the need to focus on applying faculties to the prospective task of analytically studying a relevant circumstance. In this way individuals can decipher GODs' blessings to them, which will lie within the truth of those moments.

As we formulate our plan of approach to the betterment of ourselves, we must develop a strategy for each individual element of our being. What we truly need is a system, a way of approaching our personal growth. For example, my plan or systematic approach is as follows. With regard to my soul, I know that I must seek to follow the righteous path. For me, it is giving/sharing positive energy with other beings. It may take the form of giving encouragement, or a positive touch or thought. It may take the form of helping and aiding those around me. Or it may entail my just listening attentively. Following the righteous path is to seek to pray every day. It is to seek meditation for a better understanding of myself. It is to seek to refrain from what is negative and excessive. It is hearing the positive voice inside of me and listening to what it says. It is seeking to follow the right path, the path of good and positive endeavor. With regard to my body, I seek to do the right action. For me, this is seeking to workout with regularity and intensity. It is seeking to eat better and keep to a minimum the foreign substances I ingest into my body. It is seeking to keep my body and its surroundings clean. It is to be well rested. It is preparing my body to be strong enough to handle all the stress I place upon it while I seek to channel positive energy through it, and require positive action from it. With regard to my mind, I must seek the right understanding. For me, this is to keep an open mind and an ever-changing (growing) perspective. It is seeking composure and civility as I relate to the world. It is seeking focus relative to my pursuits. It is seeking knowledge to facilitate preparedness, prosperity, and enjoyment. The essence of each of these endeavors is seeking to grow.

To reach our full potential, we must utilize our time such that work towards betterment of our <u>entire</u> being is performed. One reason for this is that our entire being is made better, rather than just one element of it. This will facilitate not only a fuller and more complete life for the individual, but also it will lessen the strain each individual places upon the social support systems. This will add longevity to the limited resources of aid that exist around us. The other vital reason for the simultaneous pursuit of all three elements of human composition is a spiritual one. Working to perfect or better all three elements of human composition simultaneously facilitates an awakening to the truth. In other words, pursuing betterment of all three elements of human composition (mind, body, and soul) at once opens the door to revelation or divine truth. As an individual performs the tasks that will lead to the betterment of each of their elements, they will begin to see the interconnection between the workings of these elements. As well, each will see how their elements related to the reality and environment within which they exist. They will begin to understand how embracing and producing positive flowing energy benefits them. If the understanding of this interconnection is interpreted from the spiritual perspective, revelation occurs. Each individual's path through the journey of their life is revealed to them such that they accomplish what the Divine Energy of Life had intended. Thus, fulfilling their individual part of GODs' plan.

There is a distinct direction for the actions of the pursuit of betterment or being more perfect. That direction is positive. We start the process by first recognizing that we must perfect or make better the functioning of the body. This is because the body is truly the "temple" that houses everything that allows us to exist and makes us what we are. We seek the perfection of our bodies through exercise, movement, and effort. Each of us must seek to make our mind better, because our mind controls the actions of our body or our behavior. A quiet series of moments to ourselves, as in meditation, is an act that contributes to the perfection or betterment of the mind, as well as our soul. Studying the doctrine (words) of a given discipline is also an important factor of seeking the perfection or betterment of the mind. Indulging our interests and desires brings us closer to manifesting our God-given gift(s). Because our connection to the Divine Energy of Life is perceived as such a subtle part of our reality, it seems we can relegate the pursuit of betterment of the soul to the third position of importance. To a large degree, this approach is conducive to our current perspective and the physical reality of our existence.

However, in recognition of the truth that reality occurs within the context of spirituality above all else, our soul and spiritual Nature truly have a higher priority than our body and mind. Spending time within an environment that contains natural elements like water, trees and other plant life, other animals, etc., is an act of seeking perfection or betterment of the soul. Individual prayer and religious fellowship is an act of seeking perfection or betterment of the soul. Looking within ourselves for the answers to the questions of who we truly are and what we truly want/desire is to bring our soul to the forefront of our being. Trusting in not only oneself, but in others is an acknowledgement of the soul. Real trust is based on the presumption of correct, or right(eous) action. Individuals must **trust** themselves. For individuals to be able to trust themselves, they must be able to trust those around them. Individuals must be able to presume that they, along with everyone else, will do the right thing. Each of us was given a spiritual mission by "GOD," trusting will allow these missions to be completed. The soul can lead us to understand the nature of these "missions," as well as see us through it. It is through the soul that each of us is guided in the proper direction. If our thoughts and actions are of a positive Nature, by trusting ourselves, we employ the soul as the "divine guidance system."

Through the Divine Energy of Life, the human has derived many gifts to use during the time we are alive. Life itself is a blessing. Yet, some lives are harder than others are. Not everyone is blessed in the same manner. Relative to GODs' gifts, some can do this thing or do that, like playing the piano, becoming police officers, being parents, etc. We can become anything we wish to become once our basic needs are met and the resources for prospering are at hand. Nevertheless, above all these other gifts, GODs' greatest gift to each of us is life itself, the opportunity to be alive and to experience. In recognizing this, we must never forget that there is always someone else somewhere that would be willing to die for that one opportunity which is not utilized. For Americans, there is always someone on our planet less fortunate than ourselves, someone with fewer blessings. For the blessing of American livelihood, we must be thankful.

Truly, achieving self-actualization is having become the individual "GOD" intended. Individuals need to understand that their pursuit of self-actualization has more meaning than is readily apparent. What is the more meaningful and/or spiritual reason to satisfy this inherent need? It is to create/generate new, tangible and intangible things from within the human collective. Each human being must embrace a right(eous) system of actions that would allow an individual to contribute to the perpetuation of positive flowing energy without negatively affecting what exists around that person. Each of us is to create and/or generate something unique here on our Earth.

If "GOD" wanted us to do something, it would seem only natural that "He" would make it something that we needed or desired to do. Upon close examination of this declaration, together with Dr. Maslow's hierarchy of needs, it is evident that both paths of human motivation will lead us to actions that satisfy both our worldly and spiritual responsibilities. Doing what is required to satisfy the first group of basic needs establishes the condition for growth for our being within the context of our bodies. Doing what is required to satisfy the next group of needs makes individuals a part of a community and establishes the soul as the guiding force in our individual lives. Doing what is required to satisfy the "esteem needs" establishes our pursuit of personal growth. Finally, doing what is required to satisfy the need for "self-actualization" establishes our search for that God-given gift that lies within each of us. Spiritually speaking, our needs become satisfied as we live within the context of our movements being aimed at the pursuit of perfection. Our physiological needs are satisfied by the pursuit of perfection of the body. The next set of needs, those for love, belonging, and acceptance, are satisfied by the pursuit of the perfection of the soul. This is done by identifying and pursuing a positive set of values that will lead to the manifestation of right(eous) character. From this comes peace of mind. Peace of mind is the launch pad for personal growth and "self-actualization," which is satisfied by the pursuit of the perfection of the mind.

To efficiently meet our needs as well as satisfy our wants/desires, we must have defined priorities. Priorities are dictated by the real conditions under which we exist. It is true that spiritual reality has domain over any other reality conceive of within the human mind. However, we cannot separately function within the confines of one interpretation of reality or the other. Just as the humans' understanding of existence must be derived from two interpretations, the spiritual and the worldly, each human action must reflect the consideration of both aspects of existence. We must interpret and understand our worldly reality, because it sustains us as living beings. However, we must also interpret and understand our spiritual reality, because it engulfs our entire existence. Our first priority may be the satisfaction of our physical reality by seeing to the necessities of the body. However, it is the human consciousness that controls the interactive movements and actions of the human being. Therefore, to deal with the priorities of the body, we must also deal with the reality of the aware mind. Our thoughts must have direction, and that direction is a necessary part of our lives, as indicated by the presence of its physical properties and manifestations (i.e. energy). The guidance for our direction comes to each of us within the context of our spirituality, through the pathway of our soul.

The expiration of time distorts the humans' perception of what surrounds it. Some will argue that there is no truth to the notion that the human must meet the needs of its spiritual reality to continue to exist, based on the amount of "time" our species has been around, as well as its prospects for the future. However, with an open mind, one must remember the relativity of time and the hypothesis of the "divine blink of an eye" theory. What this means is that, as the label "time" is a human conception, it cannot be strictly applied to the Divine System of creation. Therefore, what humans consider a decade, could be considered "the blink of an eye" when measured within the context of divine creation. In light of this, the human cannot use the length of its existence as an excuse for not facing the reality of its divine responsibilities. The most important of these divine responsibilities is to create the most perfect conditions of existence for growth, and as we live out our lives within those conditions, we ourselves must grow.

As we look to create the most perfect conditions of existence for the human (and all other life) to grow in, each of us must grow into a better person than we are already. As each of us strengthens and betters ourselves, we in turn strengthen the community. The human community is made up of many smaller communities, i.e. social groups, neighborhoods, gangs, militias, ethnic groups, and nations to name a few. A community is a group sharing common characteristics or interests, and perceived or perceiving itself as distinct in some respect from the larger group within which it exists. Every community is built on the foundation of its individual members. Therefore, the better the individual becomes, the better the community becomes. This is true whether we are talking about our neighborhood, or the human race.

Imagine what the global state of utopia would be like? There would be no famine, in America or anywhere else in the world. There would be stable borders and relations between nations, while national economics and international commerce would flourish and enrich. Individuals would have profound peace of mind, the result of the restoration of hope, morality, stability, and order. Compassion would fill the air because humans will have accepted the significance of every individual life, as well as their obligation to perpetuate it. Joy and merriment would be the norm as we allow our cultural differences to enrich our interactive, interconnected lives. Emotions like hatred and envy would be replaced by feelings of love and goodwill, once the goodness of "GOD" is instilled in the hearts of those strong enough to face the facts of our entire reality in a responsible way. The fear that grips our general populous would vanish as our youth add substance, direction, and discipline to their lives. Sportsmanship and healthy competition would strengthen each individual's character and provide the needed outlet for aggressive tendencies. Employment would be nearly 100%, for those willing to work. Homelessness would become part of a not-too-distant past. We can have all these things, by the blessings of "GOD".

We must recognize that as we pursue the satisfaction of our individual needs as well as our wants/desires, we can and must establish a pattern of civilized human behavior that can and will cross the lines of all groups within our communities. We can have a unified, harmonious system of social interactions in America even though our collective American culture is made up of many different, individual ones. This is true because the foundation of this common pattern of behavior is based on our having common motivations for our pursuits. Accepting that we have common motivation should reemphasize why all Americans must embrace a common value system. Our personal value system is based upon our individual wants and/or desires. If each of us reached a point where we achieved satisfaction relative to a common value system, the state of that collective existence would be called "utopia."

Utopia is the epitome of a positive state of existence. America was on the road to establishing a utopian society when we as a nation were <u>collectively</u> pursuing the American dream. This is because it created for us a common value system. Having a common value system is one of the important factors of establishing an overall, common direction and set of goals. It is a crucial part of the foundation of a civilization and a utopian society. Values are based upon needs as well as wants/desires. It is true that wants and/or desires can be positive or negative. It is also true that we all need to pursue a positive conclusion to the moments we face (perfect resolution). Therefore, our value system must be based upon positive wants and/or desires. Values refer to the ideals, customs, institutions and the like, of a society toward which the people of the group have a high regard. Values constitute any object or quality desirable as a means to an end or as an end in itself. There are a number of elements that make up a value system. We refer to some of these elements as personal values, family values, spiritual values, social values, political values, economic values, moral values, and ethical values. With respect to these categories of values, each is composed of what is needed and desired with regard to that area of our lives. Each of us truly needs, wants, and desires positive things for ourselves. Face this truth. Individuals should use positive action to attain what they would have for themselves. Positive stimulation and satisfaction will be the reward derived from the Divine System of Nature.

The journey of human life can now take one of two paths. There is the path that embraces reality, truth, and spirituality within their relevant context. Then, there is the path of arrogance and ignorance. This is where humanity continues to stumble through its existence, being manipulated by powers far greater than anyone realizes. It is the path where divisiveness and individualism provide a firm foundation upon which a few can stand while many are destroyed. We must pursue a utopian state of existence because it represents the epitome of balance between the existence of animal life and the life of our Earth itself. Selfish and greedy behavior is excessively consuming the limited resources of our Earth. This is because with this behavior comes little or no regard and/or concern for the perpetuation of the human species, or life in general. This negative direction of action will lead us all to damnation. It will lead to death and a barren planet.

Moving harmoniously together as we work to satisfy our individual needs serves to move our species collectively ahead into the creation of GODs' kingdom here on our Earth, as was GODs' original intent. To create "GODs" kingdom," we must first satisfy the basic needs of all Americans, so that individuals can focus on betterment. We must then create the perfect conditions for growth by giving and receiving love. We then work at growing by satisfying our need for esteem and achievement. We then become the being "GOD" intended through self-actualization. Each individual must seek to develop his or her own "self" relative to Maslow's law. It is the job of the community and of the society to support the individual and vice versa, as defined within the context of being a member of an interdependent, socialized species. What we must create is a "more perfect union."

To direct our movements in a way that keeps our actions within the parameters of right(eous)ness while seeking a more perfect understanding of the significance and relevance of our being, we have only to employ two rules that are natural to each of us individually, and our species collectively. One is to seek to always move (and/or act) in a positive way rather than a negative one. The other is to utilize our individual sense of equilibrium to achieve balance with our positive actions, for the mutual benefit of all within our dominion. Relative to the personal pursuit of needs, they are to be met utilizing positive means. A balance must be sought to the degree that no individual being working toward achieving these things is deprived of them because of the excessive acquisitions of other individuals. As a conscious, socialized, interdependent species, our nature is to help and support one another's efforts to survive.

If our choices and judgments are positive in nature and directed toward the manifestation of equation and balance, the result will be harmonious movement for all living things. We must seek to achieve mutual benefit using compromise and tolerance in a collectively supportive existence, i.e. civilization. Balance and equation can always be attained by virtue of compromise and tolerance. Compromise can be likened to the action of moving a fulcrum under a balance beam. The position of the fulcrum depends upon the weight of the subjects on either end of the position of division created by the fulcrum. Within this comparison, tolerance is the distance under the balance beam that the fulcrum can be moved. If balance and equation are truly being sought, then compromise and tolerance should be limited only by the physical properties involved in that circumstance. Within the analogous comparison, the physical properties that limit the degree to which an individual can exercise compromise and tolerance are the strength and length of the balance beam that supports that which is to be balanced. That "balance beam" is the human mind. It is the human mind where the choices and judgments that produce balance occur. The strength of the human mind is massive and seemingly limitless. The length of the rational human mind is limited only by the circumstance of death. Therefore, there are no true objective limits to a rational individual's ability to compromise and tolerate relative to choice and judgment. When it is said that only the strong survive, this is not only related to one's physical stature and prowess. Balance is the essential factor within the formula of existence. Human survival requires a continual strength of will and of character. Compromise exercises and therefore strengthens one's will. As well, tolerance exercises and therefore strengthens one's character. Just as each of us must routinely exercise our body to strengthen it, each of us must also routinely exercise compromise and tolerance to strengthen our will and character respectively.

The movements and/or actions of one individual cannot solve our collective problems. Those of one hundred individuals cannot do it either. It will take the movements and/or actions of each and every American citizen making a positive contribution or effort towards common goals. What are these common goals? They are mutual satisfaction, mutual protection, and mutual benefit. That is what society is all about. Society is the system of community life within which individuals form a continuous and regulatory association for mutual protection and mutual benefit. This is achieved through balanced action, compromise, and tolerance. We must pursue equation because it is a vital, fundamental element of the Divine System of Nature. By combining our body's efforts and our mind's efforts together with the efforts of our soul, each of us will be guided to satisfying our needs in a balanced, positive manner while still aiding what surrounds us to do the same. In doing these things, we fulfill our role as a positive part of the Divine System of Nature.

The complete satisfaction each of us seeks can only be achieved by all of us together through our accepting, embracing, and utilizing the gifts and tools of our spirituality. Each of us needs to examine ourselves honestly, while separating ourselves as individuals from the rest of existence. If we were to apply the truthful understanding we derived from this examination, we would know that this is what we need as a society, as well as what each of us needs as individuals. What is needed is peace and stability, both physically and mentally. That is what an objective understanding of our spiritual reality brings to us. We have known it all our lives, but have been hesitant to take advantage of it because the foundation of spirituality is the giving of oneself to benefit others. This is verified as true because of the scientific designation of our species, which is "socialized." Our tangible existence causes us to "grab" materials for possession, so we tend to be in competition for things. Because of this, many of us find it hard to "give" as a way of living. However, we must collectively understand our existence with regard to positive energy, and how this energy travels through a parallel circuit. Each of us must embrace the truth within this understanding. Then, we will be able to see that polarized energy travels along a directed circular path. This means that emitting or utilizing the positive energy of goodness will bring back to us the positive energy of benefit and blessing, to complete the circular path the energy within this earthly circuit travels. To receive this blessing, we must expand our consciousness so that we may accept this as reality, and we must have faith in what is true. We must live within the context of our spiritual existence, defining and accepting the limited boundaries in which our individual lives occur.

As individuals and as a collective, all-inclusive species, we must evolve to the next stage of human development. The human species now has to deal with the information superhighway, national and international economic circumstances, the vanishing borders as well as other barriers, dwindling natural resources, war, disease, etc. To successfully deal with them in a positive way will require the human to evolve in consciousness and intellect. We as a species group must evolve to deal with our future in a way that will benefit all of humanity. To evolve is to get better. For us to do this in the most successful and beneficial way, we must reach a higher plane of understanding. We must open up our minds to reach that level of understanding, through the comprehension and utilization of the spiritual side of our nature. We as a species, a conscious group, a society, need serenity in our lives now. Serenity, or peace of mind, is the missing element. To achieve it, each of us must be satisfied in our lives.

We must have understanding and direction, along with an acceptance of the limitations of reality. To eliminate the negative elements of envy, hatred, and violence that result from selfishness and greed, individuals must manifest discipline both physically and emotionally. We must acknowledge and release the goodness that is inside each of us, which we repress because of the pressures that result from our worldly, material existence.

Spiritually speaking, the essence of the human being is true, righteous, and positive. To conform to this reality and to take our place within Nature in a physical sense, our movements must produce energy of the same polarity (that travels in the same direction) as corresponds with what is true, righteous, and positive. Because our minds direct the actions of our bodies, we must consciously direct ourselves toward responsible actions or behaviors that are aimed at truth, righteousness, and the positive resolution of the events we experience during the journey of our lives. We cannot just sit back and act or behave irresponsibly, and hope the story of human life has a happy ending. It is up to us to make that happen. As defined by the nature of community life, and as members of the family of living things, we are all connected. Therefore, each living thing is bound by natural and spiritual law to have motion in a positive direction, by the reality of its physical existence. All action that utilizes divine energy (which is all action) needs to be positive to fit into the divine flow of life. "Interaction" is therefore spiritual and must be positive, leading to harmonious coexistence through the balance achieved with compromise and tolerance.

As a conscious being, individuals are profoundly aware of themselves and their actions. By declaring, "I am," individuals acknowledge themselves. To claim respect for the fact that we "are," "am" as it were, to the degree that any of us expects another to recognize our space, while we demand rights and expect privileges, each then acknowledges that they are conscious. Therefore, each of us is responsible for our actions, which are the result of our thoughts. Unless an individual is mentally or physically ill, that person must be "able" to take responsibility for controlling his or her actions. The opposite of this would be to act without thought, i.e. on impulse and instinct alone, like a wild and uncivilized animal. The human existence occurs within the context of civilization. This revelation negates any effort to act without thought, or to deny responsibility. humans have evolved to a point where the state of our existence is considered by us to be "civilized," so the behavior of all members of this society is suppose be a representation of the characteristics that define that condition of existence.

By definition, we cannot truthfully ignore our responsibility to act in a civilized manner. We must direct our behavior as we live. The direction of this behavior is to be positive and within the parameters of civilized standards. Our behavior must be civilized because this word defines our state of existence. Our behavior must be positive because the rules of both civilized society, and the Divine System of Nature required positive action from us. We must face the reality that the words we use set precedent characteristics of controlled human behavior (or action). When that control is positively exercised, it leads to a continually successful growth of consciousness derived from the actions of discipline (work), sacrifice (understanding), perseverance (hope), and patience (peace of mind).

These qualities produced civilization. Civilization is an advanced state of intellectual, cultural, and material development in human society. It is marked by progress in the arts and sciences, the extensive use of writing, and the appearance of complex political and social institutions. It is also the conforming of human behavior to the controlled standards of civility. The parameter of this set of standards being defined by such words as "polite," "courteous," "helpful," "nice," "obedient," and the like. What this all means is that what each of us thinks translates into what we do; our behavior is predicated on what goes on in our minds. Since we live in a civilized society, there are parameters that set a standard for what goes on in our minds, and the behavior that results from those thoughts. To rebel against this truth is to rebel against the conditions under which each of us desires to live. To rebel against this truth while demanding the privileges bestowed by the group structure is hypocrisy. Surely, most have heard the word "hypocrisy," and have a general understanding of what it means. Hypocrisy is a fundamental tool of truth manipulation. In this case, it is a pretense of having a virtuous character, moral or religious beliefs or principles, etc., that one does not possess. It is an act or instance of such falseness.

The very first step we must all take toward bettering the social system of the United States of America is to recognize that it is necessary for us to be (not proud, pride is one of the cardinal sins, consider it actually just being) happy and/or thankful to be American citizens. The strength of a nation is built on the strength of each individual of that nation. Therefore, it is important for each and every American citizen to be strong for our country to be strong. The reason we are a world power is more perfect union of our economic, political, military, scientific, and intellectual powers. The strategies of our existence, our style of living, what we are as free Americans, are what make us great. Next to being a child of "GOD," being an American should mean everything to a citizen of this nation.

The true purpose of saying the "pledge of allegiance" in school before beginning the educational pursuits of the day was to reaffirm our commitment to our country on a daily basis. Each of us was to "pledge allegiance to the flag of the United States of America, and to the Republic for which it stands as one nation under "GOD." We were to be indivisible, while giving liberty and justice for all." Our existence, our country, is not about separation. It's all about unity. Unity is so much a part of our living condition. So much so, that it is the label by which we as a nation are identified. That label being "the United States of America." Without its citizens, a nation does not exist. "We the people" are this country. Our nation is not the white house, the president, or the politicians. It is each individual citizen joined together forming the collective.

As we commit our individual efforts to our country, our minds must have a common focus. To achieve betterment in our country, we must commit the efforts of our entire being. To commit the efforts of our minds to our country is to think about our country. It is to believe in American ideals. This commitment will allow our minds to manifest within each of us, the characteristic that will provide the motivation to make America an even greater nation. This characteristic is "patriotism." Patriotism is the love of and devotion to one's country, and this is what we must have. This country is not only the land that makes it up. It is not only the buildings and other structures. The citizens of this nation are the country. Therefore, a large part of our patriotism includes our loving each other and being devoted to each. We show this love and devotion to each other by helping one another.

People tend to look at the government and the country as some abstract establishment of which they are not a part. The reality is we are just a large group of people trying to coexist harmoniously and fruitfully. Because of this, every individual's voice is important. Each individual's thoughts and feelings are relevant to reality. Our political system must be guided by the Will of "the people." "The people" means each individual person considered collectively. Each individual one of us must fully participate in the social system by carrying out our civic duties. The nature of our system places upon us the responsibility to participate in the system at a very basic level to facilitate the functioning of our system. The most basic "required actions" are working, voting, paying taxes, and obeying laws. By fulfilling these basic requirements, we are afforded the liberty to fully explore and pursue our personal desires.

It is hoped that along with laws, morality and ethics will define the parameters or standards within which our behavior would be contained. Morals, ethics, and positive principles are the foundations of a civilized society. Our commitment to the system or society, is our adherence to the rules of conduct that reflect the wishes of the majority, the norm, or the average. The reward for our adherence to the social and moral codes of society is that we can act freely, and to some degree, we can expect to have the certain essential aspects of our survival provided for.

There is a moral standard that the populous should adhere to, being members of an interactive civilized community. However, these standards are flexible in a free society. We can push the limits of those standards to suit our personal indulgences from time to time as long as no one is harmed. That flexibility is left up to the judgment of the court system, one of its primary functions.

To protect our rights and to prosper within this nation's borders, we citizens must stand up and perform the required actions that are our responsibilities as citizens. The system that supports American life is the United States government. To make our social support system better, we must make the United States government better. In a free, democratic society, the job of a government is to serve the good of the people. The United States constitution is written to support this directive. Each individual citizen of this country is bound by his or her citizenship to participate actively in our social system. All who are eligible to vote must do so. It is disgraceful to note that of the eligible voters in our country, the average turnout for an election is 35%. This means that less than 35% of the American population is shaping the course of American life. An individual may not desire to be completely involved in every facet of civic duty, but there are minimum requirements to be met. These would be voting, obeying the laws, and taking care of one's own. Failing this, that person becomes a burden to the system, and the other members of the system must work harder to support this burden. This being a "free" society, there are no pressures to produce beyond the minimum requirement.

To negotiate the next stage of human evolution successfully, our species must work together with sincerity, meaning, focus, commitment, determination, and planning. In coming together as a collective, we enhance our lives as individuals greatly. We as Americans have given so much to this planet. Without regret, we must now focus on our country and ourselves, if we are to right the wrongs of our collective and individual existence. This country was founded and built on the efforts of individuals not native to this land. Each group came here under varied circumstances. Their efforts helped build a prosperous, free society. This occurred during a time when land, resources, and jobs were, to one degree or another, plentiful. The United States of America now has one of the highest, stable standards of living. It is one filled with abundance and leisure. As one of many nations, Americas' position in global affairs is considered one of leadership. Militarily, the United States of America is the dominant power of the planet. Our nation is the anchor of the global economy. The United States of America has strong political and economic alliances with the overwhelming majority of the nations of our planet. By and large, humanity has a common direction aimed toward democracy, liberty, and prosperity. Along with the other major military forces of our planet, a quick response to violence and disorder can be expected as the nations of the world ban together within the context of the United Nations to establish lasting peace. The global community of our species has in place a structural system that adequately sustains its interdependent Nature.

With the condition of the global community and the state of existence within Americas' borders, every nation of the planet will understand that now is the time for our country to focus on the problems within our own borders for our own betterment. The United States of America has reached a point in its national existence where it has become necessary to apply the nation's resources to the problems within our borders. We as a nation need to re-evaluate everything, i.e. the entire code, rule, and structure of our social and economic system. Our entire system of existence needs to be updated to the degree where it applies to present-day requirements and encompasses all the circumstances we face. America has entered into a new millennium with new technology, and new problems as well. We are also going to need to restructure our resource allocation to insure our continued survival within a civilized, prosperous social system. This includes the need to commit our nation's financial resources to repairing and upgrading our infrastructure. We all recognize that our present-day reality indicates that our social system may be spreading itself too thin by taking on more financial responsibility than it has the resources to provide for.

A good percentage of this financial responsibility is aimed in areas that are not related to the direct benefit of American citizens. as a sovereign country with defined borders, we the citizenry are entitled to be concerned about our future as a nation, irrespective of the other nations of the world. Globally, it is true that most all countries have domestic problems that they focus on without regard for the rest of the world. An example of this would be how other countries limit imports, maximize exports, and apply tariffs to goods. These policies are reflective of what is in the best interest of their people, and it illustrates our need to make some restrictive moves for our own best interest.

We too must internalize our concerns and resources. If we were to spend 5 years or more <u>focusing</u> on our domestic problems with the resources available to us right now, we could all but eliminate some of the unnecessary suffering that goes on in this country. We could accomplish this while continuing to help and influence the rest of the world. We have now reached a point in our collective American existence where we must assess our resources, and plan for our future. With every system that operates within the confines of a "fixed budget," there comes a time when a "balance sheet" or resource assessment must be made to determine the stability of the system at a given moment of reality, as well as its needs for the future. We have reached that time. We must now more clearly define our assets and our liabilities. We must determine the value of our resources (assets), and divide them by the number of the citizenry of our nation (liabilities). This determination cannot be made over night; it may very well take years. We must have an accurate accounting of the number of legal American citizens that exists, even if we have to conduct an "emergency" census, one that includes every legal American citizen.

The United States will need time and resources to refocus its energy and money towards internal problems like unemployment, homelessness, poverty, urban decay and destruction, etc. Our foreign aid may need to be reduced during this period. It may be necessary to make formal and impose a 3-8 year non-immigration/reduced foreign aid period that will provide for us the time and money this nation needs to rescue itself from impeding ruin. between 1946 and 1990, the U.S. government disbursed over $374 billion in foreign aid. In March of 1994, this nation doubled aid to the Ukraine, to a figure of $700 million. This was a "reward" for it having moved toward economic reform and nuclear disarmament. That same month in another news article, it was reported that U.S. aid to Russia and other former soviet states was not getting to the people who needed it, and that "major problems" plagued the management of the $3 billion assistance program, meaning some U.S. resources are being wasted abroad. In May of 1995, the kickoff by U.S. officials of a $25 million project to help rebuild Bosnia was reported. In a news article published Dec. 18, 1995, it was reported that according to the general accounting office (the investigative "arm" of congress), at least 23 U.S. government agencies had committed $5.4 billion for 215 separate programs in the former Soviet Union. There was also another $10 billion made available for loans, guarantees, and insurance. These numbers must be given consideration when a truthful assessment of the economic stability of the American social system is being considered.

Just like the welfare system in this country, foreign aid creates and perpetuates cultures of dependency. Many of the countries that have been receiving long-term foreign aid are poorer today than they were 30 years ago. Foreign aid during our period of refrain should continue to provide education and farming equipment, etc., possibly creating more U.S. jobs. The United States of America must come together with other nations to help them develop their resources in such a way that mutual benefit can result from the use the entire resources of the globe for the betterment of the planetary population. An example of this would be with regard to aid to Russia. The area of Chernobyl could become the world's designated toxic waste dump, because it can never be cleaned up or restored to its natural state. A global waste disposal process center could be setup there that serves the needs of the entire planet.

When an assessment is made of our nations' resources allocation, one must also consider how this applies to immigration. It has been estimated by a research organization based in Washington, D.C. that nearly 10 million immigrants entered the U.S. in the 1980's. This figure includes both legal and illegal entries. That accounts for roughly 37% of the population growth for our nation during that period. In an article published in the news dated Nov. 22, 1994, it was reported that some politicians were moving to deny welfare benefits to most legal immigrants. The estimated saving was $22 billion dollars over five years. That is an average cost to the American taxpayer of $4.4 billion dollars per year of welfare benefits alone to legal immigrants in the U.S. In another news article dated Feb. 24, 1994, it was reported that congressional investigators found that immigrants were being coached by some "unscrupulous" translators, attorneys, and "store-front" business to fake mental illness and retardation to qualify for federal disability benefits. Under the law, supplemental security income pays disability benefits of a maximum $446 per month (usually with a lump sum payment of $2,500 to $3,000 in the beginning created by the benefit being retroactive to the time of the application) to poor people who cannot work due to a fatal or long-term disabling condition. Abuse of the system only magnifies the need to reassess how American resources are allocated.

In a news article published Feb. 14, 1994, it was reported that the U.S. immigration and naturalization service estimates there were six million <u>illegal</u> aliens in this country at that time. We have seen what problems this has caused relative to our nation's security. Well, under the law, <u>illegal</u> parents are not entitled to welfare or Medicaid benefits themselves. However, if their children are born on U.S. soil, the children are entitled to the full array of benefits because they are full U.S. citizens. This is afforded them, despite the fact that their parents came here illegally. This article also asserted that the center for immigration studies estimated that federal prisons housed some 29,000 <u>illegal</u> aliens, at a cost of more than $800 million a year to the American taxpayer. Their estimates further indicate that when Medicaid, welfare, schooling, and other costs are added up, <u>illegal</u> aliens cost the taxpayers $5.4 billion per year, and this is based upon numbers derived from 1994. In another news article published March

6, 1994, it was reported that <u>illegal</u> aliens were working in jobs that could be held by legal U.S. citizens. One of the <u>illegal</u> aliens insisted he was making "the going rate" of $32.50 an hour, while most earned $7.50 an hour. Most of these jobs were obtained because these individuals held falsified documents that indicated they were in this country legally. Stopping illegal entry into this country would take more extreme measures than are already applied to the problem. This effort would require money, possibly from funds redirected from foreign aid. If it takes building a long fence, this would create construction jobs. If it takes increased manpower for stepped up border patrols, this also creates jobs.

Consider this, what if 60% of the people in other nations decide to come to America to share in our livelihood and prosperity. What would we do then? For one, there is not enough land within our borders to accommodate such an exodus. Secondly, does our nation have an obligation to ensure the welfare of its citizenry before giving aid to "guests"? If you the reader were living on a fixed income, would you first feed and clothe your family before you fed and clothed a stranger from another town? If our nation is going to provide someone with food, shelter, and clothing, it should ensure that all its citizenry has these basics first.

As we focus on ourselves, we need the support and understanding of the rest of the world also, so that we may all benefit from the remaining resources of our planet and the opportunities before humanity. Our collective destiny is now. All the events and elements that are relevant are present simultaneously. This is the period of our existence when we must all make the decisions that will define the direction of our journey through the remaining spans of time. We the people, must demand the changes that will benefit us all, rich and poor, and in between. The leaders in Washington represent us. They must do what it is we want them to do, or we must replace them with people who will.

To accomplish these things we must become involved. We must all work together for the good of the collective. This will benefit us as individuals. The possibilities and/or opportunities before us are endless, but we must evaluate and utilize them realistically. We must recognize the reality that at this juncture in our social development, we need to embrace radical blanket reform with an open mind, being innovative to the degree that we get the most benefit out of the opportunities that lie before us. As a nation, we must again focus on creating a better world for our offspring to inherit.

As we move forward as a nation towards the perfection of our collective and individual existence, we must identify the areas we must perfect or make better. One of the areas is government. To make our government more better, to create a "more perfect union," the system of government must function in a way that conforms to the way it was created to function. We have a government that is for the people, of the people, and by the people. We, the citizen of the United States of America, are the governed. Because of our constitution, the citizenry is the power of this nation. We elect individuals to represent our collective interests on Capitol Hill. They are there to do our bidding, not their own. In taking the path of least resistance, i.e. the easier way, we elect these people, then blindly allow them to take responsibility for our collective future. These people are elected by the masses. They do not know what each individual wants out of government. Individuals must tell elected officials what they want them to know and what they want them to do. The most powerful weapon that a citizen welds before the government in a democratic society is the individual vote. The magnitude of the power of that one vote is increased when that vote is added to another, this is the formation of a "coalition."

The population of the United States is around 288.5 million, give or take some millions. For all of us to work together towards a common goal requires organization. We need a unit of interdependent individuals having a system for our interactions. That system is in place. It is our government, supported by our social structure. For our government to give us what we want, it must know what we want. We as individuals must tell our government what we want. How do we do this? Well, an individual could call his or her local representative in congress and express their desire. This viable option will get results. However, with a population as large as ours, there is no way to achieve <u>mutual</u> satisfaction if you act individually. This is because in that case you are seeking to have your desires satisfied, without consideration for your neighbors. Your local representative, however, represents your neighbor as well as you. If your desire conflicts with that of your neighbor, there must be a compromise. As your representative is in Washington doing the job you elected him or her to do, with the many people they represent, they cannot be expected to mediate every conflict of interest. To achieve mutual satisfaction through balance, compromise, and tolerance, the individual must interact with their neighbor. Each of us must share our interests with each other to come to a mutual understanding and compromise. This is working together to achieve mutual satisfaction.

As this task requires organization, organize is what we must do. It can start on your street or block. All the residents of a street or block come together as a group with a purpose in mind, that purpose being the betterment of their shared living condition. Everyone makes a list of what is wanted in the neighborhood. It could be clean streets, paved alleys, playgrounds, a new school, whatever. Recognizing that you cannot have everything without a substantial increase in taxes, you narrow the list down to the things that are common concerns of everyone. You then formalize your mandate and deliver it to your local representative at the municipal, congressional, or senatorial level. Then you tell them that if they cannot deliver, when the next election comes around, you will all vote together to elect someone who can deliver. You must then follow-up your effort by monitoring the progress your elected official makes. You will have just created a "voting bloc." The bigger the voting bloc, the more power it wields. This is what lobbying groups do. There is absolutely no reason why individual citizens cannot form groups to lobby for their interests, in the same manner as do lobbyist for "special interests groups."

The most important power that the individual has in America is the vote. To make it as affective as possible requires this type of organization. This "organization" would then "lobby" for the needs of those it represents. It starts with organizing a block, then a neighborhood, then a municipality, etc., etc. If the entire nation wielded its political power as a unit, the power of the government would be in the hands of the people, as it is designed to be. People look at their one vote and think it does not amount to anything. They think that they cannot effect change with one vote, so they feel as though they do not count. To magnify the power of the vote, we need to form neighborhood voter lobbying groups that champion the immediate needs and interests of our local communities.

I cannot emphasis enough that the important thing to understand as you examine these elements of social and governmental restructuring or "reform" is that, as humans, we must come together as a united species of animal. As Americans, we must come together as members of a large, diverse family. We must come together as Americans under the one true "GOD." If each individual wants to reap the benefits of our society, then that individual must be willing to give the civil behavior back, i.e. conformity. Each of us can conform to common social behavior and values, while still maintaining our ethnic identities. This is truly the American way. We all have to start thinking of ourselves as Americans to regain our focus and work ethic. People will say, "Yes, we must come together, but there are problems that keep us apart." Every one of the political and social options proposed here are merely possible solutions to our problems. Whether or not they are considered viable by all, they stand in testament to the radical degree of change (evolution) we must embrace, and the direction those changes must take. We must be at least as innovative as we make changes in our social and political arenas as humanity embraces the new millennium. Remember that over 226 years ago, the forefathers of this great nation were able to put together and finalize a document so profound, it is still the foundation upon which our government's structure stands. Are we not equal to or greater than these men were? Our present-day circumstance affords us more insight from practical experience and formal education than was available to those men. We also have added resources those men did not utilize. These resources are contained within the minds of women and of those of other cultural backgrounds. Together, we must all tackle the future of our nation with the same vigor and commitment as the founding fathers of our country.

The next step in bettering the social system of the United States of America is the restoration of our belief and trust in those we choose to lead us. We must again trust the institution of government. In our minds and in our hearts, we must grant amnesty to our government for old conspiracies and atrocities. To some degree, we are partly responsible for whatever has happened because of our lack of participation in the governing system. Therefore, we must accept that things have happened in the past that were not in the best interests of all concerned, and resolve that these circumstances never again occur. We must take the necessary steps to insure this. Then we the people, and our government, must move forward with a new commitment to each other. However, we must first forgive, so that we can again trust and believe in the system that we have. Our system of government is called "democracy." There are other systems of governing that have been utilized on our Earth and that are currently in use. There is the dictatorship or totalitarianism, communism, and socialism, to name a few. There are elements of each of the systems found in the other systems in some form or fashion. An example is how a family functions like a government (democracy with a hint of dictatorship). In our democracy, we have social programs setup to aid people who need and deserve our collective consideration. Does that mean that our system is a socialist form of government rather than a democracy? No, it means that in our wisdom, we identified an area of concern and utilized the knowledge and resources at hand to address the circumstance in a positive manner.

If there is some component of a social structure that could be considered a part of another social system and can be implemented in our society to benefit the common good, we cannot ignore it simply because of a label. We must be more intelligent and disciplined than that. This new millennium will require us to broaden our application of truth and wisdom in a more objective manner to achieve a balanced system of existence through the application of compromise and tolerance.

Our physical presence as human animals and as American citizens, i.e. our reality is America. Life as we know it, our "lifestyle," the context within which we exist is only within the borders of our nation. If something happens to America, all of our realities, objective or subjective, are affected. To embrace reality and truth, we must conform to the norms, standards, ethics, morals, and laws of this nation.

None of us as individuals can make America conform to our personal desires or standards. Therefore, we must come to common terms, to allow us to experience our reality to the fullest. We must respect each other, and live in harmony. America allows for the satisfaction of our needs and desires like no other place. It provides a human living condition unlike any other on our planet.

There are examples (signs) all around us that show us the way to the truth. A good example of this would be an analogy of the journey down the road of life. It may seem as though it is not possible for all of us to live harmoniously in a civilized manner. It may appear that a utopian existence is beyond human capacity. The reason these interpretations of our collective reality seem right is because of our individual perspectives. We as individuals have closed our minds to sharing and mutual benefit because of our desire for self-satisfaction. We would rather use our energy to satisfy our personal whims, instead of expending energy to overcome the struggles, as well as exercise the compromise and the tolerance needed to achieve unity and mutual benefit. This is the conscious and/or subconscious manifestation of selfishness and greed. It leads to a self-centered approach to indulgence and satisfaction. Because of this perspective, most of us believe that "utopia" cannot be manifested into reality. This is not true, and there is precedent for this assertion.

In a broad sense, the actions of our lives can be viewed in much the same way as any journey that occurs during the course of an aware existence. There is a beginning. It is the point at which one sets out in whatever direction is chosen. There is the actual movement along the path that is chosen. Then there is the destination, the goal, or the point at which one wishes to arrive. An analogous comparison of the span of our lives and a journey can be made as a means of achieving a clearer understanding of the flow of our collective interactions. Our ability to negotiate the roads we travel has already demonstrated our ability to exist harmoniously relative to mass human interaction. This precedent must serve as the example that demonstrates our ability to respect each other and live by rules. We all <u>can</u> and <u>must</u> balance our individual pursuit of satisfaction with the pursuits of others. We can all harmoniously interact within the parameters of the rules of conduct that are applicable to the given circumstance, as we all move in a positive direction toward our individual "destinations" or personal goals. Let us explore some of the similarities between a human "living" and a "journey," within the context of American citizenship.

If we were an unstructured, uncivilized, non-industrialized group of beings, the setting for this journey would be the wilderness. For each individual, there would be a starting point. From that moment, until their moments end, there would be chaos along their journey. At the outset, each person's destination or goal would be the acquisition of basic necessities. Without a civilized behavioral structure comprised of compromise and tolerance to adhere to, each of us would be bumping into others without defined directions. Fighting and killing would ensue. However, we are a structured, civilized, industrialized group of beings, so our setting is what it is, urban and rural America. From the moment we begin our individual journeys, the expectation is not one of chaos, but of enjoyment. This is because with our standard of living, generally speaking, the necessities like food, shelter, and clothing can be more easily met.

The chosen direction of a person's journey is supposed to be aimed at enrichment. As civilized beings, to avoid the chaos created by each of us "doing our own thing," rules of conduct are established so that the flow of all the movement does not lead to conflict. As the setting of our journey is here in present-day America, the roads upon which these journeys would be made are paved. For the purposes of this analogy, the way that we will travel these paved roads is by bicycle and by car. For the American citizen, a clear comparison between the journey of life and the journey on a bicycle and in a car can be made. Relative to the bicycle, we can come to a clearer understanding of the use and direction of energy, both positive and negative. Relative to the car, things become clearer with regard to a human's interaction with another. In each analogous situation, the human and the vehicle must be interpreted as one entity composed of distinct parts. As well, what is true regarding the vehicle is true regarding the human being.

Let us first look at the journey upon a bicycle. It is the bicycle that provides a clear understanding of the use of human energy and the direction of it. The journey does not begin unless the human moves. Energy generates the movement that causes the vehicle to move. The energy that moves the bicycle comes from within the human. The energy that the human produces to move the bicycle is considered positive because it moves the vehicle forward toward the rider's goal. The energy can be used in a negative way, to move the bicycle backwards, but this is not the natural path to take. The negative path can be negotiated successfully, but it is uncomfortable to do so. Though this path can be traveled successfully for a short period, over the long-term, the odds are that tragedy will befall the person traveling this path. The speed with which the bicycle travels is the direct result of the effort the rider wishes to exert. This determines when that individual will arrive at where they would like to be. An individual can go in many different positive directions. Along the way, there are times when the path is easier to travel (downhill), and times when it is more difficult (uphill). We know that our energy for the ride is limited, and for that reason, we cannot get to our destination instantaneously. So, we consciously pace ourselves, enjoying the ride as we go. Along the way we pass many things, these are our experiences. Every time we pass something, it becomes a part of what we know. However, just because we see it, does not mean that we know all there is to know about it. If we want to know more about one of these "experiences," we can stop and indulge ourselves in that moment as we learn. Then the journey must continue if we are to arrive at our desired goal or destination.

Let us now look at the journey of our lives within the context of an analogous relationship to a journey in a car. In this analogy, the car is likened to the human in that the car is the human body. The carburetor is like the heart, as the gas is like the blood. The driver inside the car is like the brain inside the body. The wheels are like the limbs, etc. With the journey in a car as well as the journey of life, thoughts alone have no effect on reality. It is what thoughts lead one to <u>do</u> that affects reality. When persons are in their cars, they become the brain of that physical body which houses them. They can be calm, humored, or irate and going nuts. None of these occurrences alone has any effect on the other cars. It is what the car itself does that affects the reality around it. It is the actions of the person that truly matter. As long as the cars/persons do not swerve, collide, or come into conflict with one another, the turmoil remains within the car itself and there is no negative impact on the reality around it. Our personal problems are just that, and we should take our cars/ persons to the appropriate "mechanics" to have those problems corrected. The cars/persons we interact with along the paths of our journey are not responsible for our troubles, so we should not be imposing our frustrations on them.

In life, we are supposed to move in one direction and in harmony with one another. This "right" direction is positive. Again, we could also say that this direction is forward. There are times when we cannot avoid going backwards, but whatever happens, we must regain our right direction. This direction is forward, or positive. As we move forward, we must recognize that we are not the only individuals on the road/planet, and others have as much right to exist and move freely as we do. Rules were established to allow us all to move about in harmony and without conflict. It is not a choice, but an obligation to obey these rules. Obeying these rules allows us all to coexist in an orderly fashion, using compromise, tolerance, and balance. There are rules, both inferred and define, that govern the conduct of vehicles as they travel along the system of roads that is the path of their journey. Likewise, there are rules, both inferred and define, that govern the conduct of humans as they travel along the system of existence that is the path of their journey. Making a comparison of the similarities between the rules of conduct associated with these like journeys will perhaps simplify our understanding of the need and benefit of staying within the parameters of the system of interaction.

When we set out to travel to a destination, it is the same as working to achieve a goal. Each of us begins at point a, and our goal is to arrive at point b. Relative to vehicular travel, each of us understands that we are supposed to make this trip lawfully and without creating conflict along the way. None of us readily travels in the wrong direction down a one-way street (which is unlawful), or drives through buildings, or over median strips. The reason we resist the temptation to do these things is not only because they are unlawful, we also recognize the possible harm that can be caused by our actions. The same applies to the journey of life. We must choose a lawful, positive path for the course of our lives. We must resist the temptation to do wrong not only because of any fear of judicial repercussion, but also to avoid doing harm.

Every individual car/person has a destination that the other cars/persons cannot discern as they pass each other within the flow of the system of interaction. The right of way is the customary or legal right of a person, vessel, or vehicle to pass in front of another. To yield is to give up (an advantage, for example) to another. It is to concede. To yield is to exercise compromise and tolerance. Relative to human interaction, these rules of conduct are elements of civility. They are the foundation of common courtesy. We must be courteous and yielding because we have no way of knowing whose "destination" is more significant at that specific moment in time. The significance of a car's/person's journey is obvious if that individual entity is wearing a uniform (fire engine/man or woman, police car/man or woman, ambulance/doctor, etc.). However, things are not always so obvious. In addition, a courteous, civil pattern of behavior makes all movement occur with less resistance, thereby saving the expenditure of energy that would otherwise be used to overcome relative hindrances.

By looking at it from the perspective of its analogous relationship to the flow of vehicular traffic, there are countless ways in which we can come to a more objective understanding of the "flow" of life. One reason that life's circumstances can be synonymous with traffic circumstances is because both entails traveling along a path of a journey towards a destination with an objective in mind. If individuals do not have a destination or an objective in mind, they wander aimlessly about. Let us examine a few other similarities. Anyone who has a valid driver's license is given the privilege of freely operating a vehicle in a legal manner. This privilege is theirs as long as they continue to operate legally or within the code of conduct required by the social system. This allows them to arrive at the destination of their choosing without having infringed upon the privileges of others. In American life, citizenship gives that individual the privilege of freely operating as he or she sees fit. This privilege is theirs as long as they continue to operate legally or within the code of conduct required by the social system. This allows them to arrive at the goal(s) of their choosing without having infringed upon the privileges of others.

In a traffic situation, individuals are traveling down a road, steering themselves in whatever direction they choose, to whatever destination they choose, while only being in control of the physical structure that carries their person.

In the situation we call life, individuals are traveling down the road that is the journey of that life, steering themselves in whatever direction they choose, to whatever destination they choose, while only being in control of the physical structure that carries their conscious mind. In neither circumstance can an individual presume to control any other car/person. The object is for each individual car/person to reach their respective destinations at their own pace, safely and satisfactorily. As with the system of traffic interaction and the system of human interaction, the "pathways" these "vehicles" are to travel was designed to produce a consistent, balanced, harmonious "flow" of movement through compromise and tolerance.

The "flow" of traffic generally goes in one direction, forward (positive). This is also true of life. Along these respective journeys, there are sometimes mishaps. In cars, we can refer to them as troubles and accidents. In life, we can refer to them as trials and tribulations. Some are circumstances that affect only the one car/person involved, i.e. running out of gas, flat tires, mechanical problems, etc. Some are circumstances that affect more than one car/person, i.e. cutting someone off, running lights and stop signs, wrecks, etc. During these travels, when two cars/ persons come into physical contact with each other, we call this a "collision/conflict." Sometimes the collision/conflict is slight and sometimes it is extensive. Sometimes the driver/brain is harmed in some way, and sometimes not. Whatever the nature of the mishap (trial or tribulation), every car/person can expect to have them during the course of their existence simply because of the magnitude of motion and interaction. Some are lucky to avoid these "mishaps," but each of us must be conscious of their possible occurrence.

Within the context of traffic, each of us must respect the area that the individual cars comprise, because regardless of what an individual may feel about the other car, they know that it physically exists. Each of us knows the damage that will ultimately occur if an encounter becomes physical. Individuals also know that to hit another makes them liable or legally responsible for the damage they cause. They also know that they will cause harm and damage to themselves. So regardless of the intensity of an encounter, rarely does one car ram or purposely hit another. It is the same in life's interactions. Each of us must respect other persons in much the same way. It does not matter how we feel about one another, each of us must still respect the fact that the other exists. Moreover, we must consciously refrain from physical violence.

When a person enters the collective movements of traffic, which can be liken to the mainstream of the human collective movement, he or she accelerates and/or passes, doing what is appropriate to get into the "flow" of interactive movements. Once that person has found a place among the many, that person can move along at his or her own pace. As long as that person obeys the rules and does not get in anyone's way, that person can go as he or she pleases within comfortable limits. That is also how it works with life interactions. In traffic, if a person is near someone with an irritating pattern of driving or acting, by indulging in confrontational behavior individuals exceed the parameters of compromise and tolerance. all persons need do is to tolerate that circumstance (usually lasting only a few seconds or minutes of an individual's <u>70-year</u> lifespan) until they can pick a safe time to put distance between them and that other person, putting as much distance between them as is possible. That is the way it should be within the context of human interaction.

When individuals pull up to stop signs and stop, this is a manifestation of the discipline required to live within the rules, i.e. the limits of social order. Persons are supposed to come to a complete stop at stop signs. If there is no one around to witness or enforce compliance, persons stop out of an understanding of the possible harsh ramifications that will result from behavior that blatantly disregards established standards. If persons obey all the rules of the road, obeying the speed limit and going with the flow of the traffic, there will be places along their journey where they will have an opportunity to exceed the prescribed parameters. Persons can cruise at a speed higher than the limit and perhaps they will not be caught. This is not right, but if individuals stay within the traffic pattern, i.e. the flow of their life, each can sometimes get away with minor excesses. In traffic, if individuals do the right thing all the time, each will get where they are going safely. This is accomplished by obeying all the laws and following the rules, yielding in the interest of harmony, and showing discipline through compromise and tolerance. In traffic, the pedestrian always has the right-of-way. As in life, the one with the least advantage in an encounter is to be given extra protection and consideration.

What follows are a few more examples that also serve to clarify how readily we can come to understand the movements of our individual lives within the context of a vehicular journey. One traffic rule is "keep right except to pass." The principle behind that being, people go through their respective journeys at different speeds. If most everyone stays within the same vein of progression, those people who consciously choose to go at a faster pace than others have a safe avenue through which to travel. However, there are those who think they are moving at the same speed as everyone else, so it does not matter what vein they are in, and they sometimes drive in the left lane. That is their choice, but they must deal with the repercussions of their actions. As keeping right except to pass is a law, those people are in violation, and if they are caught, they must pay the price. There are people who are in that lane because they are passing or for whatever valid reason. You also encounter people who are there intent on impeding the progress of others for a variety of unfounded reasons. They impose their will on others by not letting them pass. The thing to be remembered by the one who wishes to pass is that they should not exhibit malicious intent resulting from these actions because that only increases the level of negative flowing energy. Yes, that person is an ass. However, you do not have to like that person, you only have to respect the fact that they exist and occupy a space on our Earth. In addition, the direction of action (behavior) to pursue is positive, regardless of the choice others make. There will definitely be an opportunity to pass that person. It is just a matter of patiently waiting for that opportunity to present itself safely. That person who impedes the flow can very well be likened to one who exhibits discriminatory tendencies. Their actions are based on assumptions they make about people they have no knowledge of, nor prior contact. They allow their competitive spirit to inter-mix with their bias (subjective) views, and it causes them to react in a malicious manner towards people who, more often than not, have no relevance in their life.

When racism is examined within the context of the analogous relationship between life's journey and vehicular journey, the excessive subjectivity and irrationality of this way of thinking becomes crystal clear. racism is the result of "an <u>excessive</u> and irrational belief in or advocacy of the superiority of a given group, people, or nation, usually one's own, on the basis of racial differences having no scientific validity; it is social action or government policy based upon such assumed differences." The first part of the definition identifies two aspects of reality that are contrary to our true spiritual Nature, and the laws of the Divine System of Nature. The first is the fact that it is excessive. This indicates it will lead to imbalance, inequality, and sin. The second is that it is a subjective interpretation of reality, a manipulation of the truth. Road rage is the result of an excessive and irrational belief that one individual has superiority over another, thereby granting that individual the right to impose their will to move onto another. It is the action that is based upon such an assumption. Not one of us believes the mentality that produces road rage is valid. Likewise, we must all see that the mentality that produces racism is not a valid perspective either.

There are many more examples that illustrate the analogous relationship between life's journey and a vehicular journey. What all these examples show is that humans can move harmoniously on a mass scale while pursuing individual goals. The difference in these two circumstances is that relative to vehicle interaction, the consequences of wrongdoing or negative action is immediate and obvious.

While the repercussions of wrongdoing or negative action relative to personal interaction is not. In the interest of our individual and collective future, we must take the precedent set by our patterns of behavior during our vehicular travels, and apply the truth there to our full, civilized existence.

There is a normal pattern to traffic. Therefore, according to the foregoing analogy, there should be a normal pattern to human behavior. Existence or time is generated by continuous movement in a specific direction. This "continuous" movement translates into a "series" of actions defined by degrees. With regard to the human and its relationship to the system of Nature, it is every choice that individuals make added together that defines their life, not each individual one. Every choice that is made is connected to the last choice. Every moment and the action contained in it is connected to the next. It is the series of choices made that defines the direction of one's life. As persons connect their actions together, each builds up "momentum." Once individuals establish momentum in their lives, it becomes easier to maintain direction. To stop momentum takes a strong, radical effort. If persons buildup positive momentum, it usually takes extremely weighty negative occurrence to alter the direction of the positive momentum, and vice versa. Humanity has established momentum. To effect corrections to the course of our existence, we must embrace strong, radical change to be effective. This is why each of us must be continually positive, and continually objective. It is about a pattern of behavior that can truly be regarded as normal relative to the definition of our social structure. We live our lives within a social structure defined as civilized. Acting within the context of what is normal or common relative to the definition of a living entity is a part of the physical responsibility that an entity has to the Divine System of Nature. In America, the definition of the living entity we label "human" is that of a civilized being. If something is a reality, it sets precedent that must be considered in the formation of individual perspective.

As the word "normal" refers to a statistically average type of behavior, we must recognize it as an essential part of the flow of our lives within the context of both Nature and spirituality. The term "normal" refers to an action and/or movement-filled series of moments that transpire as a natural occurrence, thereby allowing for a systematic analysis from which a pattern can emerge. The standard by which to measure normal is average. Average includes both success and failure. Comparing the behavior of the best of us and the worst, and everything in between is how average behavior is determined. We must all work toward and aspire to being the best we could possibly become within the structure of our existence (more perfect). Our goal should be to meet the civilized standard determined to be average, and we must be satisfied with whatever achievement we reap. This is because whatever happens is still a part of the average. The standard of the average encompasses our individuality, because everyone must be included to derive an average. The standard of the average is the measure of our collective existence, so it encompasses our relationship as a species group. To pursue the behavior and performance of the average person is to function within the parameters of the standards that give structure to our civilized value system.

Within a collective social group, no individual is expected to be anything more than average. This truth is relevant to the fact that individuals are different, some better and some worst. An individual can accurately determine their own response to a circumstance of existence, or measure their own achievement in an endeavor, as it compares to others in their same range of existence. Whatever the condition of an average person of similar demographics in a given circumstance was, when faced with that same circumstance, one can compare themselves against the standard of the average because they can be only better or worse in that instance. Each of us must try to function at a level that is equal to or better than what could be concluded to be the average as it applied to the given condition. This is how we achieve growth. As each of us strives to be better, the achievement of the average becomes higher. This elevates the prosperity of the entire group. As long as an individual is working to produce and therefore contribute, they are a factor in arriving at the average. The performance and contribution of everyone from the highest achiever to the lowest achiever is important.

While everyone wants to be thought of as an "individual," each of us is still a part of a group and a member of an interdependent species. To the degree that this is true, we must accept and utilize this knowledge to the full limits of its benefit. Because there is the inherent system or pattern of human behavior, how each of us acts must reflect the standard set by the system within which we exist or move. What is extremely important about this is that there is nothing inherently wrong with general conformity or assimilation. The current level of freedom in American society allows persons to exert their individuality at times and in areas where it is beneficial for them to do so. However, this does not necessarily need to include every waking moment of a person's life, simply because that person wants to be seen as totally in control of his or her life. The revelation here is that as individuals, we are never "totally" in control of our existence because we are a socialized species, and are therefore required by the laws of Nature to be dependent upon each other for our collective survival.

In a capitalist society such as ours, freedom and control is based upon economic position. Time is not cheap. We all know and understand that things of value have a price. Within this context, the phrase "free time" does not accurately apply to the moments to which are being referred. The more accurate label for the time that individuals have bought for themselves is "leisure time." Even for the child, the time that is his or hers is bought or paid for by someone, usually the parents. Leisure time is something that is earned. In a capitalist society, leisure time is more of a privilege than a right. Within the context of the Divine System of Nature, leisure time is naturally earned after any animal has completed the necessities of its existence, i.e. its divine responsibilities. The time to indulge and submerge oneself in individuality is leisure time. This is the time when individuals are free from the demands of work or duty. Leisure time is the reward individuals receive from having worked.

All in all, each of us only deals with society, or better put, the public, during a specific part of our day. That part being the time we spend outside our dwelling place. During the time we are out and about, we should focus our energies on the circumstances and tasks at hand, so as to facilitate the positive impact upon our existence that righteous spiritual movement promises. When the activities of the "workday" are satisfactorily completed, we can then shift the focus of our energies to our personal lives and the elements therein (i.e. our families, ourselves, our friends, etc.). During leisure time is when individuals are with the people who comprise the group they interact with on a personal level. This is a subgroup or subculture. It is during this that individuals can interact anyway they choose. However, when persons are dealing with the general public, i.e. the mainstream, each must relate as we all do, because there has to be trust and responsibility. It is all about balance and compromise. Individuals want things from the system, like the ability to live freely. The system of Nature is a balanced system, action leading to reaction. If an individual wants, that individual must also give. Each of us must compromise to achieve balance. If a person wants to act a certain way all the time, then he or she has to accumulate the resources that supports the time to do that. Positive action dictates that all individuals do that legally. Therefore, persons must pursue the difficult path of learning and attaining knowledge or skill, so that each may contribute to the mainstream and prosper within this capitalist system. This is so that each can have all that leisure time to indulge as is liked. It is a process that more often than not takes time. That time is supported in a natural sense through the family structure, the nucleus of the nation. The timeframes of this process are labeled as infancy, childhood, puberty, teen years, and adulthood. Once an adult, the better-prepared persons are to gain whatever it is they want out of life, the faster and easier it is going to be to attain those goals. Each of us must not use negative action to achieve our goals in a short period of time, because this action is not a part of our system of existence. Spiritually speaking, negative action conflicts with our natural presence here on our planet. Regardless of what individuals are doing, they must always be consciously guiding their actions in the direction of positive change. Change is an inevitable result of the combination of action and reactions, together with moving reality, or time.

To pursue a utopian existence within the context of the physical properties of this electromagnetically charged circle that we are all on is to seek to have every system of reality work correctly, rightly, or positively. In essence, each system is supposed to have action or move in the right or positive direction. As we work to achieve this, we must start from the smallest systems of existence and progress in sequence to the larger systems of existence. From the standpoint of the individual human being, the smallest system is that of the self. Each person is composed of the body, which houses the mind and the soul. These three elements of human composition work together to form the system that brings to life the individual human existence. There is a system of reality that supports each element of our being. As we seek to perfect ourselves, we must also seek to perfect these worldly support systems if we are to maintain the gains we have made.

In dealing with the components of our existence that support the elements of our being, there is the spiritual system that supports the workings of our soul. Each of us must come to understand that the spiritual system includes all structured and unstructured references to our natural being. These are things like our personal feelings and emotions (i.e. laughter, happiness, sadness, intuition, instinct, etc.), Nature itself, churches (religion as a belief system), all our interactions with other beings, and all natural objects (animal, vegetable, and mineral), etc. There are the education and recreation systems (i.e. schools, recreational facilities) that contribute to and support our minds. All mental and recreational exercise serves to support our mind and its positive function. Things like crossword puzzles and word games, along with physical activities that are fun work these areas while reducing stress. Finally, society itself supports our bodies. As a socialized species, our physical existence relies upon the interdependent interactions related to human-to-human contact. This method of interaction has developed itself into what we have labeled the "social system." The social system is composed of the family, of the community, of the city, of the state, of the federal government, and of the global community.

Within these institutions are other "support" systems, like the economic system, the political system, the healthcare system, and more. As we seek betterment for ourselves, we must make our living conditions better relative to the "worldly" and the "spiritual" support systems. We have to perfect ourselves as individuals for obvious reasons. We have to perfect the support systems because we are an interdependent species. It is the support systems we have collectively constructed that provide the basis for our interdependent interaction, as well as the ability to maintain our gains. However, when we look to make better the human living condition, we must start to better ourselves as individuals before we can require the respective support systems around us to be better.

When reference is made to the support systems of the soul, the first component of that system that comes to mind is the church. Houses of worship are vital to the humans' effort to make his or her soul function better. When an individual who embraces the system of spirituality walks into a house of worship, the focus of that person's mind becomes altered. The control of their being is consciously released to whatever may <u>naturally</u> occur. This is because of the inherent understanding that the Divine Energy of Life is indeed an unseen force of spirit or energy. What we are doing is opening ourselves up to or allowing ourselves to become receptive to the direction this energy or spirit takes us. When in this environment, an individual can "tune in" to the frequency within which they are individually connected to the Divine Energy of Life. Because of the focus derived from prayer and the receptiveness manifested in this environment, we make for ourselves the opportunity to feel and sense the changes that occur within the body as the energy or spirit surges through us. Fellowship magnifies the power and presence of the Divine Energy of Life within that worshipping structure because of the concentration of so many like-minded people (electrical branches). Yet, each of us must understand that it is not the house of worship that manifests the presence and power of "GOD" (the Divine Energy of Life). Truly, the minds within the structure congregate for fellowship, and this brings about the presence and power of "GOD." GODs' power and presence is brought into the dimension of our existence through the focus of the human mind.

To Hue America

My love, appreciation, and commitment to my country, the land of my birth, America, is a very strong element of my character. It is the foundation upon which my values and ideals are built. Nevertheless, my love and appreciation for my ethnicity, my blackness, is another strong element of my character, and it is the reason that I am driven to make an effort toward bringing the truth of salvation to the reality of my ethnic group. In no way do I want to imply any disregard or apathy for Caucasians or any other nationality. However, it is the Black-American people who are about to become an endangered Hu- of man. The words of this book are for all to read, but Black-Americans must recognize these truths with urgency. As determined by the content and direction of their actions, many Black-Americans are not seeing reality for what it is, choosing instead to create a reality that fits their perspective, as most all humans have a tendency to do. Black-Americans must pull their collective heads out of the sand and face the truths that surround them.

This is a message for <u>all</u> my brothers and sisters, be they black, white, Hispanic, Asian, Indian, or whatever. It is for us all because we are all members of the <u>human</u> family. We are a single species of animal. However, this is a book that must be read by <u>all</u> Black-Americans. We determine the course of the human species' future. These words have been put together to cause Black-American males in particular to make this world a better place. All humans must face reality, and Black-American males are no exception. These words apply to us all as Americans, but irrespective of what any other sub-culture or ethnic group does with this knowledge, Black-Americans and specifically males, must recognize these things or they will be systematically annihilated. My use of the word "systematically" is not intended to imply that the "white establishment" is conspiring to eliminate blacks from the face of our Earth. What I do mean to imply is that within our "system" of existence, continual negative action begets continual negative reaction. The Divine System of Nature does not systematically support negative flowing energy. As a natural response to energy flowing (which infers continual) in a negative direction, the Divine System of Nature will seek to correct or right this wrong against the system of Nature, of which we are all a part. This will be accomplished by whatever means necessary. The "means" available to the Divine System of Nature are derived from the actions of both the elements of Nature and of the natural objects within Nature's system. The elements are Earth (what we stand on), wind, fire and water. The objects are animals (<u>including humans</u>), vegetables, and minerals. This means that Mother Nature's response to the negative energy un-natural to her system of existence could be any disastrous series of events, leading to the demise of Black-American males.

Realistically, if all Black-Americans were to act in a positive manner collectively, supported by all the respective support systems, literally the whole world would go in a different direction. The human conditions of existence would be utopian in as short a time as perhaps 10 years. If we applied ourselves in education and business we would accomplish so much because as a people, we are capable of such great things, as evidenced by our true history upon this planet. In tribute to Anglo-Americans, they have built one hell of capitalist system here in America, with our (unacknowledged) help. If Black-Americans were to be honest, we would have to admit that Anglo-Americans have made efforts to integrate us into this system. It is not only the divisive attitudes of some within the white infrastructure of American society that is keeping Black-Americans from experiencing prosperity. What is now holding us back are our own racial attitudes. Black-Americans are the ones who must now truly let go of "racism." We are the ones most affected by racism, and we have a biased view of those of Caucasian ancestry. By letting go of the past deeds of the "white" race, we can begin to put our own race back together. Black-American men must let go of the hatred and look to our spiritual teacher as the example by which we measure ourselves, that figure being Jesus Christ, our brother.

Black-Americans who have not entered into the mainstream of American life have to face reality. They must turn away from the direction the negative impulses generated by selfishness and greed lead to, and go in the positive direction toward the advantages and opportunities already existing within our society. Each must embrace whatever help is offered, while being committed to the idea of helping themselves. We must all build on our assets with our creativity and energy. We all know there is a part of the Black-American population that is negative and hateful towards Anglo-Americans, just as there is a part of the Anglo-American population that is negative and hateful towards Black-Americans. This makes the task of "mutual" acceptance difficult, and to some degree, undesirable for those of that persuasion. Coexistence and integration of all citizens into the mainstream social structure is not negative within the context of Nature (spiritually), nor in a practical sense (worldly) because of the rewards of this society. For Black-Americans, the example of the viability of integration exists in the precedent set by those desiring a "normal" American way of life. Differences and conflicts based on race existed in the suburban community where I grew up. However, it was our common value system that held us together as a community despite those differences and conflicts. This is not to say that all the work on the racial problems in our land has been done. However, not one of us, white, black, or whatever, can let the issue of race hold us back as individuals, as a community, or as a country.

American citizens, regardless of their ethnic lineage, have an advantage because the system is tilted to benefit the taxpaying consumer. Each of us must utilize the advantages of the system without regard to difference. If an individual encounters discrimination, then deal with it as a single occurrence. Not one of us can allow this one circumstance to paralyze our ability to deal with the rest of the circumstances of our lives. Every individual has the right to identify with his or her own ethnic group. There is nothing wrong with an individual having a good feeling about his or her ethnic group, so long as that person accepts the fact that others may feel this same way about their ethnic heritage. There is a competitive streak in individuals that is a part of their human Nature. If one is not open-minded enough to recognize and rationalize this fact, he or she will interpret these feelings in a very superficial manner, which is a contributing factor in racial bigotry. As Americans, we cannot allow our personal desires to cause us to do anything that adversely affects our system, because it is this system that allows us the opportunity to be individuals and have attainable personal desires. When one lives within the confines of a social structure, that person is a part of that cooperative structure regardless of what that person may think. Everything that person does affects that structure whether it is negative or positive. Presently, the word "freedom" is taken too literally. Our individual freedom must be exercised within the parameters of the social structure. Written laws and implied codes of conduct relative to the definition of the word "civilized" define these parameters. The freedoms experienced within this country are to be had by all. The "wrongs" that Black-Americans experience are basically the result of the subjective administration of policy and law. This must be changed from within. It is accomplished by those seeking change becoming an active element of the internal workings of the social system. Beyond this, the only way we as individuals can exercise our liberty to experience any freedoms is if we all respect each other as individuals.

Being a Black-American myself, I understand this system seems to have racist barriers built into the institutions of our social system's infrastructure. Black-Americans must understand that this is merely a perception based upon the interpretation of individual actions. It is not based upon the interpretation of the words that constitute the foundation of the system. Largely, the barriers faced are created by the people administering the system rather than by the system itself. The fact that racism exists does not relieve its victims of the responsibility that each human individual has for their own existence. Each of us must continue to strive to become a functioning part of every aspect of the social system so that we can bring equal consideration to the administration of the social system. We must strive to become everything from police officers, to judges, to politicians, to doctors, to CEOs, and the like, so that we are counted among those "administering" the system.

We must provide for our own existence within the social system, as is the responsibility of every (matured) living entity within the Divine System of Nature. The social system can be utilized to such a degree that Black-Americans could almost work around racism if we functioned as a unit. This is because of the nature of free enterprise. Individuals have to clean up their own houses before they can tell someone else his or her house is dirty. We as Black-Americans have to pull ourselves up by our own bootstraps. There are government programs out there to help. The word "help" has to be taken literally in that those programs are set up merely to aid citizens with their personal efforts. If an individual has no personal effort, then the aid seems insufficient because too much is expected of it.

We all need to stop fighting the American social system and become a positive part of it. Dr. Martin Luther King protested peacefully rather than with violence because he felt integration, not revolution, was in the best interest of the people he represented as well as America as a whole. Revolution in America is a monumental task and beneficial to no one. The citizens of this country do not need to start a revolution. Revolution is a circumstance that occurs when a citizenry unite under one philosophy that is contrary to the philosophy of the government. In a revolution, it is the people who revolt against the government because the government does not work in the best interest of the people. In our time, our government is perhaps the best it can be with our present level of participation. It is not the government that the people must revolt against, it is the negative forces affecting our lives that we must tackle in unison with one another to depress what is negative and elevate what is positive.

Black-Americans do not examine their problems as a united community, nor from a global perspective. The standard of living this civilization has achieved for its general populous is unprecedented in the history of homosapiens on our planet. We must become a productive, positive part of the American populous. As bad as things seem here, the opportunities for individuals to have comfortable lives are better here than they are anywhere else on our planet. Elsewhere in the world, there are populations that have much greater barriers to overcome to meet basic everyday needs. When compared to those circumstances, the conditions of existence for average Black-Americans are luxurious. As each of us reaches for the satisfaction of our basic needs, those needs are closer to our grasp than in most countries of the world. Globally there exists an economy unparalleled in the history of this circle we are on, and we live in the anchor of it all. We should all capitalize on the opportunities before us regardless of our difference, and continually work to change the problems that exist within this social system for everyone's benefit.

Many in the black community blame their current position in life on past transgressions committed against our ancestors. The fact that whites brought blacks over here as slaves is a horrible tragedy. However, it is not terribly relevant to the degree that now we are here, and we must function within the circumstances and situations that currently exist. White-Americans will never be able to make up for what they have caused Black-Americans to lose as an ethnic group. However, the past is just that, the past. It is gone. We must learn from the mistakes that are evident in it. The present is now, as these words are being read. The future is there for us to change. The world is moving ahead, and Black-Americans must move ahead with it.

Most everyone has heard the phrase "keep on pushing"; this is what we must do. When one examines the road to maturity within any civilized social system, it is evident that all entities must push themselves and work hard to make gains, while overcoming the hardships that are inherent to the journey of life. All individuals must work for any gains they make in this social system, whether they are economic, political, personal or whatever. Each of us must always continually strive to accomplish. The nature of the existence of the hue of man termed "black" is one of everyday struggle. Each of us must recognize this as our reality and deal with it. What we work for in this country is a comfortable "style of living" that can be maintained over a lifetime. To enjoy a comfortable standard of living, one must share in the things that are within the mainstream of society. To enjoy any sort of a long-term, normal, comfortable lifestyle, one's income must be earned legitimately. All the movements or actions of living things need to conform to the system within which they exist. This is not the law of the human. It is the law of Nature.

Each mature adult within American society must strive to be the best individual they can become. This is because we are <u>all</u> role models to every child we come into contact with. Black-American men must aspire to positive things because like it or not, our youth look up to us as role models. All children do this. It is a part of the Divine System of Nature. The young ones study and mimic the older ones to learn the ways of the world. As they desire to be like us, which is to do what we do and have what we have, they have to learn from us that the true avenue to prosperity is a legitimate one. Not one related to some sort of anti-social endeavor. The Black-American populous hanging out on the corners of our communities and generally up to nothing constructive are not making a positive contribution to our communities. Nor are they providing good examples for our children. Therefore, we must stop them from doing this. We in the black community should be continually protesting their presence on our street corners, but we do not.

Black-Americans are not recognizing the truths in the moments before them, and they are not responding to those truths with conscious actions aimed at getting positive results. Our lives have always been a struggle, recognize that and deal with it positively. There is still racism here in America, recognize that and deal with it in a positive manner. There are serious problems in our communities, recognize this and deal with it by using positive action. There is a divine truth that all mature, competent humans understand. It cannot be manipulated by changing a word here, or inserting a word there, or leaving out words altogether. It is the truth of what actions are positive, and what actions are negative. As humans, we control or choose our movements or actions through conscious thought. because of this ability to "control" ourselves, all humans are responsible for manifesting the discipline it takes to choose the right action that corresponds to a respective moment and a given circumstance. Since this is true, individuals bear a good deal of the responsibility for whatever situation they find themselves in, stopping short of the use of armed force. If persons find themselves in a negative situation, they must choose the action that changes that situation into a positive one. The right reaction to that circumstance is not to do something negative, it is to do something positive.

A major factor in human existence that has brought about our progress as a species has been technology, a product of the human mind. An element of this factor is about to have an effect not only on human existence, but also on the human species itself. This element of technology is the computer. It will drastically change the way humans <u>think</u> and <u>move</u>. It will therefore alter the structure of human life. The structure of human life is civilization. The structure will change on all social, political, and economic levels. To be a part of this evolution requires consistent access to a computer capable of allowing one to plug into the internet, or World Wide Web. This requirement infers a particular level of economic status. This is because ideally, what will be needed is a stable residence, with consistent telephone or cable service to go along with the computer system and the internet access provider. The reality here to be recognized is that, before a person reaches the point where they are a part of this evolutionary process, all their basic needs must be met. What good is a computer if you are starving? A person must be clothed and fed, and they must be without the stress produced by worrying about their basic day-to-day existence, so they can fully embrace the opportunity for growth.

Black-America must wake up to the information renaissance that is occurring in the civilized world. They must face the revelation of the oncoming social, cultural, and economic changes that are occurring around them. Societies will evolve as a result of the information superhighway. As this process occurs, if anyone finds himself or herself in a position of not being prepared to compete for prosperity, that person will have none. To be a part of this evolutionary information exchange, one must be able to communicate using the words common to the system. This requires individuals to be <u>literate</u> and <u>educated</u>. If an individual is not "plugged into" the computer age, the quality, direction, and nature of that person's existence will be irrevocably changed for the worse. during this period, if an individual does not have consistent access to a computer and the internet, within a time span of a few years, that person's earning power and lifestyle will diminish to levels they will consider unacceptable.

That person's understanding of the social system will be archaic and out of touch with the times. Our capitalist economic system is based on supply and demand. If there is no market for something, it does not sell. Being out of touch with the times, that person's presence and abilities will have no market, therefore, their prospects for sustenance and prosperity will be very limited.

Whether or not we are open-minded enough to recognize it, Americans of all ethnic backgrounds truly want the same things out of life. Some Black-Americans rebel against the efforts made to achieve integration, or what could also be called, "assimilation." However, the reality is that if an examination is made of every black individual or family that has "made it," it would be found that in general, each has pursued and attained the things that produce a standard of living that mirrors that of what would be commonly associated with White-Americans. Black-Americans are truly a people of great intelligence, strength, and ability, but there are those that lack direction. The world of the Anglo-American can provide that direction if we accept America for what it is (reality) and build upon the foundation it has laid for each of us. For the Black-American, America is the land of our birth. It is our homeland. Africa is our "motherland." The American dream may seem like a White-American aspiration. However, if given a choice, it is one we would choose for ourselves. If it is beneficial to each individual regardless of who it is associated with, then why not embrace this dream as a possibility and strive for it?

It must not be believed that all whites hate blacks because this is not true. It is a fact that there are organizations devoted to the hatred of blacks (and other groups). It is also a fact that all whites are not members of these organizations. A lot of the discord and hostility that exists in America is related to the fact that the majority of White-Americans have a certain vision of how American society should be, and a large percentage of the Black-American population is not contributing to this vision. This vision is of peaceful, prosperous existence through the mainstream system of American life. This is not an unrealistic desire, since we are in America. Black-Americans must embrace the reality that this society was founded on Anglo-Saxon beliefs. We live in this society and our greatest chance of success as defined by the nature of civilized comfort, and middle-class values, is here in America. Therefore, it is up to us as individuals to make the most of the opportunities before us, and to work to right the wrongs we are confronted with.

The hostility that some individuals within the white race have toward black people or other minorities cannot be condoned. We are all Americans, and we all must start working toward our own prosperity within that context. White-Americans hold the major of the positions with power in this country. Because of this, there is a good possibility of a black individual will encounter a person who is biased. Truly, what difference does that make with regard to one's own responsibilities? Each of us must still do what we need to do. Each of us must perform our required actions. In other words, each of us must live up to our responsibilities. With respect to those within the black ethnic group, each of us must face the realization that we have minority status in this society. Even so, this society is capable of providing us with the style of living we desire. To achieve this desired standard of living, we must work within the social structure. Black-Americans who work hard, to a large degree have opportunities very similar to, if not the same as White-Americans within our social structure. There are prejudices within the structure, and we manifest some of those biases because of the direction of some of our actions.

All subgroups within our nation have patterns of behavior that must be changed. If the social system needs changing, the social system provides a lawful vehicle for affecting change. All Americans must use the social system to their advantage, rather than rebelling against what is still our best road to prosperity.

There is a reality to the circumstance of slavery that all of America must recognize. Whites must recognize that to re-establish the balance of existence created by "GOD," they must fully embrace their responsibility for having destroyed the Black-Americans ability to be utterly and immediately self-sustaining by uprooting them from their natural living condition, and destroying their past. Whites destroyed the foundation upon which blacks were to build their future. Because of this, Black-Americans do not understand their relevance to the future. This is significant because time is continuous and connected. In essence, the past is connected to the present, the present to the future, and the future to the past. Imagine what it would do to the population of any large nation of today to forcibly conquer the citizenry, and separate them from their land. In addition, to take them into the unknown and destroy their individuality to the degree that each can be totally dominated. This is what truly happened, and the consequence of this cannot be changed, it must be overcome.

White-America must reestablish its understanding of the truth that being black in America is truly a difficult venture. The psychological pressures experienced by Black-Americans that have resulted from the actions of White-America can be beyond belief. Take for example one burden black men are forced to incorporate into their psyche. It is a subconscious burden derived from the actions of the past. It has created a state of mind that is very difficult to get rid of. Black men must function around the possibility that, simply because of the color of their skin, on any given day and without warning or apparent reason, their life can change and become harmfully different than it has been. It is anticipated that this change can occur irrespective of any of their own actions. It is, for the most part, beyond their control. It is a matter of conditioning that took many decades. This conditioning resulted from the fact that in the (not too distant) past, a group of whites could, without warning, barge into the place where any man is expected to protect his family, the family home. That group of whites could and would take any or every one of them outside and beat their ass, burn their house to the ground, rape or hang members of the family, and the victims (specifically the men) would have no recourse. It did not matter if these individuals were guilty of something or not. Moreover, it could happen because of having expressed a natural part of their humanity. These acts could be provoked by the expression of a natural emotion like happiness or anger. It could be provoked by a natural expression of one's manhood like prowess or flirtation. Today, this state of mind is perpetuated by the vision of black men being beaten by a cop when stopped for a traffic ticket, or being falsely accused of a crime by a white woman who does not want to admit her own weakness. To have to live with subjugation is a very difficult burden to bear. This burden is a factor that has contributed to some youthful black males having created the "subculture" of drugs, hip-hop, and street gangs that they have, so they have some place within which they can function where they believe they are beyond the "white man's" influence. Some place they can be dominant and free from having to deal with this burden of not controlling their destiny in a natural sense. This may be hard for White-Americans to understand. However, it is a real reaction to the past actions of white persons, and as all reality is connected, the responsibilities that have resulted from those actions must be faced.

It is hard for White-Americans to understand such problems because they are not subjected to these actions. Any individuals reading this should consider how they would react if their character, ability, confidence, or self-esteem was totally disregarded in a circumstance. In addition, if solely because of some characteristic of their physical makeup, their physical safety was in jeopardy. For white persons to get some idea of what feelings and emotions blacks must deal with and control, they should place themselves in this scenario without regard to color and see how they would respond.

To go someplace and once there, be confronted by someone who exhibited a hostile dislike for them for no apparent reason. Keep in mind that the hostile person has had absolutely no past encounter or anything in common with the "victim" other than that particular moment in time. Yet, "the perpetrator" shows intense hatred for them. Then, as that is being dealt with, it is also remembered that the group the hostile person belongs to perpetrated horrible atrocities against the group to which "the victim" belongs. On a daily basis, blacks of all backgrounds encounter people who are hostile toward them not because of some offense they have committed, but rather because of something bestowed upon them by Nature, the color of their skin. In most civilized cases, if one white person was to come upon another white person and had never encountered that person before, these individuals would not exhibit any feelings toward each other, and the dealings would be truly objective. However, when the contact is with a black person, some (and I mean a lot) exhibit negative feelings, and most times hostility towards that person and it is based solely on the color of their skin rather than anything that individual has done. White-Americans should then ask themselves how they would feel about the hostile person and the group to which they belong.

One reason some White-Americans have a hard time accepting the existence of what is referred to as "institutional" racism is because they are not subjected to it. The reason they are not subjected to it is that White-Americans have majority status in this country. The American cultural system is oriented around the Caucasian belief system and based on an Anglo-Saxon past. White-Americans have the positions and the power to "control" and/or greatly influence the lives of American "minority" groups. White-Americans hold the power positions in government, making the policies that shape all our lives. White-Americans hold the power positions in the corporations as well as in the educational system, making decisions on who works and how one gets educated. Because of this, there is no way for White-Americans to collective experience institutional racism. When one is subjected to it, it becomes all too real. Truthfully, institutional racism is not the institutions of society being racist in nature. It is the people who administer the institution's policies and practices exercising their bigoted judgments while administering to those at the mercy of the system.

Is it realistic to think that so many people with biased feelings and convictions have disappeared? Have those with biases as strong as those in the hate groups that perpetrated the horrendous acts in the south and elsewhere just suddenly given up their beliefs and adopted an unbiased approach to daily life? The real question is, where have the racists gone? A deeper examination of the actions that have generated recent events happening on a daily basis in our country reveals much of the answer to such a question. There was David Duke being embraced by a major political party shaping the policies that govern American life. A close examination of the long-range ramifications of the directives that were within the "contract with America" is startling. There are cadets in our military academies aspiring to the ideals of the KKK and Nazism. Hate crimes are evident within the ranks of our military. Corporate executives have been caught expressing and practicing racial intolerance and biases. Restaurant chains have been exposed to have biased policies. Police departments contain officers that are clearly abusing their power by using excessive force when dealing with individuals belonging to particular "victim" groups. The once openly racist individuals have shed their markings and infiltrated the workings of our social system to accomplish their objectives. This is from where the notion of institutional racism is derived.

Without safeguards like civilian lobbyist and review boards, affirmative action, quotas, and the like, there is no guarantee of fairness for all Americans. White-Americans have to understand that the lack of evident fairness manifests itself into a feeling of helplessness and hopelessness in a person who already feels oppressed to begin with, whether or not that person is truly oppressed. White-Americans cannot close their minds to the reality that this society has greatly oppressed Black-Americans (and other groups) that are in this country. In this country, Black-Americans receive the most hostility among the various minority groups.

While it is up to White-Americans to acknowledge their responsibility for this circumstance, Black-Americans must "wake up" to the fact that they are responsible for themselves as individuals and as an ethnic group. However, White-Americans must understand that for this to happen on a large scale, they must allow Black-Americans to empower themselves. They must allow and encourage them to organize, to become strong, to become prosperous. The interesting aspect of a (Black-American) collective agenda is that there is nothing wrong with maximizing one's efforts towards advancing their own interests as long as they do not harm others. There is nothing destructive for America as a whole, to have Black-Americans pooling their economic power for their benefit because it can only be beneficial if it is done within the framework of the American system. As American citizens, our prosperity will benefit all Americans.

Many white people are oblivious to the mayhem generated because of racism. Why is that? It is because racist mentally that generates that mayhem is not an inherent trait of the white ethnic group. It is a state of mind held by many, but not the majority. There is no mystical connection of the mind between those within this group generate negative energies and actions, and those who are opposed or indifferent to those energies and actions. It is the same in all other ethnic groups. For example, there is no inherent connection that links upscale, suburban blacks to inner city gangs and the street violence they commit that would allow those in the suburbs to know what those in the cities are doing. When these atrocities are exposed, any and every ethnic group can determine what is right or wrong with the circumstance. This was evident during the civil rights era of the 1960s. The abuses like the beatings, hangings, and use of water cannons were shown on TV. When a white human being not of that locale saw another human being treated in such a manner, the right and wrong of this was clear. This natural distinction between positive and negative action increased white support of the civil rights movement, because many had no idea of the magnitude of the acts that were being committed. Racism, like most sinful things, is supported by a foundation of understanding that contains a high degree of selfishness, and greed. These aspects of the human perspective are the result of a superficial level of interpretation and understanding.

For White-Americans to expect there not to be some sort of resentment by Black-Americans for the actions perpetrated upon them, regardless of the rationalization, is unrealistic. For the short term at least, White-Americans must accept the fact that some Black-Americans harbor negative feelings about them that have resulted from the subjugation and hate-motivated atrocities perpetrated by people of Caucasian ancestry. Black-Americans must also accept the fact that some White-Americans harbor negative feelings about them based upon their skin color and the actions of a few. White-Americans must exhibit even more compassionate than they are, because to heal the wounds that have been inflicted, they must ultimately see their compassion and understanding as "partial-payment" of a debt. It is the same as if it was a family and the child told the parent, "I didn't ask to come here." Because that child's being there is not the result of their own actions, parents have a responsibility to the child. Likewise, White-Americans have a responsibility to Black-Americans.

Though the (North American) Indian has never truly benefited or accepted the European version of cultured civilization, their history is what will strengthen our understanding of why we need to allow our spiritual being to guide our lives. This group of individuals has known as great a hardship as any ethnic group on our planet. Like the Black-African, they too had rich fertile land because of their faith and respect for the spirit of Nature. As well, they too were forced into a life of domination. However, they held on to their belief system. Even now, when the world around them thrives on stimulation and satisfaction, they have accepted their circumstance to the degree that they exist day-to-day as they do. It is their faith and belief in "the spirits" from which they have drawn their strength. Their example to America is that though the nation is great, this greatness is the result of the labor, hardship, lives, and contributions of others.

Though America can close its eyes to its past as it relates to Black-Americans, it must always remain humble in the eyes of both "GOD" and humanity, because the American Indian exist in monument to the fact that America does not belong to those of Caucasian ancestry. This land was taken from the natives who occupied this space in time, and it was done without equitable compensation. so for some to feel and act as though no one belongs in America but the white person is wrong. The pilgrims never "discovered" this land. It was never lost. One of my favorite analogies relates to the "discovering" and settling of America. It goes something like this: white people discovered America in much the same way as if they discovered the "red" man in his own car. "Hey man, I found you in your car, now, I want your car." Huh? There was no "discovery" of America. America was quite literally "come upon" by everyone who sailed here.

Hypocrisy is defined as being insincere. Hypocrisy is the pretense of having feelings or characteristics one does not possess. In truth, it is any state of being to which reality and the truth of it are not adhered. A state of existence where the truth from the spoken word does not match to reality created by the related actions those words produce. Hypocrisy occurs when we say one thing and do another. Hypocrisy is a lie. It is denying the truth inherent to reality. An example of this occurs when some white persons say other ethnic groups should leave America and go home. "Home" is meant as the land from which their ethnic group originated. Yet, those who utter these words are not native to this land themselves. Their ancestors came here from England or some other European nation because they sought greater control over their lives. The original white settlers took this land from the indigenous population, i.e.

the "red man." The truth of what they are saying does not match the reality of the actions that occurred. Therefore, they are denying reality. They are manipulating the truth so that it validates the self-centered perspective they wish to have. By doing this, they are creating their own personal reality rather than dealing with the reality "GOD" created for all of us to dwell in.

It must never be forgotten that the Native American, the North American Indians, the Red Man, was here when the pilgrims got here. This was their land. It is a reality that this is now by most considered the "white man's" America. However, how that transpired is also a reality. Therefore, it is now and will always be a debt for which the "white man" must make restitution. Likewise, the "white man" must make restitution (reparations) to the Black-American for uprooting them and taking them from their motherland. The form of these reparations is debatable. However, one element of them is clear. They must include compassion for, and tolerance of the Black-Americans existence and the behavior derived from it. This is because the condition of their existence and their behavior are a natural occurrence, and they are in a large part due to the actions of the Caucasian ethnic group.

It was reported in July of 1994 that Audley Moore, then 95-years old and known as the queen mother by her neighbors in Harlem, had been fighting for decades to win government compensation for the suffering of Black-Americans that resulted from slavery. At that time an annual convention for N'COBRA, or the National Coalition Of Blacks for Reparations in America, had attracted several hundred people from across the nation. That movement is growing, especially after the 1988 success of Japanese Americans in winning cash payments of $20,000 for each of the 60,000 survivors who were denied freedom and forced to live in internment camps during World War II. Since then, it was reported in 1998 that the U.S. chamber of commerce planned to solicit donations from U.S. corporations to compensate (white) slave laborers and others who were forced to work in German factories that were owned by American companies during World War II. One German fund contained $5.2 billion dollars, and many survivors claimed that amount was not enough. It was reported in February of 2000 that an Oklahoma state commission recommended the state pay reparations for "one" of the nation's deadliest racial clashes. It was a little-known rampage by a white Tulsa mob. It occurred on May 31, 1921, and result in the death of nearly 300 people who were mostly black.

The commission called for such things as direct payments to survivors and the descendants of victims. It also called for scholarships and a tax check-off program to fund economic development in a mostly black area there, along with a memorial to the dead.

America is not in a position to pay financial reparations to Black-Americans for the tragedy of enslavement. The magnitude of the wrong itself, together with the length of time over which it transpired and the incalculable damage this atrocity caused make monetary compensation economically overwhelming. The interest alone on the proposed compensation of 40-acres and a mule would cripple, if not destroy the American economy. These facts do not alleviate this nation of its financial responsibilities relative to the Black-American community. However, what America lacks in the area of financial reparations, it must make up for with compassion, understanding, and tolerance. White-America created and still perpetuates the plight of Black-America. It was their negative action that started it all. American history is truly a difficult past for White-Americans to face. It is costly to face because concessions and compromises must be made in the interest of balance and harmony. The balance that is inherent in nature applies to every aspect of existence. This is because everything that exists is a part of Nature. That means everything. We all must now take the positive steps toward our collective, prosperous future. To embrace reality and accept the truth is an exercise in humility for us all.

There are things in the history of every ethnic group that each must come to grips with and make amends for (repentance). For one group, it is the murder of Jesus Christ. For another, it is reneging on the covenant with "GOD." For still another, it is the subjugation and domination of the other peoples of the world, etc., etc. We all must humbly embrace each other and support each other as we try to get past these things. Each ethnic group cannot get beyond these things alone. just as the Holy Scriptures say one must confront their sin and confess it to those affected by it, we must all accept and confession our sins to each other in a collective manner. I heard a holy man describe forgiveness in a very effective manner. He said that forgiveness is not forgetting the wrong of another. It is not tolerating it. It is not ignoring it. It is not accepting it. It is not making excuses for it. It is not denying it ever happened. It is putting aside the wrong of another. It is releasing oneself of the burden of concern for the wrong. The citizens of America as well as the rest of the human race must embrace this definition of forgiveness for the sake of our collective future on our planet.

As we recognize reality and come together as a species, we must understand that the differences that generated what we classify as races are truly the result of geographic location and environmental conditioning. Race is simply a factor of our collective reality. What the collective American society has to accept as a simple fact is that whites belong to an ethnic group, as do blacks, Hispanics, Asians, and others. We all have different cultural backgrounds, and this does not strip any of us of our rights or responsibilities as American citizens. In America, we can exhibit any traditional behaviors we may want. However, we have to live within the structure of our society harmoniously, by fully utilizing compromise and tolerance. As difficult and costly as it may be, whites must face and deal with the realities of their past actions, as well as the realities that lie before them. Whites in America enslaved the blacks that were forcibly brought here, and they must responsibly deal with the profound reactions of those past actions. To do otherwise is to deny reality. The ancestry of White-Americans are responsible for the situation Black-Americans find themselves in now to the degree that their group brought the black group here under negative conditions and never intended for them to be equals in this social structure. In addition, for the longest time the black group was denied access to the tools they needed to function here. Then once those tools were made available to them, no one explained this social structure to them in earnest detail, not within the context of them being a true part of it.

Once blacks were "set free," they were denied adequate education. They were left to their own devices, and their plight is the result. That is also a part of the problem America presently faces, the lack of instruction regarding common behavioral parameters. This was not the native culture for blacks brought here then, and the nuances of Anglo-American culture are not natural to Black-Americans now.

The fact that the first human of this planet is known to have been of Africa is not relevant to the importance of each individual race. We must take our understanding of reality, that of "GOD" (the Divine Energy of Life), how the human came to be, etc., and put the complete spiritual and worldly story together, so that we can all come together and believe the same thing. We must put the story of "GOD" and our material reality together and embrace it as a unit, so that we can perpetuate ourselves as a species on a new level of intellectual and spiritual development. Knowing of the past is so important. Whether it is general history, personal history, or otherwise, it is important to know because when one recognizes where they have come from, they know where their future is to lead. One can see the strides that have been made. One can see the paths that have led to various actions and realities. One will understand the possibilities that are open to them, and all this makes a person work harder to get where they want to be. The history of a nation allows it to move forward as a unit.

Black Americans are a critical part of the history of the United States of America. We may not know the full history of the ethnic group classified as black on the continent of Africa because that was taken away from us. However, we can build a positive future on the foundation of our collective history on the continent of North America. Though it may not match the regally independent one from the mother continent, it is one of struggle, survival, goodness, and achievement marked by excellence. Whatever the history is, it is still a history, and it can be a foundation to build upon. Ever since the first individual stepped off a slave ship into this country, Black-Americans have been making vital contributions to the development of American society. Therefore, it is unrealistic for some White-Americans to think that society is not indebted to Black-Americans to one degree or another. As well, it is also unrealistic for Black-Americans to feel as though they are not a part of the American social system. The following is a list of a few contributions blacks have made to further American civilization.

Crisps Attucks (1723-1770) was the <u>first</u> American to die in the struggle for our nations' independence. He was killed in the Boston massacre on March 5, 1770, while leading a group of his followers in an attack on British soldiers in the streets of Boston. A monument to him was erected in 1888 in recognition of his sacrifice and contribution to the "first" victory of the American Revolution.

Benjamin Banneker (1731-1806) was, among other things, a mathematician, an astronomer, a surveyor, and an inventor. He made the first wooden clock in America. He wrote the first scientific book written by a Black-American. He published an almanac that became the main reference book for farmers. He was the first black presidential appointee in this country. He was the surveyor on the six-man team that helped design the blueprints for Washington, D.C.

Jean Baptiste Pointe Dusable (1745-1818) was a Haitian who had a trading post on Lake Michigan. Among his accomplishments was his ownership of 800 acres of land. He was the founder and first settler of what became Chicago.

George Washington Bush (1790-1863) led a group of American settlers from Missouri to Oregon in 1844. Once there, he was not allowed to live in the territory because he was black. So he crossed the Columbia River and settled somewhere near Puget Sound. This was part of Canada at the time. It was his presence there as the first "American" settler that was the basis for the United States' claim to the area, which later became part of the U.S. Once it became part of the Oregon territory, his white friends petitioned congress to allow him to retain his ownership of his property.

Norbert Rillieux was born a free man in 1806. He transformed sugar from a high-priced luxury product into one that everyone could afford. He did this by inventing a multiple effect vacuum pan evaporator. This invention was also used to manufacture soap, glue, gelatin, and evaporated milk.

William Alexander Leidesdorff (1810-1848), a pioneer in the development of California, was Americas' first black millionaire. His holdings included a 35,000-acre estate, and a 160-ton sailing vessel of which he was captain. He built San Francisco's first hotel, and opened California's first public school. He was an American diplomat, a member of the San Francisco city council, chairman of the school board, and the city treasurer.

Elijah J. McCoy (1843-1929) was born in Canada and educated in Scotland. In this country, he was denied employment in engineering because he was black. As a mechanical engineer and inventor, he invented a variety of things, including the ironing board and the lawn sprinkler. He found work as a fireman for a railroad, oiling the moving parts of trains. It was so boring to him, that he invented a machine to do it. At first, his "lubricator cup" made it possible to oil machines without having to turn them off. Most have no doubt heard the popular expression "the real McCoy." This is a reference to him. It is indicative of the trust people had in his inventions.

Andrew Jackson Beard (1850-1921) was a farmer, inventor, and businessman. In 1889, he invented and received a patent for a rotary steam engine that was said to be safer and cheaper than other steam engines of the time. He also invented and patented improved plows for farming. He invented the "jenny coupler," the automatic railroad car coupler, and his other railroad inventions saved many workers from possible injury.

Jan Earnst Matzeliger (1852-1889), the son of an engineer, was born in Surinam, South America. He traveled around the world as a sailor before coming to the U.S. in 1873. He patented several inventions, including one that revolutionized the shoe-making industry. It was a machine that made an entire shoe. Sewing the sole to the upper part of the shoe was done completely by hand before he invented the "shoe lasting machine." This invention is the foundation of the modern shoe industry. His invention led to the emergence of companies that formed the united shoe machine corporation, which was worth over a billion dollars by the year 1955.

Granville T. Woods (1856-1910) was a brilliant inventor awarded at least 35 patents. The first time he applied for a patent, it was for an improved steam-boiler furnace. During that same year, he invented a telephone transmitter that carried voices further distances with a better sound. He received a patent for a device that made it possible to send messages back and forth between a moving train and a railway station, the synchronous multiplex railway telegraph.

He invented an overhead conducting system for electric railways and the "third rail" system for subways. He also greatly improved the efficiency of electrical motors. He invented the "dimmer" lighting system, which produced energy savings of up to 40 percent.

George Washington Carver (1860-1943) was a botanist, an agricultural chemist, and one of the greatest scientists of all time. From the oils, proteins, and chemicals of the peanut plant, he developed close to 300 different products, some of which were instant coffee, face cream, ink, shampoo, and soaps. He also discovered dozens of products from sweet potatoes, pecans, and southern clay. These products played significant roles in the economic prosperity of the south.

Bill Pickett (1870-1932) was one of the greatest cowboys who ever lived. He was the main attraction of the famous 101 ranch and Wild West show, attaining national and international fame as a rodeo performer. Known as the "Dusty Demon," he was the first black cowboy admitted to the national rodeo hall of fame in 1971.

Garrett A. Morgan (1875-1963) was credited with a number of discoveries and inventions. One such discovery was a substance that straightened hair, which was sold for profit. His very first invention was a belt fastener for sewing machines. He brought safety and order to our country's streets with the invention of the traffic signal.

With the widely used gas mask he patented in 1914, he became a hero by rescuing some workers that were trapped inside a fiery tunnel. The thick smoke and fumes kept everyone else from entering the tunnel, even policemen and firemen. Wearing his gas mask, Garrett and three friends were able to rescue the men from the tunnel.

Frederick McKinley Jones (1892-1961) was an inventor whose accomplishments completely changed the food transporting industry. He invented the first practical refrigeration system for long-haul trucks. He was a partner and vice president of the Thermo Control Company, which grew into a $3,000,000 a year business. He was a consultant for the United States defense department as well as the bureau of standards on refrigeration problems in during the 1950s. To help the war effort during World War II, he designed a special refrigeration unit to keep blood serum fresh for transfusions. His first patent was for a ticket-dispensing machine that is found in most movie theaters. Other inventions and products to his credit are such things as transmitters, movie projectors, air-cooling devices, and racing cars. Where would America be without air-conditioning or refrigerators?

Dr. Charles Richard Drew (1893-1926) was among other things, an author of scientific books. He was an instructor of biology and chemistry, as well as the director of athletics at Morgan State University in Maryland. Every blood bank in the world exists because of his genius, since it was he that developed a method for preserving blood plasma. Dr. Drew was the first director of the American Red Cross Blood Bank.

Otis Boykin was born in 1920. He was a college graduate that became a research engineer. He invented some 25 electronic gadgets, many of which are used in computers and guided missiles. He also invented an electrical regulating unit for the first heart pacemaker. Another of his inventions was a type of resistor that is still used in radios, televisions, and computers to this day.

Benjamin S. Carson, Sr. was born in 1951. He earned his bachelor's degree at Yale University. after attending the University of Michigan's Medical School and being the first black person to do a residency at Johns Hopkins Hospital, he went on to become a great doctor and neurosurgeon. Johns Hopkins Hospital made him the youngest director of pediatric neurosurgery in 1984. Being considered a pioneer in brain surgical techniques, he led the first surgical team to successfully separated Siamese twins that were born joined at the head.

Ida B. Wells Barnett (1723-1770) was a speaker, reporter, partner and editor of the *Free Speech*, a black newspaper. She was a co-founder of the NAACP. She was driven to crusade against lynching, traveling throughout the U.S. and Europe. Her primary weapon was *a red record*, which she published. It was a serious statistical analysis of the tragedy of lynching in our country.

Sojourner Truth (1797-1883) was a woman who could not read or write, but she became an eloquent public speaker who for close to 40 years, lectured on the issues of abolition and women's rights.

Harriet Ross Tubman (1820-1913) escaped from slavery, then made 19 trips back into the south to guided more than 300 slaves to freedom via the "underground railroad." She also helped free 750 others from slavery by leading some units of the union army on a raid into the south. During the civil war, she was a scout, spy, and nurse for the north.

Madame C.J. Walker (1867-1919) was Americas' first black female millionaire. It all started in 1905, when she invented and patented a straightening comb for hair. She went on to build a manufacturing company that employed over 3,000 people. Her hair and beauty products were very popular in the use and the Caribbean. She helped black artists and writers get noticed, and set up scholarships at black colleges and other schools. Her efforts continued after her death, as she left money to build a school for girls in West Africa.

Maggie Lena Walker (1867-1934) was the founder of the St. Luke consolidated bank and trust company. She became Americas' first female bank president. Besides these great accomplishments, she was a national director of the NAACP. She was also a member of the board of the national urban league.

These are but a few of the many black individuals that have made personal, practical, cultural, conventional, primal, economical, industrial, political, territorial, agricultural, medical, and social contributions to the American social structure and way of life. From these and the many more positive works of Black-Americans, each and every American citizen must see that the greatness of our nation is the result of the efforts of every ethnic group contained within the social structure. Black-Americans specifically must allow these achievements to solidify their commitment to the nation of their birth, and inspire them to greater heights. Many may think of this as difficult to do. One has only to place himself or herself in the shoes of the Tuskegee airman. What must it have been like for them during the heat of battle, knowing they lived in a society that would treat them as though they were less than human after the war was over? All the while that they were fighting, they knew they lived in a land in which they were treated in a repressive manner. Yet, they <u>volunteered</u> to fight for the ideals of this country. With an examination of the reality of the circumstance, the only understanding one can come away with is that in their hearts these men knew that both America and democracy were right for all people who chose freedom over tyranny. These men knew that once the war was over, they would have to come back and fight again, against the social structure to make gains towards equality. They knew that fight would also be won, because it was right. These rewards could only be achieved within this social system, one they fought for and for which some gave their lives. This system is worth the effort to save, for all Americans of whatever hue.

Right this very minute and at any moment in the future, regardless of the difficulties or pains I may experience because of the circumstances of our American society, I would die for the perpetuation of democratic freedom in America. I would give my life so that America should live. I get such strength and power from my faith in the Divine Energy of Life along with the patriotism and commitment that is in my heart for American ideals. Sometimes I feel like the most powerful person on our planet. I fear no single law-abiding individual. Nor do I fear any element of American society because I know who I am. I know I am equal to anyone because we are <u>all</u> created equal. I am a Black-American male who acts in righteousness, has a positive direction, and has the lawful strength of the American social structure supporting him. That is nearly as strong as one gets on our planet, a Black-American male with the power of America behind him. When he reaches deep down inside himself, only the black male knows the degree of that power. It takes strength to effect and endure change. The Black-American has had his and her fortitude tested by years of slavery and oppression. Our people have survived it with strength. Black-Americans have the power of America behind them because they are legal citizens of this nation. It is their birthright, and they must claim it. Black-Americans must face the realities of their citizenship, and White-Americans must allow them to do that. Black-Americans in turn, as a matter of responsibility, must commit themselves to this social system. For Black-Americans to benefit from the social system that the white founders of this country setup, they must commit themselves and their efforts to the system. It is an Anglo-American system. We must concede this fact and accept it because it is our American heritage. One's existence in America is a reality, so committing oneself to the right actions of the system that makes it exist is the same as committing oneself to reality. All Black-Americans must make this commitment. On pure faith, we as Americans must commit our individual efforts to "GOD," to our country, to our families, and then to ourselves. If we work to perpetuate these entities, and live up to our obligation as a living being within Nature's system, we can only prosper. Then, the degree of our prosperity becomes a reflection of our efforts.

Through hard work (the body), perseverance (the spirit/energy/the soul), discipline (mind), and a strong foundation of belief ("GOD"), I have created a comfortable, stable existence for myself. This is the result of the pursuit of what I categorize as divine perfection. It is the result of striving to get the most out of my abilities relative to my mind, body, and soul, and also out of the circumstances I face. I have not achieved perfection, divine or otherwise, by any means.

Yet, the fruits of that pursuit (or the best I could achieve) have brought me security (peace of mind), comfort (peace of body), and love (peace of soul). These are the three divinely perfect things that bring satisfaction to human existence. These things are what we all consciously or unconsciously pursue with our efforts (actions). I am definitely one of a number of "average" human beings. However, I have pursued objective understanding and sought to apply it. Because of the humility I manifest in recognition of the reality of my subordinate position to that which created me, I can be satisfied with the blessings I have received through my efforts, as guided by the spirit of "GOD." The spirit or energy of "GOD" is the Divine Energy of Life, and it flows in a positive direction.

It may seem hard to imagine the circumstances of "damnation" because with all of the hardship in America and the rest of the world, the future seems full of prosperous opportunity. Computers are connecting us together and making our lives easier. There are some good jobs out there for people who have prepared themselves for them. There are people of all nationalities coming to our land and making money. Every other ethnic group in America can see the opportunities this country provides. If only the black community would begin to structure itself the way that the rest of the system is structured (i.e. working together with a common set of values, working hard, pursuing the American dream, etc.), we too could begin to prosper in America collectively. Black people are an intrinsic part of the global system. We must consciously "do" what is required of us to become a positive part of the human social system. We allow ourselves to be victims of racism by not "commanding" the respect of our peers. We gain this respect by coordinating our behavior and having it occur within the parameters set by the normal social standards of the social system within which we live. We accomplish this through positive action. Take the Japanese people for example; they are a very strong people. They were defeated in war. They had "two" Atom bombs dropped on them, for crying out loud. In the view of the whole world they surrendered, a terribly humiliating experience. However, they consciously decided that if they were not going to be a military world power, they would be an economic world power. They began to work within the social system of their existence to effect positive change. They suffered through a negative action, and responded to it with positive action. Their population began to soak up knowledge as though it was their life's blood. Look where it has gotten them. Japan is a country the size of one of the states within America, and now it is a world economic power.

Black-Americans in this land must come together as a sub-group of the American collective, and do what must be done to help the whole group prosper. We must exercise our birthright here in the land of our birth. We must become a positive part of America. We must help to stop the violence, the drug abuse, and the crime in the communities of this nation. Look at all the black males (as well as females) on the streets of our cities. Image what it would mean to the black community and America as a whole if all those men (and women) were in college? what if all those men just went out, got jobs, and paid taxes? What would happen if all Black-Americans gave $10 a month to the NAACP to establish a human aid fund? Black-Americans could solve their problems in America, in Africa (our motherland), and almost everywhere else. It is up to the Black-American male to take the first steps to ushering in the utopian state of existence. By helping himself, the Black-American male helps the world. This is not to infer that all the problems of the world will disappear overnight. It is not to imply that there will be no difficulties before the black male in his quest for prosperity. However, the problems of the world are the result of the actions of all humans. It is up to each individual member of the global population to contribute energy toward solving those problems. Here in America, blacks and whites must form a partnership aimed at making America greater than it already is. We must give love to receive love.

Having a working understanding of "GOD" and goodness will bring to each of our lives the peace of mind it takes to accomplish our dreams through adversity. This does not entail becoming a saint. It means to accept the humility that is inherent in the finite nature of individual existence.

It means to praise the greatness of "GOD" to have created one as unique and special as oneself and others. It means to respect, aid, and protect all that "GOD" has created. It means to strive to find the gift(s) that "GOD" has given each person, and to share it (or them). This will enrich not only that individual, but also all of humanity. Our society is on the verge of greatness beyond our collective comprehension. If we can stop the destruction that is taking place in all our communities and the black community specifically, we can achieve mutual satisfaction through compromise and tolerance. If the black community can become a completely positive contributing factor in our society, along with all the other ethnic communities, America will truly be the greatest country on the face of the Earth.

The system that "GOD" (the Divine Energy of Life) created takes into consideration the fact that with the immensity of free spirit within the human population, we cannot all think in exactly the same way. Our natural system of existence has been set up to compensate for this fact. If we all have the same feelings in our hearts and our actions have the proper direction, this will be good enough. The human has a need to satisfy a sense of belonging. This is a part of what it is to be a member of a socialized species. Because of this, each human will seek out people or groups that have the same attitudes and perspectives. This is why if individuals seek to transform themselves, i.e. become more spiritual and positive, salvation and prosperity will be created from a "domino" effect. Those that resist will be in the minority. Therefore, their harmful effects upon our society and our Earth will be minimal. Do not be concerned with the prejudices and misbehavior of others. In recognition of spirituality, know that each individual is divinely held accountable for his or her actions. Each of us must be concerned with our own realities.

Everything on our planet can be viewed from the perspective of balance. All difference is to be combined to form "a more perfect union" of everything within the system of existence. The intent of this is to make the system of existence function at its best through the harmonious interaction of the elements the system is composed. Relative to human interaction, each ethnic group has attributes that we can all embrace to enhance our individual and collective lives. As civilized existence has spread across our planet, native cultures have embraced and adopted elements learned from and associated with other "foreign" cultures. We know this to be true because there are examples of this fact all around us. There are basic attributes inherent to each cultural ethnic group that are strong points of that particular ethnic group, but that are prevalent within each of us as individuals. This is not to imply that each individual population group does not contain the elements profoundly inherent in others. It does mean to imply is that one group is no better than another is, because each group was given gifts that were to be shared to form a "more perfect union."

As we work towards forming a more perfect union, we must come to terms with the differences that exist between us and embrace those differences so that they may enrich all our lives. What we must be objective about is ethnic background. As a nation of individuals, each of us must be concerned about the future into which our country is headed. Let us all collectively focus on that. let us then leave to each individual the task of growing into the best person he or she can be, built upon the foundation of the knowledge they derive from knowing of where they came from ethnically.

Just as we as individuals seek to get better, the support systems of our nation must get better as well. As this growth takes place, we must work to ensure that the systems that support our lives are not administered in a discriminatory manner. There are advantages inherent to our support systems that are available to some groups of people and not others. This occurs within the context of compromise, and it must be tolerated. The administration of our social system must be balanced and fair, so that all the citizenry of our nation can trust that their individual growth can be built upon the foundation laid by the greatest civilization in human history. That civilization exists, here in the United States of America.

We must recognize the truth and act upon it, always. The humans' problems involving difference are truly the result of the humans' wholly subjective interpretation of reality. To overcome this, our attitudes and aspirations must transcend bigotry and greed, disregard and domination, rape and neglect. We must all seek to coexist in a balanced and stable way so that our positive flowing energy produces mutual satisfaction. Our individual movements must aid in the perpetuation of the flow of positive energy. Imagine the resulting reality that would be manifested in America if White-Americans, Black-Americans, and other minority groups put aside both negative thought and negative action, and combined their positive flowing energy to produce actions aimed towards mutual benefit. The divine truth is our reality in America would resemble utopia, and it is there for all who look to see. We must use the history of human action on our Earth to bind us together by nations. Each nation must be allowed to maintain its heritage and culture with patriotic dignity and respect. The country established by our forefathers provides us with the liberty to be individuals that move freely within the context of a civilized society. However, there is a large percentage of us that are now behaving in an uncivilized manner. If this continues unchecked, not a single one of us will continue to have liberty.

What each of us must do is to better ourselves as individuals. Making our bodies strong is only the beginning. We must seek to grow in a multitude of ways. We must become a healthy society before we can reach for a utopian existence. By producing muscle that feeds and nourishes our nerves, our nerves are better able to receive the energy pulses of the Divine Energy of Life. Within our pursuit of utopia, we must make the plant life flourish upon the surface of our planet. We must all contribute positive energy through positive action. We must elevate our minds and souls to higher levels of interaction in our lives. Then we can reach for utopia. However, we must recognize it all as being a part of one system. We must recognize everything that we do within the confines of that system. Therefore, from bodybuilding, to energizing the mind and the soul, to making positive choices in our day, we must interpret it all as a part of one system aimed at producing a common goal. That common goal is the freedom to pursue life, liberty, and happiness. This is the American dream. The United States of America is where utopia must begin.

As individuals, each of us is to work to create a more perfect union between our body, mind, and soul. Each of us must work to create a more perfect union between family members. Each of us must work to create a more perfect union between the various human communities. Each of us must work to create a more perfect union between business, government, and the citizenry. Each of us must work to create a more perfect union between animal kingdom, the vegetable kingdom, and the mineral kingdom. Each of us must work to create a more perfect union between ourselves and our Earth. These more perfect unions with make it easier for everyone and everything to move. The first step toward a utopian living condition is the continual exchange of love.

The Ending or The Beginning?

Understanding spirituality (i.e. the Divine System of Nature) and the Divine Energy of Life from a physically real, electromagnetic perspective allows us all to embrace the revelation that there are <u>physical</u> reasons, defined within the context of Nature, for us to have a positive attitude. There are <u>physical</u> reasons for all of humanity to share and coexist in harmony with all other living creatures, as well as the Earth itself. There are <u>physical</u> reasons for all of us to exhibit responsible, mannerly, civilized behavior. The realities of the teachings of "GOD" (the Divine Energy of Life) are not merely a philosophic concept, but a tangible manifestation of our planetary system that requires things of us. There are spiritual realities that we cannot escape simply by closing our minds to them for self-satisfying reasons. The word "Nature" is merely the label we hide behind to allow us to avoid our responsibility to act within the context of the system we recognize around us. Nature is not something exterior to us as human animals. We are as much a part of it as any other natural object. Therefore, there are natural actions that are required of us that we must perform, whether it satisfies us to do so or not. In a word, required action is **RESPONSIBILITY**.

By thinking of ourselves as being separate from Nature, we omit a key element of understanding that will lead to a clearer picture of our spirituality. In a physical context, the source of the energy that keeps us alive is the spinning action of our Earth. By incorporating this fact into our understanding, the importance of positive and negative energy and action becomes clearer. The Divine Energy of Life is the source that keeps our Earth spinning. Our reality comes from this spinning action. We are a component of the electric circuit created by the spinning action. True, it is necessary for each of us to develop a direct relationship of understanding with "GOD" (the Divine Energy of Life). However, relative to our collective actions, our electrical connection to the source that gives us life, our Earth, cannot be overlooked or ignored.

The gift of "time" is the opportunity to exist. This is the ultimate miracle. The greatest gift that "GOD" gave to each of us is truly opportunity. The truth about "opportunity" is real. It is so real in fact, it has manifested itself in our lives such that it has become a doctrine that we have subconsciously subscribed to and followed. This doctrine is "opportunism." The dogma indicates that we limit our judgment (or choice) of what positive actions are to what quickly suits our own purposes, rather than what is truly right. It is to follow the policy or practice as we have in politics or business, or life in general. It is one of embracing decisions and actions based upon what we subjectively deem as advantageous to our self-interests, rather than what is right or just, regardless of any sacrifice of our physical needs or our personal beliefs. Because of the opportunity to live, each of us must truly experience the things that exist around us. Each of us has to indulge our senses. However, each of us must also understand that because of the magnitude of this gift combined with the multitude of living things and the limits of Nature and "her" resources, there are rules within which each of us must conduct ourselves. This is what we must all accept as civilized beings with dominion over our planet.

This book is about Americans facing and dealing with the realities of our existence in a civilized manner. There is only one reality. It includes everything we are conscious of, as well as everything of which we are not conscious. Within this context, we must recognize that the truths of reality apply to our existence whether or not we recognize or accept them as such. For example, some say the past is the past. They say that we must forget about it and move on into the future. The truth is that all time is connected, so what happened in the past cannot be separated from the present or the future. All human reality is connected by time. Newton's third law of motion, the law governing actions and reactions, connects moments in time. That is because once an action occurs, the reaction occurs in a different span of time. So those two spans of time are connected by action or movement, and they make up one circumstance of reality, what we label an "event."

Therefore, the past is connected to the present, the present is connected to the future, and the future is connected to the past (drawn figuratively, this forms a circle). We cannot disregard the actions or events that have occurred in any of these time periods if we are to deal with the reality of another time period. In addition, since all reality is connected, truth is universal and our interpretation of reality should be based on this universal truth, creating for all humans a common objective perspective.

We, as Americans, must recognize and live within the context of the truth. The direction of American society specifically, and humanity in general, is on a collision course with chaos and destruction. This outcome can be changed, if the direction of our actions is changed. To change the direction of our actions, we must change the polarity of our minds. This is because the humans' mind controls the humans' actions or behaviors. In changing our minds, we must recognize and examine the basic truths of existence. The first is that energy is the foundation of all creation. We must then recognize and deal with the reality that as a species of animal, we are a part of the system of Nature. What this means is that everything that comes naturally to us is part of this system. One of the things I am referring to are the thoughts we have. The words we use to share those thoughts, the actions that result from those thoughts, and the results those actions produce. Once we accept these realities, we can achieve a clearer understanding of our existence.

We are the United States of America. We are a nation of pioneers. We are a family. Our nation has the right(eous) combination of power, resources, strength, liberty, and opportunity to establish a utopian existence. The only obstacle before us as a citizenry is that we do not have the necessary understanding of the true need for a common faith, a common focus, and a common direction. Living within the context of spirituality and truth will give us all these things. For as bad as things are in America and around the world in terms of suffering and domination, along with the cruelty and aggression, the human is as great as it has ever been in its whole existence. The embracing of reality, spirituality, common truth, and a common direction, would be the ultimate action aimed at the perpetuation of human existence. To create an understanding within all of humanity that results in the release of tensions and hostilities, America must take a stand and lead by example. However, we must let it be known that we as a nation intend to exist forever. We must let the world know that we are embracing our nationalism, just as smaller countries embrace theirs. We must embrace the reality that we are a nation like any other, free to be concerned about ourselves.

As a nation, we must draw strength from every moment of experience in our collective past, our history. Through all the conflict that has befallen us as a nation, both internally and externally (slavery, civil war, world wars, terrorism, natural disasters, etc.), we have survived it as one, a dominant civilized society. This should give us the confidence to face our future head-on, recognizing that what we <u>have</u> accomplished has been achieved without a completely unified, committed effort. If all the people within our borders truly came together to form a body of united states within the land of America, and we worked <u>together</u> to make our future as rich as humanly possible, no problem would be too great to overcome. Individually, most claim they cannot make a difference, so they do not try. This book is the result of my profound attempt to make a difference. My personal and academic pursuits during the course of my life were based on interests that did not include delivering a message to all humankind. However, "GOD" has chosen me to communicate the relevance of the knowledge derived from words and numbers that have been with us for ages.

**Spread the word,
"Do it DEWsWay"**